S0-CFM-667

A COMPLETE GUIDE

THE SARASOTA, SANIBEL ISLAND & NAPLES BOOK

3RD EDITION

THE SARASOTA, SANIBEL ISLAND & NAPLES BOOK

Chelle Koster Walton

The Countryman Press
Woodstock, Vermont

Copyright © 1993, 1998, 2001, 2005 by The Countryman Press

Third Edition

All rights reserved. No part of this book may be reproduced in any way by any electronic or mechanical means, including information storage and retrieval systems, without permission in writing from the publisher, except by a reviewer, who may quote brief passages.

ISBN 1-58157-072-4
An ISSN application has been filed with the Library of Congress.

Front cover photo © Karen T. Bartlett
Interior photos © Karen T. Bartlett unless otherwise specified
Book design by Bodenweber Design
Composition by Melinda Belter
Maps by Mapping Specialists Ltd., Madison, WI © The Countryman Press

Published by The Countryman Press, P.O. Box 748, Woodstock, Vermont 05091

Distributed by W. W. Norton & Company, Inc., 500 Fifth Avenue, New York, NY 10110

Manufactured in the United States of America

10 9 8 7 6 5 4 3 2

No complimentary meals or lodgings were accepted by the author and reviewers in gathering information for this work.

GREAT DESTINATIONS TRAVEL GUIDEBOOK SERIES

Recommended by *National Geographic Traveler* and *Travel & Leisure* magazines.

[A] CRISP AND CRITICAL APPROACH, FOR TRAVELERS WHO WANT TO LIVE LIKE LOCALS.
— *USA Today*

Great Destinations™ guidebooks are known for their comprehensive, critical coverage of regions of extraordinary cultural interest and natural beauty. The authors in this series are professional travel writers who have lived for many years in the regions they describe. Each title in this series is continuously updated with each printing to insure accurate and timely information. All the books contain over 100 photographs and maps.

Neither the publisher, the authors, the reviewers, nor other contributors accept complimentary lodgings, meals, or any other consideration (such as advertising) while gathering information for any book in this series.

Current titles available:

THE ADIRONDACK BOOK

THE BERKSHIRE BOOK

THE CHARLESTON, SAVANNAH & COASTAL ISLANDS BOOK

THE CHESAPEAKE BAY BOOK

THE COAST OF MAINE BOOK

THE FINGER LAKES BOOK

THE HAMPTONS BOOK

THE HUDSON VALLEY BOOK

THE MONTEREY BAY, BIG SUR & GOLD COAST WINE COUNTRY BOOK

THE NANTUCKET BOOK

THE NAPA & SONOMA BOOK

THE SANTA FE & TAOS BOOK

THE SARASOTA, SANIBEL ISLAND & NAPLES BOOK

THE SHENANDOAH VALLEY BOOK

THE TEXAS HILL COUNTRY BOOK

TOURING EAST COAST WINE COUNTRY

If you are traveling to, moving to, residing in, or just interested in any (or all!) of these enchanting regions, a Great Destinations guidebook is a superior companion. Honest and painstakingly critical, full of information only a local can provide, Great Destinations guidebooks give you all the practical knowledge you need to enjoy the best of each region. Why not own them all?

To Gene Koster,
who first instilled in me
a love for the road

Contents

ACKNOWLEDGMENTS

I can't list all of the people on whose patience and understanding I counted to see me through this project. First dibs on my gratitude must go to my husband, Rob, for not divorcing me, and my son, Aaron, who helped particularly with my beach and "kids' stuff" research. Thanks to Ron and Mindy Koster, who visited during my most intense stretch of writing-under-deadline and helped out in many ways.

Special thanks to Prudy Taylor Board, who checked up on my historical facts and who will no doubt cringe at the pirate legends I couldn't bring myself to omit. Thanks to Amy Ligon and Susie Holly, who spent hours on the phone doing the nitty-gritty final fact-checking.

Nancy Hamilton at the Lee County Visitor & Convention Bureau and the Sarasota Convention & Visitors Bureau have been particularly helpful. Beth Preddy, a personal friend and travel industry colleague, always provides me with insights and assistance when it comes to Naples research.

Thanks to photographer Karen T. Bartlett, who contributed creative energy to the project, and to my supportive editors at The Countryman Press: Philip Rich, Dale Evva Gelfand, and Jennifer Thompson. You all helped me to extract the inherent agony of guidebook detail work and to make this book a joyful undertaking.

INTRODUCTION

Morning dawns like a boater's dream. The sky is clear except for a trace of last night's moon: wispy, like a wadded-up cloud. The water stretches like cellophane pulled taut between Sanibel and Pine Islands. It is a morning to wonder why one ever does anything else on days off but return to the sea. On cue, a family of three dolphins pierces the surface with their fins and their smiles. The show has begun.

In the course of our leisurely, two-hour cruise between Sanibel Island and Boca Grande, we are entertained by leaping stingrays, a school of mackerel, and the usual dive-bomb squadron of brown pelicans.

At lights-out call—after lunch in a marina-side fish house, beach time on an unbridged island, and a duck-the-afternoon-rains cocktail at a historic island inn—nature's revue reaches its spectacular finale. In the moonless dark, the wake behind our boat sparkles like a watery fireworks display. The gulf has thrown an electric breaker switch. Liquid lightning strikes all around us as our 21-foot Mako powerboat parts the seas. Whitecaps puff like nuclear popcorn.

Scientists call the phenomena *dinoflagellates*. Lay folks call the glowing organisms phosphorescence. Jamaicans call them sea-blinkies. The Ancient Mariner called them death-fires. I call their unpredictable visits to our summer waters magic, imparting a topsy-turvy, ethereal feeling that someone—without warning—has transformed the sea into a starry sky.

Such a perfect day isn't required to fully appreciate this inimitable slice of Gulf Coast Florida, but such days do help to remind me why I moved here from long-johns land 20-some years ago. Like so many who constitute our hodgepodge population, I escaped, I loved, I dug in. I stayed for the exotic, warm quality of tropical nature. I remain because of the miracles I discover—and watch my young son discover—every day.

— Chelle Koster Walton, Sanibel Island, Florida

THE WAY THIS BOOK WORKS

Organization

The area bounded on the north by the Braden River and on the south by Ten Thousand Islands is often lumped under the heading Southwest Florida. Sometimes the Bradenton –Sarasota area is omitted from the region this heading defines and otherwise grouped with Tampa as Central West Florida. For the purpose of this guide, it is included. The book often refers to the region covered as Gulf Coast Florida, or West Coast Florida, although, of course, it does not cover the entire coast. It does cover in depth the cities, towns, and communities from Bradenton–Sarasota in the north to Naples–Marco Island and the Everglades in the south.

I have sliced this delectable pie into four geographical region chapters, north to south: Sarasota Bay Coast, Charlotte Harbor Coast, Island Coast, and South Coast. Within these chapters I scan under separate headings each region's lodging, dining, culture, recreation, and shopping.

Other chapters deal with the coastline's history as a whole, transportation, and nitty-gritty information.

A series of indexes at the back of the book provide easy access to information. The first, a standard index, lists entries and subjects in alphabetical order. Next, hotels, inns, and resorts are categorized by price. Restaurants are organized in two separate indexes: one by price, one by type of cuisine.

List of Maps

The Gulf Coast of Florida
Gulf Coast Access Maps
Sarasota Bay Coast
Charlotte Harbor Coast
Island Coast
South Coast

High Fives

In the *Information* chapter, I have rated listings within a number of fun—and sometimes quirky—categories, from Splurge Accommodations and Martini Meccas to Kid Cool and Paddle Happy. They begin under the Chelle's High Fives heading on page 317.

Within the chapters, listings that have earned a High Five get a star ✪ next to their names.

Prices

Rather than give specific prices, this guide rates dining and lodging options within a range.

Lodging prices are normally based on per person/double occupancy for hotel rooms and per unit for efficiencies, apartments, cottages, suites, and villas. Price ranges reflect the difference in off-season and high season (usually Christmas through Easter). Generally, the colder the weather up north, the higher the cost of accommodations here. Rates can double during the course of a year. Many resorts offer off-season packages at special rates. Pricing does not include the 6 percent Florida sales tax. Furthermore, many large resorts add gratuities or maid charges, and some counties also impose a tourist tax, proceeds from which are applied to beach and environmental maintenance.

If rates seem high for rooms on the Gulf Coast, it's partially because many resorts cater to families by providing kitchen facilities. Take into consideration what this could save you on dining bills. A star after the pricing designation indicates that accommodations include at least continental breakfast with the cost of lodging; a few offer the American Plan, serving all meals, which is then explained within the description copy.

Dining cost categories are based on the range of dinner entrée prices or, if dinner is not served, on lunch entrées. To save money at the more expensive restaurants, look in this guide to see which ones offer "early-dining specials." Restaurants at some large resorts add gratuities to the tab. This is also customary for large parties at most restaurants, so check your bill carefully before leaving a tip. Satisfied diners are expected to tip between 15 and 20 percent.

Heavy state taxes on liquor served in-house can mount up a drinking tab quickly. Paying as you drink is a wise measure to prevent sticker shock.

Price Codes

	Lodging	Dining
Inexpensive	Up to $75	Up to $10
Moderate	$75 to $150	$10 to $20
Expensive	$150 to $200	$20 to $30
Very Expensive	$200 and up	$30 or more

(An asterisk after the pricing designation indicates that the rate includes at least a continental breakfast in the cost of lodging and possibly more extensive meal service as noted in the listing.)

The following abbreviations are used for credit card information:

AE – American Express   MC – MasterCard
D – Discover Card   V – Visa
DC – Diners Card

Area Code

Until 2001 the 941 area code applied to the entire region. Now, the Island Coast and South Coast regions use 239.

Numbers prefixed with 800, 888, 866, and 877 are toll free.

Tourist Information

Local visitors bureaus, tourism development councils, and chambers of commerce are adept at the dissemination of materials and information about their area. These are listed in Chapter Seven, *Information.*

For information on the entire region and other parts of Florida, contact Visit Florida, 661 E. Jefferson St., Suite 300, Tallahassee, FL 32301; 888-7FLA-USA; www.flausa.com.

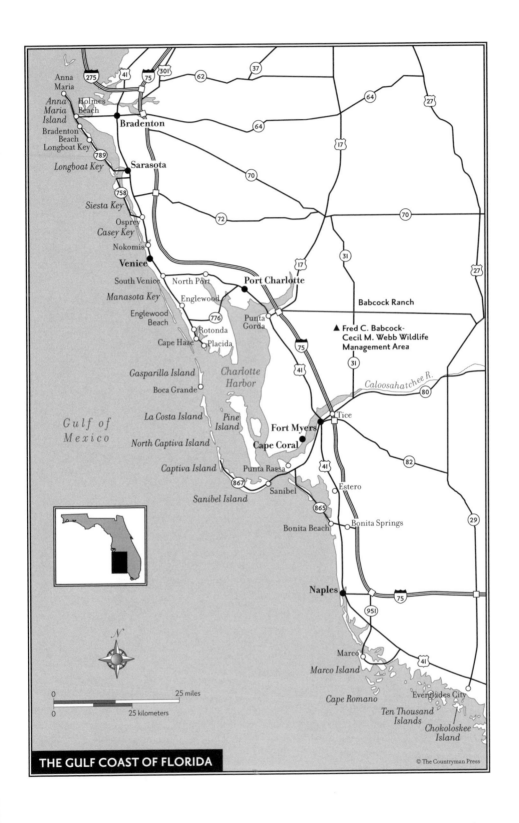

THE GULF COAST OF FLORIDA

© The Countryman Press

1

HISTORY

Mangroves, Man, and Magnates

The essence of Gulf Coast Florida seems to be a balance of polar extremes: the ultimate in both natural wilderness and social civility. To understand the region and the richness of its heritage, culture, and environment, one must understand its roots, learn the names, and revel in the legends of its past—a past steeped in romance, adventure, and power.

The story begins with a single mangrove tree and evolves around man's need to conquer that tree's primeval world. Enter the characters: Ambition, Wealth, and Social Grace. How does the story end? Happily, we can hope, with the modern rediscovery of the coast's unique natural and historical heritage.

NATURAL HISTORY

From Grains of Sand

Each wave helps build a ridge of accumulating sand and shell that runs roughly parallel to the beach. Over a period of hundreds or thousands of years, a ridge may become a barrier island.
                                        —*Lynn Stone, Voyageurs Series,*
                                            Sanibel Island, 1991

On the floor is a straw mat. Under the mat is a layer of sand that has been tracked into the cottage and has sifted through the straw. I have thought some of taking the mat up and sweeping the sand into a pile and removing it, but have decided against it. This is the way keys form, apparently, and I have no particular reason to interfere.
                                        —*E. B. White, "On a Florida Key," 1941*

Billions of years ago, the Florida peninsula existed only as a scattering of volcanic keys, akin to the Caribbean islands. The passing years, silt, and the sea's power eventually buried all evidence of these volcanic origins. What is now Florida remained submerged until some 20 million years ago, when matter buildup brought land to the surface in the form of new islands.

Ice Age sea fluctuations molded Florida into solid land, and islands continued to grow along its fringes. From a single grain of sand or a lone mangrove sprout they stabilized into masses of sand and forests composed of leggy roots and finger shoots. As shells and marine encrustations accumulated, islands fell into formation along the Gulf Coast, protecting it from the battering of a storm-driven sea. In the gaps between the islands, the gulf's waters scoured the shore to forge inlets, estuaries, bayous, creeks, and rivers. The sea chiseled a mottled, labyrinthine shoreline that kept the southern Gulf Coast a secret while the rest of the state was being tamed.

During its infancy, the region hosted a slow parade of ever-changing creatures. In prehistoric graveyards modern archaeologists have found mummified remains of rhinoceroses, crocodiles, llamas, camels, pygmy horses, saber-toothed tigers, mastodons, and great woolly mammoths—Florida's first winter visitors at the advent of the Ice Age. Another era brought giant armadillos, tapirs, and other South American creatures. Fauna and flora from these ancient eras survive today: cabbage palms (the state tree), saw palmettos, garfish, seahorses, horseshoe crabs, alligators, manatees, armadillos, and loggerhead sea turtles.

Islands continue to grow along Florida's fringes.
Karen T. Bartlett

The Miracle of the Mangrove

The mangrove forest is both a fertile incubator and a marine graveyard, the home of an island construction crew and a vegetative ballet troupe. It is a self-sustaining world marked by vivid contrasts. The Mangrove Coast (as one local historian terms it) is riddled with red, black, and white species of the tree. Red mangroves strut along mainland coastlines, canals, and the leeward sides of islands on graceful prop roots—or at least they look graceful until low tide reveals the oysters, barnacles, and tiny marine metropolises that weigh them down and keep them connected to the sea.

Farther inland, black-and-white mangroves create thick, impenetrable forests that buffer waves, filter pollutants, send out shoots, and always busily build. Encrustations of shellfish grab algae, silt, and sand, creating rich soil out of decaying material. Fish, crabs, and mollusks skitter among the roots, nibbling dinner, depositing eggs, and tending to their young. Birds rest and nest in the mangroves' scraggly branches, ready to dive for the fish on which they feed. Mother trees send their tubular offspring bobbing upon sea currents to find a foothold elsewhere and begin, perhaps, a new island. The cycle is ancient and ongoing, threatened only by the chainsaws of developers. A few decades ago these natural builders, the mangroves, were leveled in favor of cement seawalls. Today, strict regulations prohibit mangrove destruction. The crucial role of the mangrove in the survival of Florida's sea life finally has been realized. And cherished.

An Early Picture

> *In the bay of Juan Ponce De León, in the west side of the land, we meet with innumerable*
> *small islands, and several fresh streams: the land in general is drowned mangrove swamp. . . .*
> *From this place [Cape Romano, latitude 25:43] to latitude 26:30 are many inconsiderable inlets,*
> *all carefully laid down in the chart, here is Carlos Bay, and the Coloosa Hatchee, or Coloosa river,*
> *with the island San Ybell, where we find the southern entrance of Charlotte harbour. . . .*
>
> —*Bernard Romans, 1775*

One of the earliest recorders of Florida native life and topography, Bernard Romans is credited with naming Charlotte Harbor after the queen of his adopted homeland, England, and Cape Romano after himself. Native Americans and earlier Spanish explorers are responsible for other regional place names.

The harbor was already the center of west coast life when the first explorers discovered it. Its deep waters and barrier-island protection created a pocket of unusually mild climate, attracting early aborigines and their descendants.

Romans and his contemporaries found the Gulf Coast alive with wild turkeys, black bears, deer, golden panthers, bobcats, possums, raccoons, alligators, otters, lizards, and snakes. Wild boars and scrub cattle roamed freely, descendants of stock brought by Spanish missionaries. Land birds and waterfowl of all varieties filled the skies and back bays, some permanent, some migratory. Majestic ospreys and bald eagles swooped; kites soared effortlessly; sandhill cranes dotted the countryside; wood storks nested; pelicans came in colors of brown and white; gulls, terns, and sandpipers patrolled seashores; cormorants, ducks, anhingas, ibises, egrets, roseate spoonbills, and herons fed among the mangroves.

Marine life flourished. Manatees cleared waterways, dolphins frolicked in the waves, and mullet burst from bay waters like cannon shot. Tarpon, rays, snapper, snook, flounder, ladyfish, and mackerel churned the otherwise calm backwaters. Grouper, tripletail, tuna, and shark lurked in deep waters offshore.

Giant armadillos roamed prehistoric Florida. Their descendants still seek insects by night. Karen T. Bartlett

On land, a wide variety of indigenous vegetation abounded. Sea grapes, mahoes, sea oats, nickerbeans, and railroad vines anchored sandy coasts. Thick, impenetrable jungles clogged inland areas. Cabbage palms and gumbo-limbo trees stood tall. Papayas flourished along with flowering shrubs. In mixed-wood forests pines climbed skyward, and live oaks wore their eerie veils of Spanish moss. Cedars fringed islands along the Sarasota Bay coast. Ferns and grasses carpeted the marshes. Swamplands were home to great cypress trees with bony knees and armfuls of parasitic mistletoe and epiphytic orchids and bromeliads.

Primeval and teeming, Florida held an exotic and mysterious aura. The swamp nurtured all of life, from the Everglades upward along the lowlands of the Gulf Coast. It was a perfect ecosystem, designed by nature to withstand all forces—except man.

Face-lifts and Implants

With the arrival of the first settlers, the natural balance that existed along the Gulf Coast began to tilt. The Spanish brought citrus seedlings and livestock. Naturalists and growers introduced specimens from the north and south: mangoes, avocados, bougainvillea, hibiscus, frangipani, coconut palms, pineapples, sapodillas, tomatoes, and legumes. For the most part these exotics proved harmless to the fragile environment.

Three nonnative plants brought to the area in the past century, however, have harmed the ecosystem and changed the pro-file of the land. The prolific melaleuca tree (or cajeput), casuarina (Australian pine), and Brazilian pepper choke out the native vegetation that wildlife feeds on and harm both man and property. Many communities are attempting to eradicate these noxious plants, particularly the pepper tree.

The juicy mango was introduced into Florida by naturalists and growers. Karen T. Bartlett

The complexion of the west coast was changed further by dredging and plowing. In times when swampland was equated with slimy monsters and slick realtors, developers and governments thought nothing of filling it in to create more buildable land. This, too, threw the ecosystem off balance. Fortunately, such mistakes were recognized before their effects became irreversible. Today government strives to preserve, even restore, the deli-cate balance of the wetlands.

SOCIAL HISTORY

Dateline: Gulf Coast Florida

The modern settlement of Florida's southwest coast can be traced like a dateline that begins on the shores of Sarasota Bay in 1841 and ends at Naples in 1887. At first glance this time frame makes the region look young, without the gracious patina of age and the wrinkles of

Once an Indian trading post, Smallwood's Story today serves as a museum in the secluded Everlades outpost of Chokoloskee Island. Karen T. Bartlett

an interesting past. Common is the belief, in fact, that the Gulf Coast has no history because it lacks Williamsburg's colonial homes or Philadelphia's monuments.

True, the Gulf Coast's early pioneers left no standing architecture. Termites, flimsy building styles, erosion, and tropical storms saw to that. But earlier settlers did leave other proof of their existence, artifacts that date as far back as 10,000 years. If that isn't history, what is?

Calusa Kingdom

Archaeologists of this century have discovered remnants of early architecture and lifeways in the shell mounds of the Calusa and Timucua tribes, who settled the coastlines more than 2,500 years ago. The Timucua inhabited the Sarasota Bay coast for many years and then migrated northward and to the east; the Calusa later moved into the Sarasota area and were centered around Charlotte Harbor.

Evidence of still earlier civilizations has been found, placing Florida's first immigrants, possibly from Asia, in the upper coast regions circa 8200 BC. Little is known about these early arrivals except that they used pointed spears.

Archaeological excavations and the writings of Spanish explorers give us a more complete picture of the Calusa and other tribes, who built shell mounds to bury their dead and debris. Learned consensus brings the Calusa and the Timucua to southern Florida from Caribbean islands—evidence of similar lifestyles and sustained contact suggests a connection to the peaceful Arawak Indians of the West Indies. Similarities have also been found between the Calusa and South American tribes, leading some historians to consider Florida's tribes to be wayward relatives of the Mayans or Aztecs, given the indications of their great engineering skills. Others trace the connections to trade rather than origin.

The name Calusa, or Caloosa, was used first by Spanish conquerors, who understood the name of the tribe's chief to be Calos. They were said to be tall people with hip-length hair that men wore in a topknot. When clothed, men dressed in breeches of deerskin or woven palmetto fiber, and women fashioned garments out of Spanish moss. They cultivated corn, pumpkins, squash, and tobacco; fished for mullet and mackerel with harpoons and

Early Florida explorers encountered savage beauty on Gulf Coast shores. Karen T. Bartlett

palmetto-fiber nets; hunted for turkey, deer, and bear with bow and arrow, deer-bone dirks, and Aztec-style weapons; and harvested wild sea grapes, fruit, yams, swamp cabbage (hearts of palm), and the coontie root, out of which they pounded flour for bread. Conch and whelk shells were crafted into tools for building and cooking. The natives spent their leisure time wrestling, celebrating the corn harvest, and worshiping the sun god. Great men of the sea, the Calusa built canoes and traveled in them to Caribbean islands and the Yucatán. A different style of pirogue took them along rivers and bay waters to visit villages of their own tribe and those of other Nations.

Much of our information about the Calusa comes from the son of a Spanish official stationed in Cartagena, in what is now Colombia. The youngster, Hernando de Escalante Fontaneda, was shipwrecked along Calusa shores en route to Spain. He lived among the tribe for 17 years, learned its language, and, upon returning to Spain in 1574, recorded its customs. In 1895 Frank Hamilton Cushing explored Charlotte Harbor's Amerindian heritage. He surmised that the Calusa's religious structures and palmetto piling homes had perched on shell mounds along riverbanks and coastlines. Terraces and steps bit into the towering mounds where gardens and courts had been built. Manmade canals up to 30 feet wide connected neighboring villages. Pine Island, Mound Key, Manasota Key, and Marco Island were important religious and governmental centers for the Calusa.

Excavations along the Gulf Coast continually provide new information about the region's native inhabitants and their symbiotic relationship with nature.

Spanish Imposition

Greed and religious fervor eventually warped this idyllic picture, and the Calusa showed themselves to be vicious warriors in an attempt to preserve the life they knew. Juan Ponce de León first crashed the party in 1513. It's possible that early slavers from the Caribbean were responsible for the Calusa hostility he encountered, or perhaps the Amerindians' early hatred of the *conquistadores* was gained secondhand, trading with island natives. Whatever the reason, Ponce was "blacklisted" by the Calusa shortly after he began his search, according to legend, for Bimini, a storied land of treasure and youth.

Ponce de León made his first landing on Florida's east coast. This celebrated Eastertime event went off without a hitch, and the conqueror named the land after the Spanish holiday Pascua Florida. However, his second landing, days later, was met by shell-tipped spears and bows and arrows. His three wounded sailors were the first Europeans known to shed blood in Florida. Ponce de León's ship continued to the west coast, where it stopped in the vicinity of Marco Island. Here one native astounded him by speaking to him in Spanish—learned, perhaps, from West Indies contacts. Impressed, Ponce de León allowed his party to be tricked by a marauding native army in canoes but escaped with the loss of only one man's life.

After several trips to Florida and the Gulf Coast, Ponce de León returned to Puerto Rico—still treasureless and now middle-aged—to plot a new scheme. In 1521 he set out to establish a Gulf Coast colony as a base for treasure explorations. This time the party he crashed had been forewarned, possibly by smoke signals. Calusa arrows pierced the heavy armor of the Spaniards, killing and wounding many, the latter including the great seeker of youth himself. Returned to Havana for medical attention, Ponce de León died there at the age of 60.

Lust for gold overcame common sense as more explorers and invaders followed in Ponce de León's tragic footsteps. In 1539 Hernando de Soto sailed from Havana and headed up the

Gulf Coast, seeking, it would seem, a way to confuse future historians. Three different crewmen described the expedition three different ways. The Smithsonian Institution has published a report some locals still dispute, which claims that de Soto landed first on Longboat Key and then, looking for fresh water, headed toward Tampa Bay. Others are convinced that his first landfall was at Fort Myers Beach. According to the Smithsonian, de Soto set up his first mainland camp at an abandoned native village at the mouth of the Manatee River, near modern-day Bradenton. Regardless of where the landing took place, we know that de Soto scoured the coast for gold, all the while torturing and killing Native Americans who would not, or could not, lead him to it.

Sarasota and its environs embrace the Smithsonian study's findings. Some say the name of the town itself, initially written as "Sara Sota," comes from the conqueror. Others prefer a more romantic legend regarding his fictional daughter, Sara. Sarasota's first hotel, in any case, took its name from de Soto. Near Bradenton, a small national park marks the alleged spot of his first landing.

In 1565 Pedro Menéndez de Avilés came to the Gulf Coast, searching for a son lost to shipwreck and a group of Spaniards being held captive by the Calusa. With the aid of one of Chief Calos's Spanish captives, Menéndez befriended Calos with flattery and gifts, then built a fort and a mission at a spot called San Anton, believed to have been on Pine Island. But Menéndez insulted the great chieftain by rejecting his sister as a wife and allying himself with enemy tribes. Sensing Calos's anger, Menéndez tricked the leader into captivity and had him beheaded. When Menéndez later executed Calos's son and heir to the throne, along with 11 of his subchiefs, tribesmen burned their own villages, forcing the settlers to bail out in search of food.

The century that followed is considered the Golden Age of the Calusa. It was marked by freedom from European intrusion and great cultural advances, heightened by the contribution of Spanish captives who had refused to be saved by Menéndez's rescue party and others who found Calusa ways preferable to "civilization."

Eventually, peaceful trading softened the hostility between Spanish settlers and the Calusa. Cuban immigrants began building a fishing industry around Charlotte Harbor. But although the Calusa had won the war against Spanish invaders, they were defenseless against the diseases the Europeans brought with them. By the turn of the 19th century, smallpox and other diseases had killed off most Calusa; the remainder were absorbed by inbreeding with the Cubans and newly arriving tribes. The most prominent of the latter were the Seminole—a name meaning "wanderer"—a mixture of Georgian Creek, African, and Spanish bloodlines.

The Varmint Era

"A haunt of the picaroons of all nations," wrote explorer James Grant Forbes in 1772, referring to Charlotte Harbor—layover, if not home, for every scoundrel who sailed its island-clotted waters. The Gulf Coast's maze of forbidding bayous and barely navigable waterways made it a favorite hideout for escaped criminals, bootleggers, government refugees, smugglers, and—that most popular of all local folk characters—buccaneers.

Pirate legends color the pages of regional history books in shades of blood red and doubloon gold. Besides willing to residents a certain cavalier spirit, these pirates have left —if one believes the tales—millions of dollars in buried treasure. "After researching the subject in 1950 . . . then State Attorney General Ralph E. Odum estimated that some $165 million is still buried beneath Florida's sands and waters," reported a 1978 issue

Kingdom of Gasparilla

Of all the rum-chugging and throat-slashing visitors to have set foot upon southwest Florida's tolerant shores, José Gaspar (known by the more properly pirate-sounding name "Gasparilla") is the one remembered most fondly. Gaspar set up headquarters, it is said, on Gasparilla Island, where Boca Grande now sits. In his time it was called High Town. He built a palmetto palace there and furnished it with the finest booty. Low Town he placed on a separate island so as to distance himself from the crude lifestyles of his rowdy shipmates. Gasparilla's fort stood on Cayo Costa.

Legends say Gasparilla got his start as a pirate after some nasty business with the wife of a crown prince. He gave up his cushy position as admiral of the Spanish navy for the hardships of life at sea and in the jungles of late-18th-century Florida.

His address might have changed, but his love of beautiful women did not. He kidnapped the fairest and wealthiest of them from captured ships and whisked them off to another Gulf Coast island named for its inhabitants—Captiva—until ransom money arrived. Gasparilla took the most beautiful of his captives to High Town, to woo them with fine wines, jewels, and Spanish poetry. One object of his affection, a Mexican princess named Joséfa, would have nothing to do with such a barbarian. Finally, driven to madness by her insults, Gasparilla beheaded his beloved. He carried her body to another key in his island fiefdom, where he buried her with remorse and sand. He named the island Joséfa, which, through the years and the twistings of rum-swollen tongues, has been perverted to Useppa. And so the exclusive island is called today.

Nearby Sanibel Island, according to one legend, got its name from the abandoned lover of Gaspar's gunner. However, variations abound and improve with each telling. The legend began with the ramblings of old "Panther Key John" Gomez and was perpetuated by railroad press agents and optimistic treasure hunters.

Serious historians doubt the existence of a man named Gasparilla but concede that one of the many Gulf Coast pirates might have borrowed the island's name. Others hold tenaciously to the legend, plying coastal sands with shovels and dredges in search of his ill-gotten booty.

of the *Miami Herald's Florida Almanac,* "$30 million of it originally the property of Jose Gaspar."

Besides the mostly mythical Gaspar, other picaresque names resound along the Gulf Coast: Jean Lafitte, of New Orleans fame; Bru Baker, Gaspar's Pine Island cohort; and a dark soul named Black Caesar. Henry Castor supposedly buried treasure on Egmont Key in the mid-1700s. Local legend places the notorious Calico Jack Rackham and his pirate lover, Anne Bonny, on the shores of Fort Myers Beach for a playful honeymoon. Black Augustus lived and died a hermit on Mound Key, to the south. On Panther Key, John Gomez, Gaspar's self-proclaimed cabin boy, lived to be 122 and sold maps purportedly leading to Gasparillan gold to many a gullible treasure hunter.

According to more reliable historical records, island pirate havens were replaced by or coexisted with crude Spanish fishing ranchos, which cropped up as early as the 1600s. The camps—which provided Cuban traders with salted mullet and roe to eat—consisted of thatched shacks, some built on pilings in shallow waters. Here families lived, according to customs inspector Henry B. Crews, "in a state of Savage Barbarism with no associate but the Seminole Indians and the lowest class of refugee Spaniards who from crime have most generally been compelled to abandon the haunts of civilized life."

Ice-making and railroads changed the direction of fish exportation from southern points to northern destinations. Punta Gorda, with the area's first railroad station, became the center for the transshipment of fresh fish. Major fish-shipping companies built stilt houses for the more than 200 men who harvested their mullet crops. These structures straddled shallows from Charlotte Harbor to Ten Thousand Islands, providing homes for the fishermen and their families until the late 1930s, when modern roads and the burning of Punta Gorda's Long Dock brought the era to a close. Fewer than a dozen of the historic fish shacks have survived hurricanes, erosion, and the state's determination to tear them down as a public nuisance. They strut along the shallows of Charlotte Harbor, in greatest concentration offshore of North Captiva Island.

"It is highly important that no person should be permitted to settle on the Islands forming 'Charlotte Harbor' . . . which are of no value for the purpose of agriculture, being in general formed of sand and shells," advised Assistant Adjutant General Captain Lorenzo Thomas in 1844. Nonetheless, out of this era of varmints sprouted a tradition of farming. Coconuts, citrus, tomatoes, and other crops were raised, despite hardship and heartbreak, as plucky pioneers trickled in to coax their livelihood from a hostile environment.

Years of Discontent

The bloody years of the Wars of Indian Removal began in 1821, when Andrew Jackson—then governor of the territory—decided to claim northern Florida from the Seminole tribes that were wreaking havoc on American settlers. By 1837 fighting had spread to the southern reaches of the peninsula, and two forts were built upriver from present-day Fort Myers. The following year the government reached an agreement with the Seminoles, restricting them to mainland areas along the Charlotte Harbor coast, the Caloosahatchee River, and southward.

News of imminent peace prompted Josiah Gates to build a hotel on the banks of the Manatee River, near modern-day Bradenton, in anticipation of the influx of settlers from Fort Brooke (Tampa) that the treaty would bring. A modest community rose up around this precursor of southwest Florida resorts. Families of soldiers and wealthy southern planters settled in the area. The latter brought their slaves and built sugarcane plantations on vast expanses of land that they bought for $1.25 an acre.

Sarasota got its first permanent settler in 1842 when William Whitaker, a fisherman, built his home on Yellow Bluff, overlooking Sarasota Bay. He and his new wife, daughter of one of the Manatee planters, had 10 children and later went into cattle ranching and farming. The year after the peace treaty was signed, a tribe of Seminoles attacked a settlement across the river from their village, on the same site as present-day Fort Myers. The Harney Point Massacre rekindled the war. Fort Harvie was built near the site of the violent attack. Chief Billy Bowlegs led his people in evasive tactics through the wild and mysterious Everglades, but by 1842 the government had captured 230 of his people and shipped them west. Further pursuit was abandoned. Only Fort Harvie and one other fortification remained operational. A new agreement contained the Seminoles along the Caloosahatchee and barred them from the islands, to protect the fishermen and their families. The treaty made no mention of the swampland, probably because the government considered it useless; the Seminoles assumed the territory was theirs.

By 1848, three years after Florida's admission to the Union as the 27th state, there was a surge of interest in the wetlands. The government, envisioning drainage projects to create more land, offered the Seminoles $250 each to relocate in the West. When they refused, a

The story of Chief Billy Bowlegs finds an audience along Venice's main thoroughfare. Karen T. Bartlett

systematic plan to conquer them went into effect. This plan included the repair of Fort Harvie, which was renamed Fort Myers after a U.S. colonel who had served for many years in Florida and was engaged to the commanding general's daughter. Manpower was increased there, and the fort was reinforced and enlarged. Scouting parties stalked the Seminoles but usually found only the remains of abandoned and burned villages when they arrived.

In December 1855, after soldiers destroyed Billy Bowlegs's prize banana patch, the Seminole chief and his people retaliated. Fort Myers became the center of war activity. The government placed a bounty on the head of any Seminole brought to the fort and offered $1,000 to each Seminole warrior ($100 to each woman and child) who agreed to leave the area. Finally in 1858, after soldiers had captured his granddaughter and other women of the tribe, Billy Bowlegs capitulated, thus bringing an end to 37 years of killing and deception by the government and the military. Fort Myers was abandoned, and the remaining Seminole dispersed deep into the Everglades. Farmers, planters, fishermen, and cattlemen continued peacefully in their trades, although government vigilance against alliances with the Seminole forced some of the island fishing *ranchos* to close during the war's final years. Today the Seminole live on reservations, earning an income from tourism, fishing, and casinos.

In the late 1850s, Virginia planter Captain James Evans purchased Fort Myers on the auction block. He brought in his slaves to work the crops he envisioned—tropical fruits, coconut palms, coffee, and other exotic plants. The Civil War interrupted his venture, sending him back home. Florida joined the Confederacy in 1861. West coast inhabitants generally remained uninvolved until a federal blockade at Key West cut off supplies, at which point they turned to the profitable business of blockade running.

Cattle Kings, Carpetbaggers, and Crackers

Jacob Summerlin epitomized the Florida cattle king. He dressed in a floppy hat, leather boots, and trail dust. Having established a steady trade between Florida and ports south before the Civil War, Summerlin was in a good position to provide the Confederate Army with contraband beef. Working with his blockade-running partner, James McKay Sr., he drove his cattle from inland Florida to Punta Rassa, where the causeway from Sanibel Island makes landfall today. There he sold his scrub cattle, descendants of livestock left by the early Spaniards. The U.S. Navy eventually learned of these illegal dealings and stationed boats at Sanibel and Punta Rassa. In spite of attempts to thwart their trade, however,

Summerlin and McKay sold 25,000 steers to the Confederates between 1861 and 1865.

Jake Summerlin lived by the seat of his pants, driving cattle to Punta Rassa and collecting big bags of Cuban gold—which he spent at the end of the line on drinking and gaming. In 1874 he built the Summerlin House at Punta Rassa, where he and his men could bunk and invest the profits of the business in frivolity.

The rough, free-and-easy lifestyle of the cow hunter attracted young post–Civil War drifters. In addition, Summerlin's success lured Civil War officers into the prosperous life of the cattle boss, including Captain F. A. Hendry, founder of an ongoing Fort Myers dynasty. Between 1870 and 1880 stockmen sold 165,000 head of cattle at Punta Rassa for more than $2 million. Into the 1900s, the cow hunters drove their herds through the streets of downtown Fort Myers, past the homes of wealthy investors and bankers.

Reconstruction brought other settlers to Florida's west coast. One notable rebel refugee, Judah P. Benjamin—who had served as the Confederacy's secretary of state—ducked indictment as a war criminal by hiding out in Florida. His week-long asylum at the old Gamble plantation near Bradenton ensured the landmark's preservation by the United Daughters of the Confederacy.

The first postwar visitors to Fort Myers were the vultures who picked the fort clean of coveted building materials. Then came men who remembered the old fort in its heyday and hoped to settle with their families in this land of plenty. The first settler, Captain Manuel A. Gonzalez, had run a provisions boat from Tampa during the Seminole War. He and his family moved from Key West with another family named Vivas. Other war officers and refugees settled in and around the ruins of the old fort, planting gardens, opening stores, and living a blissful existence unknown elsewhere in the devastated South.

Captain James Evans returned to Fort Myers from Virginia to find his land comfortably occupied. After struggling in the courts to keep the land out of government hands, he split it with the squatters in exchange for a share of his legal fees. In 1872 the first school in Fort Myers was built. County government was centered 270 miles away, in Key West.

Some historians credit the cow hunters with contributing the name "Cracker" to early Florida settlers, which they say derives from the cracking of the long whips the cowmen used to drive their herds. Others say it originated with the Georgia settlers who cracked corn for their hush puppies, corn pone, and fritters. Georgians did, in fact, drift down to southwest Florida, most notably the Knight clan, which founded a settlement at Horse and Chaise, named by seamen to describe a landmark clump of trees. (The name was changed to Venice in 1888 by developer Frank Higel, who was reminded of the Italian city by the area's many bayous and creeks.)

The Homestead Act, passed in 1862, entitled each settler in Florida to 160 acres of land, provided they built a home and tended the land for five years. As it intended, the act brought a flood of intrepid settlers into the area from all over the eastern seaboard and Deep South. Traveling by foot or boat, they built rough palmetto huts, burned cow chips to ward off mosquitoes that carried yellow fever, ate raccoon purloo and turtle steaks, and stubbornly endured the heat, hurricanes, and freezes that stymied a number of enterprises: sugar refining, fish-oil production, and pineapple and citrus farming.

Florida's cow hunters eventually proved detrimental to the agriculturally based ventures associated with the Crackers of the Sarasota Bay region. They allied themselves with greedy land speculators who, by 1883, underhandedly nullified the beneficial effects of the Homestead Act. These speculators had discovered a loophole in Florida's land development legislation, namely the Swamp Land Act, which allowed them to purchase flooded land at rock-bottom prices while overriding homestead claims. They succeeded in declaring arable property swampland and ultimately bought up a good 90 percent of present-day Manatee County, much of which had been worked for years by hardy pioneers. Together the speculators and the cattlemen fought farmers' protests against "free ranging," the practice of letting herds roam and feed without restriction. A Sara Sota Vigilance Committee formed in opposition, and by the time the fighting ended, two men lay dead.

As thatch homes gave way to wooden farmhouses—the tin-roofed vernacular style today termed Cracker—Gulf Coast settlements entered a new era, an era that made "riffraff" out of Crackers, rich men out of schemers, and exclusive getaways out of crude frontier towns.

At the Drop of a Name

When your first guests are Juan Ponce de León and Hernando de Soto, whom do you invite next? With such a standard set, it wouldn't do to host just anybody. So began west coast Florida's tradition of larger-than-life visitors with impressive names and pedigrees, all of whom just as impressively influenced the region's development. Thomas Edison, Henry Ford, Harvey Firestone, John and Charles Ringling, Charles Lindbergh, Teddy Roosevelt, Henry du Pont, Andrew Mellon, Rose Cleveland, and Shirley Temple were among the wide array of early southwest Florida winterers. Their fame and following quickly elevated the status of the lower Gulf Coast from crude and backward to avant-garde and exclusive, attracting the cutting-edge elite. They set national trends by declaring new hot spots— fresh, wild, unspoiled places about which no one else knew, especially the paparazzi. It was they who balanced the very wild coast with a very civilized clientele. The area's natural endowments of fish, fowl, and game attracted adventurers, fishermen, and hunters with the means to make the long, slow journey.

The first and most influential name in any Gulf Coast retrospective is Thomas Edison. Disappointed by the cold winters of St. Augustine, the ailing inventor embarked on a scouting cruise along the Gulf Coast in 1885, the same year Fort Myers was incorporated. As Edison sailed along the Caloosahatchee River, he sighted a stand of bamboo trees. Then and there he decided to move to Fort Myers. And he wanted that property!

The bamboo worked well as filament in Edison's lightbulb experiments, and the climate bolstered his failing health, helping to add another 46 years to his life. On the banks of the Caloosahatchee the inventor fashioned his ideal winter home, Seminole Lodge, complete with laboratory and tropical gardens. Holder of more than a thousand patents, the genius experimented with rare plants in his quest to produce inexpensive rubber for his friend, tire mogul Harvey Firestone. So enamored with Fort Myers was Edison that he persuaded Firestone to spend his winters there. He also set up fellow visionary Henry Ford on an estate next to his. A self-styled botanist, Edison planted the frequently photographed row of royal palms lining the street that eventually ran past his home, McGregor Boulevard, thereby earning the town its nickname: City of Palms.

Meanwhile, the Florida Mortgage and Investment Company—connected with such notables as the archbishop of Canterbury and estate owner Sir John Gillespie—lured a colony of politically disgruntled Scotsmen to Sara Sota, a paradise of genteel estates, bountiful orange groves, and cheap land. Or so the brochures promised. But instead of the Garden of Eden and ready-made manor houses about which they had read, the newcomers found shortages of food and building materials. Only through the kindness of the Whitakers and other pioneers did they survive their first month. Then the Gulf Coast's unpredictable winter weather dealt another cold blow, causing most of the colonists to return to their homeland. Those who stayed, however, brought life to the struggling village and sparked it with a determined spirit.

Most influential among the Scottish ranks was John Hamilton Gillespie, son of Sir John. He built the city's first hotel, the De Soto, and introduced the game of golf to Florida. Gillespie initially transplanted the sport from his homeland by building a two-hole links down Main Street, near his hotel; he later built the area's first real course and clubhouse nearby. When the town of Sarasota was incorporated on October 14, 1902, Gillespie became its first mayor.

It was an American woman, however, who firmly and definitively upgraded Sarasota's image. At the turn of the 20th century the name Mrs. (Bertha) Potter Palmer stood for social elitism—not only in her hometown, Chicago, but also in London and Paris, where she kept homes and hobnobbed with royalty. When the widowed socialite decided to visit Sarasota in 1910, hearts palpitated: She could make or break the new town. Enchanted by the area's beauty and the town's quaintness, Mrs. Palmer immediately bought 13 acres that eventually grew to 140,000. She built her home, The Oaks, and a cattle ranch in a community south of Sarasota called Osprey and from there proceeded to spread the word.

Mrs. Palmer's much-publicized love affair with the Gulf Coast drew the attention of John and Charles Ringling, the youngest of the illustrious circus family's seven sons. The two brothers, in a contest of one-upmanship, began buying property around town. They became active in civic affairs, built bridges to Sarasota's islands, and stoked the economy by making the town the winter home for the Ringling Circus. John Ringling, especially, and his wife, Mable, brought to Sarasota a new worldliness born of their extensive travels and love of European art.

The fate of the Charlotte Harbor coast lay mostly in the hands of one powerful man, Henry B. Plant. The west coast's counterpart to Henry Flagler—builder of the east coast's railroad and great hotels—Plant brought the railway to Tampa, where he built a fabulous resort of his own, always in competition with Flagler. At the same time, another railway company extended its tracks to an unknown, unsettled spot in the wilderness of Charlotte Harbor's shores and erected the Hotel Charlotte Harbor. It reigned briefly as the latest posh outpost for wealthy sportsmen and adventurers, counting Andrew Mellon and W. K. Vanderbilt among its patrons. But in 1897, after Plant had acquired the railway to Punta Gorda, he decided that the town's deepwater port and resort posed too much competition for his Tampa enterprises. So he choked the life out of a thriving commercial and resort town by severing the rails to Punta Gorda's Long Dock.

Deepwater ports, railroads, and fabulous hotels went hand in hand in those days: Developers had to provide transportation before they could attract visitors. At the end of the line, the visitors needed a place to stay. In Boca Grande, where a railroad had been built in 1906, the deep waters of Boca Grande Pass attracted Rockefellers, du Ponts, J. P. Morgan, and other industrialists who used the port for shipping phosphate from central Florida. To accommodate them, the graciously refined Gasparilla Inn was built in 1913.

Another man who was to influence the discovery and development of the Gulf Coast came to town in 1911. John M. Roach, Chicago streetcar magnate and owner of Useppa Island, introduced Barron Collier to the area. Collier eventually bought Useppa from his friend and there established the Useppa Inn and the Izaak Walton Club. Both attracted, according to local lore, tarpon fishing enthusiasts the likes of Shirley Temple, Gloria Swanson, Mae West, Herbert Hoover, Zane Grey, and Mary Roberts Rinehart; the latter author then bought nearby Cabbage Key for her son and his bride.

Today's Historic Spanish Point spans eras of Sarasota history from shell-mound-builders to Berthe Palmer, on whose estate it stands. Karen T. Bartlett

Collier went on to infuse life into the southwest coast by underwriting the completion of Tamiami Trail, stalled on its route from Tampa to Miami. He acquired land throughout the county that today bears his name, after earlier attempts by Louisville publisher Walter Haldeman had failed to put Naples on the map.

Along the lower Gulf Coast of Florida, Collier bought more than 1,000,000 acres, much of it under the infamous Swamp Act. Although he dreamed of development on the scale of Flagler and Plant, anticorporation outcry, hurricanes, the Depression, and war stymied his success. His sons inherited his kingdom, which they ruled with a heart for the unique environment their father so loved. Collier's influence increased the awareness of the Gulf Coast as a refuge for crowd-weary stars and illuminati. Its islands still are popular with the rich and famous who seek anonymity.

But what about the ordinary people—Native Americans, fishermen, cattlemen, Crackers, pioneers, and common folk—who loved this land long before it became fashionable to do so? For the most part they lived side by side with this new brand of resident, called the "winterer" or "snowbird." (In Boca Grande they were termed "beachfronters" for their unusual-at-the-time idiosyncrasy of building dangerously close to the shore.) The locals became their fishing guides, cooks, and innkeepers. In some cases their heads were turned by brushes with great wealth. In other instances heightened standards pulled the curtain on cruder lifestyles, especially that of the cow hunter, whose boisterousness and preference for free-running stock hastened his extinction.

Sometimes the common folk protested big-bucks development and were classified as riffraff. The "Cracker" label today, despite the culture's enriching influence on architecture and cuisine, is considered an insult by some native Floridians.

Old fish houses around Charlotte Harbor survive from the 1930s, when fishermen's families lived in and worked out of the stilted structures. Lee County Visitor & Convention Bureau

Booms, Bursts, and Other Explosions

The Gulf Coast's resort reputation came of age at the turn of the 20th century. Sarasota's De Soto, the Hotel Charlotte Harbor, Boca Grande's Gasparilla Inn, the Useppa Inn, Fort Myers's Royal Palm Hotel, the Naples Hotel, and the Marco Inn pioneered in the hotel field, hosting visitors in styles ranging from bare bones to bend-over-backward. They sparked an era touched with Gatsby-type glamour, giddiness, and graciousness.

The Gulf Coast's halcyon days peaked in the early 1920s as the state entered a decade known as the Great Florida Land Boom. Growth came quickly to the young communities of Bradenton, Sarasota, Fort Myers, and Naples. In fact, the good people of the Gulf Coast grew dizzy with the whirl of growth and success.

According to the 1910 census, Sarasota's population was 840; before the 1920s drew to a close, almost 8,400 people called it home. In the meantime the city shaped itself with sidewalks, streets, schools, a newspaper, a pier, an airfield, and the establishment of its own county, having split from Bradenton's Manatee County. A bridge to Siesta Key added a whole new element to the town's personality by plugging it into the gulf and attracting a seaside resort trade.

World War I briefly interfered. Prohibition brought to the coast yet another roguish character: the rumrunner. Homes and hotels popped up like toadstools after a summer rain shower. Increased lodging options opened the Gulf Coast to a wider range of vacationers. The average traveler could now afford Florida's Gulf Coast, no longer just a socialites' haven. A new class of winterer arrived in force, known as the "tin-can tourist" for the trailers and campers they pulled behind their vehicles. Tourist camps sprang up overnight, and southwest Florida became an Everyman's paradise. Real estate profits added to the lure of tourism, and many visitors decided to remain permanently.

The 1920s created Charlotte County along the Charlotte Harbor coast. A bridge was built across the Peace River, connecting the pioneer towns of Charlotte Harbor and Punta Gorda, spurring growth, and spawning subdivisions by the score.

Fort Myers became the seat of a new county named for Confederate General Robert E. Lee. Between 1920 and 1930, the population grew from 3,600 to 9,000, boosted by the completion of Tamiami Trail in 1928. Fort Myers evolved from a raucous cattle town to a modern city with electricity (thanks to Edison), telephone lines, and a railroad. The Royal Palm Hotel treated guests to a regal departure from the cow trails that ran adjacent to the property. A country club put Fort Myers on the golfing map, and a bridge to Estero Island's beautiful beaches further boosted tourism. Real adventurers took the ferry to Sanibel Island, to be accommodated at Casa Ybel or the Palm Hotel.

South of Fort Myers, the farming community of Survey was renamed Bonita Springs. In 1923 Naples (previously a well-kept secret among buyers from such faraway places as Kentucky and Ohio and distinguished vacationers from the upper echelons) became a city, just in time to feel the effects of the tourism boom. The same year, Collier County seceded from Lee County. Everglades City became the first county seat; later, growing, thriving Naples took the honors. In 1927 the Naples Pier, which had served as a landing point for visitors and cargo since 1887, was replaced in importance by a railroad depot.

Gulf Coast skies had never been sunnier: Visitors spent lots of money. Residents prospered. Real estate prices soared. It seemed too good to be true. And indeed it was.

A 1926 hurricane hit Fort Myers, worsening a condition of already deepening debt. In Sarasota, John Ringling suffered severe financial losses from which he never recovered.

On the southernmost coast, however, the national economy had little impact on the surge of interest sparked by the opening of Tamiami Trail.

The Depression blunted the momentum with which the Gulf Coast had developed during the 1920s but in many ways affected the region less drastically than it did other parts of the country. Since it most tragically affected the middle class, wealthy Gulf Coast residents were largely spared. Works Progress Administration (WPA) recovery projects built Fort Myers its waterfront park, yacht basin, and the city's first hospital. The WPA also funded the building of Bayfront Park, a municipal auditorium, and the Lido Beach Casino along the Sarasota Bay coast. And despite serious financial problems, Ringling kept his promises to build bridges and an art museum.

By the beginning of World War II, southwest Florida had firmly joined the 20th century, with modern conveniences that made it popular among retirees. New golf courses accommodated active seniors, who often participated in the civic affairs of their adopted communities more vigorously than they had in those of their hometowns. Professional golf tournaments were introduced, first in Naples and then along the coast, making the area golf's winter home. Later, spring baseball camps brought another spectator sport to this land of year-round recreation.

Heat seekers turned their attention to the Gulf Coast's islands and beachfronts. Golfing communities and waterfront resorts swallowed up local farming and fishing industries. High-rise condominiums replaced Cracker houses, posh resorts toppled tourist fishing camps, and the Gulf Coast continued to grow—albeit not quite as loudly or erratically as in pre-Depression times.

Some areas learned to control their growth. Sanibel Island served as a model, taking grip of its fate after a causeway connected it to the mainland in 1963. It incorporated and introduced measures to protect wilderness areas and limit takeover by developers. The southward expansion of Interstate 75 during the 1970s and 1980s changed the Gulf Coast from a series of towns connected by two-lane roads to communities keeping pace with the world. Communication and transportation systems improved. Commercial development spread to the freeway corridor, leaving downtown areas to fade in bygone glory. Light industry and winter-weary entrepreneurs relocated. Postsecondary schools worked to prepare local youth for the changing marketplace. The construction and tourism industries continued to prosper.

The Gulf Coast remained seemingly untouched by the fluctuations of the American economy. Urban blight was a distant reality. Northerners fled to the Gulf Coast to escape overcrowding, smog, and crime. In previous decades this had caused unnatural development in some of the metropolitan areas. The delicate balance of infrastructure, human services, nature, heritage preservation, and the arts spun out of kilter. The coast lived very much in the present, deaf to the demands of residents, both human and otherwise.

Finally, though, the new trends of ecotourism and social responsibility amplified the voices of the few who had screamed over the decades for preservation of the environment against tourism and cultural sterility. While Sarasota and Naples served as cultural prototypes, Sanibel and Gasparilla Islands provided environmental models. The 1990s saw the dawn of an awareness of the frailty of the west coast's islands, wetlands, and shorelines. At the same time, interest in the area's history grew, and movements were launched to preserve architectural treasures that so far had been spared by the bulldozer. Eventually the dipping economic trends of the early 1990s affected the Gulf Coast. Construction slowed its racing pulse, and unemployment figures jumped as northerners continued to arrive, looking for jobs in this legendary land of treasure and youth.

All of these factors have contributed to the current perspective on the Gulf Coast. Economic fluctuations give city planners occasion to pause and rethink. Future growth is being mapped out with more care than ever before. Dying downtown neighborhoods and abandoned Cracker homes are being revitalized, now recognized as an important part of the area's heritage. Government is drawing into its blueprints the need for environmental preservation, cultural enrichment, and historic renovation. With the new millennium's economic boom comes a more enlightened attitude that promises to return the sunshine to Gulf Coast skies, free of the recent past's dimming clouds. The grain of sand and the mangrove pod from which this land was wrought will once again play a role in its future.

Coastal Culture

One of southwest Florida's great contradictions is that it lies more to the north than to the south on the cultural map. North of it, or inland, you will find Deep South cookery, clog dancing, bluegrass music, and traditional southern arts. In southwest Florida, however, Midwestern and Northeastern U.S. influences sway heavy. The only truly indigenous art forms have their origins in the Seminole Indian traditions of weaving, dancing, and festivals. Other cultures have arrived through the centuries to create one of the nation's richest melting pots. African-Americans, East Indians, Hispanics, and Germans have most indelibly enriched the coastal makeup.

The arts have been heavily influenced through the years by the region's winter population. Many northern-based artists have relocated here, lured by the sea and tropical muses. Others bring with them their appetite for culture, sparking the finest in visual, performing, and culinary arts.

Seminole Henry John Billie crafts canoes the traditional way. Karen T. Bartlett

Southwest Florida Architecture

Years of simmering together Seminole, Cracker, "Yankee," and Caribbean traditions have yielded a unique southwest Florida style, particularly in architecture and cuisine. If one overall style could be said to represent local architecture, it would have to be Mediterranean—specifically, Italian and Spanish-mission forms.

Lumped together under the label "Mediterranean Revival," these southern European influences are found primarily in public and commercial buildings constructed during the boom years of the Roaring Twenties. They're revealed in stucco finish, mission arches, red barrel-tile roofing, bell towers, and rounded step façades. Re-revived Mediterranean Postmodern—updated Mediterranean Revival blended with elements of tropical styles

A Seminole trademark, chikee (pronounced chi-KEY) huts have dotted the Everglades landscape since the Seminole Wars forced the Indians into hostile swampland. Karen T. Bartlett

adopted from the Cracker era—serves as a popular style for upscale housing developments and commercial enterprises.

Cracker vernacular runs a close architectural second. Pure Cracker style began as folk housing. From the single-pen home—a wood-frame one-room house featuring a shady veranda, a high tin roof, an elevated floor, and wood siding—grew more sophisticated interpretations of the style. With Gothic touches, Victorian embellishments, Palladian accents, and New England influences, the humble Cracker house evolved into a trendy, modern-day version termed "Old Florida." Boxy and built on stilts, its most distinctive characteristics include a tin roof and wide wraparound porch.

The latest influence on the Cracker house comes from the Caribbean and the Bahamas via the Keys. Since indigenous West Indian styles are greatly similar to Cracker, especially in their suitability to tropical weather, the convergence was inevitable. The result: sherbet colors and hand-carved fretwork—used as much for ventilation as for decoration—that add charm and whimsy to the basic unit.

Like the Cracker home, the Seminole Indian's chikee (pronounced *chi-KEY*) hut conformed to the tropical climate with its high-peaked roof, wide overhangs, and open sides. Today the thatched roofing that is the chikee's most distinctive feature has become an art form. Still a popular style of housing for the Seminoles and Miccosukees of the Everglades, the chikee has evolved as a trademark of the Gulf Coast watering-hole tradition known as chikee, or tiki, bars.

With the mid-1920s influx of "tin-can tourists," the mobile home replaced the Cracker house on the low end of the architectural totem pole. Mobile home parks still provide low-cost housing, mostly to part-time winter residents, homes that would "look a lot better as beer cans," according to an old Jimmy Buffett tune.

The concrete-block ranch, a popular residential style of the 1970s, was built to withstand hurricanes. The flood regulations of the 1980s raised these up on pilings; lattice and fretwork added interest. Art Deco returned later in the decade as Miami Beach's Art Deco District attracted attention.

Today's Gulf Coast towns are seasoned with period styles and spiced with contemporary looks that strive for compatibility with nature. Screened porches (often called lanais), windowed "Florida rooms," and lots of sliding doors let the outside in, to take full advantage of the unique, enviable climate and environment.

Coastal Cuisine

As for culinary *richesse*, southwest Florida has wowed hungry visitors since the first Europeans came ashore and discovered nature's abundantly stocked pantry. The seas were teeming with Neptune's bounty, and exotic fruits and vegetables flourished on land. In fact, one former Fort Myers newspaper columnist, Bob Morris, adheres to a theory that this was the original Paradise, and it was a sweet, luscious mango, not an apple, that caused Eve's downfall—hence the fruit's name: Man! Go!

Mangoes, though, are not actually native to southwest Florida but grow plentifully along with other naturalized tropical fruit: bananas, coconuts, pineapples, avocados, sapodillas, carambolas (star fruit), and lychees. Citrus fruit, particularly oranges, is of course the region's most visible and profitable crop. Key lime trees grow in profusion, as well. Practically year-round producers, they are a standard part of any good Florida cook's landscaping scheme. Here on the Gulf Coast, as in the Florida Keys, where the tree got named and famed, key lime pie is a culinary paradigm, and each restaurant claims to make

Stone crab claws were "discovered" in the Everglades, and you don't find 'em any fresher than at local restaurants and fish markets. Karen T. Bartlett

the best. In the finest restaurants with the most extravagant dessert menus, key lime pie inevitably outsells the rest. The classic recipe, created by Florida cooks before refrigeration, uses canned sweetened and condensed milk and is elegant in its simplicity. The most important factor is the freshness of the limes—sometimes a problem for restaurants since the fruit does not lend itself to commercial farming. One sure sign of an inauthentic version is the color green. Key limes turn yellow when ripe and, unless the cook adds food coloring, should impart a buttery hue to the pie.

Historically, crop farming has provided coastal residents with economic sustenance. Weather conditions bless farmers with two growing seasons for most ground crops. As land becomes too valuable to farm, agriculture has been pushed inland. Bonita Springs, where acreage remains devoted to tomatoes, and Pine Island, known for its tropical fruits, are the region's final bastions of the agricultural tradition.

Seafood is most commonly associated with Gulf Coast cuisine, including some delicacies unique to Florida. Our prize catch, the stone crab (Florida author Marjorie Kinnan Rawlings once described the taste as being "almost as rare as nightingales' tongues"), was discovered as a food source in the Everglades. They are in-season from October 15 through May 15, and restaurants serve them hot with drawn butter or cold with tangy mustard sauce. Their aptly named shells are usually precracked to facilitate diners' enjoyment.

The gulf shrimp is an emblem of local cuisine. Its poorer cousin, the rock shrimp, gets less publicity because of its hard-to-peel shell. More economical and with a flavor and texture akin to lobster, it's certainly worth tasting. Restaurants change their menus—or at least their daily specials—according to what's in-season. Grouper, the most versatile food fish in the area, traditionally has been available year-round, but environmental pressure is limiting its availability. A large and meaty fish, its taste is so mild that you hardly know it's fish. Winter months bring red and yellowtail snapper—my favorite—to diners' plates. Warmer weather means pompano, cobia, shark, and dolphinfish (also known as mahimahi). Tuna and flounder are caught year-round but sporadically. Some restaurants serve less well-known species, such as triggerfish and catfish, to offset spiraling costs caused by dwindling supplies of the more popular varieties. Fish farming also addresses these shortages. Catfish and a Brazilian fish called tilapia (which tastes similar to snapper) are cultivated most commonly. Fresh fish from around the world supplement local bounty.

The best Gulf Coast restaurants buy their seafood directly from the docks of local commercial fishermen to ensure the utmost freshness. The traditional style of cooking seafood in Florida is deep-frying. Although constituting a mortal sin in this age of gourmet standards and health awareness, it is a true art when properly executed. There's a vast difference between what you find in the frozen food department at the supermarket and what comes hand-breaded, crunchy, and flavor-sealed on your plate at the local fish house.

New Florida style, at the other extreme, has evolved from so-called California, new American, new world, and eclectic styles of cuisine. This type also depends on freshness—of all its ingredients. For this reason it uses local produce, prepared in global culinary styles. Regional cookery—sometimes termed Gulfshore or Floribbean cuisine—prefers tropical foods and ingredients, inspired by the cuisines of New Orleans, Mexico, Cuba, Puerto Rico, Haiti, the Bahamas, Jamaica, and Trinidad. Pacific Rim influences have become prominent in recent years. Depending on the cook, Deep South traditions take their place at the table, too. The outcome at its tamest merely twists the familiar; at its most adventurous, it can treat your taste buds to a veritable bungee jump.

Between the two extremes of old and new Florida styles, Continental cuisine survives in both classic and reinvented forms. Along with restaurants that serve the finest in French and Italian haute cuisine, you will find others that represent the Gulf Coast's melting pot, with authentic renditions or interpretations of a wide variety of cuisines: Native American, Thai, East Indian, Iranian, German, Irish, Greek, Cuban, Jamaican, Amish, Jewish, Mexican, and Puerto Rican.

In its cuisine and cultural makeup as well as its history, the map of Gulf Coast Florida resembles a patchwork quilt. It blankets its people in warmth, checkers its past with colorful and contrasting patterns, and layers its character with intriguing, international textures.

2

TRANSPORTATION

Blazing the Trail

The Gulf of Mexico and its great rivers and Intracoastal Waterway comprise the region's oldest and lowest-maintenance transportation system. From the days when the Calusa paddled the streams and estuaries in dugout canoes, through the romantic steamboat era, and until 1927 when the railroad to Naples was completed, boat travel was the most popular means of getting around. Early homes lined the waterways, and today's houses still face the water, not the roads that accommodate modern-day traffic. Even today the Caloosahatchee River, which empties into the sea along the Island Coast and connects to the east coast via Lake Okeechobee, constitutes part of a major intercoastal water route.

The railroad first came to Charlotte County's deepwater port in 1886 and created the town of Punta Gorda—much to the chagrin of Fort Myers's leaders, who had tried for years to persuade company officials to extend their Florida Southern Railroad to the Caloosahatchee River. Instead, an unpopulated location was selected and a fabulous hotel built there, according to the custom of Florida's great railroad builders of the day. Besides transporting wealthy winterers to the nation's southernmost railroad stop, the trains hauled fresh fish, cattle, and produce.

A train nicknamed "Slow and Wobbly" ran between Bradenton and Sarasota from 1892 to 1894. The Seaboard Railroad built a more reliable version to Bradenton in 1902. In 1911 it was extended beyond Venice, under the influence of Chicago socialite and major landholder Berthe Palmer. When Palmer named the railway terminus Venice, infuriated residents of Venice changed their town's name to Nokomis. Then the Charlotte Harbor and Northern Railway laid track in 1906 to ship phosphate from inland mines to the deep waters of Boca Grande Pass, off Gasparilla Island. Another refined resort came with it.

Fort Myers finally got its first railroad station in 1904. In 1922 the trestles reached Bonita Springs and were later extended to Naples and Marco Island. Famous passengers such as movie stars Hedy Lamarr, Greta Garbo, and Gary Cooper rode the rails to vacation at the posh Naples Beach Hotel & Golf Club, one of Florida's first resorts to boast golf greens on the property.

The concept of a Tamiami Trail made headway when, in 1923, a group called the Trail Blazers traveled the proposed route that would connect Tampa and Miami. Mules, oxen, and tractors were used to complete that first motorized crossing of the Everglades. Progress was slowed by dense jungles, forbidding swampland, devastating heat, and mosquitoes so thick that they covered exposed skin like a buzzing body glove. Builders lived at

Art shows, model train exhibits, and community functions give new life to the old Naples Depot, where celebrities disembarked during the Roaring Twenties. Karen T. Bartlett

the work site, and a whole body of legend grew up around the monumental task. The project was hampered by war and depletion of funds. A special new dredge had to be invented to build the section across the Everglades. Before the trail was paved, it had a sand surface. Summer rains caused flooding. Old-timers remember getting out of the car to catch fish in the road while their parents worked to get their vehicle unstuck. Even after the rains subsided, jarring muck-crusted ruts made the trip less than comfortable.

As the trail's west coast leg inched toward its destination, it changed the communities it penetrated. Thirteen years in the building, Tamiami Trail was met with euphoria when it was completed in 1928, opening communities to land travel, trade, and tourism. Today the Trail—also known as U.S. Highway 41—strings together the region's oldest towns and cities, and newer communities have grown up around it.

With the extension of parallel Interstate 75, Tamiami Trail has lost its role as the sole intercoastal lifeline. Nonetheless, it remains the backbone of the lower west coast. Probing both metropolitan interiors and rural vistas, it provides glimpses of a cross-section of life —as it was and as it is—in southwest Florida.

Highway 41 runs through the middle of the area covered in this book. At the Gulf Coast's northern and southern extremes, the highway edges close to the shoreline. In mid-sections it reaches inland to communities built along harbors and rivers.

Interstate 75 draws the eastern boundary for this guide's coverage. The freeway glimpses, at top speed, Gulf Coast life as it enters the 21st century. Although convenient and free of traffic lights, it misses the character that the more leisurely pace of the Tamiami Trail reveals. However, it does extend the boundaries of Highway 41's family of communities and create new ones.

GETTING TO THE COAST

By Car

Southwest Florida is plugged into Florida's more highly charged areas by both major conduits and small feeders. Tampa/St. Petersburg lies at the Sarasota Bay coast's back door, via Highway 41, Interstate 75, and Interstate 275. Tamiami Trail ends here, but Highway 41 continues on. The interstate proceeds north and connects to Orlando and the east coast via Interstate 4. Highway 19 takes up the coastal route in St. Petersburg, heading toward Georgia. Highway 70 cuts across the state above Lake Okeechobee, to connect the east coast to the Sarasota Bay coast at Bradenton, and at Sarasota and Punta Gorda via Routes 72 and 17 respectively. These roads meander into Native American reservation territory, Arcadia's cowboy country, and the expansive Myakka River State Park. The route runs jaggedly between the Island Coast, the big lake, and West Palm Beach, following a series of lazy two- and four-lane roads, including Routes 80, 27, 441, and 98.

Alligator Alley (Interstate 75) crosses the Everglades with a certain mystique. Once a two-lane toll road on which encounters with crossing gators and panthers were common (tragically, cars inevitably fared better in such encounters), today I-75 has been widened to four lanes, with underpasses for wildlife. Certain times of the year, it continues to earn its name, and a sharp eye can spot hundreds of gators sunning on water banks. But it's still a toll road and still less than user-friendly. Gas up before you approach: Fuel station/restaurant exit breaks are few and far between on the two-hour drive until it reaches the east coast at Fort Lauderdale. Highway 41 takes you into Miami and branches off into Highway 1 to the Florida Keys.

This namesake of Alligator Alley (Interstate 75) enjoys the sun—as do many Florida inhabitants.
Karen T. Bartlett

By Plane

Two major airports service the lower Gulf Coast: **Sarasota-Bradenton International Airport** (SRQ) and **Southwest Florida International** (RSW) in Fort Myers. The Sarasota-Bradenton facility gives a proper introduction to the region, with shark tanks and tropical orchids from local attractions, a two-story waterfall, and works from its prolific artist community. RSW recently expanded facilities from 17 gates to 28. The new terminal opens in June 2005.

Smaller airports and fields service shuttle, charter, and private planes. The Charlotte County airport caters mainly to private craft. North Captiva Island and Everglades City have their own landing strips for private planes, and seaplane service is available to some islands.

GULF COAST ACCESS

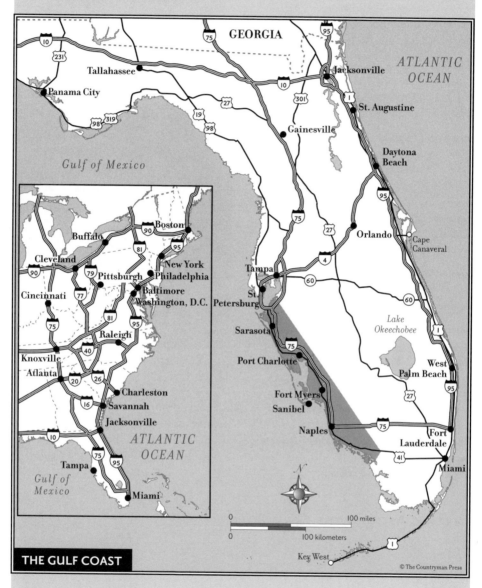

THE GULF COAST

© The Countryman Press

From Florida Cities

From	To Sarasota Bay	To Island Coast	To South Coast
Miami	212 mi./4.25 hr.	148 mi./2.5 hr.	110 mi./2 hr.
Orlando	132 mi./2.25 hr.	167 mi./3.5 hr.	187 mi./3.75 hr.
Daytona	185 mi./3.75 hr.	219 mi./4.25 hr.	241 mi./4.5 hr.
Jacksonville	239 mi./4.5 hr.	311 mi./6 hr.	325 mi./6.25 hr.

Sarasota-Bradenton International Airport (SRQ), 941-359-2770, 941-359-2777; www.srq-airport.com; 6000 Airport Circle, Sarasota 34243. Air Sunshine, ATA, CanJet, Continental, Delta, Northwest, US Airways.

Charlotte County Airport (PGD), 941-639-1101; www.charlottecountyairport.com; 28000 Airport Rd., Punta Gorda 33982.

Southwest Florida International Airport (RSW), 239-768-1000; www.swfia.com; 16000 Chamberlin Pkwy., Fort Myers 33913. Air Canada, Air Tran, America West, American, American Trans Air, Continental, Delta, Frontier, JetBlue, Midwest Express, Northwest/KLM, Song, Spirit Airlines, United, US Airways.

Naples Municipal Airport (APF), 239-643-0733; www.flynaples.com; 160 Aviation Dr. N., Naples 34104.

Welcome to paradise: Southwest Florida International Airport in Fort Myers. Karen T. Bartlett

Marco Island Executive Airport (MKY), 239-394-3355; www.collierairports.com; Collier County Airport Authority, 2003 Mainsail Dr., Naples 34114.

By Bus

Greyhound Lines (www.greyhound.com) Depots are found along the west coast at Bradenton (941-495-3639; 3028 First St. W.), Sarasota (941-955-5735; 575 North Washington Blvd.), Port Charlotte (941-629-4808; 900 Kings Hwy.), Punta Gorda (941-575-2781; 26505 N. Jones Loop), Fort Myers (941-334-1011; 2250 Peck St.), and Naples (941-774-5660; 2669 Davis Blvd.).

GETTING AROUND THE GULF COAST

By Car
Best Routes
Tamiami Trail (Highway 41) forms the heart of the Gulf Coast's major metropolitan areas and provides north-south passage within and between them.

SARASOTA BAY COAST
In Bradenton and Sarasota, Highway 41 runs along bay shores and converges with Highway 301, another major trunk road. Principal through streets for east-west traffic in this area are generally those with exits off Interstate 75, north to south: Manatee Avenue (Route 64), Carter Road (Route 70), University Parkway (closest to the Ringling Museums), Fruitville Road (closest to downtown and the islands), Bee Ridge Road (closest to Siesta Key), Clark Road (Route 72), and Venice Avenue. Note that in 2002 Florida interstate exit numbers

changed to correspond with actual mileage rather than numerical order. Old exit numbers are still noted on the exit signs, along with the new numbers.

Bradenton's 75th Street West (De Soto Memorial Highway) skims the town's western reaches close to the bay front. At exit 220 (old 42), Route 64 travels straight into downtown and out to Anna Maria Island. From the south, take exit 217 (old 41) and follow Route 70 to Highway 41. Head north on Highway 41, then turn west on Route 684 (Cortez Road/44th Avenue), which takes you across the south bridge. Both bridges lead to Gulf Drive (Route 789), the island's main road. Longboat Key lies to the south of Anna Maria Island, across a bridge, along Gulf of Mexico Drive. Lido Key is connected to Longboat Key by yet another bridge and also by bridge from the mainland in downtown Sarasota.

Streets hiccup through downtown Sarasota, starting and stopping without warning. Main Street runs east-west, crossed by Orange Avenue, one of the neighborhood's longest streets. Bayfront Drive arcs around the water and skirts a lot of the town's water-sports action. Bahia Vista intersects Orange at its southern extreme and constitutes a major route. To cross town from north to south between Highway 41 and Interstate 75, take Tuttle Avenue, Beneva Road, McIntosh Road, or Cattlemen Road.

To get to St. Armands Key and Lido Key from downtown Sarasota, follow the signs on Tamiami Trail to cross the new Ringling Causeway, which recently replaced a drawbridge with a high span. To reach Siesta Key from I-75, take exit 205 (old 37/Clark Road) or 207 (old 38/Bee Ridge Road). From Bee Ridge Road, turn north on Highway 41 and west on Siesta Drive, which leads to the north bridge. Clark Road (Route 72) crosses the south bridge and becomes Stickney Point Road. On Siesta's north end, Higel Avenue and Ocean Boulevard are the main routes into the shopping district. Beach Road runs gulfside and intersects with Midnight Pass Road, which travels to the island's south end, intersecting Stickney Point Road.

Take Venice Avenue off Interstate 75 to get to Venice's beaches and old Mediterranean-influenced neighborhoods. Highway 41's business route splits from Tamiami Trail at Venice and takes you to the older part of town. Harbor Drive travels north-south along the beaches. The Esplanade and Tarpon Center Road reach into waterfront communities.

CHARLOTTE HARBOR COAST

Highway 41 heads inland, running within miles of Interstate 75 at some points. In these parts getting to the gulf entails crossing several bodies of water. Most of the routes qualify as back roads and are listed under that heading. A toll bridge links Gasparilla Island (Boca Grande) to the mainland, costing $3.50 for cars to cross.

ISLAND COAST

Bonita Beach is touted as the closest sands to Interstate 75 in this area. Highway 41 again distances itself from its modern counterpart to take you into downtown business districts and past upscale golfing communities. Pine Island Road, Route 78, diverges from the major arteries and crosses North Fort Myers and Cape Coral to reach Pine Island. Del Prado Boulevard and Cape Coral Parkway, which intersect, are Cape Coral's main commercial routes. Stringfellow Road, which lies at the end of Pine Island Road, is Pine Island's principal north-south artery.

On the south side of the Caloosahatchee Bridge, Fort Myers's main east-west connectors are Martin Luther King Jr. Boulevard, Colonial Boulevard (which feeds into the Mid-Point Toll Bridge to Cape Coral), College Parkway (which also crosses the river between Fort Myers and Cape Coral at Cape Coral Parkway with a toll), and Daniels Parkway/Gladiolus Drive.

Thomas Edison is credited with planting the royal palms flanking Fort Myers's prestigious McGregor Boulevard, thereby earning the city its nickname, City of Palms. Karen T. Bartlett

Traveling roughly from north to south, historic and royal-palm-lined McGregor Boulevard (Route 867) follows the river past the old homes that line it. Summerlin Road (Route 869) and Metro Parkway run parallel, to the east. Tamiami Trail becomes Cleveland Avenue. Take McGregor or Summerlin west (they eventually merge) to get to Sanibel and Captiva Islands, land of no traffic lights. There's a $6 toll for crossing the bridge to Sanibel without a transponder gate-pass gizmo. Stay in the right lanes unless you have one. This drawbridge, too, is being replaced by a high span. Periwinkle Way is Sanibel's main drag and connects to Sanibel-Captiva Road via Tarpon Bay Road. Policemen with white gloves direct traffic at the main intersections during high-traffic hours. Sanibel-Captiva Road turns into Captiva Drive at the pass between the two islands. San Carlos Boulevard off Summerlin Road takes you to Fort Myers Beach and the islands that lie to its south along Route 865 (Estero Boulevard in Fort Myers Beach, Hickory Boulevard in Bonita Beach).

SOUTH COAST

Here, Highway 41 (also known as Ninth Street) closes in on the sea once again as it travels through Naples. At Bonita Springs, Old Highway 41 branches off toward the town's business district. Bonita Beach road (exit 116/old exit 18) crosses Highway 41 to travel to Bonita Beach. I-75 exit 111 (old 17) gets you to the Vanderbilt Beach/North Naples area via Route 846; exit 107 (old 16) dumps you into Pine Ridge Road, which leads to the north end of Naples. Interstate 75 then swings east, so that Route 951 at exit 101 (old exit 15) is closer to downtown Naples in a north-west direction but farther in an east-west direction. Depending on the time of year, you're sometimes better off taking exit 107 (old exit 16) to Highway 41 when approaching from the north, then heading south to get downtown. When coming from the south, take exit 101, and hook up with Highway 41.

Parallel to Highway 41 in Naples, major city dissectors include Goodlette-Frank Road (Route 851) and Airport-Pulling Road (Route 31). East-west trunks are, from north to south, the Naples-Immokalee Highway (Route 846) at the north edge of town; Pine Ridge Road (Route 896), Golden Gate Parkway (Route 886), Radio Road (Route 856), and Davis Boulevard (Route 84) in town; and Rattlesnake Hammock Road (Route 864) at the southern extreme.

To get to Marco Island from the north, take Route 951 (interstate exit 101), which will take you to the main high bridge at the island's north end. Route 951 becomes Collier Boulevard and continues through the island's commercial section and along the gulf front. Bald Eagle Drive (Route 953) heads north-south to Olde Marco and mid-island.

It connects to San Marco Drive (Route 92), which crosses the south bridge. The south-end bridge is a better access if you're approaching from the east along Highway 41. Turn south-west off of Highway 41 onto Route 92 to cross the south bridge.

Route 29 takes you from Highway 41 to Everglades City. Take a right onto Camellia Street to get to School Drive along the river, lined with old fishing boats, stacks of crab traps, and fish houses. Copeland Avenue crosses the causeway to Chokoloskee Island.

Alternate Back Roads and Scenic Routes

This section of Gulf Coast has many scenic back roads that bypass traffic and plunge the traveler into timeless scenes and unique neighborhoods. These routes are especially good to know when you tire of counting out-of-state license plates during rush hour in high season.

SARASOTA BAY COAST

Follow the twisty road through a string of barrier islands, from Anna Maria in the north to Bird Key at the end. Route 789 adopts a different name on each island: John Ringling Parkway, Gulf of Mexico Drive, etc. To avoid Highway 41 traffic between downtown Sarasota and Siesta Key, turn west onto Orange Avenue, and follow it through scenic neighborhoods along McClellan and Osprey Avenues to Siesta Drive, and then turn west again. Route 758, along Siesta Key, makes a short, beachy bypass between Siesta Drive and Stickney Point Road. The loop through lovely Casey Key begins between Sarasota and Venice at Blackburn Point Road, off Highway 41, then proceeds south through Nokomis Beach and back to the mainland.

CHARLOTTE HARBOR COAST

To reach Englewood from Venice, cross quiet, out-of-the-way Manasota Key along Route 776 through Englewood Beach. Then follow Routes 775 and 771 back to Route 776 for a scenic drive through the peninsula, separated from the mainland by Charlotte Harbor, or to get to Gasparilla Island. (It costs $3.50 to cross the causeway onto the island.) Park Avenue is the shopper's route in Boca; Gulf Boulevard takes you to the beaches. Staying on 776 takes you more directly to Highway 41. To skirt Highway 41's chain-outlet anonymity in the Port Charlotte area, take Collingswood Boulevard off 776 to Edgewater Drive and back to 41.

Between Charlotte County and the Island Coast, Route 765, or Burnt Store Road, rambles through the county's Cracker era: scrub cattle, rusty tin roofs, and old fishermen bobbing cane poles. This connects to Highway 78, which leads to Pine Island when taken west, or Highway 41 and I-75 when followed east. To enter Cape Coral the back way, follow Veteran's Parkway to Chiquita Boulevard, turn right and then left on Cape Coral Parkway.

Don't let winter-season traffic ruffle your feathers. Hit the scenic back roads. Karen T. Bartlett

ISLAND COAST

The back roads along the Island Coast's shores plunge you briefly into the frenzied activity of Fort Myers Beach along Routes

968 (San Carlos Boulevard) and 865 (Estero Boulevard), then carry you along at a more mellow pace as you cross into Lovers Key and Big and Little Hickory Islands, where 865 becomes Hickory Boulevard. The road returns you via Bonita Beach Road to Highway 41 at Bonita Springs.

SOUTH COAST

Gulfshore Boulevard, which stops and starts to make way for Naples's waterways, is the town's most scenic route, skirting beaches and beautiful homes.

South of Naples, Routes 951, 952, and 953 carry you to Isles of Capri, Marco Island, Goodland, and back to Highway 41 just before the Everglades.

Car Rentals

Rental agencies with airport offices or shuttle service are listed below:

Alamo: 800-327-9633; www.alamo.com (SRQ, 941-359-5540; RSW, 239-768-2424)

Avis: 800-331-1212; www.avis.com (SRQ, 941-359-5240; RSW, 239-768-2121; APF, 239-643-0900)

Budget: 800-527-0700; www.budget.com (RSW, 239-768-1500; APF, 239-643-2212)

Dollar: 800-800-4000; www.dollarcar.com (SRQ, 941-355-2996; RSW, 239-768-2223; APF, 239-793-2226)

Hertz: 800-654-3131; www.hertz.com (SRQ, 941-355-8848; RSW, 239-768-3100; APF, 239-643-1515)

National: 800-328-4567; www.nationalcar.com (SRQ, 941-355-7711; RSW, 239-768-2100; APF, 239-643-0200)

Thrifty: 800-367-2277; www.thrifty.com (SRQ, 941-355-8884; RSW, 239-768-2322)

Airport Taxis/Shuttles

Some hotels and resorts arrange pickup service to and from the airport. Taxi and limousine companies operate in most areas.

Taxi companies that provide transportation to and from the Bradenton-Sarasota airport include **Diplomat Taxi** (941-355-5155), **West Coast Executive Sedans** (941-355-9645, 941-359-8600), and **Longboat Limousine** (941-383-1235, 800-525-4661; www.longboatlimousine.com). For more companies that service the Bradenton-Sarasota airport, call x941-359-5225.

Boca Grande Limo (239-964-0455, 800-771-7433; www.bocagrandelimo.com) provides 24-hour connections to all Florida airports. For a more dramatic arrival or departure, call **Boca Grande Seaplane** (941-964-0234, 800-940-0234). **Charlotte Limousine Service** (941-627-4494) will pick up from and deliver to all airports in the region.

From Southwest Florida International Airport in Fort Myers, **Aaron Airport Transportation** (239-768-1893, 800-998-1898) makes pickups and deliveries throughout the region. Or call **AAA Airport Transportation** (800-872-2711). **Pine Island Taxi** (239-283-7777) provides 24-hour service anywhere with advance notice.

In the south coast area, call **Checker Cab** (239-455-5555), **Naples Taxi** (239-643-2148), or, in Marco Island, **A-Action** (239-394-4000).

By Bus

The Sarasota Bay coast boasts dependable public transportation, with discounts for school-children and seniors. Buses run every day but Sunday, 6am to 6pm. A new downtown trolley runs around Sarasota and St. Armands Circle. For route information, call **Sarasota County Area Transit** (SCAT) (941-316-1234) or **Manatee County Transit** (MCAT) (941-747-8621).

On the Island Coast, city buses follow routes around Fort Myers, Cape Coral, and south Fort Myers. Call **Lee Tran** (239-275-8726) for schedules and information about trolley rides to and around Fort Myers Beach's beach accesses, including Lovers Key.

The **Naples Trolley** (239-262-7300; www.naplestrolleytours.com) conducts sightseeing and shopping tours in the Naples area. The **Marco Island Trolley** (239-394-1600; www.marcoislandtrolley.net) visits 13 different historical sites.

By Carriage

The **Naples Horse and Carriage Company** (239-649-1210) provides evening tours of Old Naples, the beaches, and the fishing pier in season.

By Train

The **Seminole Gulf Railway** (239-275-8487, 800-SEM-GULF; www.semgulf.com), stationed at the corner of Colonial Boulevard and Metro Parkway in Fort Myers, does dinner trips, Murder Mystery Tours, and other excursions throughout the area.

By Water

Water no longer provides functional transportation routes on the Gulf Coast, except to the unbridged islands. Today boat travel is mostly recreational. The region boasts two trademark water vessels: The noisy, power-driven **airboat**, designed especially for the shallow waters of the Everglades, and the **swamp buggy**, an all-terrain vehicle built to carry 2 to 20 passengers that travels on fat tire treads. In addition, **pontoon boats** offer a more conventional way to explore the Everglades and coastal shallows.

Numerous sightseeing tours and charters originate daily at marinas and resorts. Some specialize in fishing, others in shelling or birding. Many include lunch at an exotic island restaurant, while a few serve meals on board. All cater to the sightseer. Most tour operators are knowledgeable about sights and history on local waterways. These are all listed in the "Recreation" section of each chapter.

Ed Frank (second from far right) invented the swamp buggy, an amphibious form of transportation engineered for travel in the Everglades. He poses here in 1947 with his brainchild and his hunting buddies. Collier County Historical Society, Inc.

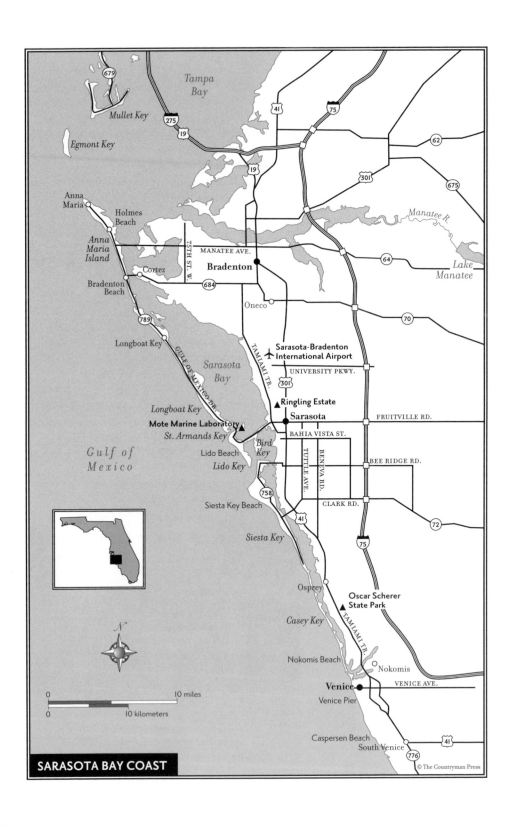

Tampa
Bay

Mullet Key

Egmont Key

Anna
Maria

Holmes
Beach

*Anna
Maria
Island*

Cortez

Bradenton
Beach

789

Longboat Key

GULF OF MEXICO DR.

*Sarasota
Bay*

Longboat Key

Mote Marine Laboratory

St. Armands Key

Lido Beach

Lido Key

*Gulf of
Mexico*

*Bird
Key*

25TH ST. W.

MANATEE AVE.

Bradenton

684

Oneco

TAMIAMI TR.

✈ **Sarasota-Bradenton
International Airport**

UNIVERSITY PKWY.

301

▲ **Ringling Estate**

● **Sarasota**

BAHIA VISTA ST.

TUTTLE AVE.

BENEVA RD.

FRUITVILLE RD.

BEE RIDGE RD.

679

275

19

41

75

62

301

675

Manatee R.

64

Lake
Manatee

70

758

Siesta Key Beach

41

Siesta Key

CLARK RD.

75

72

Osprey

▲ **Oscar Scherer
State Park**

Casey Key

TAMIAMI TR.

Nokomis Beach

○ Nokomis

Venice

VENICE AVE.

Venice Pier

Caspersen Beach

South Venice

776

41

0 ——————————— 10 miles

0 ——————————— 10 kilometers

N

SARASOTA BAY COAST

© The Countryman Press

3

SARASOTA BAY COAST

Seashore Sophisticate

The cities of Bradenton and Sarasota dominate the Sarasota Bay coast, an expanse of metropolitan sprawl barricaded behind sybaritic, beach-centric islands. History and a heritage of high culture add dimension to this world of sand and city streets.

Bradenton draws much of its historical identity from the supposed landing of Hernando de Soto on local shores. Old Hernando—scoundrel and sadist though he turned out to be—gives the town a reason to celebrate its heritage each year when it reenacts the momentous occasion. A national park further recognizes the Indian-slaying conquistador.

Later in the history of Bradenton and the surrounding mainland communities, two pioneering influences dictated a low-key attitude and light development. The first, the wealthy plantation owners of the 1840s, ranked Manatee County as the largest area in the state for sugar and molasses production. Sugar's aristocratic families set the social standards of the town until the Civil War turned the sweetly lucrative sugar industry sour. The second, 19th-century land speculators, exploited Florida's Swamp Act, which had an opposite, stunting

Fountains and playful sculpture define Sarasota's bayfront with its island high-rise backdrop. Karen T. Bartlett

effect on the area's development. By having homestead properties fraudulently declared wetlands, they prevented agricultural expansion and delayed its by-product, the building of railroads.

Wealthy social godparents guided Sarasota's early development. Mrs. Potter (Bertha Honore) Palmer, known as "queen of Chicago society," settled south of town in 1910, which eventually drew John Ringling and his circus to Sarasota. Though lesser known today, Mrs. Palmer exerted an influence equal to Ringling's in attracting attention to the area around Sarasota Bay. Sarasota continues to grow as a wealth-conscious town—not too big, not too small, just right. In past years, growth has been upward as the downtown bayside skyline fills in with luxury condo and resort towers, the Ritz-Carlton and Renaissance among them.

Most of Bradenton's modern growth has occurred since 1970, when tourism and shipping into deepwater Port Manatee became major income sources. Today, preservation of the Gamble Plantation and original village structures along with downtown waterfront restoration projects and a new artists' colony make Bradenton a vital city textured with an interesting past.

The village of **Cortez** lies southwest of Bradenton and several eras to the past. Fishing made this peninsular community, and fishing remains its livelihood. Along its southern waterfront, a working fishing operation and its toilers reside in a time-stilled setting.

Fishing, resorts, and heterogeneous neighborhoods mark the three incorporated towns of **Anna Maria Island: Anna Maria, Holmes Beach**, and **Bradenton Beach**. The first Anna Maria Island settlers of record were George Emerson Bean and his family, circa 1890. He developed the island in the early 1900s for tourists, who arrived by boat at the Anna Maria City pier. In 1921 the first bridge to the island was built from Cortez.

Longboat Key to the south was mentioned often on the maps and journals of early Spanish explorers. It supposedly got its name from the longboats that Hernando de Soto's scouting party used to come ashore. Aside from one tucked-away village with a salty, local flavor, Longboat Key is known for its prim and properness. A series of seven historic markers relate Longboat Key's history as a 16th-century destination for Timucuan canoes and Spanish galleons, a World War II bombing target, and a major shipping port destroyed by the hurricane of 1921.

Old fishing traditions endure in the village of Cortez. Karen T. Bartlett

The Town the Circus Built

The circus comes as close to being the world in microcosm as anything I know: in a way it puts all the rest of show business in the shade. Its magic is universal and complex.
—E. B. White, Ring of Times, 1956

Legend has it that Bird Key and St. Armands Key, two of Sarasota's barrier islands, became John Ringling's possessions in a poker game. Tales of the circus master's influence on the area's development have grown to mythic proportions: elephants that built bridges, midgets who built fortunes, and an eccentric who built himself an Italian palace. However true the legends, during the 20 years after John Ringling came to Sarasota to house his circus here in winter, he demonstrated a three-ring influence over the city and its barrier islands.

After falling in love with the fledgling mainland village and purchasing real estate offshore, Ringling erected his lavish mansion, Cà d'Zan ("House of John" in Italian, modeled after a Venetian palazzo). He also began the construction of a causeway to Lido Key by filling and dredging, and he dreamed of a city park and a shoppers' haven on St. Armands Key. For Longboat Key he envisioned a world-class hotel. With unbridled fervor he set out during his worldwide travels to acquire a fine collection of Baroque art for public display in a museum.

The dreams Ringling failed to realize before he died in 1936 were not abandoned. The causeway was completed and donated to the state. St. Armands Circle today is famed for its shops. The steel skeleton of what was to be the world's finest hotel sat rusting on Longboat Key for years until it was reborn as a modern resort. The John and Mable Ringling Museum of Art encompasses acres of bayside estate, and its collection and grounds include Baroque statuary, original Rubens masterpieces, a rose garden, the restored Venetian Gothic mansion Cà d'Zan, a circus museum, and an antique Italian theater.

Aside from John Ringling's concrete legacy to Sarasota, he bequeathed an undying commitment to beauty, fantasy, art, and showmanship. The circus remains an important industry in Sarasota—in fact, at the high school, circus is an extracurricular activity, like football. Theaters and galleries thrive, thanks to Ringling's patronage of the arts. Without his influence, the entire coast might well have remained a cultural frontier for many more decades.

Remote **Siesta Key** resisted settlement until the turn of the 20th century, when a hotel launched the island's reputation as a restful place. A bridge built in 1917 finally brought permanent residents to the island. Siesta Key has historically attracted creative types. One of its best-known citizens was prolific writer John D. Macdonald, most famous for his Travis McGee detective novels. While living on Siesta Key he is believed to have written more than 70 novels. Witty essayist E.B. White was a regular visitor around the '40s. Pulitzer Prize–winning author MacKinlay Kantor and late abstractionist Syd Solomon also settled on the island, and Pulitzer Prize–winning cartoonist Mike Peters lived there for many years. Other cartoonists and artists have also found the area conducive to creativity. Hagar the Horrible's Dik Browne lived here while alive; now his son Chris has moved in. Garfield's Jim Davis has wintered on Longboat Key. Surrealist Jimmy Ernst, son of Dada master Max Ernst, spent much time on Casey Key during his life. Artist Thornton Utz and jazz notable Jerry Jerome still have homes in the area.

The Webb family first arrived in the Sarasota area in 1867 to plant the seed for a town they named **Osprey** 17 years later. Here is where Bertha Honore Palmer headquartered when she arrived in 1910.

The original village of **Venice** sat where Nokomis does today. It moved south and seaward after the railroad bypassed it in 1922 toward a station in the middle of nowhere. Actually an island separated from the mainland by narrow waterways, the original Venice reflects the influence of Ringling and visionary urban planner John Nolen, who was hired by the Brotherhood of Locomotive Engineers union, which purchased much of the town in the 1920s.

Casey Key was built on the principle that island real estate should be reserved for the well-to-do. This has kept it exclusive and lightly developed, particularly at its north end, where a narrow road snakes through a forest of mansions à la Palm Beach. Nokomis Beach, at the southern end, contrasts as a more casual, beachy, fishing-oriented resort area.

The Sarasota area has conveniently organized its environmental and historical attractions on a *Gulf Coast Heritage Trail* map, available at visitor information centers around town or by calling 941-957-1877.

LODGING

Most vacationers on the Sarasota Bay coast gravitate toward the barrier islands. On Siesta Key you won't find chain hotels other than a Best Western; however, you will find accommodations large and small by the score. The others have their chains but more mom-and-pops, B&Bs, inns, destination resorts, and privately owned places. On the mainland, especially around the airport, business travelers find no-nonsense franchise and small motels, plus a couple of luxury options old and forthcoming. In 2001 two luxury condo resorts opened: a Ritz-Carlton and a Renaissance. With downtown's renewal, more and more vacationers are choosing mainland accommodations.

Privately owned second homes and condominiums provide another source of accommodations along the Sarasota Bay coast. Vacation brokers who match visitors with such properties are listed under "Home and Condo Rentals," at the end of this section.

I've listed here a well-rounded selection of Sarasota area accommodations, including a few of the better chain hotels. Toll-free 800, 888, 866, or 877 reservation numbers, where available, are listed after local numbers.

Pricing codes are explained below. They are normally per person/double occupancy for hotel rooms and per unit for efficiencies, apartments, cottages, suites, and villas. The range spans low- and high-season rates. Many resorts offer off-season packages at special rates and free lodging for children. Pricing does not include the 6 percent Florida sales tax or Sarasota County's 3 percent tourist tax, which is allotted to beach revitalization, arts funding, and tourism promotion. Some large resorts add service gratuities or maid surcharges.

Rate Categories

Inexpensive	Up to $75
Moderate	$75 to $150
Expensive	$150 to $200
Very Expensive	$200 and up

(An asterisk after the pricing designation indicates that the rate includes at least a continental breakfast in the cost of lodging and possibly more extensive meal service as noted in the listing.)

The following abbreviations are used for credit card information:

AE: American Express
MC: MasterCard
D: Discover Card
V: Visa
DC: Diners Club

Accommodations

ANNA MARIA
ROD & REEL MOTEL
Managers: Todd and Janet Test.
941-778-2780.
www.rodandreelmotel.com.
877 North Shore Dr., PO Box 1939, Anna
Maria Island 34216.
Price: Inexpensive to Moderate.
Credit Cards: MC, V.
Handicap Access: No.

This motel sits prettily on a narrow slab of
bayside beach, with flowery landscaping,
shuffleboard, picnic facilities, a sunning
deck, and a tiki-roofed pavilion. Each of the
10 one-room efficiencies is fully furnished
with a kitchenette (microwave, stovetop,
and refrigerator), ironing board, couch,
plastic dining room chairs, and spic-and-
span housekeeping. The motel is next to the
independently owned Rod & Reel Pier.

BRADENTON
✪ HOLIDAY INN RIVERFRONT
General Manager: Roy Padgett.
941-747-3727, 800-23-HOTEL.
www.holiday-inn.com/bradentonfl.
100 Riverfront Dr. W., Bradenton 34205.
Price: Moderate to Expensive.
Credit Cards: AE, D, DC, MC, V.

Perched riverside, this is mainland
Bradenton's loveliest property, pertly landscaped and designed to mesh with
Bradenton's Spanish colonial heritage.
Dark, heavy wood and wrought iron embellish the striking atrium lobby, off which lies
a pleasant fountain courtyard dripping with
hibiscus and oleander blossoms. Here
you'll also find the pool and spa and the
entrance to the hotel's various indoor and
outdoor restaurants and bars. A few steps
away flows the Manatee River, edged by
Bradenton Waterfront Park. Other amenities include a tiny fitness center, complimentary morning coffee and newspaper,
and a gift shop. All 153 dark-wood rooms
and suites in the five-story hotel have narrow private balconies that overlook the
river or courtyard and are stocked with coffeemakers and hair dryers; the suites have
wet bars and refrigerators. Brand-new carpeting and bedspreads offset worn aspects
awaiting an update.

BRADENTON BEACH
BRIDGEWALK
General Manager: Angela Rodocker.
941-779-2545, 866-779-2545.
www.silverresorts.com.
100 Bridge St., Bradenton Beach 34217.
Price: Moderate to Very Expensive.
Credit Cards: AE, D, MC, V.
Handicap Access: No.

There's a renaissance afoot in Bradenton
Beach, and this shiny new resort gives it a
huge kick upward. Key West–Caribbean in
look, it colorfully houses 28 studio suites,
townhouses, and so-called apartos (mini
apartments) in three tin-roofed low risers

Newcomer to the Bradenton Beach resort scene,
BridgeWalk adds color and style. Karen T. Bartlett

along the town's refurbishing historic district. Units are comfortably spacious with full or mini-kitchens. Deluxe touches include granite countertops, Jacuzzi tubs in some units, and gulf views from one of the buildings. The resort also houses upscale shops, eateries, and a day spa along the street. The beach is a short walk across the street, and a heated pool in the parking area cools off guests on property.

SEASIDE INN & RESORT
Owners: Kevan and Fawn Ker.
941-778-5254, 800-447-7124.
www.seasideresort.com.
2200 Gulf Dr. N., Bradenton Beach 34217.
Price: Moderate to Very Expensive.
Credit Cards: D, MC, V.

Like the rest of Bradenton Beach, things are constantly looking better here. Spotless and decorated with charm, the seven efficiencies and three rooms have new kitchen counters, toasters, refrigerators, and microwaves, with stovetops in the efficiencies, plus remodeled tiled bathrooms. Fawn, one of the owners, is adding lovely trompe l'oeil touches to the white walls. The penthouse (expensive to very expensive) has a separate bedroom and luxury appointments, and can connect to two other rooms for large family gatherings. Each room looks out on the gulf with a patio or deck balcony, and the inn has its own private walled beach, above the public beach, which was widened in 2001. Use of kayaks is complimentary to guests. It's a good value for beachside lodging with pleasant amenities.

HOLMES BEACH
✪ HARRINGTON HOUSE B&B
Innkeepers: JoAdele and Frank Davis.
941-778-5444, 888-828-5566.
5626 Gulf Dr., Holmes Beach 34217.
www.harringtonhouse.com.
Price: Moderate to Expensive.* (Two-night minimum weekends and holidays.)
Credit Cards: MC, V.

One of Florida's loveliest and best-maintained bed & breakfasts, Harrington adds to its homey, historic allure with a beachfront. Built in 1925 of local coquina rock and pecky cypress, with Mediterranean flourishes, the home was refurbished with casual elegance and magical touches. Each of the seven rooms is labeled—Renaissance, Birdsong, Sunset, etc.—with a needlepoint door sign. Room sizes vary from spacious, with a king-sized bed, to comfortably cozy. Each guestroom has its own bathroom, refrigerator, and TV. An eclectic collection of handpicked antique furniture enhances guests' comfort. A dramatic cut-stone fireplace dominates the sitting room, where taped classical music is interrupted only by an occasional piano solo and homemade chocolate chip cookies in the afternoon. Guests enjoy gourmet home-cooked breakfasts at individual tables amid Victorian pieces and filmy white curtains. Outdoor areas include sun decks, a pool, a wide beach, and charmingly colorful landscaping around picket fences and arched alcoves. Eight more rooms, some with Jacuzzi-style tubs and fireplaces, occupy two beach houses down the beach (ranging in the Very Expensive category). Bikes and kayaks are available for guests' use.

LIDO KEY
GULF BEACH RESORT MOTEL
General Manager: Sue Culpepper.
941-388-2127, 800-232-2489.
www.gulfbeachsarasota.com.
930 Ben Franklin Dr., Sarasota 34236.
Price: Inexpensive to Expensive.
Credit Cards: D, MC, V.

Just a couple of doors down from the towering Radisson, Gulf Beach takes you to a circa 1950 era of Florida vacationing. All 49 rooms of this "condo-tel" are privately owned and therefore decorated with individual personality. They range from tiny motel rooms with mini-fridges, microwaves, and coffeemakers to roomy two-bedroom gulf-front apartments with all the comforts of home. Three one- and two-story cement-block buildings file between the main beach drag and the wide sands of Lido. There's a homey feel here. Owners have been coming for years, taking advantage of the welcoming pool, grilling area, shuffleboard, and sunset-perfect view. In 2003 Lido Key businesspeople saved this, Lido's first motel, from demise and high-rise takeover by getting it designated a historic landmark.

RADISSON LIDO BEACH RESORT
General Manager: Rick Benninghove.
941-388-2161, 800-441-2113.
www.radisson.com/sarasotafl.
700 Ben Franklin Dr., Sarasota 34236.
Price: Moderate to Very Expensive.
Credit Cards: AE, D, MC, V.

Located next to Lido Key's public beach, the 222-unit Radisson provides attractive, pleasant accommodations and a full range of water sports in the thick of beach activity. A new tower that opened in 2003 holds 12 floors, a city-view restaurant named Christopher's, and business facilities. Between it and the original four-story hotel squirms a goldfish creek crossed by wooden walkways with tin-roofed gazebos. The two pools sit on the shell-scattered beach and have their own beach bar. Another café feeds guests in the lobby. Modern, nicely furnished rooms come with or without full kitchens. Some have a small refrigerator and microwave, instead; all have coffeemakers. The resort provides a complimentary shuttle to shopping at St. Armands Circle.

LONGBOAT KEY
✪ COLONY BEACH AND TENNIS RESORT
General Manager: Katherine Klauber Moulton.
941-383-6464, 800-4COLONY.
www.colonybeachresort.com.
1620 Gulf of Mexico Dr., Longboat Key 34228.

Price: Very Expensive.
Credit Cards: AE, D, DC, MC, V.

The Colony ranks among Florida's finest resorts, a place where you could hide indefinitely behind security gates without ever having to face the real world. Here, in fact, is where President Bush was "hiding" when 9/11 happened. It stakes its reputation on top-notch tennis and dining: Ten of the 21 tennis courts are state-of-the-art soft surface. *Tennis* magazine has named it the top U.S. tennis resort for eight consecutive years. The Colony Dining Room, one of the property's two dining spots, also consistently wins awards. The 18-acre oleander-trimmed resort occupies a stretch of broad private beach. Complimentary kids' recreational programs take young guests to the courts, beach, pool, and off-property attractions. The Colony's 234 privately owned units range from adult-only beachfront units to family-friendly one- or two-bedroom suites. All units contain modern kitchen facilities; designer lamps, art, and furnishings; and marble master baths. Guests have free use of hard-surface tennis courts as well as a spa and a professionally staffed health club with an aerobic studio. Golf is available at 10 local private and semiprivate clubs.

THE RESORT AT LONGBOAT KEY CLUB
General Manager: Trevor Hind.
941-383-8821, 800-237-8821.
www.longboatkeyclub.com.
301 Gulf of Mexico Dr., Longboat Key 34228.
Price: Expensive to Very Expensive.
Credit Cards: AE, DC, MC, V.

Serious golfers are most apt to appreciate this gated 10-story beach resort in the midst of a private golf community. Besides the 45 holes of golf, 38 Har-Tru tennis courts, water sports, and a spiffy fitness center satisfy the active vacationer. Dining is another huge plus. Open only to guests and members, the club's restaurants excel at flavor-bursting seafood dishes prepared with only the top ingredients and seasoned exotically. Rooms, which underwent renovation in 2003, come in the one-bedroom or two-bedroom suite variety with complete kitchens, space to dance, and class-act appointments. Use of beach cabanas, umbrellas, and bikes is complimentary. Add-on extras include massage and body treatments, seasonal kids' programs, and water sports rentals. The resort has a no-cash policy; all charges go on a room tab.

✪ ROLLING WAVES COTTAGES
Owners: Theresa and Ed Woodland.
941-383-1323.
www.rollingwaves.com.
6351 Gulf of Mexico Dr., Longboat Key 34228.
Price: Moderate to Very Expensive.
(Minimum stay required.)
Credit Cards: MC, V.
Handicap Access: No.

What more could you ask of a beach vacation: a cute little 1940s cottage furnished modernly in bright colors, containing a remodeled full kitchen and bath, and complete with picnic table, grill, sea grapes, huge pink hibiscus blossoms, and a quiet beach outside the door? Rolling Waves's eight cottages are kept meticulous and decorated with touches of character: clay-tile kitchen floor, a rag rug over wood floors in a couple of the cottages, full-sized futons in the living room, VCRs, and an exterior paint job that evokes the chattel houses of the Caribbean. Located in Longboat Key's old, historic section, it escapes the glitz and the throngs with classic class.

NOKOMIS BEACH
A BEACH RETREAT
Owner: Gregory Snyder.
941-485-8771, 866-232-2480.
www.abeachretreat.com.
105 Casey Key Rd., Nokomis 34275.
Price: Inexpensive to Moderate.
Credit Cards: MC, V.
Handicap Access: Yes.

A Beach Retreat has efficiencies and apartments on both the beach and the bay. Fancied up with a jaunty yellow paint job and lattice trim, it also has a swimming pool on the bay side, where boat docks and 10 units accommodate guests and their vessels. The gulfside rooms, mostly ground level, are steps from a lovely, natural beach, but because of the wonderful tall sea oats, they have no view of the water. They cluster around a tropically vegetated courtyard and shuffleboard courts. The 27 units—from studios to three-bedroom suites (expensive to very expensive)—all have their own look and layout—largely modern but with some imperfections that lend beach character. All but two have a full kitchen.

SARASOTA
✪ THE CYPRESS
Innkeepers: Vicki Hadley and Robert and Nina Belott.
941-955-4683.
www.cypressbb.com.
621 Gulfstream Ave. S., Sarasota 34236.
Price: Moderate to Very Expensive.*
Credit Cards: AE, D, MC, V.
Handicap Access: No.

Details make a bed-and-breakfast inn, and the Cypress's attention to special touches, flourishes, and minutiae place it among the top in its genre. Notice the antique ice cream table with swivel-out stools in the sunny breakfast room, the fireplace and pianos in the living room, the exquisite crown molding throughout, the vintage Edison phonograph in the Martha Rose room, the fresh flowers in every room, the multicourse gourmet breakfasts, the happyhour hors d'oeuvres, the complimentary top-shelf cordials before bedtime, and the cookie turndown service. In short, the innkeepers spoil their guests. This trio of talent took a 1940s home that the original owner's daughter refused to sell out to encroaching condos. That leaves the Cypress—named for its sturdy building

Artistic and gracious. Cypress B&B blends well with Sarasota's downtown personality. Karen T. Bartlett

material—a flower in the shadow of high-rises. Still, the location is quite enviable. From the front deck guests can watch the sun set over the masts of yachts in the marina across the way. Downtown's burgeoning Palm Avenue district of galleries, sidewalk cafés, and specialty shops, meanwhile, is a short stroll away.

✪ THE RITZ-CARLTON SARASOTA

General Manager: Jim Veil.
941-309-2000, 800-241-3333.
www.ritzcarlton.com/hotels/sarasota.
1111 Ritz-Carlton Dr., Sarasota 34236.
Price: Expensive to Very Expensive.
Credit Cards: AE, D, DC, MC, V.

One of the first in the Ritz-Carlton line to offer living quarters, this hotel's 266 rooms and suites deliver all the luxury you expect from the name. Perched on the edge of downtown, it's more of a city hotel than other Ritz-Carlton Florida properties. Some rooms have views of Sarasota Bay,

others overlook a neighboring marina. Marble bathrooms, oversized rooms, and state-of-the-art Internet hookups make this equally accommodating for leisure and business travelers. Opened in November 2001, the Ritz recently added a full-service spa and beach club on Lido Key to its list of amenities, which includes a fitness center, a swimming pool, a fine Mediterranean restaurant, a sophisticated cigar bar, and nearby golf and shopping.

SIESTA KEY

Most of Siesta Key's accommodations require a minimum stay (usually one week) during season.

BEST WESTERN SIESTA BEACH RESORT

General Manager: Craig Sterlace.
941-349-3211, 800-223-5786.
www.siestakeyflorida.com.
5311 Ocean Blvd., Siesta Key 34242.
Price: Moderate to Very Expensive.
Credit Cards: AE, D, DC, MC, V.

For convenience to Siesta Village and the island's luscious white sands, you can't beat this humble little property. It has taken over two classic motels that have been recently renovated with character and care. Red-tile roofs and teal awnings dress up the outside, while inside, tile floors and modern decor bring the 51 units into the 21st century. They come in varieties from standard rooms to studio efficiencies and one- and two-bedroom suites. Jacuzzi suites are also available. A swimming pool and laundry facilities complete the amenities.

TURTLE BEACH RESORT

Innkeepers: David and Gail Rubinfeld.
941-349-4554.
www.turtlebeachresort.com.
9049 Midnight Pass Rd., Siesta Key 34242.
Price: Expensive to Very Expensive.
(Minimum stay required in season.
Housekeeping is extra.)
Credit Cards: D, MC, V.

Cozy, picturesque corners make Turtle Beach Resort a romantic hideaway.   Karen T. Bartlett

One of Sarasota's Small Superior Lodgings, this place is a real find at the southern, quiet end of the island, a three-minute walk from Turtle Beach. Ten cottages on the bay contain studio, one-bedroom, or two-bedroom accommodations, plus a private hot tub. Each cottage has its own personality, reflected in names such as Rain Forest, Montego Bay, and Southwestern. Modern designer furniture and lamps, objets d'art, and other decorative pieces carry out the themes. Most have sleeper sofas; all come with complete kitchen facilities. Bathrobes, TV, VCR, and sherry are provided in each of the cottages, which spread along a lushly landscaped strip well-planned with private nooks along waterside docks, poolside, or tucked into courtyard foliage. Use of washers and dryers is free after 4pm, and bicycles, canoes, kayaks, rowboats, and boat docks are available, complimentary for guests' enjoyment. Very romantic, this resort is nonetheless conducive to families, as well, and pets are permitted. News flash: The owner tells me Stephen King recently moved in next door.

VENICE
BANYAN HOUSE

Innkeepers: Chuck and Susan McCormick.
941-484-1385.
www.banyanhouse.com.
519 S. Harbor Dr., Venice 34285.
Price: Moderate.*
Credit Cards: MC, V.
Handicap Access: No.

In the mid-1920s architects designed Venice in accordance with its Italian name; homes and buildings are modeled after northern Mediterranean styles. The town's first community swimming pool was located in the backyard of one of the original homes, next to a fledgling banyan tree. Today that small pool, with its now-sprawling tree, resides at the same home, a red-tile-roofed B&B inn known as the Banyan House. Classic statuary, fountains, multihued blossoms, a courtyard, a sun deck, and a hot tub share the property. Five rooms, each with a private bath, exert their individual personalities: the Palm Room has a fireplace, the Laurel Room features an outdoor balcony, the Tree House includes a sunny sitting room overlooking the pool; the Sun Deck has a separate entrance; the Palmetto Room offers hardwood floors and lavender hues. All units contain at least a small refrigerator; three are efficiencies. Two rooms and one apartment are also available in the carriage house, rented by the month in season. Deluxe touches include bathrobes in the closet and wine in the fridge. Susan serves homemade gourmet breakfast in a solarium off the formal sitting room, the latter furnished with an antique Italian fireplace, a circa 1890 hoopskirt bench, and other Victorian period pieces. Pecky cypress, wood-beam ceilings, terracotta slate tiling, and wrought-iron banisters are all original. Free use of bicycles allows guests to explore old Venice's nearby shopping mecca and beach. Smoking is not allowed in any of the rooms.

INN AT THE BEACH
General Manager: Pam Orr.
941-484-8471, 800-255-8471.
www.innatthebeach.com.
725 W. Venice Ave., Venice 34285.
Price: Moderate to Very Expensive.*
Credit Cards: AE, D, DC, MC, V.

This modern resort was built to include Mediterranean architectural overtones and contemporary Florida comfort and decor. Located across the street from the public access to Venice Beach, the hotel has 49 units; many of the second-floor ones overlook the gulf. Its well-maintained rooms have a clean white, light-wood, and understated-floral motif. Plantation shutters and tile floors add designer touches. All contain at least a microwave, coffeemaker, and minifridge; efficiencies and one- and two-bedroom suites add full refrigerators, stovetops, dishwashers, dishware, and pans. A small pool with spa and sundeck is tucked away behind the hotel in the parking lot—not high on atmosphere. I'd opt for the beach. Continental breakfast is included in the rate.

A touch of the Old World at Banyan House, a venerable bed-and-breakfast in Venice. Courtesy of Banyan House

Home & Condo Rentals

Florida Vacation Accommodations (941-383-9505, 800-237-9505; www.vacationinfl.com; 4030 Gulf of Mexico Dr., Longboat Key 34228; or 941-346-9505 or 800-237-2252; 5218 Ocean Blvd, Siesta Key 34242; or 941-364-9505; 3800 S. Tamiami Trail, Suite 14, Sarasota 34239) Call or write for a catalog of more than 2,000 waterfront properties throughout the region.

A Paradise Rental Management (941-778-4800, 800-237-2252; www.aparadise rentals.com; 5201 Gulf Dr., Holmes Beach 34217) Rental condos and homes on Anna Maria Island for short and long term.

RV Resorts

Horseshoe Cove (941-758-5335, 800-291-3446; www.originalgator.50megs.com/horseshoecove.html; 5100 60th St. E., Bradenton 34203) A 60-acre oak-grove riverfront site, including a 12-acre island with a pavilion and nature and biking trails. Resort has a heated pool and spa, a postal facility, hookup to phone and cable, lighted fishing docks on the Braden River, shuffleboard courts, and other recreational facilities.

Linger Lodge (941-755-2757; 7205 Linger Lodge Rd., Bradenton 34202) By dint of its old-Florida-style character and slightly bizarre restaurant, this place has gained a reputation for funky. RV sites lie along or near the Braden River. Amenities include a boat ramp, fishing, and laundry.

Sarasota Bay Travel Trailer Park (941-794-1200, 800-247-8361; 10777 44th Ave. W., Bradenton 34210; at Cortez Rd.) Located on the bay with full hookups, a boat ramp and dock, fishing, horseshoes, exercise room, recreation hall, and entertainment, it caters mostly to permanent abodes, with some spots for transients. This is an exceptionally well-kept and scenic facility.

Venice Campground (941-488-0850; www.campvenice.com/index.shtml; 4085 E. Venice Ave., Venice 34292; at exit 191 off I-75) Full hookups and waterfront sites. Amenities include security gates, heated swimming pool, shuffleboard, horseshoe, nature trail, fishing, boat and canoe rentals, laundry room, and supply store.

DINING

For Sarasotans, eating out is as much a cultural event as attending the opera. It is often an inextricable part of an evening at the theater or a gallery opening. Sarasotans take dining out quite seriously and keep restaurants full, even off-season. Their enthusiasm for newness makes kitchens more innovative than those of their neighbors to the south. (Out of 47 Golden Spoon winners awarded in 2004 by *Florida Trend* magazine, five—Beach Bistro, Euphemia Haye, Michael's on East, Summerhouse, and the Colony Dining Room—are found in this region.) Sarasota slides along the cutting edge of New World cuisine while maintaining classic favorites that range from rickety oyster bars to French cafés.

The following listings span the diversity of Sarasota Bay coast cuisine in these price categories:

Inexpensive	Up to $10
Moderate	$10 to $20
Expensive	$20 to $30
Very Expensive	$30 or more

Cost categories are based on the range of dinner entrée prices or, if dinner is not served, on lunch entrées. Many restaurants offer early-dining discounts, often called early-bird specials. These are rarely listed on the regular menu and sometimes are not publicized by tip-conscious servers. I have noted restaurants that offer them. Certain restrictions apply, such as time constraints, a specific menu, or number of people first in the door. Call the restaurant and ask about its policy. Those restaurants listed with "Healthy Selections" usually mark such on their menu.

The following abbreviations are used for credit card information and meals:

AE: American Express
D: Discover Card
DC: Diners Club
MC: MasterCard
V: Visa
B: Breakfast
L: Lunch
D: Dinner
SB: Sunday Brunch

Note: New Florida law forbids smoking inside all restaurants and bars serving food. Smoking is permitted only in restaurants with outdoor seating.

ANNA MARIA

✪ ROTTEN RALPH'S

941-778-3953.
902 Bay Blvd. S., Anna Maria Island 34216.
At the Galati Yacht Basin.
Price: Inexpensive to Moderate.
Children's Menu: No (kid-suitable items on regular menu).
Cuisine: Old Florida.
Liquor: Full.
Serving: L, D.
Credit Cards: D, MC, V.
Handicap Access: Yes.
Reservations: No.
Special Features: Dock seating on the marina; early-dining menu.

The atmosphere here is due entirely to the setting. It's a place that locals frequent, full of character and characters. The laminated placemat menu describes several finger food selections (steamed shellfish, popcorn shrimp, oysters Rockefeller, onion rings, chicken wings, nachos), Old Florida fried seafood standards, steamed seafood pots, and other, more esoteric, concessions such as shrimp linguine Alfredo, Danish baby back ribs, and Cajun shrimp. I inevitably order the blackened grouper sandwich,

totally fresh and well seasoned. We've always found the food fresh and tasty—but, truthfully, we enjoy the view more.

BRADENTON

LEE'S CRAB TRAP II

941-729-7777.
4815 17th St. E., PO Box 450, Ellenton 34222.
Right off I-75 exit 224.
Price: Moderate to Very Expensive.
Cuisine: Seafood.
Children's Menu: Yes
Liquor: Full.
Serving: L, D.
Credit Cards: D, MC, V.
Handicap Access: Yes.
Reservations: No.
Special Features: View of the water.

If you're visiting Gamble Mansion or happen to be passing by this interstate exit with a hunger on, this is a must-stop and has been as long as I can remember. The notebook-sized menu is largely given over to, of course, crab. Try it steamed (stone or king), provençal, deviled, or in a variety of other treatments. The grilled crab cakes—lightly bound chunks of prime meat—and three-crab soup with asparagus are excellent. All the soups have a distinct from-scratch, long-mulled flavor. The soup-of-the-day vegetable chowder I had there recently was the best soup I can remember. The menu doesn't limit itself to seafood; it flexes wide to include fine Angus beef, lobster, frogs' legs, catfish, chicken, ostrich, kangaroo, wild boar, octopus, alligator, and pasta. The large, wood-and-bamboo dining rooms have a comfortable, handsome feel with a view of a pond out back. Expect a wait for lunch or dinner in-season. The bar offers a more select, lighter version of the extensive menu.

NADINE'S 10TH STREET BISTRO

941-748-0434.
309 10th Street W., Bradenton 32405.
In the Riverpark Hotel.

Price: Inexpensive.
Cuisine: American.
Liquor: Full.
Serving: L.
Closed: Sat., Sun.
Credit Cards: AE, MC, V.
Handicap Access: Yes.
Reservations: No.
Special Features: Historic setting.

Nadine's resides in the historic pink neo-Mediterranean Riverpark Hotel, built in the 1920s as Manatee River Hotel and now a retirement home. But don't let that throw you off; the food here is as energetic as it is affordable. The setting is bright and cheerful, with high ceilings and windows, market umbrellas, a stone fountain, and occasional music from a player piano. Diners are greeted with a helping of skinny breadsticks for dipping into a cheese dip. Classic and imaginative salads (try the grilled chicken pita salad or seafood salad with shrimp, langoustine, and real crab on pasta and greens) and sandwiches come in generous portions. The house balsamic dressing is so flavorful, you'd never guess that it's fat free. Choose one of the River Park Favorites sandwiches for a complex meal with lots of nutritional variety. They include the Bruchetta, done up with pesto, muenster cheese, roma tomatoes, and fresh mozzarella, with a lovely orange-vinaigrette-dressed salad; the New Yorker, with beef, black pepper, and slaw; and the Fresh Italian, dauntingly ample with portobello mushroom, roma tomatoes, mozzarella, prosciutto, and garlic-basil mayonnaise. The hamburger boasts Angus beef, and other sandwiches demonstrate great variety. If there's key lime pie on the menu, order it. It's top-shelf tart, with real whipped cream.

BRADENTON BEACH
✪ **HISTORIC BRIDGE STREET PIER CAFÉ**
941-779-1706.
200 Bridge St., Bradenton Beach 34217.
Price: Inexpensive to Moderate.

CLOSED

Children's Menu: Yes.
Cuisine: American/seafood.
Liquor: Beer and wine.
Serving: B, L, D.
Credit Cards: D, MC, V.
Handicap Access: Yes.
Reservations: No.
Special Features: Outdoor seating at the city pier; early-bird specials.

Come awake to the slosh of bay waters against pier pilings and the hum of early-morning traffic crossing the Cortez Bridge. Breakfast is an event here—not a grand event but one steeped in local color and history, with nothing fancier than French toast and patio furniture. The servers have a soft southern accent, a no-nonsense friendliness, and a sense of humor. The humble shacklike café straddles the city pier, a truncated former bridge. You can take one of the few breeze-cooled tables inside, but you'd be foolish to pass up the outdoor view in any weather short of a downpour. Lunch and dinner demonstrate classic Old Florida fish-house style with seafood selections from the deep fryer plunked into a basket: oysters, grouper, shrimp, crab cakes. For a sampler, order one of the two seafood platters. The café also serves great burgers, the signature one being the Pier Burger, with onions, mushrooms, and Swiss cheese. Come for all-you-can-eat grouper, $15.95 (only $13.95 on Monday, Wednesday, and Friday 11:30–9).

HOLMES BEACH
✪ **BEACH BISTRO**
941-778-6444.
www.beachbistro.com/body.html.
6600 Gulf Dr., Holmes Beach 34217.
Price: Very Expensive.
Children's Menu: Yes, plus puzzles, fruit amusées, and more.
Cuisine: New American.
Liquor: Full.
Serving: D.
Credit Cards: AE, D, DC, MC, V.
Handicap Access: Close quarters and no

bathroom wheelchair access.
Reservations: Yes.
Special Features: Front room view of gulf.

The talk of connoisseurs for many years, this little bit of gourmet heaven has fewer than 20 tables in a two-room cottage. (Most of them cluster around picture windows in a room with one of the best local dining views of sunset. The other room has been turned into a martini bar, featuring both edible and drinkable varieties.) We came to understand what all the hubbub is about as the meal progressed, and our server attended us with skilled timing and pleasant surprises. Even before our appetizer came, we enjoyed herbed bread with a marvelous dip of tomatoes and basil, then two entwined shrimp with red pepper coulis. The exacting menu showcases the chefs' quirky talents that are difficult to define but easy to enjoy. The "lobstercargots" appetizer, for instance, replaces those "chewy little slugs" with succulent morsels of Florida lobster in bubbling garlic butter and spinach. We had a hard time letting them cool before we ate them, they were that tantalizing. A signature "kicker" sauce keeps the jumbo shrimp from drying on the grill and adds a spark nicely complemented by its Grand Marnier ginger beurre blanc. Tournedos comes with portobellos or peppered. We tried the latter, a wonderfully fiery demi-glace of black, green, and pink peppercorns and cognac. Each dish was executed to perfection. The vegetable accompaniments to our main courses were delicious enough to fight them for attention. And our wine by the glass was poured from the bottle, a touch I always appreciate. In short, if you hear critics and regular folks raving about Beach Bistro, it's all true.

LIDO KEY
✪ OLD SALTY DOG
941-388-4311.
1601 Ken Thompson Pkwy., Sarasota 34236.
On City Island.

Price: Inexpensive.
Children's Menu: No, but the menu offers child-appropriate selections.
Cuisine: American/seafood.
Liquor: Beer, wine.
Serving: L, D.
Credit Cards: V, MC.
Handicap Access: Yes.
Reservations: No.
Special Features: Outdoor waterfront seating.

A spin-off of the Siesta Key original, this one has a more properly salty setting: a tin-roofed red stucco building tucked into a marina in the shadow of the Longboat Key bridge. If you sit outside on the breezy patios, you'll be entertained by boaters, Waverunners, and water skiers. The menu lists such fun casual eats as City Island wings with dill sauce, New England clam chowder, deep-fried clams on a bed of fries, peel-and-eat shrimp, burgers, fish 'n chips, and the trademark Salty Dog (beer-battered and deep-fried, and not for the faint of heart). I ordered the grouper sandwich blackened and was pleased to have a choice of hot, medium, or mild. (Too many places assume palate sensitivity and water down the heat of a properly executed blackening.) I specified hot and got it just right, not so fiery as to overpower the full-flavored freshness of the fish. This is a great place to stop after a visit to Mote Marine and its nearby attractions. We like the wide selection of beer it offers, on tap as well as bottled. My son likes that we didn't have to wait long for our food.

LONGBOAT KEY
EUPHEMIA HAYE
941-383-3633.
www.euphemiahaye.com.
5540 Gulf of Mexico Dr., Longboat Key 34228
Price: Moderate to Very Expensive.
Children's Menu: No.
Cuisine: Continental.
Liquor: Full.
Serving: D.

Credit Cards: CB, DC, D, MC, V.
Handicap Access: Downstairs, yes.
Reservations: Yes.
Special Features: Appetizer/dessert parlor; live entertainment.

The name Euphemia Haye, odd and difficult to pronounce as it may seem, has come to define one of Sarasota's most coveted dining experiences. The appellation actually comes from the founder's grandmother. There's nothing grandmotherly about the concept and cuisine, however, although you will find elements of comfort food sprinkled among international and house specialties: a smoked salmon appetizer on buckwheat crepes from Russia, lamb shank from Greece, gnocchi Gorgonzola from Italy, shrimp Taj Mahal from India, French calves' sweetbreads, and so on. The signature roast duckling is a fine example of the details that make a meal at Euphemia Haye a blend of familiar and exotic. With bread stuffing and a seasonally changing fruit sauce (orange and green peppercorn last time I sampled it), it arrived with a simple parsley sprig garnish. Filet mignon Fritzie is another Euphemia specialty on the seasonally changing menu. It sits atop a potato pancake with caramelized shallots and bourbon demi-glace. To top off the experience, a trip upstairs to the Haye Loft for dessert is de rigueur. The selection is mind-boggling (not to mention diet-blowing, but let that thought go in this atmosphere). Besides sinful desserts, you can order coffee and after-dinner drinks. The peanut butter mousse with chocolate rum topping was much heavier than its name suggests, enough to go around a table of four; the coconut cream pie, extraordinary.

✪ MAR-VISTA DOCKSIDE RESAURANT & PUB
941-383-2391.
www.groupersandwich.com.
760 Broadway St., Longboat Key 34228.
In the Village.

Price: Moderate.
Children's Menu: Yes.
Cuisine: Seafood.
Liquor: Full.
Serving: L, D.
Credit Cards: AE, D, DC, MC, V.
Handicap Access: Restaurant, yes; restrooms, no.
Reservations: Preferred seating.
Special Features: Boat access.

Locals refer to it as The Pub, a hangover from years gone by. Casual at its best, it has that lovely, lived-in, borderline ramshackle look on the outside, crowned by an appropriately rusting tin roof. Inside, tables don't match, mounted fish and sailors' dollar bills adorn the wall, boaters hoist beers at the bar, and a view of the harbor dominates the decorator's scheme. There's also seating on the patio, on plastic chairs with heaters when it's cool (and where you may occasionally get an earful of cooks' disagreements in the kitchen). Seafood is fresh and prepared with signature twists: vegetable and conch fritters, fresh-catch Rueben sandwich, garlic-fried shrimp, Longbeach bouillabaisse, sesame tuna, and Caribbean grilled chicken. Steamer pots in four sizes brim with shellfish and vegetables. We've enjoyed the cuisine and casual atmosphere here many times.

NOKOMIS
✪ CAPTAIN EDDIE'S SEAFOOD RESTAURANT
941-484-4623.
107 Colonia Ln. E., Nokomis 34275.
Price: Inexpensive to Moderate.
Children's Menu: Yes.
Cuisine: Seafood/Florida.
Liquor: Beer and wine.
Serving: L, D.
Closed: Sun.; in summer also closed all day Mon. and Sat. lunch.
Credit Cards: D, MC, V.
Handicap Access: Restaurant, yes; restrooms, no.
Reservations: No.

Ask anyone around the Venice-Nokomis-Osprey area where to get fresh seafood, and 9 out of 10 will recommend, without pause, Captain Eddie's. The restaurant began as a fish market that took over a convenience store and set up a few picnic tables to fill the space. Those picnic tables came to be in such great demand that the market eventually grew into a restaurant where the locals know they can get their money's worth in fresh fish. The picnic tables remain; if you're a small party, you may be sharing with others. Or you can sit at the counter. This is a true Florida fish house, my favorite brand of dining. Don't expect tableware that won't get tossed at the end of the meal. Do expect a roll of paper towels for linen and neighborly service. The hostess calls most of the patrons by name. The menu carries a lot of fried fish items such as shrimp, catfish, and oysters (but fried right and in canola oil) as well as broiled options. After an appetizer of alligator bites, I tried a broiled grouper sandwich that was the best I've tasted since my husband came home from a deep-sea fishing trip. Broiled grouper can be bland, but this was tastefully prepared, served on a yummy hoagie in a plastic basket. The lone dessert, key lime pie, is the real thing, though with a discernible off-flavor that sometimes comes from bottled lime juice. (But, then, I have my own lime tree and am something of a snob!)

St. Armands Circle
✪ CAFÉ L'EUROPE
941-388-4415.
www.cafeleurope.net.
431 St. Armands Circle, Sarasota 34236.
Price: Expensive to Very Expensive.
Children's Menu: No.
Cuisine: French.
Liquor: Full.
Serving: L, D.
Closed: Lunch off-season.
Credit Cards: AE, D, DC, MC, V.
Handicap Access: Yes.
Reservations: Yes, for lunch and dinner.

St. Armands Circle's reputation for fine dining has faded somewhat over the years, but Café L'Europe remains a shining star that offers French classics with a New Age tweak. Dark woods and redbrick archways set an atmosphere that's warm in an inviting way, yet a cool cellarlike break from Florida heat. When the weather allows, you can also sit outdoors on the patio to sip your French pinot blanc and sample such stunning selections as the wild mushroom strudel appetizer or a Stilton salad served with wedges of the coveted bleu cheese and a light peppercorn dressing, brandied duckling, mustard-crusted grilled rack of lamb, steak Diane, veal piccata, osso buco, chateaubriand for two, curry-painted sea bass on cabbage apple slaw (lightly breaded and seasoned to complement the delicate meat), or snapper au poivre with a mustard cream sauce (pan-seared and light on the poivre). For dessert, it's fun to try the sampler of five crème brûlées and guess which is which: white chocolate, coffee, honey, lemon, and strawberry-balsamic. We never were able to discern the honey from the coffee.

Sarasota
BIJOU CAFÉ
941-366-8111.
www.bijoucafe.net.
1287 First St., Sarasota 34236.
Price: Moderate to Expensive.
Children's Menu: No.
Cuisine: New American.
Healthy Selections: Yes.
Liquor: Full.
Serving: L, D.
Closed: Sun. in summer; Sat. and Sun. for lunch year-round.
Credit Cards: AE, DC, MC, V.
Handicap Access: Yes.
Reservations: Recommended.
Situated in the midst of the Theater and Arts District, the Bijou is the pick of the pre- and post-theater crowd and upper-

echelon business community of Sarasota. Small and simply decorated, only lacy curtains, some heavily framed paintings, and a few stylish vases (here you'd pronounce that *vah-zes*) embellish. Linen and fresh flowers dress the tables, even at lunch, when the clientele is equally dressed up. The eclectic menu offers choices from continental, New Orleans, and American cuisine, from fruit soup to duck. One of my favorite dishes, shrimp Piri-Piri, makes a classic example of how chef/owner Jean-Pierre Knaggs perfectly balances flavors to create entirely fresh taste sensations. It is mildly spicy with citrus tones and appears on both the lunch and dinner menus. Other dinner specialties include roast duckling; crab cakes rémoulade; veal Louisville with pecans, bourbon, and pears; and braised lamb shanks in zinfandel and rosemary. The pommes gratin Dauphinois with Gruyère is a signature side dish, available à

Visual arts and culinary arts collide at the entrance to Sarasota's perennially popular Bijou Café. Karen T. Bartlett

la carte. Desserts, made in-house, have an excellent reputation. Lunch draws a brisk business crowd with handmade spinach and ricotta ravioli, boursin-glazed shrimp, grilled rosemary lamb sandwich, Cobb salad, and the like.

CAFÉ BACI

941-921-4848.
4001 S. Tamiami Trail, Sarasota 34231.
Price: Moderate to Expensive.
Early-Dining Menu: Yes.
Children's Menu: Yes.
Cuisine: Northern Italian.
Liquor: Full.
Serving: L, D.
Closed: Lunch Sat. and Sun.
Credit Cards: AE, D, DC, MC, V.
Handicap Access: Restaurant, yes; rest room, no.
Reservations: For dinner.

I describe this place as "affordably dressy." It has, after all, a porte cochere out front and linens on the tables (even at lunch) inside, the business clientele and older crowd wear nice clothes, and the Tuscan-Roman specialties dwell in the realm of fine cuisine. Yet its location on plebeian South Tamiami Trail, away from Sarasota's centers of chichi, allows for a reasonably priced menu. Lunch is especially popular with locals, who squeeze the parking lot full to capacity. I enjoy lunch there, too; it imparts a bit of affordable elegance in the middle of a hectic day alongside a road-rage street. Though Café Baci is unspectacular in atmosphere, its food has kept it at the head of growing Italian competition. Many of the dinner entrées are available in smaller portions and prices at lunchtime. I have ordered, for example, the ravioli di funghi, an exquisite plate of homemade half-moon pasta pockets filled with delicately creamed wild mushrooms and topped with a buttery tomato cream sauce. It costs only $7.25 and is, with its rich sauce, the most I could eat for lunch—thanks also to the bread basket, which was filled with marvelous tomato focaccia squares. The mussels and linguine lunch is another winner, the tomato and basil broth so tasty I requested a soup spoon. Both lunch and dinner menus touch on the four major Italian food groups: pasta, veal, chicken, and seafood. These are tended with a creative hand. Here's a taste: corkscrew pasta with mushrooms, peas, prosciutto, and cream; lasagna verde (made with spinach noodles); grilled breast of chicken stuffed with cheese and prosciutto and topped with a pancetta, mushroom, and onion sauce; breaded veal scaloppini with arugula, onion, tomatoes, and basil; pan-seared salmon with white wine, leeks, pine nuts, and sun-dried-tomato sauce; and polenta-crusted sea bass. The extensive wine list has received the Wine Spectator Award of Excellence.

✪ CAPTAIN BRIAN'S SEAFOOD MARKET RESTAURANT

941-351-4492.
8441 N. Tamiami Trail, Sarasota 34243.
Price: Inexpensive to Moderate.
Children's Menu: Yes.
Cuisine: Seafood.
Liquor: Beer and wine.
Serving: L, D.
Credit Cards: AE, D, DC, MC, V.
Handicap Access: Yes.
Reservations: No.
Special features: Fresh-fish market.

When fresh seafood is priority one and affordability priority two, go see Captain Brian. I'm not sure such a person actually exists, but the T-shirted staff here can quickly fix you up with the best available. The first thing you notice when you enter the inconspicuous storefront is that it looks like a seafood market, but it doesn't smell like one. Clean as humanly possible, it makes seafood relishing totally appealing. The daily lunch and dinner menus, besides

fried shrimp baskets, fish sandwiches, crab cakes, seafood combo platters, and such, spell out a long list of fresh catches that you can order fried, grilled, or blackened. I asked for my favorite fish—red snapper, grilled—and it was elegant in its simplicity: flapping fresh and unadorned but for a side of black bean salad. You can opt for the salad bar rather than a starch side, and there you have yourself a meal that's not only inherently good but good for you. The decor is simple: tables and booths, blue-checkered oilcloth, and fish. Keep your eye peeled for this local secret just north of the airport.

✪ FRED'S

941-364-5811.
www.epicureanlife.com.
1917 S. Osprey Ave., Sarasota 34239.
Price: Moderate to Very Expensive.
Children's Menu: No.
Cuisine: New American.
Liquor: Full.
Serving: L, D, SB.
Credit Cards: AE, D, DC, MC, V.
Handicap Access: Yes.
Reservations: Accepted for lunch or dinner.

Down in burgeoning Southside Village, the people at Morton's Market are sewing up food service along Osprey Avenue. Their Fred's is the newest, most happening place on the block, a warm and convivial spot for a polished lunch and dinner with flair. The Power Lunch costs $7 and includes soup, fries or salad, and a choice of interesting sandwiches. Other salads, soups, and small-portion entrées show the same creativity as the dinner menu. Dinner begins with a basket of Mexican-style corn muffins, breadsticks, and lavosh. On a recent visit, I chose a side of pickled green tomatoes—lightly marinated and slightly spicy—for a salad. From chipotle-barbecued chicken pizza, pan-seared diver scallops with smoked polenta, lobster cavatelli with vodka-bacon sauce, and other temptations, I selected the miso-roasted grouper with ginger-plantain crust atop a crisp and zingy Asian slaw. The grouper was meaty, moist, and perfectly done, with just the right accent of ginger. A large selection of wines, featuring several by the glass, starts in the reasonable range and climbs into the $500s. Don't find the wine you want? Just ask your server and he'll run to the neighboring wine store owned by the chain and get it for you, which was what happened when I asked for a certain type of chardonnay. Appetizers run the gamut from southern-fried calamari to baked oysters with fire-roasted pepper and manchego pesto to $85 servings of Beluga caviar. For dessert, just try to pass up the whiskey bread pudding, chocolate mousse cake, or chai tea crème brûlée. It's not hard to understand why this place has taken off like wildfire among the locals.

❂ MICHAEL'S ON EAST

941-366-0007.
www.bestfood.com.
1212 East Ave. S., Sarasota 34239.
In Midtown Plaza at Bahia Vista St. and Tamiami Trail.
Price: Expensive to Very Expensive.
Children's Menu: No, but will halve portions.
Cuisine: New American.
Liquor: Full.
Serving: L, D.
Closed: Sat. and Sun. for lunch.
Credit Cards: AE, DC, MC, V.
Handicap Access: Yes.
Reservations: Recommended for lunch or dinner.
Special Features: Early-dining menu; piano bar with late-night menu.

Michael Klauber is a well-respected name in Sarasota culinary circles. He learned successful restaurateuring early in life as a member of Longboat Key's Colony Beach Resort family. He created an immediate sensation when he opened his own place back in 1987, and Michael's on East remains the pinnacle of cutting-edge cuisine and atmosphere. Oh so Art Deco, you won't find a square corner in the wavy motif. You can dine around the circular bar or in two other rooms separated by scrims and etched glass (wavy, of course, and très chic). On the lunch menu, the best value is one of the $8.95 combinations, where you have your choice of any two: duck spring rolls, Caesar salad, angel hair onion rings, chef's soup, seasonal salad, sweet and spicy calamari, and a half turkey wrap. If your idea of calamari has anything to do with rubber bands, try Michael's cornmeal-battered, hand-breaded version—tender to a T and complemented with a wonderful sauce and corn-pancetta relish. The lunch menu also features a lengthy selection of glorious salads, such as warm chicken on greens with dried cranberries, candied pecans, and goat cheese. Such are the touches that make Michael's a consistent winner. Specialties on the dinner menu include pan-seared Chilean sea bass with vegetable couscous, artichoke hearts, and thyme-tomato coulis; rack of lamb with roasted mushroom jus and caramelized sweet onion mash; and pan-roasted crab cakes with truffle roasted potatoes. For dessert, the white chocolate cheesecake with coconut crust and mango sauce is divine. Michael's is also known, naturally, for its extensive wine list, featuring 20-plus wines by the glass, including sparkling.

MI PUEBLO

941-379-2880.
www.mipueblomexican.com.
4436 Bee Ridge Rd., Sarasota 34233.
In Palm Plaza.
Price: Inexpensive to Moderate.
Children's Menu: Yes.
Cuisine: Mexican.
Liquor: Beer and wine.
Serving: L, D.

Credit Cards: AE, MC, V.
Handicap Access: Yes.
Reservations: No.
Special features: Live mariachi or guitar
music three nights a week.

Tucked into a nondescript shopping center
(look for the most standout, colorful storefront) far from Sarasota's trendy dining districts, Mi Pueblo serves typical Mexican
(from the Chihuahua region) and Tex-Mex
specialties from a simple menu in a modest
but gaily decorated cantina. Air-brushed
paintings of beer and hot sauce labels
brighten pueblo-style walls. Painted tiles
inlay heavy wooden tables, and saltillo floor
tiles complete the south-of-the-border look.
The owners, servers, and chefs chatter in
Spanish. Traditional dishes such as fajitas,
burritos, tamales, and enchiladas (three
varieties: ropa, verde, and suiza) comprise
the menu. Specialties include pollo con mole
(nicely balanced seasonings in the sauce),
chili relleno, pollo Zargoza (marinated and
grilled chicken), and carne asada (seasoned,
grilled steak). Meals arrive quickly, so you
know much is premade, but everything has
just that extra ounce of flavor more than the
chain restaurants purveying their versions of
the same. The salsa was boldly spicy, served
with light multicolored nacho chips for a
kick of trendy. The margaritas are made with
wine rather than tequila, but light and satisfying with key lime juice. The Mexican
toothpicks appetizer—batter-fried strips of
onion and jalapeno—come recommended.
The flan had character, coarser than you find
in the assembly-line chains but flavored
with that inimitable something that smacks
of someplace warm, exotic, and folksy.

✪ PHILLIPPI CREEK VILLAGE OYSTER BAR

941-925-4444.
www.creekseafood.com.
5353 S. Tamiami Trail, Sarasota 34231.
Price: Moderate.

Children's Menu: Yes.
Cuisine: Seafood/Old Florida.
Healthy Selections: Yes.
Liquor: Full.
Serving: L, D.
Credit Cards: AE, MC, V.
Handicap Access: Yes.
Reservations: No.
Special Features: Patio and creekside float-
ing dock seating.

In Sarasota they call their fish houses "oyster bars," and Phillippi Creek sets the gold
standard. Combo pots for two are the specialty of the house: pans full of steamed
oysters, shrimp, corn on the cob, and a
selection of specialty items (clams, lobster,
crab, or scallops). The seafood is so fresh, it
ought to be slapped. We've eaten here on
several occasions; it's my husband's first
choice when we're in town. He loves the
gooey-thick clam chowder and fried oyster
sandwich. I typically pick the blackened
grouper sandwich, which comes with a
mustardy tartar sauce and sliced pickled
banana peppers for relish. You have your
choice of settings here, either indoors,
glassed-in with a boathouse motif, or out in
the breeze on dry dock. Either way you get a
backwater view and the kind of service that
puts you at ease.

YODER'S

941-955-7771.
www.yodersrestaurant.com.
3434 Bahia Vista St., Sarasota 34239.
Price: Inexpensive.
Children's Menu: Yes.
Cuisine: Amish/Home-Style.
Liquor: No.
Serving: B, L, D.
Closed: Sun.
Credit Cards: No.
Handicap Access: Yes.
Reservations: No.

A happy outgrowth of the Amish/
Mennonite community in Sarasota, home

cooking prevails in family restaurants throughout the area. These folks are principally farmers, so you can expect farmhouse-style freshness at their table. Yoder's sits squarely in the midst of the Pinecraft Amish community, and you know it's the real thing because many of the patrons are wearing long beards and suspenders or white bonnets and full-body aprons over their plain dresses. Amish photography, art, quilts, and other handiwork decorate the dining room, which is almost always full. Although you'll find typical sandwiches and hamburgers, Midwestern comfort food predominantly makes up the all-day menu: baked chicken, noodle casserole, cabbage rolls, scalloped potatoes and ham, meatloaf, and roast beef. There's no replacement for homemade goodness, and even my meatloaf sandwich benefited from red juicy tomatoes and home-baked bread. Pies are the claim to local fame here, and there's a window where fans come to pick up their whole cream or baked pies. I can only vouch for the rhubarb,

Yoder's restaurant, in the heart of Sarasota's Amish-Mennonite community, draws in locals for its home-cooking and yummy pies. Karen T. Bartlett

the perfect ending to a meal like my mother would have made: tart and encased in a crumbly sugar-glazed crust.

SIESTA KEY
THE BROKEN EGG

941-346-2750.
www.the brokenegg.com.
210 Avenida Madera, Siesta Key 34242.
Price: Inexpensive.
Children's Menu: No.
Cuisine: American.
Healthy Selections: No.
Liquor: Beer and wine.
Serving: B, L daily.
Credit Cards: AE, D, DC, MC, V.
Handicap Access: Restaurant, yes; restrooms, no.
Reservations: No.
Special Features: Sidewalk seating, attached deli, bakery, and art gallery.

If you're wondering where all the islanders are at breakfast time, turn the corner at Coldwell Banker on Beach Avenue, and take a seat indoors or out at the Broken Egg. I was warned that this was cholesterol overload, and it's true: How could a restaurant with "egg" in its name not be? Besides breakfast omelets, 15 types of fluffy platter-sized pancakes, banana nut bread French toast, deep-dish quiche, muffins, coffee cake, and other fresh bakery items, the café serves lunch, which consists of soup, salad, and sandwiches. From the bakery, I recommend a cinnamon swirl, topped with cream cheesy frosting. The portobello Benedict takes a semihealthy departure, adding mushrooms and tomatoes while subtracting meat. Try the Sheepherder: poached eggs over hash browns with cheddar and Swiss. Lunchtime, Brad's Fave is grilled, seasoned chicken breast with tomatoes, cheddar, and pineapple pepper jelly between slices of sourdough bread. If you do feel the compulsion to offset the richness of the menu, do as I did: Order a carrot-apple juice cocktail. Then ask for dessert.

✪ THE SUMMERHOUSE

941-349-1100

www.theplacetoeat.com.

6101 Midnight Pass Rd., Sarasota 34231.

Price: Expensive to Very Expensive.

Children's Menu: Yes.

Cuisine: Continental.

Healthy Selections: Yes.

Liquor: Full.

Serving: D, SB.

Credit Cards: AE, DC, D, MC, V.

Handicap Access: Yes.

Reservations: Yes.

Special Features: Glass walls surrounded by gardens and outdoor seating; piano and other live entertainment.

Summerhouse: The name connotes an upscale informality. I love the name, always have. And I love the setting. The Summerhouse is acclaimed for its design, a prime example of the so-called Sarasota School of Architecture, which brings the outdoors inside via walls of glass and junglelike grounds. You feel like you're dining in a garden, surrounded by bamboo, palms, and wild coffee plants. It's a totally pleasant experience. The servers are unpretentious; mine went out of his way to make my meal all that it could be. The menu is a study in continental gone off on a nouvelle tangent, with the accent more on flavor than lightness. Take the tournedos Rossini: fork-tender beef medallions topped with seared foie gras and the most elegant port and sage sauce. Entrées balance meat and seafood: grilled pork tenderloin with honey mustard, roast duckling, veal Oscar, lamb rib chops, grouper piccata, and lightly pan-blackened yellowfin tuna (delicious with a lemon-lime beurre blanc), as a sampling. I recommend the Caesar salad (heavy on the parmesan cheese) and macadamia-nut shrimp with a light vinegary honey-mustard dip to start and the crème brûlée for the perfect finish. The latter had the most delicate custard I've tasted beneath an ever-so-thin caramel veneer.

Siesta Key's Summerhouse restaurant lets the outdoors in. Karen T. Bartlett

VENICE

✪ THE CROW'S NEST

941-484-9551.

www.crowsnest-venice.com.

1968 Tarpon Center Dr., Venice 34285.

Price: Moderate to Very Expensive.

Children's Menu: Yes.

Cuisine: Seafood.

Liquor: Full.

Serving: L, D.

Credit Cards: AE, D, MC, V.

Handicap Access: Yes, downstairs.

Reservations: Yes.

Special Features: Early-bird menu.

A seaworthy Venice institution, it serves the finer side of fresh seafood with specialties such as roasted Bahamian lobster tail, walnut-crusted salmon, griddled crab cakes, pesto baked halibut, and snapper in Cajun brandied cream sauce. I chose the latter on a recent visit and enjoyed a nicely balanced sauce—not too heavy, not too spicy—atop perfectly prepared red snapper mounded with sweet bell peppers and mild onions.

Service was a little off, but a lot can be forgiven when you're staring out at yachts bobbing in the harbor. The two-level, window-lined dining room has a stateroom-level nautical feel. Downstairs in the faintly lit tavern, you can order sandwiches and pub fare day-long, plus there's a daily lunch menu for al fresco patio diners. As a fun alternative to key lime pie (which we would have liked better without the syrup upon which it sat), try the ice cream drink called Key Lime Treat, bolstered with Stoli vanilla vodka.

THE SODA FOUNTAIN

941-412-9860.
349 W. Venice Ave., Venice 34285.
Price: Inexpensive.
Children's Menu: No, but all regular selections suitable for children.
Cuisine: American.
Liquor: None.
Serving: L, D.
Credit Cards: AE, D, DC, MC, V.
Handicap Access: Yes.
Reservations: No.

Reward yourself with a downtown shopping break at this treat. Your inner and outer child(ren) will thank you. New, but decorated like an old-fashioned soda fountain with black-and-white checked floors and chrome-edged swivel stools at the counter, it serves all-American sandwiches and burgers. These, however, are secondary to the main course: ice cream. Have it scooped up in a cone, slathered with syrup in a sundae, or whizzed in a canister as a shake or malted. They even sell phosphates, freezes, egg creams, and freshly squeezed lemonade, limeade, and orangeade. Everything comes in umpteen flavors, including the hot dogs. The menu lists 18 varieties of the quarter-pound beef franks; some, such as the BLT dog and Hawaiian dog with pineapple, are quite unusual. We tried the day's lobster bisque, which was done surprisingly well, its sherry pronounced but well balanced. The pulled pork sandwich and Cuban sandwich, the day's special, were both tasty. But not as tasty as my chocolate peanut butter shake.

FOOD PURVEYORS

Bakeries

The Broken Egg (941-346-2750; www.thebrokenegg.com; 210 Avenida Madera, Siesta Key 34242) Yummy cinnamon swirls, muffins, coffee cakes, and pies.

Maggie's Bakeshop (941-795-1719; 6753 Manatee Ave. W., Bradenton 34209; at Northwest Promenade) A true bakery, with luscious cakes, cookies, desserts, pastries, muffins, bagels, and fragrant coffees.

Pastry Art (941-955-7545; 1508 Main St., Sarasota 34236) Exquisite pastries, cakes in every flavor, tortes, cookies, cheesecakes, European-style fruit tarts, French press coffees, and espressos.

Sarasota Bread Company (941-957-3200; www.theplacetoeat.com; 208 Westfield Shoppingtown Southgate, Sarasota 34239) From Chef Paul of Siesta Key's Summerhouse fame (see above), this bakery-café sells "artisan breads" such as pesto and Greek olive loaves, plus cakes, pastries, and gourmet sandwiches for take-out or eat-in.

Breakfast

Blue Dolphin Café (941-383-3787; 5370 Gulf of Mexico Dr., Longboat Key 34228; at The Centre Shops; and 941-388-3566; 470 John Ringling Blvd., Sarasota 34236, at St.

Armands Circle) Stylish eatery serving breakfast all day: muffins, banana granola pancakes, Belgian waffles, omelets (try the spinach-feta). Also lunch.

✪ **The Broken Egg** (941-346-2750; www.thebrokenegg.com; 210 Avenida Madera, Siesta Key 34242) See review above.

Café on the Beach (941-778-0784; 4000 Gulf Dr., Holmes Beach 34217; at Manatee County Park) Locals know this as one of the most affordable and scenic places to start the morning. Belgian waffles are a specialty, and the all-you-can-eat pancakes with sausage ($4.95) are a draw.

✪ **Gulf Drive Café** (941-778-1919; 900 Gulf Dr., Bradenton Beach 34207) A longtime, wildly popular spot for hotcakes, eggs, or Belgian waffles on the beach, all day long. Also lunch and dinner.

Candy & Ice Cream

Big Olaf Creamery (941-349-9392; 5208 Ocean Blvd., Siesta Key 34242) A vintage purveyor of fresh fudge, handmade waffle cones, homemade ice cream, skinny dips (low-fat frozen dessert), espresso, and cappuccino.

Joe's Eats & Sweets (941-778-0007; 219 Gulf Dr. S., Bradenton Beach 34217) Forty gourmet flavors of ice cream (pumpkin, cotton candy, and pineapple coconut, among them) made on the premises, including sugar-free, lactose-free, and fat-free varieties, plus low-fat yogurt. Homemade fudge in dozens of unusual flavors, sodas, creative sundaes (black forest, Hawaiian delight, apple picker, and wet walnut, for instance), shakes, espresso, and cappuccino.

Kilwin's Chocolates & Ice Cream (941-388-3200; 312 John Ringling Blvd., Sarasota 34236, at St. Armands Circle) Homemade ice cream, specialty sundaes, Mackinac Island fudge, and handmade chocolates.

Mama Lo's by the Sea (941-779-1288; 101 S. Bay Blvd., #A2, Anna Maria 34216) Near the city pier, this has become the talk of local sweet-tooth types with scrumptious sundaes, a long line of ice cream flavors such as jamocha nut and trash can, an espresso bar, teas, plus breakfast and lunch specialties.

Coffee

Mama Lo's by the Sea (941-779-1288; 101 S. Bay Blvd., #A2, Anna Maria 34216) Milky Way latte, Almond Joy mocha, Peppermint Patty latte, macchiato, brevé, and other intriguing coffee offerings, plus sandwiches, ice cream, and breakfast.

Sarasota Sweets & Coffee Company (941-388-9190; 28 N. Blvd. of Presidents, Sarasota 34236, at St. Armands Circle) Gourmet brews, bakery goods, sandwich wraps, and Internet access.

Venice Wine & Coffee/Island Gourmet (941-484-3667; 201 Venice Ave. W., Venice 34285) Buy gourmet coffee by the bag or cup at the espresso bar. Also teas, wine, spices, and hard-to-find gourmet food items.

Deli & Specialty Foods

The Chop Shop (941-794-MEAT; 5906 Manatee Ave. W., Bradenton 34209) Prime meats, fresh seafood, deli items, oven-ready entrées, wine, and beer.

Geier's Sausage Kitchen (941-923-3004; 7447 Tamiami Trail, Sarasota 34231) European-style sausage and smoked meats, prime fresh meats, imported cheeses, beer, wine, pastries, and other gourmet items.

✪ **The Gourmet Market** (941-953-9101, 888-953-9101; www.thegourmetmarket.com; 1469 Main St., Sarasota 34236) A delightful place full of good smells, cheeses, Godiva chocolates, pastas, oils, vinegars, coffees, wine, and hot sauces.

Miami Avenue Ice Cream & Deli (941-484-5008; 229 Miami Ave. W., Venice 34285) Boar's Head deli sandwiches, homemade soups, homemade ice cream in 32 flavors.

✪ **Morton's Market** (941-955-9856; www.epicureanlife.com; 1924 S. Osprey Ave., Sarasota 34239; Southside Village) The ultimate gourmet's delight, it sells hot and cold prepared items for take-out, fresh produce, deli and fresh meats, seafood, coffees, shelves of gourmet products, you name it.

Productos Latinos (941-955-2071; 1145 S. Tamiami Trail, Sarasota 34239; at Bahia Vista St.) Fresh yucca and other produce, tortillas, hot pepper sauces, Mexican cheese, and other packaged Latin food products.

A Taste of the Columbia Restaurant (941-388-1026, 800-426-5862; www.columbia restaurant.com; 421 St. Armands Circle, Sarasota 34236) Dressings, black beans mix, sangria jelly, cookbook, coffee, wine, cigars, and other items sold in the renowned Spanish restaurant.

Too Jay's (941-362-3692; Westfield Shoppingtown Southgate, 3501 S. Tamiami Trail, Sarasota 34239) This import from the Tampa area is the ultimate in deli food, with sandwiches, hot comfort-food dishes, and the real thing in New York cheesecake.

Fruit & Vegetable Stands

Albritton Fruit (800-237-3682; www.albrittonfruit.com; 1825 S. Tamiami Trail, Sarasota 34239) With five locations throughout the area, Albritton is a well-known name in citrus. Grove and packing house trolley tours available in the growing season.

Bradenton Farmers' Market (941-747-2498; on 13th St. between Sixth and Eighth Avenues downtown) Runs 7:30 to 12:30 on Saturday. Fresh local produce, plants, flowers, and baked goods.

Mixon Fruit Farms (941-748-5829, 800-608-2525; www.mixon.com; 2712 26th Ave. E., PO Box 25200, Bradenton 34206) Large old family-owned business specializing in citrus. Tours of the grove and processing plant, free samples, shipping, and a gift shop selling fruit, fudge, ice cream, and jellies. Open November–April.

Sarasota Farmers' Market (941-951-2656; Lemon Ave. between First St. and Main St., downtown Sarasota) Florida fruits, vegetables, flowers, plants, and honey. Every Saturday 7 to noon.

Natural Foods

Anfley's (941-778-4322; 5340 Gulf Dr., Holmes Beach 34217) Juice bar, teas, produce, vitamins, homeopathic treatments, organic beer and wine.

Good Earth Natural Foods (941-795-0478, 800-638-5201; www.goodearthfoods.com; 6717 Manatee Ave. W., Bradenton 34209; at Northwest Promenade) A full line of organic produce and healthy food products, with two other Bradenton locations.

The Granary Natural Foods Market (941-924-4754; 1930 Stickney Point Rd., Sarasota 34231; east of the Siesta Key bridge) A full-service mart with juice bar, hot and cold deli, salad and burrito bar, sushi, and a large fresh produce and grains area.

Richard's Whole Foods (941-966-0596; www.richardswholefoods.com; 1092 Tamiami Trail S., Osprey 34229) One of several area locations, it carries a good stock of bulk natural foods and organic groceries.

Pizza & Take-out

Circle Deli-Diner at the Pharmacy (941-388-2110; 19 N. Blvd. of Presidents, Sarasota 34236, at St. Armands Circle) Breakfast items (all day), sandwiches, soups, and salads to go or eat in.

Crusty Louie's Pizza (941-366-3100; 3800 Tamiami Trail S. #29, Sarasota 34239; at Paradise Plaza) Stuffed, pan, Chicago-style, or thin-crust pizza made with whole-wheat crust and low-fat, low-salt cheeses.

Main Bar Sandwich Shop (941-955-8733; 1944 Main St., Sarasota 34236) A long list of sandwiches, hot and cold, plus salads and desserts. Specialties include the Aztec sandwich with roast beef, provolone, and jalapeño dressing and the New Orleans Muffuletta and Veggiletta.

Morton's Market (941-955-9856; www.epicureanlife.com; 1924 S. Osprey Ave., Sarasota 34239; at Southside Village) Wildly popular (practically legendary), Morton's sells hot pre-pared items, pizza, deli sandwiches, salads, bakery goods, and homemade desserts for take-out, plus fresh produce, deli and fresh meats, seafood, coffees, and gourmet products.

Seafood

✪ **Star Fish Company** (941-794-1243; 12306 46th Ave. W., PO Box 1, Cortez 34215) To get any closer to the source, you'd have to get wet. This long-standing tradition is the anchor of Cortez village's working waterfront, where crusty old fishing boats pull up and murals and plaques deliver lessons on history and heritage. Buy fresh, fresh fish in the market to take home, or order it off the menu to enjoy dockside on picnic tables

Urbanek's Fish Market (941-488-3177; 110 Circuit Rd., Nokomis 34275) Fresh seafood and ready-to-cook and prepared dishes.

CULTURE

Culture arrived on the Sarasota Bay coast with the early settlers of wealth and means. Eager at first to escape metropolitan ways for the simplicity of life on the beach, they eventually craved access to theater and fine arts, and so ensured their existence.

Sarasota benefited most from the generous cultural endowment of the Ringling broth-ers. Not only did the Ringlings bring circus magic to a quiet frontier town, but they also exposed the pioneers to the wonders of Gilded Age European art and architecture. In their wake they left a spirit still palpable and entirely unique to the Gulf Coast. Art schools and theater groups in Sarasota breed a freshness, vitality, daring, and avant-garde attitude unusual for a town its size. Siesta Key, especially, has an atmosphere that has attracted writers, artists, actors, and cartoonists since folks began settling there.

Sarasota's cultural heritage began with an influx of Scottish settlers at the turn of the century. Now widely varied, its population includes a colony of Amish/Mennonite residents in a district known as Pinecraft, around Bahia Vista Street and Beneva Road. Here you'll see long-bearded men driving tractors down the streets, a Mennonite Church, simple homes, a neighborhood park, and an Amish restaurant or two. The African-American district is known as Newtown and lies between Highways 41 and 301 between 10th Street and Myrtle Road.

Architecture

In the **Bradenton** area, the Greek-Revival style of plantation house has left its mark. The best example of it survives grandly at ✪ **Gamble Plantation** (see "Historic Sites"). Pioneer styles are preserved at the **Manatee Historical Village,** including a Cracker Gothic farmhouse, a one-room schoolhouse, and an early brick store. In downtown Bradenton you'll find primo Mediterranean influence at the pink **Riverpark Residence Hotel** (in its former life, rumored to have hosted Al Capone) and in later-generation buildings such as the South Florida Museum. Old Florida-Victorian style survives in the homes of neighborhoods around downtown.

On **Longboat Key,** resorts and mansions are modern and ostentatious. In the village once known as Longbeach, one finds a return to comfortable, older styles with a bit of New England charm.

Sarasota's downtown and bay areas hold a smorgasbord of old European styles, from the lavish Italian-inspired ✪ **Cà d'Zan** at the Ringling Estate to the ✪ **Spanish Opera House** downtown. Fine examples of old residential architecture are found on the fringes of the downtown area. In contrast, the Frank Lloyd Wright Foundation's ✪ **Van Wezel Performing Hall** makes a big purple shell statement on the bay shoreline.

In the 1950s Sarasota revolutionized local architecture by developing a contemporary style suitable to the environment. Examples of the "Sarasota School of Architecture" are spread throughout the area, notably at **Summerhouse Restaurant** on **Siesta Key.** Often overlooked, **Venice** houses many architectural treasures created in the 1920s, when the Brotherhood of Locomotive Engineers selected it as a retirement center and subsequently built a model city in northern Italian style. Two shining examples are the **Park Place Nursing Home** at Tampa Avenue and Nassau Street—originally the Hotel Venice—and the nearby **Venice Centre Mall,** once the San Marco Hotel, later the Kentucky Military Institute. The length of **West Venice Avenue** reveals stunning shops and homes in the prevailing Mediterranean Revival style, as does the **Venezia Park** neighborhood along nearby Nassau Street. You'll find architectural treasures throughout the city, which strives to preserve its treasures. To help in your search, look for a copy of *Venice Historical Walking/Driving Tour,* available at Venice Archives and Area Historical Collection (see "Museums") or other locations.

Cinema

Film

Sarasota is a hotbed for film, with its celebrated film festivals, alternative film cinema, and ideal locations for filming.

Sarasota Film Society (941-364-8662, box office 955-FILM; www.filmsociety.org; Burns Court Cinema, 506 Burns Ln., Sarasota 34236; downtown; PO Box 3378, Sarasota 34230) This group is devoted to screening quality international films year-round, both first-run and classic. It sponsors the Cine-World Film Festival (see "Calendar of Events" at the end of this chapter).

Movies

AMC 12 Theatres at Sarasota Square Mall (941-921-7781; 8027 Beneva Rd., Sarasota 34238; at Tamiami Trail S. and Beneva Rd.)

Burns Court Cinema (941-364-8662; www.filmsociety.org; 506 Burns Ln., Sarasota 34236) Bright-pink movie theater, showing art and other out-of-the-mainstream films on three screens.

Hollywood 20 (941-954-5768; www.regalcinemas.com; 1993 Main St. at Hwy. 301, Sarasota 34236; downtown) New state-of-the-art theaters with stadium seating and surround-sound stereo.

Oakmont 8 (941-954-5768; www.regalcinemas.com; 4801 Cortez Rd. W., Bradenton 34210)

Venetian 6 Theatres (941-954-5768; 1735 Tamiami Trail S., Venice 34293; Venetian Plaza)

Dance

American International Dance Centre (941-955-8363; 556 S. Pineapple Ave., Sarasota 34236) Ballroom dancing instruction and competition for adults and children.

Sarasota Ballet (941-359-0099, box office 351-8000, 800-361-8388; www.sarasota ballet.org; 5555 N. Tamiami Trail, Sarasota 34243) Classic and interpretative dance performances are staged by professionals at the FSU Center for the Performing Arts and Van Wezel Performing Arts Center, from September to April.

Sarasota Dance Center (941-377-1751; 5000 Fruitville Rd., Sarasota 34232) Lessons in Latin, Argentine, ballroom, swing, and other dance.

Sarasota Scottish Country Dancers (941-485-7488; 194 Sunaire Terrace, Nokomis 34275) Evidence of the town's Scottish heritage, the group meets regularly and participates at special events.

Gardens
HISTORIC SPANISH POINT
941-966-5214.
www.historicspanishpoint.org.
337 N. Tamiami Trail, PO Box 846, Osprey 34229.
Open: 9am–5pm Mon.–Sat., 12–5pm Sun.
Admission: $7 adults, $3 children 6–12.

This multi-era historic attraction (see "Historic Homes & Sites," below) features the ornamental and native gardens built by Sarasota matriarch Bertha Honore Palmer in the 1910s.

The Duchene Lawn, the most dramatic, is lined with towering palms and holds a Greek-column portal that once framed a view of the sea. To create the lovely jungle walk, Mrs. Palmer built a miniature aqueduct system. A sunken garden and pergola, fern walk, and ornamental pond also provide oases of lush respite along the path at this 30-acre site.

MARIE SELBY BOTANICAL GARDENS
941-366-5731.
www.selby.org.
811 S. Palm Ave., Sarasota 34236.
Admission: $12 adults, $6 children ages 6–11, free for children 5 and under.
Open: 10am–5pm daily.
Closed: Christmas Day.

This 1920s residence on Sarasota Bay occupies 8.5 acres planted in gardens that wow plant lovers with plots of palm, bamboo, hibiscus, tropical food plants, herbs, and other exotic flora. Selby is world-renowned for its collection of more than 6,000 orchids in a lush rainforest setting among bromeliads and rare tropical plants.

RINGLING ESTATE ROSE GARDEN AND GROUNDS
941-355-5101.
www.ringling.org.
5401 Bay Shore Rd., Sarasota 34243.
On the Ringling Estate.
Open: Daily 10am–5:30pm.
Closed: Holidays.
Admission: Free.

Mammoth banyan trees (gifts from Thomas Edison, who had an estate in Fort Myers), a showy poinciana, statuesque royal palms, and a rose garden planted in 1913 are the centerpieces of the lovely bayfront Ringling Estate. Family graves are situated in the Secret Garden near Cà d'Zan, rediscovered 25 years ago and recently rededicated. The Dwarf Garden lies between the art museum and Asolo Theater.

SARASOTA JUNGLE GARDENS
941-355-5305.
www.sarasotajunglegardens.com.
3701 Bayshore Rd., Sarasota 34234.
Open: Daily 9am–5pm.
Admission: $11 adults, $10 seniors, $7 children 3–12.

Although this is largely a kiddie attraction,

Flamingos grace the exquisite gardens of Sarasota Jungle Gardens. Karen T. Bartlett

plant lovers will enjoy the botanical gardens and cool, tropical jungle. Winding paved paths lead easily through the grounds' 16 acres, a hundred varieties of palms, and countless species of indigenous and exotic flora, all identified. Private nooks and bubbling brooks make this a lovely spot for quiet reflection, especially in the early morning before the throngs arrive. Exotic birds and other attractions are gravy for the connoisseur of nature. (See "Kids' Stuff" in this section.) Snack bar and gift shop.

Historic Homes & Sites
BRADEN CASTLE RUINS
27th St. E. and Rte. 64, Bradenton, FL.
Open: Sunrise to sunset.

At the juncture of the Manatee and Braden Rivers, antebellum memories crumble gracefully in a setting recognized by the National Register of Historic Sites. Just short of spectacular, the plantation house ruins are chain-linked and posted with KEEP OUT DANGER signs. They hide at the center of a retirement trailer community in a riverside park that's not easy to find. A marker tells the story of Dr. Joseph Addison Braden from Virginia and his ill-fated Braden Plantation.

CÀ D'ZAN
941-355-5101.
www.ringling.org.
5401 Bay Shore Rd., Sarasota 34243.
On the Ringling Estate.
Open: Daily 10am–5:30pm.
Closed: Holidays.
Admission: $15 adults, $12 seniors 65 and over; covers admission to all Ringling attractions. Children 12 and under free with adult. Florida students and teachers free with proper ID.

Newly renovated Cà D'Zan, a salute to Gilded Age prosperity on the Ringling Estate. Karen T. Bartlett

Six years and $15 million of restoration, completed in April 2002, have brought this 32-room showpiece back to its Gilded Age glory. Entrance is now by half-hour guided tour only, and you must reserve a tour time when you buy your ticket at the complex's art museum. Using the Doges Palace in Venice as a model, circus king John Ringling spared no expense building this monument to success and overindulgence in the 1920s. He imported styles, materials, and pieces from Italy, France, and elsewhere around the world to embellish his eponymous (in Italian) "House of John." Baroque, Gothic, and Renaissance elements, marble, colored tiles, and jesterlike, multicolor-tinted leaded windows contribute to a breathtaking and ornate look of Roaring Twenties opulence in the 30-room, $1.5 million (nearly $17 million in today's money) mansion on the bay at the John and Mable Ringling Museum of Art (see "Visual Arts Centers & Resources," below).

CORTEZ VILLAGE
Cortez Rd. and 123rd St., Bradenton, FL.

Remnants of an 1880s fishing village include old tin-roofed fish houses, boat works, and a waterfront store. Exhibits and painted murals throughout the salty district describe local culture and environmental practices. A new maritime museum in a historic schoolhouse will be completed by summer 2006.

✪ DE SOTO NATIONAL MEMORIAL PARK
941-792-0458.
www.nps.gov.deso.
75th St. NW, PO Box 15390, Bradenton 34280.
Open: Visitors center 9am–5pm daily, park open sunrise to sunset.
Admission: Free.

Somewhat off the beaten path, this is a place where you can imagine yourself back in the 16th century among conquistadores in heavy armor trying to survive among irate Native Americans, mosquitoes, and sweltering heat. Engraved plaques, a re-created Amerindian village, and a half-mile-long trail tell the story of Hernando de Soto's life and adventures here, where supposedly he first breached the shores of the Florida mainland to begin his heroic trek to the Mississippi River. A visitors center holds artifacts and shells, and a 22-minute video presentation is available. In the winter, rangers dress and play the part of 16th-century inhabitants, demonstrating weaponry and methods of food preparation.

DOWNTOWN BRADENTON
Main Street and Manatee Avenue (Route 64).

Old Main Street and the city yacht basin are the historic downtown district's backbone. Compact, it's easy to walk and experience the old architecture, a fine museum, an intimate theater, park benches, sidewalk eateries, antique stores, and brick-paved crosswalks. Locals are trying hard to pump new life into a river town that died with the advent of the automobile. A walking plaza is in the works. The future looks bright. In the meantime, visit the shops on Main Street and have lunch, then stroll around nearby Point Pleasant for a taste of Bradenton's oak-studded homeyness and heritage. Every Saturday, October through April, visit the farmers' market.

GAMBLE PLANTATION STATE HISTORICAL SITE
941-723-4536.
3708 Patten Ave., Ellenton 34222.
Route 301 near I-75, exit 224.
Open: Visitors Center 8am–4:30pm (closed 11:45am–12:45pm); tours depart at 9:30, 10:30, 1, 2, 3, and 4.
Closed: Tues., Wed.
Admission: Mansion tour, $4 adults, $2 children 6–12. Free admission to visitors center museum.

Major Robert Gamble, originally from Scotland, learned about sugar planting in Virginia and Tallahassee before he moved to the Manatee River. He eventually cleared 1,500 acres of jungle using slave labor and built a Greek Revival–style home. He constructed the mansion's

Sugar built the antebellum plantations along Bradenton's Manatee River—perhaps literally in some cases. It is rumored that molasses was mixed into the Gamble Mansion columns' tabby (seashell) mortar.
Karen T. Bartlett

crowning touch—18 Greek columns—with a mortar known as "tabby," made of crushed and burned seashells. The spacious (by the time's standards) palace was inhabited by bachelor Gamble alone but served as the area's social hub until the major was forced to sell it in 1856 because of hurricane, frosts, and market losses. In 1925 the United Daughters of the Confederacy rescued the mansion from decades of neglect. The site was declared a Confederate shrine for its role in sheltering Confederate Secretary of State Judah P. Benjamin, when he fled for his life after the Civil War. The United Daughters donated the monument to the state a couple of years later. Visitors can see the inside of the home by tour only, which takes less than an hour. The two floors contain period furnishings and housewares, which the park ranger explains in lively, interesting dialogue. You'll learn, for example, how such expressions as "hush puppy," "sleep tight," and "pop goes the weasel" came to be, and about the lives of 19th-century plantation owners and slaves. The museum in the visitors center tells the plantation's story through the eras. A picnic shelter accommodates lunchers.

✪ HISTORIC SPANISH POINT

941-966-5214.
www.historicspanishpoint.org.
337 N. Tamiami Trail, PO Box 846, Osprey 34229.
Open: 9am–5pm Mon.–Sat., 12–5pm Sun.
Admission: $7 adults, $3 children 6–12.

This historic site spans multiple eras of the region's past—2150 BC through 1918. Its importance lies not only in its historical aspects but also in its environmental and archaeological
significance. Assembled on the 30-acre Little Sarasota Bay estate, once owned by socialite
Bertha Palmer, are prehistoric Indian burial grounds, a cutaway of a shell midden mound, the
relocated homestead and family chapel of the pioneering Webb dynasty, Mrs. Palmer's
restored gardens (see "Gardens" in this section), and a late Victorian pioneer home. Local
actors give living-history performances Saturdays and Sundays in the winter. Guided tours
and tram rides are available; reserve ahead. Another tip: Bring mosquito repellent in warm
weather.

MANATEE VILLAGE HISTORICAL PARK

941-741-4075.
604 15th St. E., Bradenton 34208.
At Manatee Ave.
Open: 9am–4:30pm weekdays.
Admission: Free.

Several buildings with local historical significance have been restored and moved to a
pleasant, oak-shaded park strongly representative of Bradenton's old wooded and winding
neighborhoods. The County Courthouse is the oldest, completed in 1860. Others include a
circa 1889 church (the oldest congregation south of Tampa), a Cracker farmhouse, a one-
room schoolhouse, a smokehouse, and a brick general store from the early 19th century. A
museum of artifacts, photographs, and hands-on exhibits for children is located in the
general store. The Cracker-Gothic Stephens House is stocked with preserves, period
kitchen items, furniture, and farm implements. Fogarty Boat Works reflects Bradenton's
boat-building heritage. The staff sometimes wears historically accurate dress. Across the
street lies the Manatee Burying Ground, which dates from 1850. All in all, the park is a
romantic site, grossly underrated and lightly visited.

Kid's Stuff
BAYFRONT PARK
Downtown Sarasota.
Admission: Free.

Toddlers especially love the shallow pool with squirting fountains and sculptures of frogs,
manatees, turtles, gators, and fish they can climb. It's a good place for strolling, people-
watching on a park bench, jogging, 'blading, and shopping for boat charters. There's a
small, inexpensive restaurant and water sports concession within. In 2001 the park began
hosting a seasonal Bayfront Exhibition of street sculptures. The exhibitions have now
become year-round, featuring artists from around the world.

✪ G. WIZ

941-309-4949.
www.gwiz.org.
1001 Boulevard of the Arts, Sarasota
34236.
Selby Library Bldg.
Open: Tues.–Sat. 10am– 5pm, Sun.
1pm–5pm.
Admission: $7 for adults, $6 for seniors,
$5 for ages 2–18. Free admission first Wed.
5pm–8pm.

G. WIZ is even more fun on the inside! Karen T. Bartlett

G. WIZ stands for Gulfcoast Wonder &
Imagination Zone. But G. Wiz about sums
it up. And wow! All shiny and high-tech, it
brings hours, worth of enrichment entertainment in an uncrowded, gallerylike,
glass geodesic structure. The state-of-the-
art playground outside is free and far
beyond mere swings and slides. Inside on
two levels, theme areas explore various
scientific and artistic phenomena. Kids
love the timed dash against one another
and the jump measurer. Kids' Zone is
geared toward toddlers with a table for fossil digging, a bubble table, and fun-house
mirrors. Upstairs, we like the animation
workstations best. Here kids can pose and
click action figures and other toys one
frame at a time to create a short film. For constructive play, this is the best place around to
take the kids. New, Sutton's Garden/Habitat Zone has butterflies on the loose and snakes
and bees contained. A special camera lets you spy underwater at the fish pond. Don't forget
to stop in the gift shop (as if the kids would let you) for educational playthings.

SARASOTA JUNGLE GARDENS

941-355-5305.
www.sarasotajunglegardens.com.
3701 Bayshore Rd., Sarasota 34234.
Open: Daily 9am–5pm.
Admission: $11 adults, $10 seniors, $7 children 3–12.

A birds of prey exhibit and show, reptile and rainforest bird shows, a Meet the Keeper program, free-strolling peacocks and other feathered friends, a playground with a jungle
theme, a bird posing area, pony rides ($3 each, $5 with photo), black leopards, monkeys,
flamingos, swans, wallabies, and other live animals make this one of the area's favorite
children's attractions. Peaceful, junglelike gardens appeal to others. (See "Gardens" in
this section.)

SOUTH FLORIDA MUSEUM

941-746-4131.
www.southfloridamuseum.org.
201 10th St. W., Bradenton 34205.
Open: Mon.–Sat.10am–5pm, Sun.12–5pm.
Closed: Mon. May–Dec. (except July) and first two weeks of Sept.
Admission: $9.50 adults, $7.50 seniors, $6 students, $5 children 5–12.

The newly renovated downtown museum has a designated Discovery Place for kids' hands-on enjoyment. The Doll House exhibit on the museum's second floor displays toys from throughout the past century. Saturday Fun programs include admission to Discovery Place, manatee presentations, and crafts activities.

VAN WEZEL SATURDAY MORNINGS FOR KIDS

941-953-3366, 953-3368.
www.vanwezel.org.
777 N. Tamiami Trail, Sarasota 34236.

January through May, *The Emperor's New Clothes*, *The Adventures of Tom Sawyer*, other kiddie classics, and contemporary favorites take the stage one Saturday morning each month at 10:30.

VENICE LITTLE THEATRE FOR YOUNG PEOPLE

941-488-1115.
www.venicestage.com.
140 W. Tampa Ave., Venice 34285.

One of the most successful nonprofit community theaters in the U.S., the Little Theatre hosts off-season summer theatrical instruction (call 941-486-8679) and three musical performances for youngsters October through May.

Museums

(For art museums, see "Visual Arts")

ANNA MARIA ISLAND HISTORICAL MUSEUM

941-778-0492.
402 Pine Ave., Anna Maria 34216.
Open: 10am–3pm Sept.–May, 10am–noon other months.
Closed: Mon., Fri., Sun.
Admission: Donations accepted.

A homey little museum inside an icehouse of the 1920s holds a wealth of photos, maps, records, books, a shell collection, a loggerhead turtle display, and vintage movies on video. Next door sits the old jail, its humorous graffiti worth a chuckle.

✪ RINGLING MUSEUM OF THE CIRCUS

941-355-5101.
www.ringling.org.
5401 Bay Shore Rd., Sarasota 34243.
On the Ringling Estate.
Open: Daily 10am–5:30pm.

Closed: Holidays.
Admission: $15 adults, $12 seniors 65 and over; covers admission to all Ringling attractions. Children 12 and under free. Florida students and teachers free with proper ID.

The Museum of the Circus was Florida's way of saying thank you to John Ringling back in 1948. Its re-creation of Big Top magic paid tribute to a man many believed invented the circus, a man who bequeathed to the city—along with the giddy world of the Big Top—a legacy of exotica, sophistication, and art appreciation. The museum reflects Ringling's seemingly contradictory interests. Fine-arts displays counterbalance high-wire exhibits. Black-and-white photography is juxtaposed with gilded fantasy. Tasteful cloth mannequins model plumed and sequined costumes. My favorite parts are the animated scale model of the circus grounds and a narrated behind-the-scenes look at circus lifestyles. The museum is located on the grounds of the John and Mable Ringling Museum of Art (see "Visual Arts Centers & Resources," below).

✪ SARASOTA CLASSIC CAR MUSEUM

941-355-6228.
www.sarasotacarmuseum.org.
5500 N. Tamiami Trail, Sarasota 34239
Open: 9am–6pm daily.
Admission: $8.50 adults, $7.65 seniors, $5.75 juniors 13–17, $4 children 6–12.
More than 125 antique and celebrity cars combine under one roof. See the DeLorean from *Back to the Future*, the original Batmobile, Elvis Presley's car, John Ringling's Rolls Royces and Pierce Arrows, and vintage motorized vehicles dating from 1903. The kids will get a kick out of the vintage game arcade, where for as little as a nickel they can make Peppy the Musical Clown dance, get their fortune told by the Great Swami, and motor cross-country on the Drive Mobile. It's lots more fun than modern-day arcades.

SOUTH FLORIDA MUSEUM

941-746-4131.
www.southfloridamuseum.org.
201 10th St. W., Bradenton 32405.
Open: Mon.–Sat. 10am–5pm, Sun. 12–5pm.
Closed: Mon. May–Dec. (except July) and first two weeks of Sept.
Admission: $9.50 adults, $7.50 seniors, $6 students, $5 children 5–12.

This two-story museum recently completed a $5 million renovation that installed shiny new, impressive displays. The all-new first floor focuses on ancient history with pre-historic skeleton casts, realistic life-size Native American dioramas, and appropriate sound effects. One of the museum's most prized exhibits, the Tallant Collection, displays artifacts excavated mostly from Manatee County. Upstairs holds some of the

Snooty, South Florida Museum's celebrity manatee, takes the stage. Karen T. Bartlett

museum's original exhibits along with new ones that replicate home and other building settings throughout the area's history. The star of the museum is Snooty, the oldest known manatee born in captivity (1948) in the United States. You can watch him and his current playmates underwater from aquarium windows or from above at the Parker Aquarium, where interactive exhibits explain the plight of the endangered manatee and educational presentations take place throughout the day. The outdoor Spanish Plaza holds a 16th-century chapel, manor house, and typical village home. The Bishop Planetarium, recently destroyed by fire, is being rebuilt for a projected 2005 opening.

VENICE ARCHIVES AND AREA HISTORICAL COLLECTION
941-486-2487.
351 S. Nassau St., Venice 34285.
Open: Mon. and Wed. 10am–4pm.
Admission: Free or by donation.

The most interesting relic here is the building that houses the facility. A 1927 Italianate structure with a triangular base and a Renaissance tower, it once was called the Triangle Inn. Stop for a peek at whatever exhibit is showing, a room full of local fossils, and another room honoring city father Dr. Fred Albee, whose operating table you'll find, among other memorabilia. A city park lies across the street.

Music & Nightlife
Sarasota dances with action throughout the week and especially on weekends. Local bands and up-and-coming stars appear in theaters, cabarets, and nightclubs. Cores of activity include downtown, the neon-bright Sarasota Quay, and posh St. Armands Circle. Every Friday check the *Sarasota Herald-Tribune*'s "Ticket" and *Bradenton Herald*'s "Weekend" to learn what's happening in area clubs.

BRADENTON BEACH
Beachhouse (941-779-2222; 200 Gulf Dr. N., Bradenton Beach 34217) Live reggae and island music most evenings.

ST. ARMANDS KEY
Cha Cha Coconuts (941-388-3300; 417 St. Armands Circle, Sarasota 34236) Contemporary music and dancing Thursday–Sunday, some Wednesdays.

SARASOTA
Cantina Latina (941-954-1330; 3800 Tamiami Trail S., Sarasota 34239; at Paradise Plaza) Salsa, merengue, rumba, flamenco, and cha-cha music and dancing every Friday and Saturday.

Club Envy (941-951-0335; 1927 Ringling Blvd., Sarasota 34236) Hot new club, featuring top 40, hip-hop, and alternative rock.

Concerts at Ringling (941-359-5700; www.ringling.org; John and Mable Ringling Museum of Art, 5401 Bay Shore Rd., Sarasota 34243) Local and international musicians perform November through March in the courtyard and in the Rubens Galleries.

Florida West Coast Symphony (941-953-3434; www.fwcs.org; 709 Tamiami Trail N., Sarasota 34236) Besides classical symphony concerts held in Bradenton and Sarasota from November to April, this group sponsors chamber orchestra and other special performances.

✪ **The Gator Club** (941-366-5969; www.thegatorclub.com; 1490 Main St., Sarasota 34236; downtown) One of the hottest places downtown, in historic digs with a pressed-tin ceiling and straw ceiling fans. Live music nightly and free Latin dance lessons Thursdays.

Jazz Club of Sarasota (941-366-1552; hot line 941-316-9207; www.jazzclubsarasota.com; 330 S. Pineapple Ave., Suite 111, Sarasota 34236) This organization dedicates itself to the perpetuation and encouragement of jazz performance by presenting various monthly and annual events, Saturday jazz jams, members' concerts, special presentations, and youth programs, with a musical instrument lending library. It sponsors a week-long Jazz Festival in March, featuring top musicians (see "Calendar of Events").

JB's Nightclub & Grille (941-924-4999; 6240 S. Tamiami Trail, Sarasota 34238) Live music Wednesday through Sunday: world beat, Motown, country.

Sarasota Concert Band (941-364-2263; www.sarasotaconcertband.homestead.com; 1345 Main St., Sarasota 34236) This ensemble's 50-some members perform October through May at Van Wezel Performing Arts Hall and other venues and at outdoor concerts through-out the area.

Sarasota Friends of Folk Music (941-377-9256; www.sarafolk.org; 3874 Wolverine St., Sarasota 34232) Group specializing in Florida folk music performs free monthly concerts on City Island at the Sarasota Sailing Squadron.

Sarasota Pops Orchestra (941-795-7677; PO Box 14191, Bradenton 34280) Presents a series of concerts each year November through March.

Venice Symphony (941-488-1010; www.thevenicesymphony.org; PO Box 1561, Venice 34284) Classical and pops concerts December through April at Church of the Nazarene (1535 E. Venice Ave.), with a free outdoor pops concert in March.

SIESTA KEY

Beach Club (941-349-6311; 5151 Ocean Blvd., Siesta Key 34242) Once a rowdy college bar, this newly yuppified restaurant and nightclub hosts local rock, jazz, and reggae groups nightly.

Fandango (941-346-1711; 1266 Old Stickney Point Rd., Siesta Key 34242) Live jazz on weekends.

VENICE

Crow's Nest (941-484-9551; www.crowsnest-venice.com; 1968 Tarpon Center Dr., Venice 34285) Features live jazz musicians and singers on a changing calendar, every night but Sunday.

Phat Cats Piano Bar (941-484-5639; http://phatcats-venice.com; 121 W. Venice Ave., Venice 34285) Fine French estate and other wines and international beers, with live piano music nightly.

Specialty Libraries

Family Heritage House (941-752-5319; www.mccfl.edu/heritage/contacts.html; Manatee Community College, 5840 26th St. W., Bradenton 34207) Part of Florida's Black Heritage Trail, it contains children's books, videotapes, audiotapes, books, magazines, and other materials relevant to black heritage, arts, and culture.

John and Mable Ringling Museum of Art Research Library (941-359-5743; www. ringling.org; 5401 Bay Shore Rd., Sarasota 34243) Specializes in 17th-century Dutch, Flemish, and Italian paintings. Open to the public Wed. and Fri. 1-5pm or by appointment.

Manatee County Central Library (941-748-5555; 1301 Barcarrotta Blvd. W., Bradenton 34205) The Eaton Room contains a collection of Florida and county historical photographs, newspapers, books, census records, and articles.

Selby Public Library (941-861-1100; 1331 First St., Sarasota 34236) The region's central library, it schedules cultural events throughout the year.

Verman Kimbrough Memorial Library (941-359-7587; www.lib.rsad.edu; Ringling School of Art and Design, 2700 N. Tamiami Trail, Sarasota 34234) Art history and instruction.

Theater

Anna Maria Island Players (941-778-5755; http://home.earthlink.net/~islandplayers; 10009 Gulf Dr. at Pine Ave., Anna Maria Island 34216) Year-round community theater in an Old Florida–style building.

✪ **Asolo Center for the Performing Arts/Florida State University Acting Conservatory** (Box office 941-351-8000, 800-361-8388; www.asolo.org; 5555 N. Tamiami Trail, Sarasota 34243; across from the Ringling Estate) The Asolo tradition began in Italy in 1798, in a theater built in the queen's castle. It ended up on the Ringling Estate in the 1940s, where it was reconstructed and, in 1965, designated State Theater of Florida. In the early 1980s a new center was built, incorporating into the interior of one of its venues another dismantled, historic European theater: a circa 1900 Scottish opera house. Carved box fronts, friezes, and ornate cornice work from the old theater decorate the new, lending an aura of Old World heritage. Opened in 1989, the 500-seat Harold E. and Esther M. Mertz Theatre hosts the excellent 40-plus-year-old Asolo Theatre Company November through May. Free tours are available Wednesday–Saturday at 10 and 11am, November through June. A separate, more intimate, 161-seat theater, called the Jane B. Cook Theatre, is the home of Florida State University's graduate-actor training program. Its season runs concurrently with the Mertz's.

Banyan Theater (941-358-5330; www.banyantheatercompany.com; PO Box 49483, Sarasota 34230) Professional theater group that performs the classics during the summer season at Asolo/Ringling Estates.

✪ **Circus Sarasota** (941-355-9335; www.circussarasota.org; PO Box 18638, Sarasota 34276; performances at Fruitville Rd. and Tuttle Rd.) This new troupe resurrects Sarasota's deeply entrenched Big Top tradition with a February-to-March schedule of performances. Conceived by Sarasota native Dolly Jacobs (daughter of the late, great circus clown Lou Jacobs), it's a not-for-profit, educational organization.

Florida Studio Theatre and Cabaret Club (941-366-9000; www.fst2000.org; 1241 N. Palm Ave., Sarasota 34236; downtown) A major testing ground for budding playwrights and new works. Florida Studio Theatre's professional troupe presents seven productions during its October–June season and a summertime Florida Playwrights Festival at its intimate main stage (see "Calendar of Events" at the end of this chapter). Musical revues and other light entertainment November–May in the Parisian-style Cabaret Club, with full-service dining.

Golden Apple Dinner Theatre (941-366-5454, 800-652-0920; www.thegoldenapple .com; 25 N. Pineapple Ave., Sarasota 34236; downtown) Year-round Broadway dinner entertainment since 1971.

Manatee Players Riverfront Theater (941-748-0111, box office 748-5875; 102 Old Main St., Bradenton 34205) Community theater in an intimate, historic setting. Family and children's theater.

The Players of Sarasota (941-365-2494; www.theplayers.org; 838 N. Tamiami Trail, Sarasota 34236) Community theater group that stages Broadway musicals October through April, plus year-round live music and other programs.

Sarasota Opera House (941-366-8450, 888-673-7212; www.sarasotaopera.org; 61 N. Pineapple Ave., Sarasota 34236; downtown) Don't even try to park or dine downtown on opera opening nights during the January–March season. Southwest Florida's oldest opera company's opening galas are popular events that require ticket purchase months in advance. In operation for more than 30 years, the Sarasota Opera Association stages all the classics in its beautifully restored 1926 Spanish-mission-style structure, located in the Theater and Arts District. You can tour the facility (and see the chandelier from the set of *Gone With the Wind*) for $2. Advance arrangements required.

✪ **Van Wezel Performing Arts Hall** (941-953-3368, 800-826-9303; www.vanwezel.org; 777 N. Tamiami Trail, Sarasota 34236) If a performance is worth seeing, it's at the Van Wezel—that purple eye-catcher radiating outward like a scallop shell on the shores of Sarasota Bay, designed by the Frank Lloyd Wright Foundation. Tickets should be purchased at least a month in advance. Newly renovated and expanded, the Van Wezel hosts name comedians, musicians, and dance groups; Broadway shows; major orchestras; ethnic music and dance groups; chamber and choral music; and Saturday children's shows.

The sculpture Applause *greets visitors to the Van Wezel Performing Arts Center.* Karen T. Bartlett

The John and Mable Ringling Museum of Art, one of the circus's most enduring legacies to Florida.
Karen T. Bartlett

Venice Little Theatre (941-488-1115; www.venicestage.com; 140 W. Tampa Ave., Venice 34285; downtown) A community-theater company that has outgrown its name as it spread to three venues. The troupe performs six Mainstage shows in a Mediterranean Revival structure, October through May, and four contemporary plays at Stage II, November through April. It conducts theater classes, workshops, and summer camp for adults and kids (call 941-486-8679).

Visual Arts Centers & Resources

The canvas of Sarasota Bay arts reveals a complex masterpiece, layered with the diverse patterns and local color of its many communities. With its backdrop of artistic types dating back to avid collector John Ringling, Sarasota leads the region to avant-garde heights. The following entries introduce you to opportunities for experiencing art as either an appreciator or a practicing artist. A listing of commercial galleries is included under "Shopping," below.

Art Center Sarasota (941-365-2032; www.artsarasota.org; 707 N. Tamiami Trail, Sarasota 34236) Exhibition and sales galleries feature the paintings, jewelry, sculpture, pottery, and enamelware of local and national artists. Art instruction and demonstrations are available. The gallery features an outdoor sculpture garden. Most activities take place November through May. Open Tuesday–Saturday 10am–4pm.

Art League of Manatee County (941-746-2862; www.almc.org; 209 Ninth St. W., Bradenton 34205) Classes and demonstrations in all media for all ages; sales gallery.

The Fine Arts Society of Sarasota (941-330-0680, 371-7719; www.vanwezel.org/aboutUs/guidedTours.cfm; Van Wezel Performing Arts Hall, 777 N. Tamiami Trail, Sarasota 34236) Van Wezel houses a permanent collection of Florida artists' works on loan from the Society, which conducts tours weekdays November through April.

✪ **The John and Mable Ringling Museum of Art** (941-355-5101; www.ringling.org; 5401 Bay Shore Rd., Sarasota 34243) Sarasota's pride and joy, and designated the State Art Museum of Florida, this is not only an art museum but also the nucleus of tourism activity and the heart of the local art community. It shares its 66-acre bay front estate with Ringling's extravagant Cà d'Zan palace (see "Historic Homes"), a circus museum (see "Museums"), a rose garden (see "Gardens"), and a Big Top-shaped restaurant. The collection specializes in late-medieval and Renaissance Italian works, covering 500 years of European art, most of which was purchased by Ringling. The Old Masters collection contains five original Rubens tapestries as well as Spanish Baroque, French, Dutch, and northern European works, mostly portraits of a religious nature. A hands-on gallery deals with conserving artworks, including an exhibit on X-radiography. The museum continually augments its collection of American and contemporary works and is currently raising funds to add galleries and an educational facility. The lushly landscaped courtyards feature reproduction classic statues and Italian decorative columns, which Ringling originally purchased for the hotel he hoped to build on Longboat Key. Musicians play in the courtyard and Rubens Galleries November through March. Admission covers all property attractions: $15 adults, $12 seniors 65 and over. Children 12 and under free; Florida students and teachers free with proper ID. Admission to the museum only is free every Monday.

Longboat Key Center for the Arts (941-383-2345; www.longboatkeyartscenter.org; 6860 Longboat Dr. S., Longboat Key 34228) Hidden from mainstream traffic, here is a find for the buyer and would-be artisan. Galleries sell works mostly by Florida artists. Changing and permanent exhibits feature local, emerging, and experimental artists. A crafts shop sells wares made at the center's surrounding workshops, where classes are taught in basketry, watercolor, jewelry making, metal craft, pottery, and more. In-season, Tuesdays bring a Jazz Concert Series to the center.

Museum of Asian Art (941-954-7117; www.museumasianart.org; 640 S. Washington Blvd. at Sarasota Art & Antique Center, Sarasota 34236) Part of an upscale and heavily secured center of antiquities, it displays works dating back to the Han Dynasty (206 BC –220 AD) originating in China, Thailand, Cambodia, Nepal, and Burma. It is known for its exquisite Yangtze River Collection of Chinese jades, the most impressive part of the exhibit, aside from the sheer age of other pieces. Some of the exhibit is permanent, but the "vault room" (actually built in to a locking vault) rotates relevant exhibitions. Admission is $5 for adults, free for students with ID and children. Open Wednesday, Thursday, and Friday 11am–5pm.

Selby Gallery (941-359-7563; www.rsad.edu; 2700 N. Tamiami Trail, Sarasota 34234; at the Ringling School of Art and Design) An intimate, modern space exhibits the works of contemporary student, faculty, local, national, and international artists and designers. Free admission. Open 10am–4pm Monday–Saturday, 10am–7pm Tuesday in-season. Call for hours May–August.

✪ **Towles Court Art Association** (941-955-4546; www.towlescourt.com; 1943 Morrill St., Sarasota 34236) A delightful, blossomy village of restored and brightly painted tin-roofed bungalows turned art colony. Art schools, showings, studios, and galleries. Most galleries and studios are open Tuesday through Saturday 11–4. Third Friday gallery walks, 6–10pm. Guided studio tours available.

Venice Art Center (941-485-7136; 390 S. Nokomis Ave., Venice 34285) Local artists' exhibitions, gift shop, café, and art instruction.

✪ **Village of the Arts** (941-747-8056; www.villageofthearts.com; PO Box 729, Bradenton 34206, 18-block radius around 12th Street and 11th Avenue West, Bradenton) Officially welcomed in January 2001, this new artist colony revitalized a former drug neighborhood, turning it into a work of pride for the community. Artisans from all disciplines—visual arts, healing arts, culinary arts—have moved into the neighborhood to work and sell their art and services. Most are concentrated on 12th St. and open Friday and Saturday 11–4; look for the Village of Arts signs in front of houses. The village hosts a First Weekend Art Fest each month.

RECREATION

Known both for its superlative white sand beaches and as the birthplace of Florida golfing, Sarasota and its environs draw outdoors lovers to its year-round playgrounds.

Beaches

The Sarasota area claims more than 35 miles of sandy seashore. Island beaches are, for the most part, highly developed, with lots of facilities and concessions. Recent years have seen a concession of another sort—to nature—as boardwalks and sea oat plantings restore the dunes. On the islands, erosion takes its toll, and beaches must be periodically renourished. This stretch of the Gulf Coast boasts some of the whitest beaches this side of the Florida Panhandle—and some of the darkest. Parking is free at all area beaches. Pets (except where noted) and glass containers are prohibited. So is walking across dune vegetation any way but on the boardwalk crossovers.

ANNA MARIA BAYFRONT PARK

Northeast end of Anna Maria Island.
Facilities: Picnic areas, restrooms, showers, playground, recreational facilities, fishing pier.

One of the region's more secluded beach parks, this one is narrower than the rest of the island's beaches. You get a magnificent view of St. Petersburg's Sunshine Skyway Bridge from the bay. A historical marker tells about the islands' early settlers. Heed danger signs that mark where heavy tidal currents make swimming perilous.

BROHARD BEACH

941-316-1172.
1600 S. Harbor Dr., Venice 34285.
Facilities: Picnic areas, restrooms, showers, fitness trail, fishing pier, restaurant.

This narrow, dark-flecked sand beach threads under the Venice Fishing Pier and around covered picnic tables. Folks come here to fish, hang out at the pier tiki bar, and hunt for sharks' teeth. It is a designated dogs-allowed beach.

CASPERSEN BEACH

941-316-1172.
South end of Harbor Dr., Venice.
Facilities: Picnic areas, restrooms, showers, nature trail.

At the end of the road lies natural, lightly developed Caspersen Beach, where a series of boardwalks cross scrub-vegetated dunes onto diminishing dark sands. It's popular with shark-tooth hunters and young beachgoers. From here you can walk to Manasota Key Beach, to the south.

✪ COQUINA BEACH

Southern end of Gulf Dr., Bradenton Beach, Anna Maria Island.
Facilities: Picnic areas, restrooms, showers, lifeguard, café, concessions, boat ramps.

Recently renourished, this large and popular park boasts plump wide sands edged in Australian pines. Waters at the south end provide good snorkeling. The park continues on the bay, where swimming should be avoided because of currents and boat traffic. The Coquina BayWalk takes you to environmentally restored Leffis Key, with its newly replaced mangrove habitat, a $321 million restoration project.

CORTEZ BEACH

North end of Gulf Dr., Bradenton Beach, Anna Maria Island.
Facilities: Picnic tables, restrooms, showers, lifeguard.

Here's a long stretch of revamped sands that meets up with Coquina, its more popular cousin. Surfers like it here. It's convenient for the heavily laden beachgoer because you park right along the sand's edge.

LIDO BEACH

941-316-1172.
400 Benjamin Franklin Dr., Lido Key 34236.
Facilities: Picnic areas, restrooms, showers, lifeguards, swimming pool, snack bar, swings, volleyball, beach wheelchairs.

This is the main beach on Lido Key, heavily developed and popular. Canvas cabanas and stylish, umbrella-shaded lounge chairs may be rented along the stretch of sand carpeted with small shells and shell hash. South of the pavilion at the Radisson Resort, you'll find water-sports equipment rentals.

LONGBOAT KEY

Public accesses at Broadway St. on the north end of island.

Longboat Key has beautiful beaches, mostly enjoyed by resort guests and waterfront residents. Public accesses are marked subtly (and have no facilities or lifeguards) at Atlas Street, Gulfside Road, and Broadway Street. Parking is limited. The beach stretches wide as well as long, with fluffy white sand and dramatic sunset views.

✪ MANATEE COUNTY PARK

Gulf Dr. and 40th St., Holmes Beach.
Facilities: Picnic area, restrooms, showers, lifeguard, playground, restaurant, ice cream, shop, beach rentals, volleyball.

The hot spot of Anna Maria Island beachgoing, this park appeals to families because of its full complement of facilities. The beach is wide enough to accommodate rows and rows of beach towels. Australian pines shade picnic areas.

NOKOMIS BEACH/ NORTH JETTY

941-486-2311.

South end Casey Key Rd., Casey Key.

Facilities: Picnic area and shelters, restrooms, showers, lifeguards, concessions, boat ramp.

Remote and exclusive Casey Key gives way to beachy abandon at its southern end. The town of Nokomis Beach is a fisherman's haven, and North Jetty, at its southernmost point, lures anglers. (South Jetty lies across the pass on Venice Beach.) A bait shop keeps them supplied. The beach's wide sands, festooned with Australian pines and sea grape trees, are well loved by serious local beachgoers.

NORTH LIDO BEACH

941-316-1172.

North end of Ben Franklin Dr., Lido Key.

The beach less traveled on Lido, this one extends from the main beach up to New Pass. Lack of facilities and limited parking keep the throngs away at this naturally maintained park. Wide, with fine spic-and-span sand plus trails for hiking and running.

PALMA SOLA CAUSEWAY BEACH

Anna Maria Bridge, Route 64.

Facilities: Picnic area, restrooms, restaurant, water-sports rentals.

Fairly narrow sands edge the causeway between mainland and Anna Maria Island. They gain some character from Australian pines and are popular with windsurfers and jet skiers. Most beachgoers congregate around the restaurant and rental concession at the western end.

POINT OF ROCKS BEACH

941-316-1172.

Access #12, south of Siesta Public Beach on Midnight Pass Rd. near Stickney Point Rd. intersection, Siesta Key.

Part of Crescent Beach—named for its shape—this beach is popular with snorkelers and fishermen because of an accumulation of rocks that attracts marine life. Like the main public beach (see below), it boasts sands whiter than white but has neither the facilities nor the ease of parking.

SERVICE CLUB PARK

941-316-1172.

S. Harbor Dr., Venice

Facilities: Picnic areas and shelters, restrooms, showers, tot play area, volleyball.

An extensive system of boardwalks crosses scrub pinelands (watch for rare scrub jays and gopher tortoises) and provides picnic nooks off the beach. This is quieter than neighboring Brohard Park and its fishing pier but within walking distance.

✪ SIESTA KEY COUNTY BEACH

941-861-2150.

Midnight Pass Rd. at Beach Way Dr., Siesta Key.

For a change, try making sand angels— in Siesta Key's heavenly white sand. Chelle Koster Walton

Facilities: Picnic areas and shelters, restrooms, showers, lifeguard, snack bar, playground, volleyball courts, tennis courts, ball fields, soccer field, fitness trail, sun decks, beach wheelchairs.

Siesta Key's Crescent Beach sand was once judged "the finest, whitest beach in the world" by the Woods Hole Oceanographic Institute. (Anna Maria Island's beach placed third.) In 2003 the Travel Channel named it the "Best Sand Beach in America." The blinding white-ness comes from its quartz (99 percent) origins; the fineness, from Mother Nature's effi-cient pulverizer, the sea. Unfortunately, these facts have not been kept secret. The park averages about 20,000 visitors a day. Arrive early to find a parking space. Condos and motels line the wide beach. Swimming is wonderful, with gradually sloping sands and usu-ally clear waters. Public accesses along Beach Road to the north provide more seclusion, but parking is on the street and limited.

SOUTH BROHARD PARK
941-316-1172.
S. Harbor Dr., Venice.

South of Brohard Park, parking and boardwalks over mangrove wetlands provide access to the beach away from noise, fishing hooks, and crowds. The undeveloped natural beach appeals to escapists, who are nonetheless within walking distance of facilities at Brohard.

SOUTH JETTY
941-316-1172.
End of Tarpon Center Dr., Venice.
Facilities: restrooms, picnic tables, food concession.

Also known as Humphris Park, the jetty at Casey's Pass—a favorite of fishing types—is shored with huge boulders. Past them stretches a span of condo-lined beach that's popular with surfers and sailboarders. Here, people while away time eating lunch and watching boat traffic through the pass. Across the pass lies Nokomis Beach's North Jetty.

SOUTH LIDO BEACH
941-316-1172.
2201 Benjamin Franklin Dr., Lido Key.
Facilities: Picnic areas, restrooms, showers, playground, volleyball, ball fields, horseshoes, soccer field, fitness trail, nature trail, canoe trail, observation tower, sun decks.

A wide sugar beach wraps around the tip of the island from the gulf to the bay, facing Siesta Key to the south. Picnic areas are overhung with Australian pines and carpeted by their needles. Within its 100 acres several brands of Florida ecology thrive on different waterfronts. Squirrels are the most evident wildlife throughout the park. Hiking trails lead you along the mangrove worlds of Little Grassy and Big Grassy lagoons. Brushy Bayou is a good place to canoe.

TURTLE BEACH
South end of Blind Pass Rd., Siesta Key.
Facilities: Picnic areas, restrooms, showers, playground, volleyball, boat ramp, horse-shoes; restaurants and bars across the street.

The sands become coarser and more shell studded at Siesta's lower extremes as the high-rise buildings become scarcer. Along here and Midnight Pass Road the island's upper echelon resides behind iron gates. Less crowded than the other Siesta beaches, it's sports- and family-oriented but without lifeguards. If you walk southward, you'll reach ✪ Palmer Point Beach (otherwise only reachable by boat), where Midnight Pass between Siesta and Casey keys has filled in, and sharks' teeth are easy to find.

✪ VENICE BEACH
941-316-1172.
100 The Esplanade, Venice.
Facilities: Picnic area, restrooms, showers, food concession, lifeguards, volleyball, beach wheelchairs.

This beach feels cramped and more urban to me compared to the spaciousness of Venice's south-end beaches. Buildings border the sands, which spread wide here. Wooden benches provide places to gaze at the normally calm sea. It's especially popular with divers because a reef fronts the sands a quarter mile out.

Bicycling
Sarasota's best bikeways lie on barrier islands, in parks, and in rural areas to the east. Most biking elsewhere is on the sides of roads or sidewalks.

By state law, bicyclists must conduct themselves as pedestrians when using sidewalks. Where they share the road with other vehicles, they must follow all the rules of the road. Children under 16 must wear a helmet.

Best Biking
The ✪ **Historical Manatee Riverwalk** takes in downtown Bradenton for strollers and cyclists. It crosses the Green Bridge (Business 41) from Palmetto and zigzags through downtown. Brochure maps are available through the local Chamber of Commerce.

✪ **Longboat Key**'s 12 miles of bike path and lane parallel Gulf of Mexico Drive's vista of good taste and wealth on both sides of the road. Bike paths travel through parts of **Lido Key** and **Siesta Key**. The new **Venetian Waterway Park** in Venice runs along both sides of the Intracoastal Waterway and will stretch for nearly 10 miles when completed. Oscar Scherer State Park provides a more natural backdrop for biking. In Sarasota, county buses are equipped with bike racks for pedal-and-ride passengers.

Rental Shops

Resorts and parks often rent bikes or provide free use of them.

Beach Bikes & Trikes (941-412-3821; 127 Tampa Ave. E. #10, Venice 34285) Rentals, repairs, and sales.

Bicycle Center (941-377-4505; 4084 Bee Ridge Rd., Sarasota 34233) Offers pickup and delivery on mountain bike and beach cruiser rentals.

Island Scooter Rentals (941-726-3163; www.islandscooter.com; Silver Surf Resort, 1301 Gulf Dr. N., Bradenton Beach 34217) Rents bikes by the hour, day, and week to the public. Customer pickup and drop-off available.

Siesta Sports Rentals (941-346-1797; www.siestasportsrentals.com; 6551 Midnight Pass Rd., Southbridge Mall, Siesta Key 34242) Has beach cruisers, speed bikes, kid bikes, tandems, surreys, jogger strollers, and in-line skates.

Boats & Boating
Canoeing and Kayaking

In addition to the outlets listed below, many resorts and parks rent canoes.

Almost Heaven Kayak Adventures (941-504-6296; www.kayakfl.com; 5450 Riverfront Dr. Apt. C, Bradenton 34208) Tours in and around the islands, bays, and rivers of Sarasota and Bradenton, lessons included. Daily and weekly rentals with drop-off and pickup service.

Native Rental (941-778-7757; 5336 Gulf Dr., Holmes Beach 34217) Quality rentals and guided and self-guided tours through bay waters and bird islands.

Oscar Scherer State Park (941-483-5956; www.floridastateparks.org/oscarscherer; 1843 S. Tamiami Trail, Osprey 34229) Canoe rentals and tidal creek canoeing along scrubby and pine flatwoods. River otters and alligators inhabit the waters; scrub jays, bobcats, and bald eagles, the land.

Oscar Scherer State Park's tidal creeks sweep canoeists along wildlife-rich habitat. Karen T. Bartlett

Pirate Pete's Watersports (941-366-7245; 5 Bayfront Dr. Sarasota 34236; at Bayfront Park) Rent kayaks, sailboats, and Waverunners by the half hour, hour, day, or week.

Siesta Sports Rentals (941-346-1797; www.siestasportsrentals.com; 6551 Midnight Pass Rd., Southbridge Mall, Siesta Key 34242) Rent single and double kayaks, plus snorkels, boogie and skim boards, and other beach equipment.

Silent Sports (941-966-5477; www.adventuresinflorida.net/silentsportsoutfitters.htm; 2301 Tamiami Trail, Nokomis 34275) Rents kayaks and canoes and leads three-hour tours.

Snook Haven (941-485-7221; www.venice-fla.com/snookhaven; 5000 E. Venice Ave., Venice 34292) Canoe rentals and tours on the ✪ Myakka River.

Walk on the Wild Side (941-351-6500; www.walkwild.com; 3434 N. Tamiami Trail, Suite 817, PO Box 817, Sarasota 34234) Guided nature hikes, kayaking, and canoeing.

Personal Watercraft Rental/Tours

Florida law now requires operators between ages 18 and 21 to have a boater safety card. Many rental agents can qualify you for the card.

Cortez Watercraft Rentals (941-792-5263; 4328 127th St. W., Cortez 34215; at the Cortez bridge) Waverunner and pontoon boat rentals.

Don & Mike's Boat Rental (941-966-4000, 800-550-2007; 482 Blackburn Point Rd., Casey Key, Osprey 34229; at the Casey Key Marina) Rents jet skis and Waverunners.

O'Leary's Sarasota Sailing School (941-953-7505; 5 Bayfront Dr., Sarasota 34236; at Bayfront Park) Rents jet skis by the half hour and hour; instruction available.

Pirate Pete's Watersports (941-366-7245; 5 Bayfront Dr. Sarasota 34236; at Bayfront Park) Rents kayaks, sailboats, and Waverunners by the half hour, hour, day, or week.

It may look relaxing, but watch out for "killer turtles" at Snook Haven, where legend and Florida rural style persist. Karen T. Bartlett

Powerboat Rentals

Bradenton Beach Marina (941-778-2288; www.bradentonbeachmarina.com; 402 Church Ave., Bradenton Beach 34217) Runabouts and pontoons.

Cannons Marina (941-383-1311; www.cannons.com; 6040 Gulf of Mexico Dr., Longboat Key 34228) Rentals by half day, day, and week; runabouts, deck boats, and open skiffs; also fishing tackle and water skis.

CB's (941-349-4400; www.cbsoutfitters.com; 1249 Stickney Point Rd., Siesta Key 34242) Runabouts, center console boats, pontoons, and deck boats; also rod and reel rentals, fishing licenses, tackle shop, and fishing guides.

Don & Mike's Boat Rental (941-966-4000, 800-550-2007; 482 Blackburn Point Rd., Casey Key, Osprey 34229; at Casey Key Marina) Powerboats, pontoons, and waterskiing equipment.

Snook Haven (941-485-7221; www.venice-fla.com/snookhaven; 5000 E. Venice Ave., Venice 34292) Rents pontoon boats and 12- to 14-foot motorboats for use on the Myakka River. Also sells bait and fishing licenses.

Ultimate Power Sports of Bradenton (941-761-7433; 9915 Manatee Ave. W., Bradenton 34209; on Anna Maria Island causeway) Jet ski and pontoon rentals.

Public Boat Ramps

City Island (Ken Thompson Pkwy.) Three ramps.

Coquina Beach Bayside Park (Gulf Blvd., Bradenton Beach) Picnic and recreational facilities; restrooms nearby.

Higel Park (Tarpon Center Dr., Venice Beach, Venice Inlet)

Kingfish Ramp (Hwy. 64 on causeway to Anna Maria Island) Picnic facilities.

Marina Boat Ramp Park (215 E. Venice Ave., Venice)

Nokomis Beach (Venice Inlet)

Palma Sola Causeway (Palma Sola Bay and Rte. 64) restrooms and picnicking.

Turtle Beach (Blind Pass Rd., Siesta Key) Two ramps.

Sailboat Charters

The Enterprise Sailing Charters (941-951-1833, 888-232-7768; www.sarasotasailing .com; 2 Marina Plaza, Sarasota 34236; in Bayfront Park) Morning, afternoon, sunset, and full-moon sails lasting two to four hours on a tall-masted Morgan 41-footer.

Key Sailing (941-346-7245; www.siestakeysailing.com; 1219 Southport Dr., Sarasota 34242; at Marina Jack) One-hour, two-hour, or full-day sail-away adventures aboard a 41-foot Morgan Classic.

Pirate Pete's Watersports (941-366-7245; 5 Bayfront Dr., Sarasota 34236; at Bayfront Park) Rents kayaks, sailboats, and Waverunners by the half hour, hour, day, or week. Sailing instruction is available.

Spice Sailing Charters (941-778-3240; http://charters2.tripod.com; 902 Bay Blvd. S., Anna Maria 34216; at the Galati Yacht Basin) Half-day and sunset sails to Egmont Key aboard a 27-foot vessel. Sailing lessons available.

Spindrift Yacht Services (941-383-7781; www.spindrift-yachts.com; 410 Gulf of Mexico Dr., Longboat Key 34228) Sailing ventures for up to 12.

Sailboat Rentals & Instruction

Many resorts have concessions that rent Hobie Cats and other small sailboats. Instruction is often available with the rental. For something more sophisticated, try:

Bradenton Beach Sailboat Rentals (941-778-4969; 1301 Gulf Dr., Bradenton Beach 34217) Free sailing lessons with G-Cat rentals.

O'Leary's Sarasota Sailing School (941-953-7505; Bayfront Park, 5 Bayfront Dr., Sarasota 34236) Rents sailing crafts 19 to 30 feet long; rates by the hour, half day, full day, and week. Instruction and captained boats available.

Sightseeing & Entertainment Cruises

Bay Lady (941-485-6366; 480 Blackburn Point Rd., Osprey 34229; at Dock Side Marine) Two-hour cruises along the Intracoastal Waterway to see bird sanctuaries, manatees, and the lovely homes of Sarasota and Venice.

LeBarge Tropical Cruises (941-366-6116; www.lebargetropicalcruises.com, 2 Marine Plaza, Sarasota 34236; at Marina Jack in Bayfront Park) Island-style crooning, an aquarium bar, and live on-board coconut palms put the tropical in this excursion. Sightseeing, dolphin, nature, and sunset-party cruises depart daily. Light snacks and drinks available.

Myakka Queen Tours (941-485-7221; www.venice-fla.com/snookhaven; Snook Haven, 5000 E. Venice Ave., Venice 34292) One-hour trips on the Myakka River Friday through Sunday.

Seafood Shack Showboat (941-794-1236; 4110 127th St. W., Cortez 34215) Sightseeing tours Wednesday, Friday, and Sunday. It departs from a long-standing restaurant, and dining packages are available. Cocktails available on board.

Fishing

Nonresidents 16 and older must obtain a license unless fishing from a vessel or pier that's covered by its own license. You can buy inexpensive, temporary nonresident licenses at county tax collectors' offices and most Kmarts, hardware stores, marinas, and bait shops.

In the Intracoastal Waterway between Sarasota and Venice, snook are so plentiful, it's been dubbed "Snook Alley." The Bradenton area is known for its mammoth grouper (formerly known as jewfish but now more politically correct). Other fine catches include mangrove snapper, sheepshead, and pompano in backwaters, and grouper, amberjack, and mackerel in deep seas. Check local regulations for season, size, and catch restrictions.

Deep-Sea Party Boats

Flying Fish Fleet (941-366-3373; www.flyingfishfleet.com; 627 Avenida del Norte, Sarasota 34242; at Marina Jack in Bayfront Park) Half-day, six-hour, and all-day deep-sea charters and party boat excursions.

Spindrift Yacht Services (941-383-7781; www.spindrift-yachts.com; 410 Gulf of Mexico Dr., Longboat Key 34228) Half-day offshore and bay-fishing excursions.

Fishing Charters/Outfitters

To find fishing guides, check with major marinas such as Marina Jack's in downtown Sarasota. Capacity is smaller and prices higher than for party-boat excursions.

Big Catch (941-366-3373; www.flyingfishfleet.com/bigcatch.html; 627 Avenida del Norte, Sarasota 34242; at Marina Jack's in Bayfront Park) Four- to eight-hour charters.

CB's (941-349-4400; www.cbsoutfitters.com; 1249 Stickney Point Rd., Siesta Key 34242) Light tackle sportfishing charters in Sarasota Bay, the gulf, "Snook Alley," and Charlotte Harbor, four to eight hours. Orvis endorsed.

Compleat Angler (941-778-9712; PO Box 314, Anna Maria Island 34216) Inshore fishing for a maximum of four; half- and full-day trips.

Cortez Fishing Center (941-795-2700; www.cortezcat.com; 12507 Cortez Rd. W., Bradenton 34210) Here's your one-stop place for fishing licenses, bait, deep-sea fishing, backwater fishing, and sightseeing charters. Deep-sea fishing trips aboard the Cortez Kat party boat last four to six hours.

Gypsy Guide Service (941-923-6095; www.floridaflyfishing.com; 2416 Parson Ln., Sarasota 34239) Light-tackle and fly fishing, bay and backwater fishing, half- or full-day trips.

Lucky Dawg Charters (941-951-0819, 941-587-9852 [cell]; www.sarasotafishing charters.com; 2576 Hillview St., Sarasota 34239) Light-tackle sportfishing the flats, back-country, and inshore for snook, trout, redfish, and tarpon. Half-day, six-hour, and full-day trips.

Stray Dog Charter Boat (941-794-5615; www.straydogcharters.com; 12507 Cortez Rd. W., Bradenton 34210) One of several guide charters docked along "Charter Row" at Cortez Fishing Center (see above), it takes fishermen out on a 34-foot custom boat with private head.

Catch a fishing charter from the Cortez docks—and don't forget to bring along a bone. Karen T. Bartlett

Fishing Piers

Anna Maria City Pier (Anna Maria Island) It juts 678 feet into Anna Maria Sound at the south end of Bayshore Park.

Bradenton Beach City Pier (Bridge St., Bradenton Beach) Reaching into intra-coastal waters, the pier was originally part of the first bridge from the island to the mainland. Restaurant and bait concession. Admission for fishing.

Green Bridge Pier (Business Hwy. 41 over the Manatee River, downtown Bradenton)

Ken Thompson Pier (941-316-1172; 1700 Ken Thompson Pkwy., City Island) Three small piers into New Pass.

✪ **Nokomis Beach North Jetty** (941-316-1172; south end Casey Key Rd., Nokomis Beach) Manmade rock projection into the gulf, with beach and picnic area.

Osprey Fishing Pier (west end of Main St., Osprey)

Rod & Reel Pier (941-778-1885; www.rodandreelpier.com; 875 North Shore Dr., Anna Maria 34216) A privately owned fishermen's complex 350 feet into Tampa Bay with café and bait shop. The world's record hammerhead shark reportedly was caught here. Admission for fishing only.

Tony Saprito Fishing Pier (941-316-1172; Hart's Landing, Ringling Causeway Park en route to St. Armands Key) Bait store across the road. For 24-hour tide and fishing information, call the hot line at 941-366-TIDE.

Turtle Beach (South end Blind Pass Rd., Siesta Key) Fishing pier, recreational facilities, and boat ramps available.

✪ **Venice Fishing Pier** (1600 S. Harbor Dr., Venice 34285; at Brohard Park) It's 740 feet long, complete with restrooms, showers, bait shop, rod and reel rentals, and restaurant. Admission.

Venice's South Jetty (941-316-1172; Tarpon Center Dr., Venice) A stretch of boulder buffer with a paved walkway at Venice's north end.

Golf

In 1902 Sarasota's founder and first mayor, a Scotsman, built a two-hole golf course in the middle of town. This is believed to have been Florida's first golf course. Through the years the sport has grown in Sarasota, and today there are more courses than you can swing a club at, the majority of which are private or semiprivate. Several large resorts have their own greens or arrange golf-around programs at local links. In winter season, rates are highest and greens most crowded. Carts are often required. Make tee times well in advance.

Golf Centers

David Leadbetter Junior Golf Academy (941-752-2661; www.leadbetter.com; IMG Academies, 5500 34th St. W., Bradenton 34210) A highly respected full-time boarding school that also offers summer and week-long lesson programs.

Evie's Eagle Golf Center (941-377-2399; 4735 Bee Ridge Rd., Sarasota 34233) Practice sand traps, chipping and putting greens, lessons with PGA pros, miniature golf.

Public Golf Courses

Bobby Jones Golf Complex (941-365-4653; 1000 Azinger Way, Sarasota 34232) Sarasota's only municipal course, it has 36 holes plus a 9-hole executive course. Restaurant and lounge.

Foxfire Golf Course (941-921-7757; www.golf-foxfire.com; 7200 Proctor Rd., Sarasota 34241) Highly rated public course with wildlife, 27 holes, par 72. Full-service restaurant, instructions.

Manatee County Golf Course (941-792-6773; www.golfable.com/golfcourses/courses/ bradenton_fl_manatee_county_golf_course; 6415 53rd Ave. W., Bradenton 34210) One of the county's most popular courses, 18 holes, par 72. Clubhouse and restaurant. Reasonable rates; twilight rate applies.

Sarasota Golf Club (941-371-2431; 7280 N. Leewynn Dr., Sarasota 34240) Public course with 18 holes, par 72. Restaurant and bar. Reasonable rates, especially in summer.

Health & Fitness Clubs

Arlington Park & Aquatic Complex (941-316-1346; 2650 Waldemere St., Sarasota 34239) City-owned, county-operated facility with swimming pool, fitness center, tennis, racquet-ball, and basketball.

Earth Spa (941-365-6581; 330 S. Pineapple Ave., Suite 202, Sarasota 34236) A combina-tion fitness gym and day spa, with fitness equipment and personal trainers. Yoga, massage, cardio training, and nutrition counseling in a fashionable setting.

Evalyn Sadlier Jones YMCA (941-922-9622; www.sarasota-ymca.org; 8301 Potter Park, Sarasota 34238) With an Olympic-sized pool and kids' water park, this Y goes beyond fit-ness to fun. For workouts, there's a weight room, locker room, 50-meter pool, diving boards, and Jacuzzi area. At the water park families will enjoy the activity pool, slides, water cannons, fountains, and other cool stuff. Childwatch program supervises the little ones while parents work out. Daily, weekly, and monthly memberships available and transferable to other Sarasota Ys.

Lifestyle Family Fitness (941-921-4400; 8383 S. Tamiami Trail, Sarasota 34238) Exercise equipment, sauna, whirlpool, lap pool, child care.

Sarasota Family YMCA (941-366-6778 www.sarasota-ymca.org; 1991 Main St., Ste. 200, Sarasota 34236) Weight machines, sauna and steam room, classes. Daily, weekly, and monthly memberships available and transferable to other Sarasota Ys.

South County Family YMCA (941-492-9622; 701 Center Rd., Venice 34285) Nautilus exercise equipment, outdoor Olympic-sized pool, and courts for handball, racquetball, and tennis.

Hiking

Myakka State Forest (941-255-7652; 4723 53rd Ave. E., Bradenton 34203) With access off Hwy. 41 south of North Port, it opens 14 miles of multi-use trails to hikers from sunrise to sunset.

✪ **Oscar Scherer State Park** (941-483-5956; www.floridastateparks.org/ oscarscherer; 1843 S. Tamiami Trail, Osprey 34229) More than 15 miles of level-ground nature trails, including a trail for disabled persons.

Sarasota Bay Walk (1550 Ken Thompson Pkwy., City Island, next to Mote Marine) Self-guided nature hike.

South Lido Park (941-316-1172; south end of Benjamin Franklin Dr., Lido Key) Nature trails into the wetlands of Brushy Bayou.

Break out of the beach mold and chill at J. P. Igloo's ice-skating rinks. <small>Karen T. Bartlett</small>

Hunting

Knight Trail Park (941-486-2350; 3445 Rustic Road, Nokomis 34275; east of Interstate 75 at exit 195, Laurel Rd.) Public facility maintained by the Sarasota Parks and Recreation Department. Trap and skeet, pistol and rifle range, archery range, picnic areas, shooting supplies.

Kid's Stuff

✪ **J. P. Igloo** (941-723-3663; www.jpigloo.com; 5309 29th St. E., Ellenton 34222; at Interstate 75 exit 224) Ice skating is getting hot in Florida. Of course, it's a totally indoor sport here. Keep your cool at this ice and in-line sports complex. Besides regulation-hockey ice and in-line skating rinks, you'll find a restaurant, snack stand, pro shop, fitness center overlooking the ice rinks, and video games. Public skating is scheduled daily; times vary. Admission is $6 for sessions lasting two hours. Skate rentals are $3 each. The rinks host ice and in-line hockey leagues, schools, and clinics for all ages.

Pirates Cove (941-755-4608; 5410 14th St. W., Bradenton 34207) Baseball/softball cages, go-carts for all ages, minigolf, bumper boats, kiddie rides, laser tag, game rooms, and snack bar entertain families at this older but well-maintained indoor-outdoor facility. Admission is free; charges per activity.

Smuggler's Cove Adventure Golf (941-756-0043; www.smugglersgolf.com; 2000 Cortez Rd. W., Bradenton 34207) "Adventure style" 18 holes of miniature golf and live gators, with a pirate's motif. Admission is per player per game.

Racquet Sports

Anna Maria Youth Center (Magnolia Ave., Anna Maria Island) Two lit courts.

Bayfront Park (941-316-1980; www.longboatkey.org/departments/rec/rec.htm; Longboat Key)

Gillespie Park (941-316-1172; 710 N. Osprey Ave., Sarasota 34236) Three courts.

Glazier Gates Park (Manatee Ave. E., Bradenton) Two unlit cement public tennis courts.

G. T. Bray Recreation Center (941-742-5923; www.co.manatee.fl.us/service/parks/parks_facilities/parks_gtbraypark.html; 5502 33rd Ave. Dr. W., Bradenton 34209) Eight each of cement, clay, and racquetball courts.

Hecksher Park (941-316-1172; 450 W. Venice Ave., Venice 34285) Six courts with lights.

Holmes Beach Courts (near City Hall, Holmes Beach) Three lit courts.

Jessie P. Miller (9th Ave. and 43rd St. W., Bradenton) Four lit cement courts and one handball court.

New World International Tennis Academy (941-756-9417; www.nwli.com, 3908 Bayside Circle, Bradenton 34210) Short- and long-term training programs.

Nick Bollettieri Tennis at IMG Academies (941-755-1000, 800-872-6425; www.imgacademies.com; 5500 34th St. W., Bradenton 34210) Training camp for adults and juniors, with state-of-the-art tennis, 72 courts (6 of them indoors), swimming pools, a sports-therapy care center, and high-tech sports center. Andre Agassi, Monica Seles, and other pros have trained here.

Siesta Key County Beach (941-861-2150; Midnight Pass Rd. at Beach Way Dr., Siesta Key) Four courts with lights.

South County Family YMCA (941-492-9622; www.veniceymca.com; 701 Center Rd., Venice 34285) Courts for handball, racquetball, and tennis, plus Nautilus exercise equipment and an outdoor Olympic-sized pool.

Shelling

Though not comparable to the coast's southern beaches for shelling, the islands of Bradenton and Sarasota do yield some unusual finds. Venice Beach, for instance, is known for its sharks' teeth, which come in all sizes and various shades from black to rare white. Manasota Beach and the south end of Siesta Key also boast toothy waters, but Venice's beaches have the best pickings.

Sharks continually shed teeth and grow new ones. Most of what you find is prehistoric. The white ones are recent sheddings. Teeth range in size from one-eighth of an inch to a rare three inches. Some resorts provide "Florida snow shovels"—screen baskets fastened to broomsticks for sifting through the sand. You can also buy them in local hardware stores. Digging for specimens is taboo.

Toothsome finds on Venice Beach, hailed as the Shark's Tooth Capital of the World. Karen T. Bartlett

Spas

A Dodge (941-387-0773; www.adodgeconceptsalon.com; 5370 Gulf of Mexico Dr., Longboat Key 34228, at The Centre Shops) An Aveda spa and salon offering half- and full-day packages, skin care, massage, and body treatments.

Body & Spirit (941-921-1388; www.bodyandspirit.net; 500 Southgate Plaza, Sarasota 34239) A luxury day spa with massage, body treatments, facials, salon services.

Earth Spa (941-365-6581; 330 S. Pineapple Ave., Suite 202, Sarasota 34236) A day spa with fitness gyms and personal trainers. Yoga, massage, cardio training, and nutrition counseling in a fashionable setting.

Hollywood Salon & Spa (941-953-3523; www.hollywoodsalonandspa.com; 1812 Hillview St., Sarasota 34239) Performing a complete menu of facials, massages, scrubs, polishes, and body masks as well as manicures, pedicures, waxing, air-brush tanning, and other salon services.

The Key Spa & Salon (941-349-9005; www.tropicalbreezeinn.com/siestakeyspa; 153 Avenida Messina, Siesta Key 34242; at Tropical Breeze Resort) Complete massage, skin care, and beauty treatments with lunch packages in a charming island setting.

The Met (941-388-1772; 35 S. Blvd. of Presidents, St. Armands Circle, Sarasota 34236) Up a sweeping staircase from a posh clothing store in an elegant setting, the Met offers full spa and beauty facilities and treatments, including hydrotherapy, wraps, massage, and spa lunch.

Plumeria Day Spa (941-782-1123; www.silverresorts.com/bridgewalk/bridgewalk_dayspa .htm; 109 First St., Bradenton Beach 34217, at the BridgeWalk resort) Package and à la carte treatments cover all the beauty and body-care bases, including massage, facials, and wraps.

The Springs International Spa (941-426-1692; www.warmmineralsprings.com; 12200 San Servando Ave., Warm Mineral Springs 34287; south of Venice near North Port) Water of a rare quality attracts health seekers to a 2.5-acre lake fed by 9 million gallons of salt water each day. If you know your spas, you will appreciate the springs' chemical analysis of 17,439 parts per million of fixed solid minerals, way above that of the world's most renowned springs. The lake, which maintains a year-round temperature of 87 degrees, has soothing and, some believe, healing powers that attract people from around the world. Folks bathe at a roped-off beach and children's area and sun on a grassy lawn. A thatched chikee pavilion provides shade and a picnic area is provided. Opened in 1940 as Warm Mineral Springs, the facilities look a bit timeworn, but services steadily improve. Archaeologists have discovered artifacts in the lake suggesting that Native Americans came here for a bit of mineral-washed R&R 10,000 years ago. Some claim this was the Fountain of Youth about which they told Ponce de León. Massages, facials, sugaring hair removal, and acupuncture are now available at the springs' facility, along with an on-site cafeteria. Spa enthusiasts can stay at a motel down the street. For the casual visitor, I suggest staying in one of the area's resorts instead. Admission is $14 per person. Seniors pay $12; students $9; children 12 and under, $5. Ten-day passes are available, and you can rent beachwear, chairs, and towels. Bottled spring water is for sale in the gift shop.

Spectator Sports
Greyhound Racing
Sarasota Kennel Club (941-355-7744; www.sarasotakennel.com; 5400 Bradenton Rd., Sarasota 34234) Greyhound racing November to mid-April. Pari-mutuel betting, matinee (except Tuesdays) and evening shows year-round. Thoroughbred horse racing is simulcast from Miami and other tracks year-round. Admission. Closed Sunday. Must be 18 or older to enter.

Polo
Sarasota Polo Club (941-907-0000; www.lakewoodranch.com/play/polo.html; 8201 Polo Club Ln., Sarasota 34240; 3-1/2 miles east of I-75 exit 213) Watch from the grandstands, or bring a tailgate picnic. Game time is 1pm every Sunday, mid-December through March. Admission.

Pro Baseball
Ed Smith Stadium (941-954-SOXX; www.sarasox.com; 2700 12th St., Sarasota 34237) Spring-training home (March and early April) of the Chicago White Sox and off-season home of the Sarasota Red Sox (941-365-4460).

McKechnie Field (941-748-4610; Ninth St. and 17th Ave. W., Bradenton 34205) Site of the Pittsburgh Pirates' exhibition games during March and into April; a small but fun park.

Pirate City (941-747-3031; 1701 27th St. E., Bradenton 34208) Spring-practice field for the Pittsburgh Pirates' major and minor leagues. Catch the major leaguers during spring season working out from 10am to 1:30pm. The minor leaguers train here March–May.

Waterskiing
Sarasota Ski-A-Rees Show (941-388-1666; www.skiarees.com; PO Box 1493, Sarasota 34230; at Ken Thompson Park, adjacent to Mote Marine Laboratory) Free amateur waterskiing and wake-boarding performances in the bay Saturdays and Sundays. Check Website for times and dates.

Water Sports
Parasailing & Waterskiing
Adventure Parasail (941-926-1300; 504 S. Tamiami Trail, Nokomis 34275; at Dona Bay Marina) Serving Casey Key, Nokomis, Manasota Key, Englewood, and Charlotte County.

Aquarius Parasail (941-346-3532; www.aquariusparasail.com; CB's, 1249 Stickney Point Rd., Siesta Key 34242) Rides up to 1,000 feet, with optional free fall.

How do you start this thing? Karen T. Bartlett

Cortez Parasail (941-795-2700; www.cortezkat.com/cortez_parasail/parasail .htm; 12507 Cortez Rd., Bradenton 34210; at the bridge) Rides up to 1,200 feet, with an option to free fall.

Don & Mike's Boat & Ski Rental (941-966-4000, 800-550-2007; 520 Blackburn Point Rd., Casey Key, Osprey 34229; at Casey Key Marina) Jet ski rides and lessons.

Siesta Parasail (941-349-1900; 1265 Old Stickney Point Rd., Siesta Key 34242; at Dockside Marine) Single, double, and triple rides.

Sailboating & Surfing

Gulf Coast waters are generally too tame to inspire awe in surfers, except in inclement weather. Sailboarders, however, find fine conditions all along the coast. Look in the "Beaches" section for surfing and windsurfing venues.

Snorkeling & Scuba

Of all the southern Gulf Coast, this region generally boasts the best visibility for underwater exploration, especially in spring. Manmade reefs make up for the lack of natural reefs on Florida's west coast. At Venice Beach, a reef lies just a quarter-mile from the beach, making shore dives possible. At Bradenton Beach, the sunken sugar barge *Regina* houses various forms of marine life.

Both snorkelers and divers look for sharks' teeth fossils.

Dive Shops & Charters

Dolphin Dive Center (941-924-2785; www.floridakayak.com; 6018 S. Tamiami Trail, Sarasota 34231) Local charters, instruction, snorkel and scuba rentals.

Scuba Quest (941-366-1530; www.scubaquestusa.com; 1129 S. Tamiami Trail, Sarasota 34236, at Bahia Vista St.) With several locations in the Sarasota-Bradenton area, this company offers classes, charters, and equipment sales.

SeaTrek Divers (941-779-1506; www.seatrekdivers.com; 105 Seventh St. N., Bradenton Beach 34217) Located across the street from the barge wreck, this firm offers two-tank, offshore dives and scuba certification courses.

Holy Sea Cows!

Today we know them as Florida manatees: 1,300-pound blimps, with skin like burlap and a face only a nature buff could love. They also go by the name sea cows, although they are more closely related to the elephant. In days of yore, many a sea-weary sailor mistook them for mermaids.

Well, Ariel they're not, but bewitching they can be. Gentle and herbivorous—consuming up to 100 pounds of aquatic plants daily—they make no enemies and have only one stumbling block to survival: man. Being mammals, manatees must surface for air, like whales and dolphins. Their girth makes them a prime target for boaters speeding through their habitat. Warning signs designate popular manatee areas. Instead of zipping through these waters and further threatening the seriously endangered manatee population, boaters can better benefit by slowing down and trying to spot the reclusive creatures as they take a breath. It requires a sharp eye, patience, and experience. Watch channels during low tides, when the manatees take to deeper water. Concentric circles, known as "manatee footprints," signal surfacing animals. They usually travel in a line and appear as drifting coconuts or fronds.

To report manatee deaths, injuries, harassment, or orphans, call 941-332-6972.

Shore Snorkeling & Diving

Bradenton Beach (Anna Maria Island) An old sugar barge sank here many years ago and houses various forms of marine life.

Point of Rocks (Siesta Key) South of Crescent Beach at the island's central zone; rocks, underwater caves, and coral formations make good submerged sightseeing.

Wilderness Camping

Oscar Scherer State Park (941-483-5956; www.floridastateparks.org.oscarscherer; 1843 S. Tamiami Trail, Osprey 34229) Nearly 1,400 acres in size, this natural oasis provides 104 full-service campsites in a wooded, creek-side setting of palmettos, pines, and venerable moss-draped oaks. The threatened Florida scrub jay seeks refuge here, along with bald eagles, bobcats, river otters, gopher tortoises, and alligators. There's swimming in a fresh-water lake plus a bird walk, nature and canoe trails, picnicking, and fishing. To reserve a campsite or cabin, call 800-326-3521, or go to www.reserveamerica.com.

Wildlife Spotting

Birds

The Sarasota coast is the least natural of the Gulf Coast's four regions. Determined bird spotters can find feathered friends at parks and refuges such as the Passage Key sanctuary, north of Anna Maria Island (bring binoculars—landing ashore is forbidden); Rookery Islands, north of Siesta Key (also approachable by boat only); Venice Area Audubon Rookery (at the end of Annex Road in South Venice, 0.5 mile south of the junction of Hwy. 41 and Route 776), and Oscar Scherer State Park in Osprey, home of the endangered Florida scrub jay. Look for wild peacocks roaming the streets of the village on Longboat Key.

Dolphins

Dolphins often follow in the wake of tour boats, but they're unpredictable. You can't plan on them; you can only be thrilled and charmed when they do appear. If you learn their feeding schedules, you have a better chance of catching their act.

Manatees

Named after the lovable creatures, Bradenton's Manatee County has erected MANATEE WATCH signs at manatee-frequented areas: on the bridges and city pier of the Manatee River, on the Palma Sola Causeway, and on Anna Maria Island at Bayfront Park, Coquina Beach and Boat Ramp, and Kingfish Boat Ramp.

Nature Preserves & Eco-Attractions
✪ MOTE MARINE LABORATORY

941-388-2451, 800-691-MOTE.
www.mote.org.
1600 Ken Thompson Pkwy., Sarasota 34236.
On City Island, northeast of Lido Key.
Open: 10am–5pm daily.
Admission: $12 for adults; $8 for children 4–12.

Mote Marine Aquarium invites you to pet a ray.   Karen T. Bartlett

Mote Marine is known around the world for its research on sharks, marine mammals, and environmental pollutants. Its two visitors centers educate the public on projects and marine life. A 135,000-gallon shark tank centerpieces the original facility and is kept stocked with sharks and fish typical of the area: grouper, snook, pompano, and snapper. Dozens of smaller aquariums and a touch tank hold more than 200 varieties of common and unusual species. Colorful signs challenge kids to ponder and learn about aquarium denizens. The original visitors center has expanded its shark focus in the new millennium with a Sea Cinema and cool interactive shark film. A 1,500-gallon Remarkable Rays touch tank sits outside in a chikee hut, and a new mollusk exhibit features a preserved 25-foot giant squid from 2,000 feet down off the coast of New Zealand. In the Marine Mammal Visitors' Center, the main attraction is a floor-to-ceiling glass tank that holds manatees Hugh and Buffett. It also features a marine mammal rehabilitation tank and a sea turtle exhibit, which host some of the world's most fascinating sea creatures.

OSCAR SCHERER STATE PARK
941-483-5956.
www.floridastateparks.org.oscarscherer.
1843 S. Tamiami Trail, Osprey 34229.
Admission: $4 per car, $1 per pedestrian or cyclist.

Home of the threatened Florida scrub jay, plus bald eagles, bobcats, river otters, gopher tortoises, and alligators. Experience wildlife in a canoe along a saltwater tidal creek or by hiking an extensive system of nature trails. Take heed: If you swim in the freshwater lake, you may become more closely acquainted with an alligator than you would care to be. The 1,384-acre park offers camping, swimming, canoeing, fishing, and picnicking.

PELICAN MAN'S BIRD SANCTUARY
941-388-4444.
www.pelicanman.org.
1708 Ken Thompson Pkwy., Sarasota 34236.
Next to Mote Marine Laboratory on City Island.
Open: 10am–5pm daily.
Admission: Suggested donation $6 adults, $4 for children ages 12 to 17, $2 for children ages 4 to 11. Boat tours: $16 for adults, $8 for children.

One man, Dale Shields, laid the foundation for this 2-acre refuge for injured pelicans and other birds—55 species in all. It's a must if you're a nature lover or visiting Mote Marine Lab. Don't expect exotic birds, just on-the-mend local varieties. The sanctuary recently began offering two-hour birding boat tours that depart from a mainland marina.

QUICK POINT NATURE PRESERVE
www.longboatkey.org/parks/quick_point.htm.
South end of Longboat Key.
Open: Daily.
Admission: Free.

The town of Longboat Key worked to restore the natural environment of this 34-acre plot, once covered over and nearly destroyed by sand dredged from New Pass. Park on the west side of the road, and follow a boardwalk under the pass bridge to get to the trails through beach, uplands, mangrove, and lagoon habitat. It's a popular spot for ospreys, egrets, ibises, and other shore birds.

SARASOTA BAY WALK
1550 Ken Thompson Pkwy., Sarasota 34236
On City Island, next to Mote Marine Laboratory.
Admission: Free.

Take a quiet, self-guided walk along the bay, estuaries, lagoons, and uplands to learn more about coastland ecology. Boardwalk and shell paths lead you past mangroves, old fishing boats bobbing on the bay, egrets, and illustrated signs detailing nature's wonders.

Wildlife Tours & Charters
Sarasota Bay Explorers (941-388-4200; www.sarasotabayexplorers.com; Mote Marine Laboratory, 1600 Ken Thompson Pkwy., Sarasota 34236; on City Island) A marine pontoon tour takes you into intracoastal waters between City Island and Siesta Key. Features include trawl net toss, binocular study of rookery islands, and marine biologist narration. Kids love the hands-on quality of this educational tour. It also offers custom and kayak tours. Packages with Mote Marine are available.

SHOPPING

In-season you may well be tempted, like everyone else, to save shopping and sightseeing for rainy, cold, off-beach days. Don't. You'll lose your diligently attained good beach attitude by the time you've found your first parking spot. Go in the morning for best results and the most relaxing experience.

Sarasota's **St. Armands Circle** is known far and wide for its arena of posh shops, galleries, and restaurants. **Downtown Sarasota** is steadily improving its shopping outlook, especially for art and antiques lovers. Nearby **Southside Village,** at Hillview Street and Osprey Avenue, has grown into an intriguing little shopping and dining destination. On the islands you'll find fun shops and beach boutiques that blend with the sand and sun.

Shopping Centers & Malls

De Soto Square Mall (941-747-5869; 303 Hwy. 301, Bradenton 34205) Some 700,000 feet of shop-till-you-drop opportunities in more than 100 stores, including Sears, Burdines, and Dillards, a high-end Florida department-store chain.

✪ **Downtown Sarasota** One of the Gulf Coast's most successful downtown restoration projects has returned Sarasota's vitality to Main Street and environs. The area—also known as the Sarasota Theater and Arts District—encompasses approximately 1.5 square miles, centered at Five Points, where Main Street intersects with four other streets. Renovated old buildings house galleries (particularly along Palm Avenue, where it's less rushed than Main Street), bookstores, clothing boutiques, antiques shops, restaurants, sidewalk cafés, cabarets, clubs, and gift shops. Palm Avenue Association hosts gallery walks the first Friday of each month, with music, refreshments, and gallery openings, beginning at 6pm. At Historic Burns Square (Pineapple and Orange Avenues) lies a unique shopping enclave of historic bungalows and unusual finds that hosts a lively First Friday Strolls each month.

Longboat Key You'll find a smattering of interesting shops and galleries at The Centre Shops (5370 Gulf of Mexico Dr.) and Avenue of Flowers (off Gulf of Mexico Dr.).

✪ **St. Armands Circle** (941-388-1554; www.starmandscircleassoc.com; 300 Madison Dr., Sarasota 34236; on St. Armands Key) On one of the Sarasota barrier islands that he owned, John Ringling envisioned a world-class shopping center, complete with park-lined walkways and baroque statuary. He would be gratified by St. Armands Circle. On a scale with Beverly Hills's Rodeo Drive and Palm Beach's Worth Avenue, it was named for developer Charles St. Amand (whose name was misspelled "Armand" in later land deeds—and it is this spelling that persists). Its spin-off formation is suited geographically to the pancake shape of the island. Four sections arc off the circular center drive. "The Circle," as it is known in local shorthand, encompasses shops of the most upscale nature, galleries, restaurants, clubs, and specialty boutiques. International style is well represented. The Circle is a hub of activity for the entire region. Horse-drawn carriages offer sunset rides. The Circus Ring of Fame honors distinguished Big Top entertainers. People dress in finery just to shop here, but don't feel obligated. Once monthly, it hosts Fourth Friday with Style jazz sessions from 6 to 9 pm. Parking is free on the street and in a garage nearby.

Siesta Key (www.siestakeychamber.com/shopping.htm) In the village along Ocean Blvd., Siesta Key's shopping style is refreshingly barefoot with a touch of beach bawdiness, mixed in with a generous dose of casual eateries. You'll find a more refined collection of shops around Stickney Point Road.

Folks shop till they dine in the blossomy setting of St. Armands Circle. Karen T. Bartlett

Venice Main Street (941-484-6722; PO Box 602, Venice 34248; at Venice Ave. W. and Tamiami Trail) Down a Mediterranean-type, date-palm-lined boulevard, you'll find shops and restaurants to fit every budget. Wander a block to the south for antiques and second-hand collectibles.

Westfield Shoppingtown (941-922-9609; www.westfield.com; 8201 S. Tamiami Trail, Sarasota 34238; at Beneva Rd.) Your choice of four major department stores, movie theaters, and more than 140 specialty shops and eateries.

Westfield Shoppingtown Southgate (941-955-0900; www.westfield.com; 3501 S. Tamiami Trail, Sarasota 34239; at Bee Ridge Rd.) A major shopping mall, this one houses Burdines, Dillards, and Saks Fifth Avenue.

Antiques & Collectibles

Antiques shops are plentiful and easy to find in and around Sarasota. You'll find a row of them on Pineapple Street and another on Fruitville Avenue, both downtown. In Venice, look along Miami Avenue, parallel to the main shopping drag, Venice Avenue. Pick up a copy of the *Sarasota Antique Guide & Locator Map* from the Sarasota Visitors Center.

Apple & Carpenter Gallery (941-951-2314; 64 S. Palm Ave., Sarasota 34236; downtown) One of the most deluxe antiquarians, this shop specializes in American and European paintings of the 19th and early 20th centuries as well as bronze and marble sculptures, fine furniture, French cameo glass, silver, bronze, porcelain, and other objets d'art. European drawing room atmosphere.

Coral Cove Antique Gallery (941-927-2205; 7272 S. Tamiami Trail, Sarasota 34231) A large garage-sale-like collection of vendor wares from Chinese collectibles to furniture and clothing.

Islander Market Antiques and Art (941-779-2501; 9807 Gulf Dr., Anna Maria Island 34216) Formerly an island grocery, this shop now sells predominantly country-style antiques, including lots of furniture.

Jack Vinales Antiques (941-957-0002; 539 Pineapple Ave. S., Sarasota 34236) More contemporary than most of Sarasota's antique stock, this shop concentrates on nostalgia of the 40s and 50s, Art Deco, pottery, lamps, and Bakelite and Fiesta ware.

Lucia and Paula Treasures (941-412-1939; 225 W. Miami Ave. #2A, Venice 34285) Fine estate wares; a little bit of everything, from furniture to crystal.

The Merchant of Venice (941-488-3830; 223 W. Miami Ave., Venice 34285) Fossil sharks' teeth, oil paintings, rugs, pottery, vintage clothing, nautical and military memorabilia.

Old Feed Store Antique Mall (941-729-1379; 4407 Hwy. 301, Ellenton 34222) Around Gamble Plantation Historic Site you'll find a few interesting antiques markets, including this one.

Old Main Street Antiques (941-745-1223; 406 Old Main St., Bradenton 34205) Treasures here range from garage-sale-quality kitchenware to panes of leaded glass windows, china, and jewelry. The owners also do custom stained glass, stripping, and refinishing.

Sarasota Art & Antique Center (640 S. Washington Ave., Sarasota 34236) This huge pink building holds a number of fine antiques galleries including **Crissy Galleries** (941-957-

1110; www.crissy.com), selling quality furniture, jewelry, and art; **Sarasota Rare Coin Gallery** (941-366-2191, 800-447-8778; www.sarasotacoin.com); **Yellow Bird Antiques** (941-388-1823), specializing in imported decorative items; **Sarasota Jewelry, Watch & Clock** (941-951-1962); and **Ashland Coin** (941-957-3760), dealing in timepieces, coins, and jewelry.

Sea Hagg (941-795-5756; www.seahagg.com; 12304 Cortez Rd. W., Cortez 34215) It's tough to pigeonhole this into one shopping category, but it fits here with its stock of antique periscopes, sextant, rods and reels, and other nautical and fishing memorabilia. Browse its two shops and yards for everything from old crab traps to sea glass by the scoop and metal bird and fish sculptures. This is a place to buy a piece of Cortez maritime heritage.

Shadow Box (941-957-3896; 1520 Fruitville Rd., Sarasota 34236) Along Fruitville Road's western end, which runs on the edge of downtown, you can find antiques shops mixed among thrift and consignment shops and generally more affordable than mainstream downtown's. This one carries a nice collection of 18th-century, Victorian, Art Deco, and modern home furnishings and decoratives.

Books

Charlie's Café, Books, and Hops (941-779-2665; 5904 Marina Dr., Holmes Beach 34217) Sip a beer or espresso, or munch on gourmet salads, panini sandwiches, pizza, and seafood while you dig in to your newly purchased used book.

Circle Books (941-388-2850; www.circle books.net; 478 John Ringling Blvd., Sarasota 34236; at St. Armands Circle) Small but packed with books for all ages (including an extensive young-teens section); features author signings.

✪ **Main Bookshop** (941-366-7653; www.mainbookshop.com; 1962 Main St., Sarasota 34236; downtown) A landmark store, with four floors full of new discounted (30 to 90 percent off) and used books on all subjects.

Sarasota's downtown shopping scene—bookstores, smart cafés, and art galleries. Karen T. Bartlett

✪ **Sarasota News & Books** (941-365-6332; www.sarasotanewsandbooks.com; 1341 Main St., Sarasota 34236; downtown) Specializes in art, architecture, and literature. Beyond books and lots of periodicals, Sarasota News sells cards, gifts, coffee, and lunch.

Venice Newsstand (941-488-6969; 329 W. Venice Ave., Venice 34285) Old-fashioned news-stand, selling cigars, greeting cards, magazines, out-of-town newspapers, and paperbacks.

Clothing

Bridgewear (941-778-4299; 121 Bridge St., Bradenton Beach 34217) Breezy, fun, and flam-boyant women's casual clothes among shops and cafés at the approach to the historic pier.

Cravats' (941-366-7780; 222 Sarasota Quay, Sarasota 34236) Custom hand-tailored shirts and fine clothing for men.

Dream Weaver (941-388-1974; www.dreamweavercollection.com; 364 St. Armands Circle, Sarasota 34236) Fine woven wear that crosses the line to fabric art; in silk, suede, and other extravagant materials.

Ivory Coast (941-388-1999; 15 N. Blvd. of Presidents, Sarasota 34236; at St. Armands Circle) Outstanding imported women's fashions, jewelry, and decorative items inspired by Africa.

LaCheape Boutique (941-488-6388; 530 Highway 41 Bypass S., Venice 34292) Liquidated stock from expensive boutiques sold at greatly reduced cost.

Little Bo-Tique (941-388-1737; 19 Fillmore Dr., Sarasota 34236; at St. Armands Circle) Adorable and stylish children's wear for boys and girls.

The Met (941-388-1772; 35 S. Blvd. of Presidents, Sarasota 34236; at St. Armands Circle) Expensive dressy and casual fashions for men and women (Polo, Ralph Lauren, etc.) in a divine setting.

Nana's (941-488-4108; 223 W. Venice Ave., Venice 34285) Quality kids' clothes and toys.

Peggy's (941-365-4485; 218 Sarasota Quay, Sarasota 34236) Ladies' formal and evening wear and accessories.

SunBug (941-485-7946; www.venicemainstreet.com/sunbug; 141 W. Venice Ave., Venice 34285) The most fun in women's fashions, from dressy to casual. Great cotton styles, swimsuits, and unusual, comfortable dresses.

Tropics (941-346-2950; 5251 Ocean Blvd., Siesta Key Village 34242) Cool, tropical fashions and T-shirts for women and kids, including Jams World and Fresh Produce labels.

Venice Tropical Shop (941-483-4533; 207 W. Venice Ave., Venice 34285) Stand-out women's fashions with tropical and natural accents, hand-crafted jewelry, evening wear.

Consignment

In Sarasota it's not the embarrassment that it is in some places to buy secondhand. In fact, recycled apparel is the "in" thing among the young and artistic. Because of the wealth and transient nature of its residents, the area offers the possibility of great discoveries in its consignment shops. Fruitville Road is a good place to shop for recycled goods. Some of the stores benefit local charities.

Designer Consigner (941-953-5995; 3639 Bahia Vista St., Sarasota 34232) Wedding gowns, evening wear, and sports and career fashions.

Green Butterfly (941-485-6223; 211 W. Miami Ave., Venice 34285) Antique, old, and new home accessories and furniture to benefit a local charity.

Kids Care-O-Sell Consignments (941-761-8405; 6600 Manatee Ave. W., Bradenton 34209) Maternity wear, kids' clothes, and furniture.

Kim & Co. (941-378-9002; 4214 Bee Ridge Rd., Sarasota 34233) Women's business, sports, and cocktail attire.

3rd St. Rags to Riches (941-957-0113; 1506 Fruitville Rd., Sarasota 34236) A nonprofit consignment shop with a wealth of furnishings, clothing, and kitchen goods.

Woman's Exchange (941-955-7873; 539 S. Orange Ave., Sarasota 34236; downtown) Furniture, family clothing, antiques, housewares, and china. Profits support local arts.

Factory Outlet Centers

Prime Outlets (941-729-8615, 888-260-7608; www.primeoutlets.com; 5461 Factory Shops Blvd., Ellenton 34222; at Interstate 75 exit 224) As far as the factory outlet malls covered in this book go, this is the most comprehensive, with more than 135 shops, a nice food court, and a children's playground in a Caribbean setting. Besides the typical kitchen and clothing stores, it boasts some top designer names, such as Off 5th (outlet for Saks Fifth Avenue), Versace Company, Liz Claiborne, Waterford/Wedgewood, and others.

Flea Markets & Bazaars

Bradenton Farmers' Market (941-747-2498; between Sixth and Eighth Avenues downtown Bradenton) Runs 7:30 to 12:30 every Saturday. Fresh local produce, baked goods, and crafts.

The Dome (941-493-6773; 5115 Rte. 775, Venice) A small indoor market open Saturday and Sunday 9am–4pm.

Downtown Farmers' Market (941-951-2656; Lemon Ave. and Main St., downtown Sarasota) Fresh fruits, vegetables, baked goods, plants, arts and crafts. Open 7am–noon Saturday, year-round.

Red Barn Flea Market (941-747-3794, 800-274-FLEA; www.redbarnfleamarket.com; 1707 First St. E., Bradenton 34208) More than 600 stores and booths selling baseball cards to car parts. Fully open 8 to 4 Wednesday, Saturday, and Sunday (also Friday November through April); mall area stores open Tuesday through Sunday 9-4.

Galleries

Galleria Silecchia (941-365-7414; 888-366-7414; www.galleriasilecchia.com; 12 & 20 S. Palm Ave., Sarasota 34236) These two storefronts contain some of the most interesting art we've seen in all of Sarasota. The larger, corner gallery contains large bronze sculptures and other pieces. The smaller one showcases the exquisite glass lamp works of Ulla Darni, whimsical cut-metal wall sculptures, colorful painted sculptures, and a select collection of decorative art.

Palm Avenue Gallery (941-953-5757; www.palmavenuegallery.com; 45 S. Palm Ave., Sarasota 34236) Small but eclectic and intriguing: modern icy glass sculptures, Italian masks, tropical scenes, screen body sculptures.

Seaweed Gallery (941-782-1128; www.seaweedgallery.com; 112 Bridge St., Bradenton Beach 34217) Fun and colorful painted furniture, tropical oil paintings, fused-glass jewelry, palm-pattern pottery, and other works with a sense of place.

Towles Court Artist Colony (941-330-9817; www.towlescourt.com; 1938 Adams Ln., Sarasota 34236; off Hwy. 301) A charming district of restored and brightly painted bungalows turned art colony features the galleries and working art studios of artists in all media. The Towles Court Art Center contains several galleries and a café. It is the colony's headquarters, with other studio-galleries scattered around it. We enjoy the work of Marge Bennett (941-955-0050), whose vibrant watercolors are displayed at the Art Center. Third Friday art walks, 6 to 10pm, with live music.

Tropical Scenes/Island Interiors (941-485-9869; 317 W. Venice Ave., Venice 34285) Home design elements from paper napkins and Alligator Crossing signs to affordable metal sculptures and other unusual wall hangings, framed originals, decorative items with an emphasis on the sea and tropics.

Wyland Galleries (941-388-5331, 888-588-5331; 465 John Ringling Blvd., Sarasota 34236; at St. Armands Circle) The work of artist Wyland (of worldwide Whaling Walls fame) as well as other renowned marine and wildlife artists.

Downtown Sarasota's Towles Court, a working artists' colony, colorfully took over an old bungalow neighborhood. Karen T. Bartlett

Ziegenfuss Gallery of Fine Art (941-365-3266; 76 S. Palm Ave., Sarasota 34236; downtown) One of my favorites along Palm Avenue, this gallery features pop art, tasteful city paintings, sculptures by Jack Dowd, and the work of other whimsical local artists.

Gifts

Some of the best gifts and souvenirs are found in attraction gift shops, especially those at the Ringling museums, Sarasota Jungle Gardens, G. WIZ, and South Florida Museum.

The Artful Dodger (941-925-8266; 1522 Stickney Point Rd., Sarasota 34231; at Boatyard Shopping Village, near Siesta Key) Artist-quality table and decorative ware of pottery and glass as well as jewelry and other fun and colorful gifts. Worth a stop when traveling on or off island.

Artisans' World Marketplace (941-365-5994; 128 S. Pineapple Ave., PO Box 5994, Sarasota 34277) This not-for-profit has made a commitment to selling the work of below-poverty-level artisans—from ginger soap made in Chicago to telephone-wire baskets from Africa to metal-drum sculptures from Haiti and wood carvings from Kenya. The resourcefulness reflected in the delightful scope of work is remarkable.

BB's on Old Main Street (941-747-9877; 417 12th St. W., Bradenton 34205) Hidden inside a building downtown, it keeps a treasure trove of novelties for the home and garden, including candles, aprons, silk plants, lace umbrellas, and baskets.

Elysian Fields (941-361-3006; www.elysianfieldsonline.com; 1273 Tamiami Trail S., Sarasota 34239; at Midtown Plaza) This shop's subtitle tells it succinctly enough: "books and gifts for conscious living." It's filled with wonderful New Age accoutrements, aromatherapy supplies, feng shui books and items, sushi and sake sets, cards, candles, and books.

Exit Art Gallery (941-383-4099 or 800-833-0894; www.exit-art.com; 5380 Gulf of

Mexico Dr., Longboat Key 34228; at the Centre Shops) Artistically designed home and office tools, pop art, colorful tableware, jewelry, and clothes.

Giving Tree Wood Gallery (941-388-1353; www.thegivingtreewoodgallery.com; 5 N. Boulevard of Presidents, Sarasota 34236; at St. Armands Circle) Beautiful inset and sculpted wood art, unique jewelry, glassware, and other fine and unusual gifts.

Hurricane Rita (941-346-7712; www.hurricaneritas.com; 5212 Ocean Blvd., Siesta Key Village, Siesta Key 34242. Also 941-388-2766; 319 John Ringling Blvd., Sarasota 34236; at St. Armands Circle) Unique and colorful home decorations with a tropical theme.

Toy Lab (941-363-0064; 1529 Main St., Sarasota 34236) Don't look for Playstation games here. This old-fashioned toy shop has educational toys and games, puppets, stuffed animals, and Brio and Playmobile sets.

Jewelry

Bari Jewelers (941-484-9197; 315 W. Venice Ave., Venice 34285) Buy your sharks' teeth necklaces and large fossil specimens here; also sea-motif charms, gold, diamonds, and other fine pieces.

Coffrin Jewelers (941-366-6871; 1829 S. Osprey Ave., Sarasota 34239; at Southside Village) Fine creations in gold, silver, and platinum, specializing in original designs. Also vendor of hand-painted French Quimper tableware.

Fawn Custom Jewelers (941-349-2748; 5221 Ocean Blvd., Siesta Key 34242) Specializing in Florida seashore-motif pieces and creative jewel settings, mostly for women.

Jewelry by Cole (941-388-3323, 800-572-9375; 7 N. Blvd. of Presidents, Sarasota 34236; at St. Armands Circle) Lovely set gems, a wide variety of the usual to the unusual in sea-themed pieces, custom work.

June Simmons Designs (941-388-4535; www.junesimmons.com; 68 S. Palm Ave., Sarasota 34236) Artistic exclusive edition jewelry and custom work.

Sarasota Silver Co. (941-388-5564; 9 N. Blvd. of Presidents, Sarasota 34236; at St. Armands Circle) The most unusual jewelry in the Circle, if you like silver. These are stunning, stand-out creations. Also, cubic zirconia and other inexpensive pieces.

✪ **Tilden Ross Jewelers** (9941-388-3338; 410 St. Armands Circle, Sarasota 34236) All that glitters! Damiani, Patek Philippe, and other top designers provide a showroom of exquisite sparkle, from pearls to gems to pale-blue beaded collars and unusual gold rings.

Kitchenware & Home Decor

Artisans (941-388-0082; 301 John Ringling Blvd., Sarasota 34236; at St. Armands Circle) Fun glassworks, jewelry, painted furniture, neon art, and more.

Basketville (941-493-0007; 4411 S. Tamiami Trail, Venice 34293) Region's widest selection of basketry, pottery, wicker furniture, silk flowers, and other household items.

Garden Argosy (941-388-6402; www.gardenargosy.com; 361 St. Armands Circle, Sarasota 34236) Gifts for the home and garden: extensive selection of candles, frames, painted wood bowls, garden statues, fountains.

Restoration Hardware (941-952-9666; Westfield Shoppingtown Southgate, 3501 S. Tamiami Trail, Sarasota 34239) Those familiar with the chain need no introduction to its smooth and classy line of furnishings, home accessories, and yes, hardware. That is, the fancy kind, such as drawer pulls and light fixtures.

Rolling Pin Kitchen Emporium (941-925-2434; www.myrollingpin.com; 8201 S. Tamiami Trail, Sarasota 34238; Westfield Shoppingtown) German cutlery and fine kitchenware.

The Tabletop (941-485-0319; www.thetabletop.com; 205 W. Venice Ave., Venice 34285) Hand-painted and other fun barware, kitchen and table accessories, coffee and espresso paraphernalia, gourmet items.

Tervis Tumbler Outlet (800-237-6688; www.tervis.com; 928 S. Tamiami Trail, Osprey 34229; 941-778-3121; 5358 Gulf Dr., Holmes Beach 34217) Floridians know the only way to keep your drinks cool is with Tervis Tumblers, which are made at the Osprey outlet. The Holmes Beach store also sells them at factory prices, about 17 percent less. The insulated acrylic tumblers are guaranteed for life, and you can return defective or broken merchandise at these outlets.

Whit's End (941-953-9448; 51 S. Palm Ave., Sarasota 34236) European antique pine and other furnishings, a wide variety of deluxe candles, framed art, mirrors, and other unusual finds.

Shell Shops

Beach Bazaar (941-346-2995; 5211 Ocean Blvd., Siesta Key 34242) A one-stop mart for seashells, toys, beach clothes, boogie and skim boards, sunglasses, and other vacation must-haves.

Sea Pleasures and Treasures (941-488-3510; 255 Venice Ave. W., Venice 34285) Quantity, not necessarily quality: sea-theme gifts, shells, and shell craft supplies.

Sporting Goods

Note: This listing includes general sports outlets only. For supplies and equipment for specific sports, please refer to "Recreation" in this chapter.

CB's Saltwater Outfitters (941-349-4400; www.cbsoutfitters.com; 1249 Stickney Point Rd., Siesta Key 34242) Fishing gear and sportswear.

Cook's Sportland (941-493-0025; 4419 Tamiami Trail, Venice 34293; next to Basketville) Equipment for archery, golf, camping, and fishing; also fishing licenses, tackle repair, sportswear, shoes, and western clothing.

CALENDAR OF EVENTS

For a complete listing of local cultural events, visit www.sarasota-arts.org, or call 941-365-5118.

January

Arts Day Festival (941-365-5118; downtown Sarasota) A gala confluence of Sarasota's visual and performing arts that spills from the galleries and theaters onto outdoor stages and sidewalks.

Sarasota Film Festival (941-364-9514; www.sarasotafilmfestival.com; Courtyard of the Stars next to Regal Cinemas on Main St., downtown Sarasota) Ten days of films, celebrities, outdoor screenings, and live entertainment.

February

Bradenton Beach Festival (941-778-3066; Historic Bridge Street) Boat rides, parasailing, live entertainment, and a street dance.

Cortez Fishing Festival (941-794-0280; www.cortezfishingfestival.org; village of Cortez) Food vendors, music, net-mending demonstrations, arts and crafts, boat tours, and educational exhibits describing the community of Cortez's hundred-year-old fishing industry. One weekend midmonth.

Greek Glendi Festival (941-355-2616, 877-355-2272; www.stbarbara-church.org/glendi .html; St. Barbara's Greek Orthodox Church, 7671 Lockwood Ridge Rd., Sarasota 34243) Greek food, dancing, arts, and crafts on one weekend near Valentine's Day.

Scottish Highland Games & Heritage Festival (941-953-6707; www.sarasotagames.com; held at the Sarasota Fairgrounds, Fruitville Rd.) Traditional dancing as well as competitions and entertainment.

March

Anna Maria Island Springfest (941-778-2099; Holmes Beach City Hall Park) A celebration of island arts: artist and crafts booths, local entertainment, and food concessions. Two days early in the month.

Gulf Coast Celtic Fling & Highland Games (941-645-7311; www.celticfling.com; Manatee Convention & Civic Center, Bradenton) The Scots and the Irish meet on friendly turf for dancing, games, music, and food.

Manatee Arts Fest (941-721-0405; Old Main St., downtown Bradenton) One weekend late in the month devoted to all the arts, with fine arts and crafts, music, dance, food, poetry reading, and children's art activities.

Manatee Heritage Month (941-741-4070) The entire month is devoted to the celebration of local history and traditions throughout Bradenton and Manatee County. Special tours are arranged by local attractions, and demonstrators weave, quilt, and make baskets and doilies.

✪ **Medieval Fair** (941-351-8497; Ringling Museum of Arts grounds, Sarasota) The event of the year, this fair is the culmination of Sarasota's love for art, theater, food, and circus, all within the atmosphere of a 12th-century flashback. Four days at the turn of March.

Run For the Turtles (941-388-4441; http://www.mote.org; Siesta Beach Pavilion, Siesta Key) 5K race to benefit Mote Marine Laboratory.

Sailor Circus (941-361-6350; www.sailorcircus.org; 2075 Bahia Vista St., Sarasota 34239) Proof that the circus is still in the blood of many Sarasota families. Students from grades 3 to 12 perform professional circus feats during a two-week season. Also Christmastime performances.

Sarasota Comedy Festival (941-365-1277; www.comedy.org; various locations in Sarasota) A result of Sarasota's large population of cartoonists, the festival takes place for a week midmonth and includes a parade, comedy film festival, comedy dinner shows with name stand-up comedians, a "cartoon walk," a main stage show, golf events, and workshops.

Sarasota County Fair (941-365-0818; www.sarasotafair.com; Sarasota Fairgrounds, Fruitville Rd.) Traditional county fair, with midway and carnival areas, exhibits, and entertainment.

Sarasota Jazz Festival (941-366-1552; throughout Sarasota) Big-name jazz players lead a slate of big bands and jazz combos at indoor and outdoor venues. One weekend.

April

Florida Heritage Festival (941-747-1998; Bradenton) Commemorates Hernando de Soto's discovery of the region. A reenactment of the 1539 landing highlights the schedule of month-long events that include a seafood festival, children's parade, Easter egg hunt, and plastic bottle boat regatta.

Florida Playwrights Festival (941-366-9000; www.fst.org; Florida Studio Theatre, 1241 N. Palm Ave., Sarasota 34236; downtown) Premieres the works of emerging playwrights from Florida and around the nation, launching almost 70 main stage productions. Mid-April through May.

Florida Winefest and Auction (941-952-1109; www.floridawinefest.com; The Resort at Longboat Key Club, 301 Gulf of Mexico Dr., Longboat Key 34228) A prestigious event featuring food and wine seminars, tastes from the area's finest restaurants, top entertainment, black-tie dinner, and fine wine auction. Four days.

La Musica International Chamber Music Festival (941-364-8802; www.lamusica festival.org; 1741 Main St., Sarasota 34236) Concerts held at the Sarasota Opera House, 61 N. Pineapple Ave., downtown Sarasota, during two weekends in April.

❂ **Sharks' Tooth & Seafood Festival** (941-488-2236; around the Venice Pier, Venice) A bacchanal of seafood bounty, the festival gets its name also from its reputation among shark's tooth collectors. One weekend mid month.

Seafood by the mound at Siesta Fiesta. Karen T. Bartlett

Siesta Fiesta (941-349-3800; www.art festival.com/pr/siestafiesta0404; Siesta Key) A weekend of crafts shows, food fest, live musical and kids' entertainment.

June

Sarasota Music Festival (941-953-4252, 941-953-3434; www.sarasotamusic festival.com; Florida West Coast Symphony, 709 N. Tamiami Trail, Sarasota 34236) Presents classical and chamber music by promising musicians from around the world. Sponsored by the Florida West Coast Symphony, the program includes lectures for participants. The public is welcome at the performances. Three weeks.

Suncoast Offshore Grand Prix (941-371-2827; www.suncoastoffshore.org; Sarasota Bay) A national attraction, with powerboat racers from around the world. Eleven days at month's end.

August

De Soto Fishing Tournament (941-747-1998; Twin Dolphin Marina Grill, 1200 1st Ave. W., Bradenton 34205; downtown) Inshore and offshore divisions. Entry fee and cash prizes. Takes place one weekend midmonth.

September

Sarasota Dancesport Spectacular (941-955-0039; www.sarasotadancesport.com) Two days of ballroom and other dance competition at the Hyatt.

October

St. Armands Circle Art Festival (941-388-1554; St. Armands Circle) Features more than 200 national artists.

Stone Crab, Seafood & Wine Festival (941-383-6464, 800-4-COLONY; Colony Beach & Tennis Resort, 1620 Gulf of Mexico Dr., Longboat Key 34228) Celebrates the opening of stone crab season with 2,300 pounds of claws, 700 bottles of wine, dinners, upcoming celebrity chef demonstrations, and wine tasting.

November

Blues Fest (941-377-3279; www.sarasotabluesfest.com; Sarasota Fairgrounds, Fruitville Rd.) Blues musicians of world renown. One day early in the month.

Cine-World Film Festival (941-955-FILM; www.filmsociety.org; Burns Court Cinema, 506 Burns Ln., Sarasota 34236; downtown) Screens 20 to 30 films from around the world for one week early in the month. Lectures, symposiums, and other events.

Taste of Sarasota (941-925-8841; www.tasteofsarasota.org; Phillippi Estate and Mansion, Sarasota) The best from Sarasota restaurants, live entertainment, a kids' park and petting zoo. One day early in the month.

Venice Art Festival (941-484-6722; downtown Venice) Artisans from around the U.S. for one weekend.

December

Winterfest (941-778-2099; Homes Beach City Hall Park) Two days of arts and crafts show, live entertainment, and food.

Winter Wonderland (941-708-6200; Old Main Street, downtown Bradenton) Two mounds of snow, kids' craft fair, lit boat parade, food, and entertainment.

Photo by Lee County Visitor & Convention Bureau

4

CHARLOTTE HARBOR COAST
Wild and Watery

As one of Florida's largest bays, Charlotte Harbor supplies a huge gulp of nature and a place to play on many waterfronts. The region has remained the most isolated and undeveloped of any in southwest Florida, primarily because its beaches—glorious though they might be—are so far removed from main highways. The Charlotte coast retains a quiet, natural temperament and still holds on to fishing as a way of life and livelihood.

This chapter begins where the last left off, on twisty, out-of-the-way **Manasota Key**, a refuge for wealthy isolationists at its north end and the site of the unpretentious, underappreciated resort community of **Englewood Beach** at its south.

On the mainland Cape Haze peninsula—bounded by the Myakka River and Charlotte Harbor—small residential communities such as **Englewood, Grove City, Cape Haze, Placida,** and **Rotonda West** hold Amerindian mounds, fishermen, retirees, golf course communities, and families. Placida is the jump-off point for **Gasparilla Island**, which has built its reputation and character on one fish in particular: the tarpon. Phosphate shipping and legends of bygone buccaneers first attracted attention to the area. Later the Silver King, prize of the fishing world, drew millionaires to the island community of **Boca Grande**. They're still around; the town reportedly has a median household income of more than $85,000. Privately owned **Little Gasparilla** and **Palm Islands** and mostly state-owned **Don Pedro Island** have run together with shifts of tides and time. They remain three of Florida's most pristine barrier islands.

Inland, across the harbor, **Port Charlotte** is a new city that was built around Tamiami Trail, principally as a retirement community. The town of **Charlotte Harbor** was settled shortly after the Civil War by farmers and cattle ranchers. Facing it across the Peace River's widest point, **Punta Gorda** boasts a past as deep as its harbor. The southernmost station for the Florida Southern Railroad in 1886, this deepwater port town enjoyed a bustling era of commerce and tourism before railroad builder Henry Plant decided to shut it down in favor of further developing Tampa Bay. Ice making, turpentine stilling, pineapple growing, and especially commercial fishing continued to earn local citizens a living for some time. Today Punta Gorda is working to recover its past glories through downtown and riverfront restoration. *Money* magazine regularly declares it one of America's most desirable places to live. Home of Ponce de León Park, where the explorer is believed to have met his death, it hosts subdivisions of modern-day youth seekers. Its heyday train depot has been restored to its old glory and today houses an antiques mall.

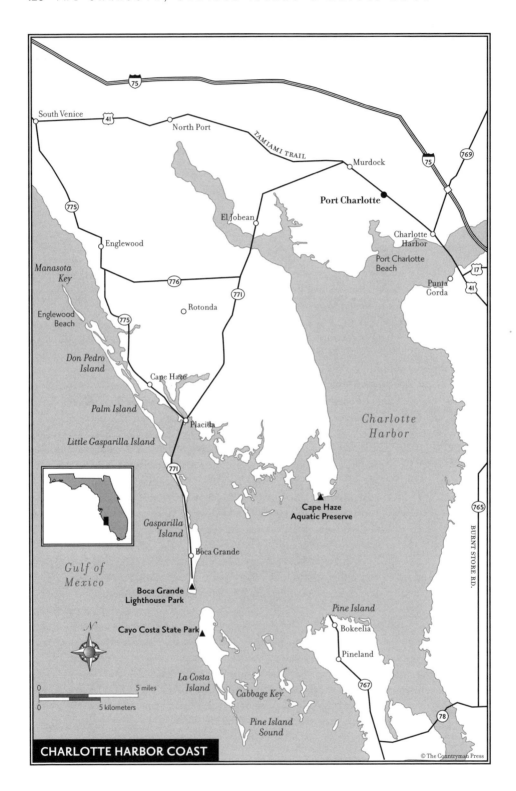

CHARLOTTE HARBOR COAST

© The Countryman Press

LODGING

Accommodations along the Charlotte Harbor coast tend to exude personality. Sure, you have your Best Western and Holiday Inn, but the remainder are either old-money polished, new-money luxurious, or money's-not-the-issue sporting. From beach cottages to the grand old Gasparilla Inn, the Charlotte Harbor coast promises something special in the way of lodging.

During high season, which begins shortly before Christmas and ends after Easter, rates may rise anywhere from 10 to 100 percent above those charged during the off-season. Some resorts schedule their rates based on as many as six different seasons, with the highest rates applying from mid-February through Easter. Reservations are recommended during these months. Some resorts and rental services require a minimum stay, especially during the peak season.

The following selection includes some of the coast's greatest lodging characters. Toll-free 800, 888, 866, or 877 reservation numbers where available are listed after local numbers.

Pricing codes are explained below. They are normally per person/double occupancy for hotel rooms and per unit for efficiencies, apartments, and cottages. Many resorts offer off-season packages at special rates. Pricing does not include the 7 percent Florida sales tax or Charlotte County's 3 percent bed tax. Some large resorts add service gratuities or maid charges.

Rate Categories

Inexpensive	Up to $75
Moderate	$75 to $150
Expensive	$150 to $200
Very Expensive	$200 and up

An asterisk after the pricing designation indicates that the rate includes at least continental breakfast in the cost of lodging; one follows the American Plan, pricing all meals into the room rate. The following abbreviations are used for credit card information:

AE: American Express
MC: MasterCard
D: Discover Card
V: Visa
DC: Diners Club

Federal law mandates that properties with 50 rooms or more provide accommodations for physically handicapped persons. I have indicated only those small places that do not make such allowances.

Accommodations

BOCA GRANDE

GASPARILLA INN

General Manager: Andy Nagle.
941-964-2201.
500 Palm Ave., PO Box 1088, Boca Grande 33921.
At 5th St. and Palm Ave.
Closed: Mid-June to mid-Dec.
Price: Very Expensive.*
Credit Cards: No.

With subtle grandeur the Gasparilla Inn sits on her throne of lush greenery. Dressed in pale-yellow clapboard with white columns, Georgian porticos, and Victorian sensibilities, the inn has been a town anchor and social emblem since 1912. The region's oldest surviving resort, the Gasparilla first opened its doors as a retreat for such families as the Vanderbilts and Du Ponts, whose descendants still visit, along with the Bushes and other illuminati. Not that the accommodations are ultraelegant: The 140 rooms reflect the era of their construction, with understated, near-institutional furnishings; the cottages are more modern and roomy. A white-linen dining room, a beauty salon and spa, an 18-hole golf course, a croquet lawn, tennis courts, playground, a beach club with fitness facilities, and two pools provide amenities. It's said that the Gasparilla Inn in quiet Boca

The Gasparilla Inn, doyenne of the Gulf Coast. Karen T. Bartlett

Grande was where Palm Beach socialites came to escape charity balls and the perpetual fashion show of their glittery hometown. Rates include full meal plan in Social Season (Christmas through Apr. 15) and breakfast and dinner only the rest of the year.

THE INNLET

General Manager: Bill Hinman.
941-964-2294.
www.innletonthewaterfront.com.
1251 Twelfth St. E., PO Box 248, Boca Grande 33921.
At 12th St. and East Ave.
Price: Moderate to Expensive.
Credit Cards: AE, MC, V.

Little stepsister to the Gasparilla Inn, the Innlet is also painted yellow, to fit in with the family. Fancy lattice touches and renovations pretty up a motel remake. The name is a double entendre on its sub-inn status and its bayou location with a ramp and docking, handy for boating and fishing

types. It has a nice little pool, playground, restaurant, and 25 rooms and efficiencies (with stovetop, microwave, and fridge) in modern, tasteful attire. Guests share communal porches and balconies.

CAPE HAZE
PALM ISLAND RESORT

President: Dean L. Beckstead.
941-697-4800, 800-824-5412; in Fla. 800-282-6142.
www.palmisland.com.
7092 Placida Rd., Cape Haze 33946.
Price: Moderate to Very Expensive (minimum stay required).
Credit Cards: AE, D, MC, V.

A true island getaway in grand style, Palm Island occupies the northernmost point of a slab of sand above Gasparilla Island. One must boat in; a car ferry runs at least every half hour from the mainland, where the resort owns one-bedroom harborside condos, in which you can also stay. On the island, Old Florida–style villas front a wide, isolated apron of beach and come with fully equipped kitchens, laundries, one to three bedrooms, exquisite appointments, and screened porches overlooking more than 2 miles of deserted beach. The 160-unit (counting the mainland accommodations) property has 5 pools and 11 tennis courts, plus restaurants and bars, an island store, a full-service marina, boat rentals, charter services, nature programs, kids' programs, playgrounds, plus bicycle, golf cart (the main mode of transport on the island), and beach equipment rentals—all the makings for an I'm-never-leaving-this-island vacation. What it doesn't have is roads, cars (you park outside resort gates), stress, and rigorous time schedules.

ENGLEWOOD BEACH
WESTON'S RESORT
Owner: Deborah L. Weston.
941-474-3431.
www.sunstate.com/westons.
985 Gulf Blvd., Englewood 34223.
Price: Inexpensive to Expensive.
Credit Cards: D, MC, V.

Taking up a good block at Englewood Beach's southern end, Weston's spreads from bay to beach to please both fishermen and sand-loving types. For the former it rents boats, motors, and gear and provides boat slips, fishing docks, and freezer storage. Free for the use of all guests are two swimming pools, tennis and shuffleboard courts, and barbecue grills. Accommodations on the 83-unit property range from studio efficiencies (inexpensive) to three-bedroom apartments (expensive) in cement-block buildings, all modernly outfitted. The rooms are clean and well kept. In some rooms the Murphy-style beds flip up into closets for more space. Kitchens are large and modern. Beach rooms look beyond seawalls to eroding beach. One pool sits in the middle of an asphalt parking lot. There's nothing luxurious about the resort, but its rates

and beach location at the quiet end of the island make it a good choice for people who love water and water sports.

MANASOTA KEY
MANASOTA BEACH CLUB
Owners: Robert and Sydney Buffum.
Manager: Warren Francis.
941-474-2614.
www.manasotabeachclub.com.
7660 Manasota Key Rd., Englewood 34223.
Price: Very Expensive.*
Credit Cards: MC, V.
Handicap Access: Yes.

A tiny, low-impact sign whispers MANASOTA BEACH CLUB. And although it occupies 25 acres of Manasota Key, the resort itself is just as unobtrusive. The unadvertised property preserves the island's natural attributes with a low-key attitude, wooded paths, and a deserted beach. Guests have reported seeing 92 bird species about the grounds. Fifteen cottages, from rustic to designer in style, the dining room, the bottle club (no alcohol is sold on the premises), and a library display Old Florida charm. The resort appeals to the "sink into oblivion" type of vacationer who wishes to hide out among natural, gnarly vegetation. (There are no televisions in the units, unless requested.) The property—which has a summer-camp feel to it—also appeals to the sportsperson, with three tennis courts, a swimming pool; bocce ball, shuffleboard, and basketball courts; horseshoes; a playground; croquet; bicycling; sailing, windsurfing, and kayaking; a children's program; and charter fishing. A private 18-hole golf course nearby is available to guests. During social season (Thanksgiving through April), cottage-room guests receive three meals a day on the American Plan; a Modified American Plan (two meals) is available during the holidays and in April. May through mid-November, the resort rents out entire cottages with kitchens and provides no meals.

Palm Island Resort: the ultimate island steal-away. Palm Island Resort, Cape Haze, FL

PORT CHARLOTTE
BANANA BAY ON CHARLOTTE HARBOR
Owner: Jana Hamilton.
Manager: Judy King.
941-743-4441.
www.bananabaymotel.com.
23285 Bayshore Rd., Charlotte Harbor 33980.
At Hwy. 41.
Price: Inexpensive to Moderate.
Credit Cards: AE, D, DC, MC, V.
Handicap Access: No.

Along Bayshore Drive in Charlotte Harbor, the feeling is Old Florida, relaxed, and fishy. Across the wide mouth of the Peace River lies Punta Gorda. Down the way, a free fishing pier juts into waters flush with fish. A few inexpensive motels in this neighborhood serve the stay-away-from-the-crowds crowd, and Banana Bay is one of the prettiest, with its mammoth potted staghorn ferns in front and banana tree murals on its one-story stucco rooms and one-bedroom efficiencies, 16 in all. The rooms have a tropical look—maybe a bit faded and floored in old-fashioned linoleum but clean and perky. Even the motel rooms have small fridges, stovetops, and microwaves. Along the bay, shuffleboard courts, grills, and picnic tables put the focus outdoors on the fetching water view.

PUNTA GORDA
FISHERMEN'S VILLAGE VILLAS
Manager: Diane Smith.
941-639-8721, 800-639-0020.
www.fishville.com.
1200 W. Retta Esplanade #58, Punta Gorda 33950.
Price: Moderate.
Credit Cards: D, MC, V.
Handicap Access: Yes.

TEMPORARILY CLOSED

One of the Gulf Coast's best lodging bargains. These spacious time-share units—all decorated in modern taste and all with a view of the water—contain two bedrooms, a loft, a living area, a big full kitchen with counter bar and stools, and one bath.

They're situated above the shops, restaurants, and courtyard hubbub of Fishermen's Village, but the rooms are well soundproofed. Guests have free use of a swimming pool, clay tennis courts, and bicycles. They are close to all the action there is to find in Punta Gorda, on land and on water. Convenient for boat-in guests, Fishermen's Village fronts a yacht harbor and a 98-slip full-service marina.

Home & Condo Rentals
Boca Grande Real Estate (941-964-0338, 800-881-2622; www.bocagrandereal estate.com; 430 W. Fourth St., PO Box 686, Boca Grande 33921) Large selection of vacation and seasonal accommodations.

Manasota Key Realty (941-474-9534, 800-881-9534; www.manasotakeyrealty .com; 1927 Beach Rd., Englewood 34223) Grand mansions, beachside cottages, and bayside homes.

Place in the Sun Vacation Rentals (941-475-6888, 800-575-3714; www.placeinthe sun.com; 2670 S. McCall Rd. #12, Englewood 34224 is at Heron Plaza) Luxury three- and four-bedroom homes.

RV Resorts
Most of the area's RV accommodations lie east of Interstate 75.

Water's Edge RV Resort (941-637-4677, 800-637-9224; www.watersedgervresort .com; 6800 Golf Course Blvd., Punta Gorda 33982) Full hookups, tent village, camping cabins, bocce court, pool, Jacuzzi, fishing lake and dock, convenience store, and rural setting.

DINING
Local cuisine smacks of Midwestern influence, but in recent years Floribbean flavors have livened things up. Fishing crews bring just-hooked seafood to the table, but that

doesn't mean some restaurants won't try to pawn off frozen products. Here I've tried to include a few eateries that believe in freshness and fanfare at the dining table.

The following listings sample all the variety of Charlotte Coast feasting in these price categories:

Inexpensive   Up to $10
Moderate $10 to $20
Expensive $20 to $30
Very Expensive $30 or more

Cost categories are based on the range of dinner entrée prices, or, if dinner is not served, on lunch entrées. The following abbreviations are used for credit card information and meals:

AE: American Express
D: Discover Card
DC: Diners Club
MC: MasterCard
V: Visa
B: Breakfast
L: Lunch
D: Dinner
SB: Sunday Brunch

Note: New Florida law forbids smoking inside all restaurants and bars serving food. Smoking is permitted only in restaurants with outdoor seating.

Boca Grande
PJ'S SEAGRILLE
941-964-0806.
321 Park Ave., Boca Grande 33921.
In the Old Theatre Building.
Price: Expensive to Very Expensive.
Cuisine: Seafood.
Children's Menu: Yes.
Liquor: Full.
Serving: L, D.
Closed: Sun. and mid-July–Sept.
Credit Cards: AE, DC, MC, V.
Handicap Access: Yes.
Reservations: Recommended for dinner.

PJ's is one of Boca Grande's most popular fine-dining experiences. Family-owned and operated for 10-plus years, it exudes an air of island familiarity, with regulars returning year after year. Dinners offer linen and candlelight; lunch is more casual —all in the setting of unfinished wood and aquariums. The menus change according to fish availability and Chef Jim's creative mood swings. At lunch, you'll find standard fare with sporadic flares of creativeness, such as pita chicken sandwich with pesto mayo and grilled portobello and veggie open-faced sandwich with roasted red peppers. At dinner, PJ's shines with an ever-changing menu featuring what the local fishermen caught that day. Some sure bets if you see them: cucumber wrapped spicy tuna tartare roll, Thai sweet and sour soup (exceptionally well-seasoned), tomato basil bisque with lump crab, char-grilled yellowfin tuna with berry sauce and wasabi, and pan-fried mangrove snapper with garlic, lemon, and white wine (much more complex in flavor than it sounds). The sides battle for attention. Try the regularly featured cheese grits or, when available, the curried acorn squash with almonds. Save room for homemade dessert. The key lime pie and chocolate cake with coconut frosting are winners.

Cape Haze
RUM BAY
941-697-0566.
7092 Placida Rd., Cape Haze 33954.
At the Palm Island Resort.
Price: Inexpensive to Moderate.
Cuisine: American.
Children's Menu: Yes.
Liquor: Full.
Serving: L, D.
Credit Cards: AE, DC, MC, V.
Handicap Access: Yes.
Reservations: Required.

Lunch or dinner at Rum Bay begins with a short (12-minute) ferry ride from the mainland—unless you have your own boat and tie up at the private resort's docks. Accessible only by boat, Palm Island and its restaurant take you away from mainland tempos and concerns to a place where water, sand, Rum Bay Smash cocktails, Danish baby back ribs, and local seafood dishes hearken back to a simpler version of Florida. The congenial bar makes its signature drink with a dose of coconut rum. Dishes are uncomplicated but diverse enough that kids, meat-lovers, vegetarians, and pastaholics will all find choices in a reasonable price range. They slather their award-winning ribs with their own sweet "swamp sauce," which they also sell by the bottle. In the seafood department, there's everything from char-grilled mahimahi topped with shrimp and tomatoes to shrimp kabobs, coconut salmon, seafood platter, and surf-turf combos. Pasta swirls around mussels, portobello mushrooms, Oriental-style veggies, and other well-matched ingredients. Come for lunch: Grab a teriyaki chicken wrap, smoked Cobb salad, or peel-and-eat shrimp; then rent a golf cart below the restaurant for a couple of hours, and head to the beach. There's no better way to make a meal into a getaway.

ENGLEWOOD BEACH
GULFVIEW GRILL
941-475-3500.
2095 N. Beach Rd., Englewood Beach 34223.
Price: Moderate to Expensive.
Children's Menu: Yes.
Cuisine: Seafood.
Liquor: Full.
Serving: L, D.
Closed: Lunch Sat. and Sun.
Credit Cards: MC, V.
Handicap Access: Yes.
Reservations: Yes.
Special Features: Window-wall views of beach and gulf; piano bar; early-bird menu.

As my old favorites on Englewood Beach have closed, I was forced to try a more modern restaurant—which happily turns out to have more appeal. To start with,

there's the knock-dead view from its stilted glass-cage perch. On a recent lunch visit, I was encouraged by the number of locals filling the tables and ultimately thrilled by the chef's special I ordered: spinach and Gorgonzola tortellini topped with perfectly cooked shrimp and a superb creamy tomato sauce. If this is any indication, I'll be back for dinner, when a multipaged menu features the day's fresh catches prepared according to your instructions and with by a number of palate-teasing sauce options, including mango beurre blanc, fra diavolo, garlic dill, and Provençal. Or choose from a chef-designed dish such as grilled salmon au poivre, lobster piccata, rack of Dijon-coated spring lamb, or prime rib. For a light lunch, the classic tuna salad with fresh tuna and ginger-soy dressing and the she-crab soup, a house specialty, look good.

PORT CHARLOTTE
CAP'N AND THE COWBOY
941-743-3969.
2200 Kings Hwy., Port Charlotte, FL 33980.
At Maple Leaf Plaza.
Price: Moderate to Expensive.
Children's Menu: Yes.
Cuisine: Steak and seafood.
Liquor: Full.
Serving: L, D.
Closed: Mon.
Credit Cards: AE, D, MC, V.
Handicap Access: Yes.
Reservations: Yes.

An old-fashioned place where steaks and shrimp come with a cup of soup and your choice of side dishes, it maintains steady popularity for its good eats, friendly folks, and clean supper-club ambiance. I can tell you, these people know how to grill. To test their abilities, I tried the barbecued shrimp and Delmonico steak combination, and both were on the perfect side of done, served with a secret sauce that's gooey and tangy with a bit of a bite. The menu, or "Grocery List," as it's called, lines up ribs, seafood, and steaks in dozens of mix-and-match configurations. Sandwiches (burgers, pork, crab cake, etc.), salads, and dinners are available all day long. Whatever time you stop, save room for the key lime pie. This one has a pastry crust and just the right amount of tartness.

Punta Gorda
AMIMOTO JAPANESE RESTAURANT
941-505-1515.
2705 S. Tamiami Trail, Punta Gorda 33950.
At Towles Plaza.
Price: Moderate to Expensive.
Cuisine: Japanese.
Children's Menu: No.
Serving: L, D.
Closed: Lunch Sat. and Sun.
Liquor: Beer and wine.
Credit Cards: AE, D, DC, MC, V.
Handicap Access: Yes.
Reservations: Accepted.
Special Features: Sushi bar.

Soothing and authentic, Amimoto satisfies the spirit as well as the stomach. The decor is simple, contemporary, and clean, decorated with tasteful Eastern art and arranged around the Formica sushi bar. The sushi menu itself presents nearly 50 choices. I like the hokkai—salmon, onions, and radish sprouts. The lunch and dinner menus list dozens more options for appetizers, such as the light miso soup with tofu and enoki, ginger shrimp, fried soft-shell crab, seaweed salad, and scads of exotic combinations involving seafood, tofu, and Oriental vegetables and sauces. *Obento* box combinations, a Japanese improvement on box lunches, are popular lunch choices. For entrées, the menus describe a few possible preparations of chicken, pork, and beef, then goes on to list a selection of seafood. Fish can be grilled with wasabi or teriyaki sauce or deep-fried. The scallops sautéed with lime and special sauce sounded tempting. The restaurant does provide forks, by the way, for those chopsticks-challenged like me.

✪ THE PERFECT CAPER
941-505-9009.
320 Sullivan St., Punta Gorda 33950.
Downtown.
Price: Expensive.
Cuisine: New American.
Children's Menu: No.
Serving: L, D, SB.
Closed: Lunch Sat.–Tues., dinner Mon. and Tues.; part of Sept.
Liquor: Beer and wine.
Credit Cards: AE, D, DC, MC, V.
Handicap Access: Yes.
Reservations: Accepted.

Something of a secret except to culinary-savvy Punta Gordans, this eatery resides among the charmingly restored bungalow-shops on brick-paved Sullivan Street. When I visited, it still didn't have a sign up, although it's been open about two years. Look for a bright-orange place next to the Purple House gift shop. Inside, the kitchen is part of the restaurant, which makes a bold decor statement with bright sky-blue walls, black tables, and a gorgeous booth with a blond onyx tabletop. Personality does not end there. My lunch of cream of mussel soup with saffron plus half a roasted pepper, baby spinach, and goat cheese

Still a well-kept secret, The Perfect Caper blends in with the restyled bungalows of Punta Gorda's Sullivan Street. Karen T. Bartlett

sandwich was divine (even though the owner told me I ordered the most boring thing on the menu). I relished the surprises: a square of herb bread for starters, lovely dressed greens and cornichon garnish, and personalized service. At only $6.25, the cup of soup and half baguette is a real value. There's a ham and brie and other baguette options. Also pan-seared halibut, burger of the day, and great-sounding salads. I'll be back for dinner, a select menu offering crispy shrimp appetizer fried in shredded phyllo, a fig and goat cheese salad, whole roasted fish with tomato-coriander consommé, pan-roasted squab with seared foie gras, and Sichuan green peppercorn strip steak. The dessert menu presents a tough choice, but you won't regret the chocolate bread pudding with vanilla-caramel sauce.

VILLAGE FISH MARKET

941-639-7959.
www.fishville.com/shops.
1200 W. Retta Esplanade, Punta Gorda 33950.
At Fishermen's Village.
Price: Inexpensive to Moderate.
Cuisine: Seafood.
Children's Menu: Yes.
Serving: L, D.

Liquor: Beer and wine.
Credit Cards: AE, D, DC, MC, V.
Handicap Access: Yes.
Reservations: No.
Special Features: River views and courtyard seating.

Fishermen's Village has several options for dining, many with scenic gazing at the Peace River. This one has been a fixture since the village opened 20 years ago, serving fresh selections from its fish market at reasonable prices. Enjoy fish-house fare plus: you'll find typical fried seafood baskets, combination platters, and fried sandwiches, but under "Finfish," "Shellfish," and "Pasta" headings and on the specials board, the preparation gets a bit more elaborate. I tried, for instance, the salmon Rockefeller, stuffed with spinach, bacon, and parmesan and topped with hollandaise sauce. Other choices from an extensive list: shrimp Milano in garlic white wine sauce over pasta, stuffed baked scrod, and blackened grouper. Nice thing about the entrées: you can order a small (3.5 ounce) or large (5 ounce) portion. You have a choice between French fries and onion rings; I recommend the crunchy rings, which arrive in such a heap that the small fish portion is more than ample.

FOOD PURVEYORS

Bakeries

Boca Grande Baking Company (941-964-5818; 384 E. Railroad Ave., Boca Grande 33921) Homemade breads, creative muffins, scones, pastries, cakes, and other desserts in an inviting setting; complete coffee bar; also pizza, lasagna, sandwiches, and other eat-in or take-out items.

Waves of Grain (941-639-3400; 264 W. Marion Ave., Punta Gorda 33950; downtown) Yeast and quick breads, muffins, scones, pastries, and cookies. Also serves breakfast and lunch.

Breakfast

Loons on a Limb (941-964-0155; 310 E. Railroad Ave., Boca Grande 33921) Open daily for breakfast and brunch, a 21-year Boca tradition, serving typical breakfast fare, smoothies, and homemade banana bread. No credit cards accepted.

Waves of Grain (941-639-3400; 264 W. Marion Ave., Punta Gorda 33950; downtown) The hot new place for breakfast and lunch, featuring fresh-baked bakery goods, quiche, omelets, and a healthy breakfast. Closed Sunday in summer.

Candy & Ice Cream

Flamingo Yogurt (941-639-5515; www.fishville.com; 1200 W. Retta Esplanade, Punta Gorda 33950; at Fishermen's Village) Premium yogurt, granita, cold cappuccino, frozen fruit drinks, ice cream, and candy.

The Loose Caboose (941-964-0440; 433 W. Fourth St., Boca Grande 33921; at Park Ave.) Katharine Hepburn, among scores of others, once left her compliments on the bulletin board at this restaurant known for its home-made ice cream and smoothies in many flavors.

The Loose Caboose in Boca Grande's Railroad Plaza carries a cargo of highly acclaimed homemade ice cream. Karen T. Bartlett

Coffee

Coffee à la Carte (941-575-4344; www.fishville.com/shops; 1200 W. Retta Esplanade, Punta Gorda 33950; at Fishermen's Village) Gourmet coffee, espresso, cappuccino, iced and frozen drinks, pastries, bagels, sandwiches, and ice cream.

Jitters (941-475-7870; 485 W. Dearborn St., Englewood 34223) In a corner at the back of a little gift gallery, find gourmet java, iced coffee, frozen fruit drinks, and chai tea.

Deli & Specialty Foods

The Artistic Gourmet (941-575-6666; 117 W. Marion Ave., Punta Gorda 33950; down-town) A small but complete and affordable selection of spices, sauces, gourmet products, table and bar ware. Catering available.

Gill's Grocery & Deli (941-964-2506; 5800 Gasparilla Rd., Boca Grande 33921; at The Courtyard) Freshly made sandwiches, salads, and heat-up entrées, plus grocery items, ice cream, party trays, and bakery goods. Delivery available.

Grapevine (941-964-0614; www.mybocagrande.com; 321 Park Ave., Boca Grande 33921; in the Old Theatre Building) Specialty wines, imported cheese, fish, prepared dishes, sandwiches, gourmet products, and baked goods Monday through Saturday.

Kallis German Butcher Sausage Kitchen (941-627-1413; 2420 Tamiami Trail, Port Charlotte 33952) Wursts of every variety, many of which you've probably never heard of;

also fine cuts of meat, rouladen, cheese, hams, and gourmet European imports. This place is a lot of fun.

Presseller Delicatessen (941-639-3990; www.pressellergallery.com; 209 W. Olympia Ave., Punta Gorda 33950; downtown) Part art gallery, it serves salads, sandwiches, pizza, and soup to eat in or take out. Also sells deli meets, import beer, wine, fudge, and other gourmet groceries.

Fruit & Vegetable Stands
De Soto Groves (941-625-2737; 1750 Tamiami Trail, Murdock 33948) Just-picked Florida citrus fruit.

Natural Foods
Reid's Nutrition Center (941-474-1115; 1951 S. McCall Rd., Englewood 34223; at Palm Plaza) Mostly vitamins but also some organic products; vegetable juice and fruit smoothie bar; certified nutritionist on staff.

Pizza & Take-out
Angelo's Pizza (941-474-2477; 2611 Placida Rd., Englewood 34223) Pizza and Italian specialties. Take-out and delivery.

Boca Grande Baking Company (941-964-5818; 384 E. Railroad Ave., Boca Grande 33921) Sandwiches, homemade pizza, lasagna, breads, desserts, and other take-out items.

Jam's (941-964-2002; www.jamsrestaurant.com; Fifth St. and Railroad Ave., Boca Grande 33921; 941-697-2080; 8501 Placida Rd., Placida 33946) New York-style thin-crust pizza and other Italian specialties to go or eat in.

Seafood
Village Fish Market (941-639-7959; www.fishville.com/shops; 1200 W. Retta Esplanade, Punta Gorda 33950; at Fishermen's Village) A small market featuring New England and Florida seafood, with dining (see above).

CULTURE

The Charlotte Harbor coast is small town—even in its larger, urban-sprawl-infected communities. Long considered a refuge for the retired, the region is not known for a vibrant arts scene or cultural diversity. Overall, it has a Midwestern flavor in coastal areas but is definitely Old Florida in inland rural parts. Awareness of the arts has developed slowly and on a hobby level. For information on local arts and culture, contact the Arts & Humanities Council of Charlotte County, 941-764-8100.

Architecture
In the smaller towns around Charlotte Harbor, single examples of historic character appear serendipitously in the midst of concrete-block homes. **Downtown Englewood,** a destination off the beaten path of Tamiami Trail, holds a few such treasures that have been reincarnated as shops, boutiques, and galleries.

Town citizens worked to beautify downtown Punta Gorda with historic and educational murals.
Chelle Koster Walton

Punta Gorda sprinkles its architectural prizes—old homes, commercial buildings, and churches—along **Marion Avenue, Olympia Avenue, Retta Esplanade**, and side streets such as **Sullivan Street** and the developing **History Park on Shreve Street.** Along the Esplanade, look for impressive newly restored homes, the jewels of the old riverfront district. In and around the town's historic section, an eclectic array of architecture ranges from old shotgun cigar workers' homes and tin-roofed Cracker shacks to Victorian mansions and a neoclassical city hall. For a guide to Punta Gorda's treasures, pick up a copy of *Punta Gorda Historic Walking Tour* at the chamber of commerce. Watch for historic murals and street sculptures along the way.

Boca Grande's most noteworthy examples of architecture, aside from the grande dame **Gasparilla Inn**, are four historic churches, each with its own style, located in a four-block area downtown. The Catholic church takes its inspiration from Spanish missions; the other three occupy early-20th-century wood-frame buildings and serve Episcopal, Baptist, and Methodist congregations.

A few blocks away, on **Tarpon Avenue**, old spruced-up Cracker homes slump comfortably in a district sometimes called **Whitewash Alley.** For a taste of wealthy eccentricity, check out the **Johann Fust Library** on Gasparilla Road. It was built of native coquina, cypress, and pink stucco.

Cinema
Regal 16 Cinema (941-623-0111; 1441 Tamiami Trail, Port Charlotte 33948; in the Port Charlotte Town Center)

Dance
Aki's Dancesport Centre (941-624-4001; 3109 Tamiami Trail, Port Charlotte 33983) Dancing socials, competitions, and lessons in swing, merengue, salsa, lindy, fox-trot, and waltz.

Country Line Dance Lessons (941-639-8721; www.fishville.com; 1200 W. Retta Esplanade, Punta Gorda 33950; in Fishermen's Village) Every Wednesday night 7 to 9; $3 per person for lessons.

Historic Homes & Sites
THE A. C. FREEMAN HOUSE
941-637-0077.
http://dhr.dos.state.fl.us/HistoricPlaces
/Counties/Charlotte.html#freeman.
639 E. Hargreaves Ave., Punta Gorda
33950.
Open: Hourly winter tours 11–3 Thurs. and
Fri Dec.–Apr.
Admission: Donations suggested.

Today home of the Charlotte County
Foundation, this house was once occupied
by Punta Gorda's turn-of-the-century
mayor and mortician. Narrowly escaping
the wrecking ball in 1985, the lovely clapboard Queen Anne mansion was saved
and restored by the people of Punta Gorda
as a memento of gracious pioneer
lifestyles.

*The A. C. Freeman House survives from Punta
Gorda's early days of prosperity.*
Charlotte County Visitors Bureau

BOCA GRANDE LIGHTHOUSE MUSEUM
941-964-0060 (GEOpark Service).
www.barrierislandparkssociety.org.
PO Box 637, Boca Grande 33921.
Gasparilla Island State Park, Gulf Blvd., Boca Grande.
Open: 10–4 Wed.–Sun.; also Tues. in-season; closed: Mon. in-season, Tues. in summer,
Aug. and major holidays.
Admission: $2 for state recreation area park; donation of $1 requested.

This 1890 structure—the most photographed and painted landmark on the island—was
renovated in Old Florida style and put back into service in 1986 after 20 years of abandon-
ment. You can self-tour both the lighthouse and the museum, which explores its history
and Boca Grande bygones—from ancient Calusa civilizations through railroad and indus-
trial eras to the island's modern-day reputation as a tarpon-fishing mecca. Historic cis-
terns, the assistant lighthouse keeper's home, and a struggling native vegetation garden
comprise the fenced-in complex. It sits within Gasparilla Island State Park.

INDIAN MOUND PARK
210 Winson Ave., Englewood 34223

It's slightly flattened now from age, but this ancient midden mound is still centerpiece to a
lovely bay front park where picnicking, boating, and exploring the trails that crisscross the
vegetated mound provide pastime.

PONCE DE LEÓN HISTORICAL PARK

End of Marion Ave., Punta Gorda.

Downsized from a rock shrine encasement to make room for more parking, a chipped-paint statue and historic plaques commemorate Ponce de León's supposed 1513 landing here and his subsequent death caused by an Indian attack. The park has a wildlife and recreational area on the harbor, with boat ramp, picnic facilities, small sea-walled beach, playground, and native trail into the mangroves.

PUNTA GORDA HISTORY PARK

501 Sheve St., Punta Gorda 33950.
Admission: Free

So far this gathering of historic buildings in a pretty park setting amounts to two old homes. Stop in first at the old Tabue House, where Punta Gorda's founder once lived. It also houses the Peace River Center for Writers and a small exhibit on the history of the two-year park and its buildings. Ask for a key to the Cigar Cottage, where the town's tobacco industry once headquartered.

The Boca Grande Lighthouse is one of the state's most picturesque. Karen T. Bartlett

Museums

CHARLOTTE COUNTY HISTORICAL CENTER

941-629-7278.
22959 Bayshore Rd., Charlotte Harbor 33980.
Open: 10–5 Mon.–Fri.; 10–3 Sat.; closed Sun.
Admission: Donation of $2 adults, $1 children 12 and under.

Relocated to a gorgeous spot on the river next to the pier at Bayshore Live Oak Park, the roomy new facility is geared toward children, with programs, signage, showcases, and interactive exhibits that illuminate facets of local history. Exhibits are devoted to the Gasparilla pirate legend, Calusa natives, fishing heritage, fossils, Seminoles, and more.

FLORIDA MILITARY HERITAGE MUSEUM

941-575-9002.
www.fmhmuseum.org.
PO Box 511141, Punta Gorda 33951.
At Fisherman's Village.
Open: 10–6 Mon.–Sat.; noon–5 Sun.
Admission: Free.

Opened in December 2001 to commemorate the 60th anniversary of Pearl Harbor, the museum features changing exhibits that focus on that infamous day as well as World Wars I and II, Vietnam, and Korea. See showcases filled with uniforms, weapons, and miscellaneous memorabilia that veterans will enjoy. Admission is free, but the staff tries to get you to volunteer at the museum. It hosts special Flag Day and other patriotic events.

GASPARILLA ISLAND MARITIME MUSEUM
941-964-GIMM.
PO Box 100, Boca Grande 33921.
At Whidden's Marina, on Harbor Dr.
Hours: Vary.
Admission: By donation.

Some might call it a shed full of old junk, but to the citizens of Boca Grande, it represents Americana and a way of life that has survived in contrast to the mansions and yachts that surround it. Part of Whidden's Marina, the museum's photo albums remember a day when the nation's top industrialists sailed here to fish and winter. Odd parts of boats and fishing gear lie strewn around the old, peeling fish shack, listed on the National Register of Historic Places. Still in operation, the marina and its store make it difficult to tell where the museum ends and the present begins.

Music & Nightlife

BOCA GRANDE
South Beach (941-964-0765; 777 Gulf Blvd., Boca Grande 33921) Contemporary bands play weekend nights. Sunset plays (almost) every evening.

ENGLEWOOD
Englewood Performing Arts Series (941-473-2787) Fine cultural entertainment from around the nation, mid-November through mid-April.

Gilchrist Park overlooks the mouth of the Peace River in Punta Gorda. Karen T. Bartlett

Mad Sam's Grille & Bar (941-475-9505; 1375 Beach Rd., Englewood 33423) Live bands playing blues, zydeco, reggae, and jazz most weekend nights.

Port Charlotte

Charlotte County Jazz Society (941-766-9422; 282 Goiana St., Port Charlotte 33983) Sponsors several jazz concerts each year at the Cultural Center Theatre (see "Theater," below).

Charlotte Symphony Orchestra (941-625-5996; www.charlottesymphony.com; PO Box 495831, Port Charlotte 33949) Performs at the Community Life Center on Edgewater Drive, November through March.

Gatorz Bar & Grill (941-625-5000; 3816 Tamiami Trail, Port Charlotte 33952) Live music throughout the week: jazz and Top 40.

Punta Gorda

Charlotte County Memorial Auditorium (941-639-5833, 800-329-9988; 75 Taylor St., Punta Gorda 33950) Waterfront host to Broadway plays, big band and swing orchestras, and national stars.

Charlotte Performing Arts Center (941-637-0459, 941-505-SHOW for box office; www.charlottesymphony.com/cpac.htm; 701 Carmalita St., Punta Gorda 33950) Opened for its first season in 2003, this modern new facility hosts jazz bands, musical shows, chamber concerts, and other performances.

Fishermen's Village (941-639-8721; www.fishville.com; 1200 W. Retta Esplanade, Punta Gorda 33950) Live entertainment most Tuesday afternoons and Friday and Saturday evenings.

Gilchrist Park (Retta Esplanade) On Thursday nights local musicians gather for impromptu jamming at dusk, to which the public is invited.

Theater

Cultural Center of Charlotte County (941-625-4175; www.theculturalcenter.com; 2280 Aaron St., PO Box 495129, Port Charlotte 33949) Home of the Charlotte Players (941-255-1022) community-theater group and Charlotte County Jazz Society (see "Music and Nightlife," above).

Lemon Bay Playhouse (941-475-6756; www.lemonbayplayhouse.com; 96 W. Dearborn St., Englewood 34223) Home of the Lemon Bay Players community-theater group. Performances Sept.–July.

Royal Palm Players (941-964-2670; www.royalpalmplayers.com; 333 Park Ave., Suite 4, PO Box 954, Boca Grande 33921) A community-theater group sponsoring plays, guest-artist performances, children's performances, and concerts November into May.

Visual Art Centers

The local "Art Around Town" movement and Historic Mural Society have turned the streets of downtown Punta Gorda into one huge outdoor gallery. Local artists lend their sculptures for display along the streets. The mural society has resulted in more than 20 historic and educational scenes painted on buildings mostly throughout the downtown area.

A listing for commercial galleries is included in the "Shopping" section of this chapter.

Arts & Humanities Council (941-764-8100; 2811 N. Tamiami Trail, Port Charlotte 33952; at LaPlaya Plaza) Hosts art displays and events.

Englewood Art Center (941-474-5548; 350 S. McCall Rd., Englewood 34223)

Visual Arts Center (941-639-8810; www.visualartscenter.com; 210 Maude St., Punta Gorda 33950; near Fishermen's Village) Home of the Charlotte County Art Guild. Exhibit halls, gift shops, library, darkroom, and classes.

RECREATION

More behind-the-scenes than the touted playgrounds of its flanking neighbors, the Charlotte Harbor coast's greatest claim to recreational fame is its fishing—particularly for that king of all sport fish, tarpon.

Beaches

You must drive way off the beaten path to find the beaches of Charlotte County. Though less convenient, that keeps them more natural, less trodden.

BLIND PASS (MIDDLE) BEACH

Route 776, mid-island on Manasota Key.
Facilities: Restrooms, showers, playground, nature trail, canoe launch.

Sixty acres of lightly developed shoreline attract those drawn more to seclusion than to the sports and activities of Manasota Key's other beaches. Low dunes edge wide salt-and-pepper sands. Next door you'll see one of the island's first buildings. Known as Hermitage House, it was once a nudist resort. Today it's a retreat for visiting artists. From the parking lot you can follow a nature boardwalk trail into the mangroves.

CHADWICK PARK BEACH

941-473-1018.
2100 N. Beach Rd., Englewood 34223.
Route 776, south end of Manasota Key at Englewood Beach.
Facilities: Picnic areas/shelters, restrooms, showers, volleyball, handicap beach chairs.
Parking: 25¢ per hour.

Many refer to this simply as Englewood Beach. A popular hangout for the local youth, it is nonetheless a well-maintained and policed area. The beach was widened, and facilities were completely renovated in 2002, including a new boardwalk, pirate-theme playground, and picnic shelters. Shops and restaurants huddle around the area, which keeps activity levels high.

DON PEDRO ISLAND STATE PARK

941-964-0375.
www.floridastateparks.org/donpedroisland.
Barrier Islands GEOpark, PO Box 1150, Boca Grande 33921.
South of Palm Island, accessible only by boat.
Facilities: Picnic area/shelters, restrooms, showers, boat docks.
Admission: $2 per boat or family arriving by ferry.

Secluded beach at a 129-acre island getaway. Once separated from Palm Island and Little Gasparilla, Don Pedro Island is now connected to the two to form one long, lightly developed barrier island. Don Pedro, the most natural component, is toward the southern end.

LIGHTHOUSE BEACH/GASPARILLA ISLAND STATE PARK
941-964-0375.
www.floridastateparks.org/gasparillaisland.
Barrier Islands GEOpark, PO Box 1150, Boca Grande 33921.
Along Gulf Blvd., Boca Grande, Gasparilla Island.
Facilities: Picnic tables, restrooms.
Parking: $2 per car for up to 8 people, $1 for pedestrians and cyclists.

Marked by a historic lighthouse with a museum inside, the park edges the deepwater tarpon grounds of Boca Grande Pass. Its plush sands encompass 135 acres, although in some parts the beach gets quite narrow. Swimming is not recommended because of strong currents through the pass. A historic chapel in the same park is under restoration.

MANASOTA BEACH
North end of Route 776, Manasota Key.
Facilities: Picnic area/shelters, restrooms, showers, lifeguard, historical marker, boat ramp.

A lively 14-acre sunning and shelling venue connected to Venice's Caspersen Beach about 1-1/2 miles to the north. It also has a reputation—but not as pointed as Venice's—for sharks' teeth. The sands are somewhat narrower here than to the south.

PORT CHARLOTTE BEACH PARK
941-627-1628.
4500 Harbor Blvd., Port Charlotte 33952.
At the southeast end of Harbor Blvd.
Facilities: Picnic areas; restrooms; showers; concessions; bocce, basketball, and tennis courts; volleyball; playground; horseshoes; boat ramps; fishing pier; swimming and kiddie pools.
Swimming Admission: $2.68 adult, $1.61 ages 3–15 (phone: 941-629-0170).
Parking: 25¢ per hour.

A highly developed recreational center that sits on Charlotte Harbor along a manmade beach, this is a good place to go if you (or the children) like to keep busy at the beach. It's better for sunning than swimming, however, as bacteria levels are sometimes high. Stick to the swimming pool, which is open daily until 4:45 (open at 10 Mon.–Fri., 11 Sat.–Sun.). A boardwalk runs along the beach and connects to the fishing pier. It looks across the way at Punta Gorda and feels more like a beach at a lake than the sea.

STUMP PASS BEACH STATE PARK
941-964-0375.
www.floridastateparks.org/stumppass.
Barrier Islands State Parks, PO Box 1150, Boca Grande 33921.
South end of Gulf Blvd., Englewood Beach on Manasota Key.
Facilities: Rest rooms, nature trail.
Parking: $2 per car, $1 for bikers and pedestrians.

This uncrowded beach offers lovely, unspoiled seclusion. Traditionally, the 255-acre park has been a magnet for fishermen who cast into Lemon Bay. Follow the 2-mile wooded trail to the south, and you'll find nice areas to spread a towel and dip your toes. The park stretches all the way to Stump Pass in a skinny strip of black-specked sand fringed by sea oats.

Bicycling

The Charlotte Coast region, with its abundance of back roads and wide-open spaces, gives cyclists an opportunity to pedal in peace. Many of its favored bikeways are on-road or designated bike lanes, which are separated from motor traffic only by a painted white line. According to state law, bicyclists who share the road with other vehicles must heed all the rules of the road. Children under age 16 are required to wear a helmet.

Best Biking

Cape Haze Pioneer Trail (941-627-1628; www.ccmpo.com) is a developing county project that runs parallel to Route 771 along a former railbed. The first 3.5 miles opened in 1999, and another 2-mile segment was completed in 2001. The third phase will be constructed in 2005.

About a mile past Gasparilla Island's causeway (which can be crossed by bicycle for $1), the **Boca Grande bike path** starts. Here you pedal along old railroad routes. Seven miles of pathway travel the island from tip to tip along Railroad Avenue and Gulf Boulevard. These paths are shared by golf carts, which one can rent and drive about the island as long as you are 14 or older. Many of Boca's downtown streets are also designated golf-cart trails.

Highway 776 through Englewood and Englewood Beach is shouldered with a bike lane that ends at the Sarasota County line. In Punta Gorda, **Gilchrist Park's bike path** runs along green space overlooking the Peace River on Retta Esplanade. Bike riding on city sidewalks is legal throughout the county.

For a map of Charlotte County bikeways, call the Charlotte County-Punta Gorda Metropolitan Planning Organization at 941-639-4676.

Rentals/Sales

Acme Bicycle Shop (941-639-3029; 258 W. Marion Ave., Punta Gorda 33950; downtown) Bikes for adults and kids, sales, and repairs.

The Bicycle Center (941-627-6600; 3755 Tamiami Trail, Port Charlotte 33952) All types of bikes, including tandems, children's, and adult tricycles. Free pickup and delivery on weekly rentals within a 10-mile radius.

Bikes and Boards (941-474-2019; 966 S. McCall Rd., Englewood Beach 34223) Bike and kayak rentals, sales, delivery, and service.

Grande Tours (941-697-8825; www.grandetours.com; 12575 Placida Rd., PO Box 281, Placida 33946)

Island Bike 'N Beach (941-964-0711; 333 Park Ave., Boca Grande 33921) Rents bikes, golf carts, and beach stuff.

Boats & Boating

Charlotte Harbor Coast offers many waterfronts for adventure: the gulf, the harbor, Peace River, Myakka River, and Lemon Bay Aquatic Preserve.

Canoeing & Kayaking

For information on paddling trails, contact Charlotte County Parks & Recreation Department at 941-627-1628; www.charlottecountyfl.com, and request a copy of the *Blueway Trails* map and listing.

Personal Watercraft

Island Jet Ski (941-474-1168; 1450 Beach Rd., Englewood Beach 34223, at Englewood Bait House Marina on the south bridge) Hourly and daily rentals.

Powerboat Rentals

Bay Breeze Boat Rentals (941-475-0733; 1450 Beach Rd., Englewood Beach 34223; at Englewood Bait House on the south bridge) Rents pontoon boats and fishing skiffs.

Boca Boat Rentals (941-964-1333, 888-416-BOAT; www.bocaboat.com; 5800 Gasparilla Rd., Boca Grande 33921; at Uncle Henry's Marina) Rents powerboats, kayaks, hydrobikes, and golf carts.

Holidaze Boat Rental (941-505-8888; www.holidazeboatrental.com; 1200 W. Retta Esplanade, Punta Gorda 33950) 17.5- to 21-foot boats and 20- to 24-foot pontoons, tri-toons, and deck boats rented hourly and by the half or full day. Also kayaks and jet skis.

Public Boat Ramps

Indian Mound Park (Englewood Recreation Center, 101 Horn St., Englewood 34223; downtown Englewood) On Lemon Bay. Access to Stump Pass, picnic pavilion, restrooms, nature trails.

Laishley Park City Marina (Marion Ave. and Nesbit St., Punta Gorda)

Manasota Beach (Manasota Beach Rd., Manasota Key) One public boat ramp across the street from a county park.

Placida (Causeway Blvd.)

Ponce de León Park (west end of Marion Ave., Punta Gorda) One boat ramp close to the gulf.

Port Charlotte Beach (941-627-1628; 4500 Harbor Blvd., Port Charlotte 33952; southeast end of Harbor Blvd.) Beach recreational area, access to Charlotte Harbor. Two boat ramps.

Sailboat Charters, Rentals, and Instruction

Captain Lynda Suzanne (941-964-2027; PO Box 1006, Boca Grande 33921; on First St.) Luncheon sails into Charlotte Harbor. Sailing instruction available.

International Sailing School (941-639-7492, 800-824-5040; www.intlsailsch.com; 1200 W. Retta Esplanade, Punta Gorda 33950; at Fishermen's Village Marina) Instruction, certification courses; rentals, sailing excursions, and club memberships.

Southwest Florida Yachts/Florida Sailing & Cruising School (239-656-1339, 800-262-SWFY; www.flsailandcruiseschool.com; 3444 Marinatown Ln. N.W., Suite 19, North Fort Myers 33903) American Sailing Association (ASA) certification courses and bareboat charters provide excellent adventures out of Burnt Store Marina (southwest of Punta Gorda) into Charlotte Harbor for live-aboard experiences.

Sightseeing & Entertainment Cruises

Boca Boat Cruises & Charters (941-964-1333 or 888-416-BOAT; www.bocaboat.com; 5800 Gasparilla Rd., PO Box 294, Boca Grande 33921; at Uncle Henry's Marina) Daily beach and lunch tours, and sunset cruises.

Grande Tours (941-697-8825; www.grandetours.com; 12575 Placida Rd., PO Box 281, Placida 33946) Tours: eco, shelling, sea life, sunset, kid fishing, pirate treasure hunt, wildlife, and narrated sightseeing. Also kayak nature and fishing tours and rentals and water-taxi service.

King Fisher Cruise Lines (941-639-0969; www.kingfisherfleet.com; 1200 W. Retta Esplanade, Punta Gorda 33950; at Fishermen's Village Marina,) Excursions to Cayo Costa and Cabbage Key and along the Peace River aboard a double-deck head boat. Also sunset and harbor sightseeing cruises.

Ko Ko Kai Charter Boat Service (941-474-2141; www.kokokai.com; 5040 N. Beach Rd., Englewood Beach 34223) Takes you island hopping to Gasparilla, Palm, Cayo Costa, Cabbage Key, Upper Captiva, and Captiva Islands as well as on lunch, fishing, and shelling charters.

Fishing

Tarpon reigns as the king of southwest Florida fish—the Silver King, to be exact, named for its silver-dollar-like scales. Boca Grande Pass is one of the most celebrated spots in the world for catching the feisty fighter.

Nonresidents age 16 and older who wish to fish must obtain a license unless fishing from a vessel or pier covered by its own license. You can buy inexpensive temporary-nonresident licenses at county tax collectors' offices and most Kmarts and bait shops. Check local regulations for season, size, and catch restrictions.

Deep-Sea Charter Boats

King Fisher Fleet (941-639-0969; www.kingfisherfleet.com; 1200 W. Retta Esplanade, Punta Gorda 33950; at Fishermen's Village Marina,) Deep-sea fishing aboard a 35-foot boat with a 22-year-old operation.

Fishing Charters/Outfitters

Boca Grande Fishing Guides Association (941-964-2559; www.bocagrandefishing.com; PO Box 676, Boca Grande 33921) Organization of more than 50 qualified charter guides especially knowledgeable about tarpon.

Tarpon, snook, sheepshead, and snapper tantalize the casting crowd. Karen T. Bartlett

Captain Jack's Charters (941-475-4511; www.sunstate.com/captjack; 1450 Beach Rd., Englewood Beach 34223; at the Englewood Bait House) Half-day, full-day, night, overnight, and weekend trips.

Fishing Unlimited (941-964-0907, 800-4-TARPON; www.4tarpon.com; 431 Park Ave., PO Box 1407, Boca Grande 33921) Outfitters, fly shop, guides and charters, authorized Orvis dealer.

King Fisher Fleet (941-639-0969; www.kingfisherfleet.com; 1200 W. Retta Esplanade, Punta Gorda 33950; at Fishermen's Village Marina) Back-bay fishing charters.

Tarpon Hunter Guide Service (941-743-6622; 265 Lomond Dr. #B, Port Charlotte 33953) Charters aboard the *Tarpon Hunter II* in Charlotte Harbor and backwaters. Specialties include fly and light-tackle fishing.

Fishing Piers

Bayshore Fishing Pier (22967 Bayshore Dr., Charlotte Harbor) At the mouth of the Peace River in Bayshore Live Oak Park, next to the Charlotte County Historical Center.

Englewood Beach (Anger) Pier (along Beach Rd. east of the drawbridge)

Gasparilla Fishing Pier South (941-627-1628; near Courtyard Plaza, north end of Gasparilla Rd., Gasparilla Island) An old railroad bridge.

Gilchrist Park (Retta Esplanade, Punta Gorda) Cast into the brackish waters where the Peace River empties into the gulf.

Myakka Fishing Pier North & South (941-627-1628; Rte. 776, El Jobean) Two piers into the Myakka River.

Port Charlotte Beach Park (941-627-1628; 4500 Harbor Blvd., Port Charlotte; southeast end of Harbor Blvd.) Part of a beach and pool recreational center, it offers fishing clinics.

Golf

Public Golf Courses & Centers

Deep Creek Golf Club (941-625-6911; www.deepcreekgc.com; 1260 San Cristobal Ave., Port Charlotte 33983) Semiprivate; 18 holes, par 70; driving range, putting green, and snack bar.

Duffy's Golf Center (941-697-3900; 12455 S. McCall Rd., Port Charlotte 33981) 18-hole executive course (nine holes lit) and lit practice range, PGA professionals, golf shop, and snack bar.

Lemon Bay Golf Club (941-697-3729; www.usga.org/green/environment/lemon_ bay.html; 9600 Eagle Preserve Dr., Englewood 34223) Semiprivate; 18 holes, par 71; restaurant. A certified Audubon Society course

Port Charlotte Golf Club (941-625-4109; 22400 Gleneagles Terrace, Port Charlotte 33952) Semiprivate; 18 holes; full practice facilities, restaurant and lounge.

Punta Gorda Country Club (941-639-1494; 6100 Duncan Rd., Punta Gorda 33950) Semiprivate; 18 holes; snack bar. Affordable rates.

Health & Fitness Clubs

Charlotte County Family YMCA (941-629-2220; www.charlottecountyymca.com; 22425 Edgewater Dr., Charlotte Harbor 33980) Aerobics, Trimnastics, body shaping, yoga, volleyball, basketball, golf tournaments, youth sports competition, steam room, and kiddie facilities and programs.

Charlotte Health & Racquet Club (941-629-2223; www.charlotteracquet.com; 3250 Loveland Blvd., Port Charlotte 33952) Racquetball, squash, tennis, dance/aerobic classes, cardio equipment, universal weights, yoga, karate, Pilates, personal training, massage.

The Punta Gorda Club (941-505-0999; www.puntagordaclub.com; 2905 Tamiami Trail, Punta Gorda 33950) Cardiovascular equipment, golf-enhancement program, free weights, yoga, Tai Chi, weight machines, tennis courts, baby-sitting, massage and other spa services.

Hiking

Charlotte Harbor Environmental Center (941-575-5435; www.checflorida.org; 10941 Burnt Store Rd., Punta Gorda 33955) Four miles of nature trails depart from this center, part of the State Buffer Preserve.

Kiwanis Park (941-627-1628; 3100 Donora St., Port Charlotte 33952; at Victoria Ave.) Here's a nice place to hike or jog while the kids entertain themselves on the playground. Nature and fitness trails thread through the woods and alongside a creek where turtles swim.

Hunting

Given southwest Florida's heightened environmental consciousness, most shooting of wildlife is done with a camera. But the Charlotte Harbor coast's wilderness does provide opportunities for hunting various species. The most popular game are wild hogs, deer, doves, snipe, quail, turkey, duck, and coot.

This rustic shed was built at Babcock Wilderness Adventures for the filming of Sean Connery's Just Cause. Karen T. Bartlett

To hunt in Florida preserves, you must obtain a state license plus a Wildlife Management Area stamp (941-637-2150). Early-season hunters need a quota permit, which is awarded randomly in a drawing in June from applications submitted to the Game and Fresh Water Fish Commission. Special permits are also required for muzzle-loading guns, archery, and turkey, migratory bird, or waterfowl hunting. Daily use permit fees are levied.

For more information about hunting seasons and bag limits, pick up a copy of *Florida Hunting Handbook & Regulations Summary* when you buy your license.

Cypress Lodge at Babcock Wilderness Adventure (941-637-0551, 800-500-5583; www.babcock wilderness.com; 8000 State Rd. 31, Punta Gorda 33982) Experienced guides take guests hunting for wild turkey, quail, and wild hogs.

Fred C. Babcock–Cecil M. Webb Wildlife Management Area (941-575-5768; 29200 Tucker Grade, Port Charlotte 33955) Some 65,000 acres, one of Florida's 62 designated hunting preserves. Advance permission is required. There is a public shooting range on the property, accessible from Tucker Grade via Rifle Range Rd. The range opens daily during daylight hours but closes the fourth Saturday of each month until 2pm for hunter education training.

Kid's Stuff

Fish Cove Adventure Golf (941-627-5393; 4949 Tamiami Trail, Port Charlotte 33980) Two 18-hole putt-putt golf courses and a bounce house. Open daily 10am to 11pm. Admission for 18 holes of golf is $4.99 to $6.99.

KidSpace (941-627-1628; Maracaibo St. and Avacado Rd., Port Charlotte) A county park created by the community expressly for kids, with a cool fortlike playground, baseball, and picnicking.

Pelican Pete's Playland (941-475-2008; 3101 McCall Rd. S., Englewood 34224) Miniature golf, kiddie train, go-carts for various age levels, batting cages, game room, and snack bar. Open daily; hours change according to season. Fees are charged per activity.

Tringali Recreational Complex Skating (941-473-1018; 3460 McCall Rd. S., Englewood 34224) Weekly skate parties for elementary and middle school kids and families; holiday kids' programs.

Racquet Sports

Boca Grande Community Center (941-964-2564; 131 First St. W., Boca Grande 33921) Two lit courts.

Charlotte Health & Racquet Club (941-629-2223; 3250 Loveland Blvd., Port Charlotte 33980) Racquetball, squash, tennis, cardio equipment, universal weights, fitness and martial arts classes.

McGuire Park (32236 McGuire Ave., Port Charlotte) Four lit hard-surface courts.

The Punta Gorda Club (941-505-1055; 2905 Tamiami Trail, Punta Gorda 33950) Tennis courts plus other sports and fitness facilities; baby-sitting available.

Tringali Recreational Complex (941-473-1018; 3460 McCall Rd. S., Englewood 34223)

Shelling

You'll find some shells on the beaches along the Charlotte Harbor coast, but if you're a serious beachcomber, you'll head south to the Island Coast.

Shelling Charters

Ko Ko Kai Charter Boat Service (941-474-2141; 5040 N. Beach Rd., Englewood Beach 34223; at Ko Ko Kai Resort) Shelling excursions on and around the islands of Gasparilla, Palm, Cayo Costa, Cabbage Key, Upper Captiva, and Captiva.

Spas

Charles of the Village Salon & Day Spa (941-639-6300, 888-753-6115; www.charles ofthevillage.com; 1200 W. Retta Esplanade, Punta Gorda 33950; at Fishermen's Village) Massage, wraps, scrubs, polish, facials, and beauty services. Packages available.

Water Sports
Sailboarding & Surfing
Bikes & Boards (941-474-2019; 966 S. McCall Rd., Englewood 34223) Rents sailboards and sells and services surfboards and skim boards.

Island Bike 'N Beach (941-964-0711; 333 Park Ave., Boca Grande 33921) Rents boogie and skim boards.

Snorkeling & Scuba
The best underwater sightseeing lies offshore some distance, where divers find a few wrecks and other manmade structures.

Wildlife Spotting
The Charlotte Harbor coast is a haven for many of Florida's threatened and endangered species, including Florida panthers (this relative of the mountain lion is yellow, not black, and is characterized by a kink in its tail), bobcats, manatees, brown pelicans, wood storks, and black skimmers. **Manasota Key** hosts the largest nesting sea turtle population on the Gulf Coast. White pelicans migrate to the region in winter. Look for them on sandbars and small mangrove islands in the bays and estuaries. They congregate in flocks and feed cooperatively by herding fish. The **Cape Haze area** between Englewood and Boca Grande is known for its nesting ospreys and bald eagles. **Lemon Bay Park** and **Cedar Point Park** afford the best opportunities to see the nests. Look for sandhill cranes on golf courses and in other grasslands.

At **Babcock Ranch,** a massive preserve east of Punta Gorda, you can see native sandhills, reintroduced American bison, and contained Florida panthers, along with lots of alligators (which are farmed there).

On **Gasparilla Island** you may spot an iguana in the wild—or trying to cross the road, for that matter. Though not native, they have established a colony along the bike path south of Boca Grande.

Intracoastal Waterway channel markers keep boaters in deep water and ospreys in nesting sites.
Karen T. Bartlett

Nature Preserves & Eco-Attractions
CEDAR POINT ENVIRONMENTAL PARK
941-475-0769.
www.charlottecountyfl.com/parks/cedarpointpark.html.
2300 Placida Rd, Englewood 34224.
Off Route 775.
Admission: Free.

Bald eagles, marsh rabbits, bobcats, gopher tortoises, and great horned owls are the stars of this 62-acre preserve, where free guided nature walks are offered on weekends and other days by appointment. It borders the Lemon Bay Aquatic Preserve.

CHARLOTTE HARBOR ENVIRONMENTAL CENTER

941-575-5435.
www.checflorida.org.
10941 Burnt Store Rd., Punta Gorda 33955.
Hours: 8–3 Mon.–Sat. and 11–3–Sun.; guided trail walks at 10am in-season, by appointment in summer.
Admission: Free.

Conducts guided tours around 4 miles of nature trails through pine and palmetto flatlands, hammocks, and marshes, where alligators and bobcats live. Also, educational exhibits about local wildlife.

LEMON BAY PARK & ENVIRONMENTAL CENTER

941-474-3065.
570 Bay Park Blvd., Englewood 34223.
Admission: Free.

Its 195 acres of mangrove forest, wetlands, pinelands, and scrub are home to bald eagles and other creatures of the sky, woods, and water. Experience its nature trails, butterfly garden, indoor environmental displays, and educational programs and guided walks.

PEACE RIVER WILDLIFE CENTER

941-637-3830.
www.peaceriverwildlifecenter.org.
3400 W. Marion Ave., Punta Gorda 33950.
At Ponce de León Park.
Hours: 11am–3pm daily.
Admission: Donations requested.

A rescue and rehabilitation facility that conducts tours among cages of baby possums, taped-together gopher tortoises, and other rescued and recovering animals. You can also self-tour the outdoor bird aviary. A board lists the current rehabilitating and recently released patients. It accepts about 1,300 orphaned, displaced, and injured creatures each year.

Wildlife Tours & Charters
BABCOCK WILDERNESS ADVENTURES

941-637-0551, 800-500-5583.
www.babcockwilderness.com.
8000 SR 31, Punta Gorda 33982.
Hours: Tours 9am–3pm Nov.–May; mornings only June–Oct.
Admission: $17.95 adults, $9.95 children 3–12 (plus tax). Advance reservations required.

On a 90-minute swamp-buggy-bus ride through 90,000-acre Crescent B Ranch and Telegraph Cypress Swamp you will spot Old Florida wildlife, including white-tailed deer, relocated bison, fenced-in Florida panthers, wild turkeys, sandhill cranes, squirrels, and alligators. The driver gives an onboard demonstration with a live baby gator and leads a boardwalk hike through a cypress swamp to see the panthers. The adventure takes place on an actual ranch that dates back to the cow-hunting era. Cattle are still raised here, as well as alligators. Off-road bike tours and night tours are also available. A restaurant, live snake

The shy panther is rarely seen in the wilds of southwest Florida, where it makes its home.

Karen T. Bartlett

display, gift shop, and a small natural history museum set in a cabin used in Sean Connery's movie *Just Cause* (filmed partly on site) provide other activities and accommodations. This is one of Charlotte Harbor coast's finest attractions.

GRANDE TOURS

941-697-8825.
www.grandetours.com.
12575 Placida Rd., PO Box 281, Placida 33946.
Hours: Most tours arranged daily.

Deck boat and kayaking tours of Myakka River and Charlotte Harbor Aquatic Preserve, led by a naturalist. The "Sea Life Excursion" features seine net pulling to collect and study marine life. The "Back Country Adventure" combines boat and kayak touring.

SHOPPING

Shopping Centers & Malls

Boca Grande (Park Ave.) Despite the millionaires and power brokers who make Boca Grande their winter home, shopping here is low-key and affordable, with shades of historic quaintness. The restored railroad depot houses gift and apparel boutiques; there's more in back at Railroad Plaza. Across the street you'll find an eccentric general store and a department store that's been there forever, both of which set a somewhat funky tone. **Sam Murphy Park** presents a serene place to rest alongside a gentle waterfall pool and under shade trees. Don't visit in August and September, when the town literally closes down.

Downtown Punta Gorda Centered around Marion and Olympia Avenues, both one-way streets, between Nesbit Street and Tamiami Trail South, you'll find a quaint historic downtown that's undergone a renaissance. Most of the shops—simple, neighborly, and much more affordable than comparables in Sarasota and Naples—reside along West Marion Avenue. Brick-paved Sullivan Street features old residences under colorful new coats of paint reborn into gift shops and galleries. Streetscaping includes old-fashioned streetlamps, alley arcades, historic murals, street sculptures, and park benches. Every third Thursday from 5 to 8pm business owners host **Gallery Walk** with live music, art, food, and a chance to meet local artists.

Fishermen's Village (941-639-8721, 800-639-0020; www.fishville.com; 1200 W. Retta Esplanade, Punta Gorda 33950) More than 40 shops and restaurants occupy a transformed crab-packing plant. This is Punta Gorda's most hyper center of activity, the site of festivals and social events. There's docking, lodging, charter boats, and fishing from the docks, besides shopping and dining, geared generally toward seniors. A preponderance

Fishermen's Village gives a nautical spin to shopping. Charlotte County Visitors Bureau

of nautical clothing and gifts are reflective of the motif. **Sunset Stroll at the Village** takes place the first Tuesday of the month during season and includes live entertainment, fashion shows, demonstrations, prizes, and food samples from 5 to 8.

Olde Englewood Village Dearborn Street, Englewood's main drag, has done some sprucing up in the past years. The old historic buildings hold fun-to-browse secondhand shops, galleries, and other surprises. Olde Englewood Village Emporium is a mini-mall with a backyard courtyard.

Port Charlotte Town Center (941-624-4447; www.simon.com; 1441 Tamiami Trail, Port Charlotte 33948) An indoor megamall with movie theaters and more than 90 commercial enterprises, including Burdines, Sears, and other chain outlets and specialty shops, such as Sam Goody and Old Navy.

Antiques & Collectibles
The Cottage Experience (941-575-5611; 105 W. Marion Ave., Punta Gorda 33950; downtown) An adorable antique shop with home furnishings and accessories: linens, teapots, tablecloths, dining room tables, and the like.

Harbour Inn Antique Mall (941-625-6126; www.theharbourinn.com; 5000 Tamiami Trail, Charlotte Harbor 33980) More than 50 dealers selling antique furniture, dolls, china, books, and art. Antique fair held the second Saturday of most months. Have afternoon tea in the Tea Room.

Mecca Antique Mall (941-575-6767; 10381 Tamiami Trail, Punta Gorda 33950) More than 30 dealers selling glassware, furniture, toys, pottery, jewelry, nautical items, and more.

Books
All Books (941-505-0345; 111 W. Marion Ave., Punta Gorda 33950; downtown) Used, rare, and hard-to-find volumes, local authors, and current books.

Ruhama's Books in the Sand (941-964-5800; www.mybocagrande.com; 5800 Gasparilla Rd., Boca Grande 33921; at Courtyard Plaza) Books of local interest and for beach reading; cards, knitting supplies, and gifts.

Clothing

Captain's Landing (941-637-6000; www.fishville.com/boutiques; 1200 W. Retta Esplanade #24, Punta Gorda 33950; at Fishermen's Village) Men's casual clothing with a nautical and fishing flair; also formal wear.

Courtyard Boutique & Gift Shop (941-637-1226; www.fishville.com/boutiques; 1200 W. Retta Esplanade #9, Punta Gorda 33950; at Fishermen's Village) Kicky women's fashions and accessories for both casual and dressy occasions.

Giuditta (941-639-8701; 322 Sullivan St., Punta Gorda 33950; downtown) Exotic patterns and finely tailored styles for the sophisticated woman; mostly formal and dress-up fashions.

The Island Bummer (941-964-2636; Boca Grande 33921; at Railroad Plaza) Casual, cotton, loose-fitting sportswear perfect for Florida climes.

Nichole's Collections (941-575-1911; www.fishville.com/boutiques; 1200 W. Retta Esplanade #12, Punta Gorda 33950; at Fishermen's Village) Fine cotton and casual women's fashions.

Sea Witch Boutique (941-460-9599; 425 Dearborn St., Englewood 34223) Cute and unusual women's casual wear.

Consignment

Carly's Consignment (941-575-1191; 215 W. Olympia Ave., Punta Gorda 33950) Designer clothing, home accessories, and collectibles.

Jim Birth's Consignment Shoppe (941-575-8685; 131-F E. Marion Ave., Punta Gorda 33950) Furniture, books, pottery, and other tableware.

Flea Markets & Bazaars

Rainbow Flea Market (941-629-1223; 4628 Tamiami Trail, Charlotte Harbor 33980) Browsing in air-conditioned comfort 9–4 Friday through Sunday.

Galleries

Grass Roots Gallery (941-473-8782; www.grassrootsfl.com; 411 W. Dearborn St., Englewood 34223) Talented artists' collections of works in metal, fused glass, burlap, ceramics, oils, and photography.

Lemon Tree Gallery (941-474-5700; Dearborn St., Englewood 34223) Bright yellow on the outside, soothing watercolors on the inside, along with art photography, whimsical copper wall sculptures, and jewelry—all tropically inclined.

Paradise! (941-964-0774; 340 Park Ave., Boca Grande 33921) Small but containing Boca's best selection, this gallery carries works by island artists and artisans and emerging Florida and national artists.

Presseller Gallery (941-639-7776; www.pressellergallery.com; 213 W. Olympia Ave., Punta Gorda 33950; downtown) Punta Gorda's most sophisticated gallery, carrying local photography, paintings, and sculptures—with a deli, to boot.

Sea Grape Art Gallery (941-575-1718; 113 W. Marion Ave., Punta Gorda 33950) Downtown Punta Gorda is growing a strong reputation for art, with its around-town murals and street sculptures. It grows stronger at the Sea Grape, which displays and sells the fine art and affordable paintings, pottery, jewelry, and three-dimensional art of co-op members, who staff the gallery, so you have a chance to meet the artists.

Smart Studio & Art Gallery (941-964-0519; www.smart-studio-fl.com; 370 Park Ave., Boca Grande 33921) Shows and sells paintings of prolific wintering artist Wini Smart as well as other decorative arts. Closed in the off-season.

General Stores
Gill's Grocery & Deli Market (941-964-2506; 5800 Gasparilla Rd., Boca Grande 33921; at The Courtyard) Beach needs, clothes, gifts, wine, deli items. Delivery available.

Gifts
Laff Out Loud (941-505-2067; www.fishville.com/shops; 1200 W. Retta Esplanade #14, Punta Gorda 33950; at Fishermen's Village) Whimsical toys for all ages: stuffed animals, dolls, puppets, lava lamps, and other nostalgic memorabilia.

Pirate's Ketch (941-637-0299; www.fishville.com/shops; 1200 W. Retta Esplanade #44, Punta Gorda 33950; at Fishermen's Village) Tasteful nautical clocks and lamps, weather vanes, seashell kitsch, framed sea charts, original art and prints.

Red Pelican (941-474-6564; 1350 Beach Rd., Englewood Beach 34223) You can find something unusual for everyone among this showroom of wall hangings, sea-themed gifts, handmade jewelry, stuffed toys and other kids' stuff, and creative beach wear.

Scrooge's Gifts (941-575-9915; 308 Sullivan St., Punta Gorda 33950; downtown) As the name hints, Christmas comes all year-round here, but you'll find more than ornaments and holiday items. Despite the somewhat tacky outward appearance, inside there are taste-ful Victorian and cottage-style gifts at delightfully affordable prices.

Jewelry
Al Morgan (941-637-0946; 119 W. Marion Ave., Punta Gorda 33950; downtown) Showcases of select, one-of-a-kind designer rings, bracelets, and necklaces for men and women.

Fine Things Jewelry (941-964-2166; www.mybocagrande.com; 321 Park Ave., Boca Grande 33921; at Serendipity Gallery, Old Theater Building) Designer jewelry.

Paradise Jewelers (941-475-2396; 3700 N. Access Rd., Englewood 34224) Custom designs, nautical pieces, diamonds, gems, and repair.

Kitchenware & Home Decor
The Artistic Gourmet (941-575-6666; 117 W. Marion Ave., Punta Gorda 33950; down-town) A small but complete and affordable selection of spices, sauces, gourmet products, table and bar ware.

The Caged Parrot (941-637-8949; www.fishville.com/shops; 1200 W. Retta Esplanade #1, Punta Gorda 33950; at Fishermen's Village) Garden accessories, wood-block models of Punta Gorda buildings, fanciful wall hangings, tin sculpture wall animals, and wind chimes.

Daylilies (941-473-1840; 477 W. Dearborn St., Englewood 34223) Furniture and decorative items in tropical-jungle and marine-life motifs.

Wish You Were Here (941-460-1829; 452 W. Dearborn St., Englewood 34223) Kitsch to cute in Florida accessories and furnishings: pink flamingoes, bamboo candles, barware, lamps, and frames.

Sporting Goods

Champs Sports (941-627-5556; 1441 Tamiami Trail, Port Charlotte 33948; at Port Charlotte Town Center) Clothes, shoes, and equipment for tennis, aerobics, weight training, and all ball sports.

CALENDAR OF EVENTS

April

Punta Gorda Block Party (Punta Gorda) Community celebration, with music, food, crafts, and a variety of events. Early in the month.

May

Charlotte Harbor–Florida Fishing Tournament (941-625-0804) Thousands of dollars in prizes; includes a Kids' Day and barbecue. Monthlong.

Florida Frontier Days (several locations in Charlotte County)

Ladies' Day Tarpon Tournament (941-964-0568) All-woman, all-release competition held on Mother's Day.

Taste of Charlotte (941-627-3539; Fishermen's Village, Punta Gorda) Feast on food, art, and music and this restaurant cook-off. One day early in the month.

June

Wildlife/Animal Awareness Expo (941-575-3007, 800-639-1054; www.fishville.com; 1200 W. Retta Esplanade, Punta Gorda 33950) A Saturday's worth of live-animal demonstrations and educational exhibits early in the month.

World's Richest Tarpon Tournament (941-964-0568; Boca Grande) A community festival held midmonth, awarding a top prize of up to $125,000.

July

Kids' Fishing Day (941-639-5723; www.fishville.com; 1200 W. Retta Esplanade, Punta Gorda; at Fishermen's Village) A day for kid casting.

October

Salute to the Arts (throughout Charlotte County) A weeklong showcase of the performing and visual arts. Late in the month.

December

Christmas Peace River Lighted Boat Parade (941-639-3720) A procession of vessels in holiday attire. Saturday evening early in the month.

Karen T. Bartlett

5

Sanibel Island & The Island Coast

Sand, Shells, and Serenity

A dreamy, tropical land adorned with a necklace of islands, this slab of coastline resembles, more than any of its neighboring regions, the laid-back islands of the Keys, Bahamas, and Caribbean. Tourism pundits brand it "The Beaches of Sanibel & Fort Myers" to capitalize on its most reputable parts. More developed than its Charlotte Harbor neighbors and more relaxed than what lies to the south and at the Sarasota end of things, the Island Coast gives us the leafy greenery for the southwest Florida sandwich. It is considered one of Florida's most ecology-minded resort areas. How it balances its dual roles as wildlife preserver and tourism mecca has served as a model for state ecotourism.

At their northern extreme, the islands are mired in an Old Florida time frame. **Cabbage Key, Useppa Island, Cayo Costa,** and **Pine Island** gave birth to the Gulf Coast's legacy of fishing lifestyles, back when the Calusa lived off the sea. On Pine Island, fishing, crabbing, and shrimping are still a way of life and survival, despite recent net-ban laws that make it less and less profitable. Many commercial fishermen have turned to charter captaining in the wake of the new legislation. In their May, 2003 issue, *Field & Stream* editors named Pine Island among the 25 hottest American fishing destinations. Protected from rampant resort development by its lack of beaches, Pine Island clings to an older way of life like a barnacle to a mangrove prop. **Cayo Costa** and **North Captiva,** both largely state owned, remain the uncut jewels in the Island Coast necklace. Useppa Island and Cabbage Key preserve another era of island bygones, days graced by celebrity sporting types in search of escape, adventure, and tarpon.

Out in San Carlos Bay, to the south, the islands of Sanibel and Captiva developed quietly but steadily through the years. At various times in the past, the islands have supported a government lighthouse reservation, citrus and tomato farms, communities of fishermen (who sometimes dealt in rum-smuggling on the side), and a coconut plantation. From 1910 through 1940, wealthy notables made their way to the islands, intent on the relative anonymity that the wilds afforded them. Teddy Roosevelt discovered Captiva Island in 1914. Charles Lindbergh and his wife, Anne Morrow Lindbergh, visited often, inspiring her to pen her well-loved seashell analogies in *Gift from the Sea*. Pulitzer Prize-winning cartoonist and conservationist Jay N. "Ding" Darling gained national attention for Captiva and Sanibel Islands by fighting for the preservation of their natural attributes during his winter visits. His efforts sparked the development of the Island Coast's environmental conscience.

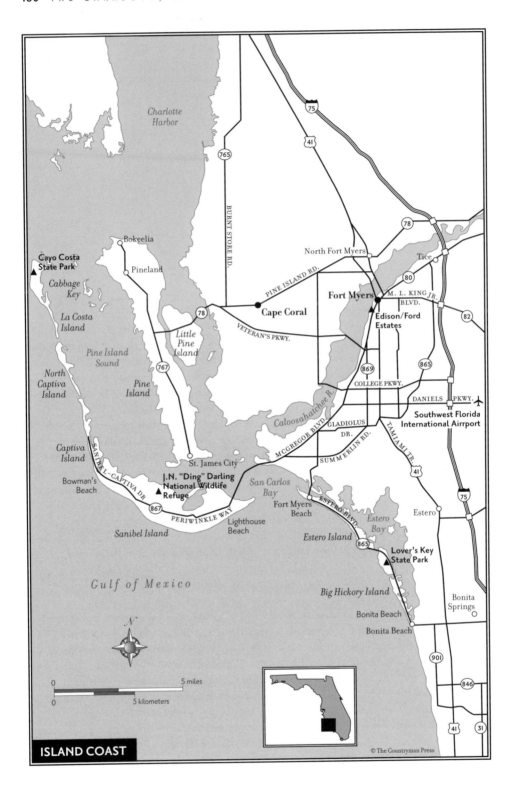

ISLAND COAST

© The Countryman Press

The Island Coast has a reputation for birds, shells, and all things natural. Karen T. Bartlett

Fort Myers Beach on Estero Island is synonymous with gulf shrimp, beach bustle, and spring breakers. Southward, the maze of islands including **Lovers Key** and **Mound Key** is reminiscent of the coast's earliest times, with primeval estuaries, intact shell mounds, whispers of buried pirate treasure, and fishing lifestyles.

On the mainland, **Cape Coral** once served as a hunting refuge for steel magnate Ogden Phipps, who vacationed in Naples. The second largest city in Florida in area, it was something of a developer's folly. The young city was cleared, canalled, and platted in 1970 and is slowly growing into itself, with a downtown revitalization effort currently underway. **North Fort Myers** borders it on the east, the Caloosahatchee River on the south.

Across the river from North Fort Myers and Cape Coral, **Fort Myers** has evolved from its fort status of Seminole wartime into the hub of communications, government, and transportation for the region. Cattle barons gave the community its early wild temperament; Thomas Edison and his class of successful entrepreneurs elevated it above its cowtrail streets.

Most unusual circumstances created the small community along Tamiami Trail named **Estero,** south of Fort Myers. The 19th-century religious cult that called itself the Koreshan Unity first settled there, led by Cyrus Teed, or Koresh, as he called himself. The Koreshans believed that the earth clings to the inside of a hollow globe like coconut meat to its shell. Members practiced celibacy and communal living. They also experimented with tropical gardening, bringing to southwest Florida the mango and avocado. The site of their brief stay has been preserved and recreated by the state, together with their buildings and the natural Florida that they discovered there.

Between Fort Myers and Estero, **San Carlos Park** escalated to booming status with the genesis of a state university a few years back. On its shirttails come shopping centers, restaurants, and other commercial enterprises that fill in the gap that once existed between quiet towns.

LODGING

Maine may boast its bed & breakfasts, Vermont its historic inns, and Colorado its ski lodges. But when vacationers envision Florida, it's the beachside resorts that flash first through the mental slide projector. The Island Coast has perfected this image of sun-and-sand abandon. Megaresorts are designed to keep guests (and their disposable income) on property. Not only can you eat lunch, rent a bike, and get a tennis lesson, you can hire a masseur, charter a boat for a sunset sail, play golf, and enroll your child in Sandcastle Building 101. These destination resorts are in business to fulfill fantasies, and they spare no effort to achieve that goal.

Side by side with the resorts, you'll also find homey little cottages that have held their ground against buyouts and takeovers. Existing between the two extremes are a wide variety of high-rise condos, funky hotels, retirement resorts, mom-and-pop motels, fishing lodges, and inns.

Privately owned second homes and condominiums provide another source of upscale accommodations along the Island Coast. For families or other groups, these can often be a better value than hotel rooms. Timeshare rental was invented on Sanibel Island, and you'll find plenty of these options still around. Vacation brokers who match visitors with such properties are listed under "Home & Condo Rentals" at the end of this section.

The highlights of Island Coast hospitality listed here—alphabetically by town—include the best and freshest in the local industry. While spanning the range of endless possibilities, this list concentrates on those properties that break out of the skyscraping, wicker-and-floral mold. Toll-free 800, 888, or 877 reservation numbers, where available, are listed after local numbers.

Pricing codes are explained below. They are normally per person/double occupancy for hotel rooms and per unit for efficiencies, apartments, cottages, suites, and villas. The range spans low- and high-season rates. Many resorts offer off-season packages at special rates and free lodging for children. Pricing does not include the 6 percent Florida sales tax. Some large resorts add service gratuities or maid charges, and Lee County imposes a 3 percent tourist tax, as well, which goes toward beach and environmental maintenance.

Rate Categories

Inexpensive	Up to $75
Moderate	$75 to $150
Expensive	$150 to $200
Very Expensive	$200 and up

(An asterisk after the pricing designation indicates that the rate includes at least a continental breakfast in the cost of lodging and occasionally other meals as described in the listing.)

The following abbreviations are used for credit card information:

AE: American Express
MC: MasterCard
D: Discover Card
V: Visa
DC: Diners Club

Accommodations

CABBAGE KEY

CABBAGE KEY INN
Innkeepers: Rob & Phyllis Wells.
239-283-2278.
www.cabbagekey.com.
PO Box 200, Pineland 33945.
Price: Moderate to Expensive
Credit Cards: MC, V.

Cabbage Key appeals to vacationers seeking an authentic Old Florida experience. Built on an unbridged island atop an ancient shell mound, the inn and its guest accommodations are reminiscent of the 1930s, when novelist Mary Roberts Rinehart used native cypress and pine to construct a home for her son and his bride. Six cypress-paneled guest-rooms in the inn and six cottages (two of them historic) accommodate overnighters. Four of the cottages have kitchens, and four have their own private docks. A couple of the cottages date back to the Rinehart era; the others are modern homes. The restaurant and its currency-papered bar attract boaters and water tours for lunch, but the island shuts down to a whisper come sundown. The inn can give you a list of boat charters from Captiva or Pine Island for transportation to and from the island. Boat rentals are available for day use.

CAPE CORAL
CASA LOMA MOTEL
Owners: Karen and Bob Bothwell, Brenda and Rick Fioretti.
239-549-6000, 877-227-2566.
www.casalomamotel.com.
3608 Del Prado Blvd., Cape Coral 33904.
Price: Moderate.
Credit Cards: AE, D, MC, V.

Cape Coral doesn't offer a lot in the way of resorts, but if you're looking for a place to stay while enjoying the town's family attractions or somewhere less costly than the beaches, this tidy little property does have its own charm and canal-front views and docks in the bargain. Its 49 efficiencies are each stocked with a kitchenette containing a microwave, minifridge, and stovetop. Reclining chairs in some rooms and stylish motel furnishings provide comfort. Porches and balconies overlook the canal and paved sundeck. Nicely landscaped grounds complement the Spanish villa architecture, with its red roof and arched balcony openings. Waterside tables, loungers, and a tiki-covered deck offer scenic places to relax.

CAPTIVA ISLAND
✪ JENSEN'S TWIN PALM COTTAGES & MARINA
Owners: David, John, and Jimmy Jensen.
239-472-5800.
www.gocaptiva.com.
1507 Captiva Dr., PO Box 460, Captiva Island 33924.
Price: Moderate to Expensive.
Credit Cards: AE, MC, V.

One of Captiva's most affordable lodging options is also one of its homier places. You get an immediate sense of neighborliness on the grounds. Perhaps it has to do with its

Cabbage Key hearkens back to the days when the rich-but-rugged made their way to the Island Coast.
Karen T. Bartlett

partiality to fisherfolk—its bayside docks, fishing charters, boat rentals, and bait supplies. I expected to find the accommodations in that same vein, where what's out in the water matters more than what's indoors. The 14 units looked plain enough from the outside: white stucco cottages with tin roofs and a splash of blue trim. Each screened-in porch holds a plain picnic table. Inside, the one- and two-bedroom cottages are entirely cheery, with their immaculate white tongue-and-groove walls, perky curtains, and simple, sturdy wooden furniture. The full kitchens are modern and spotless. Nothing fishy about 'em. Just charming old-island style dressed up comfortable.

SOUTH SEAS RESORT

General Manager: Chris van der Baars.
239-472-5111, 800-CAPTIVA.
www.south-seas-resort.com.
5400 Plantation Rd., Captiva Island 33924.
Price: Very Expensive.
Credit Cards: D, DC, MC, V.

South Seas is one of the great destination resorts of Florida, where you can enter through the security gates and leave one week later without ever having gone off property. Celebrities crave its privacy and discretion. South Seas offers any type of getaway dwelling you could imagine, from tennis villas to beach cottages to harborside hotel rooms—nine different types of accommodations in all. Rooms are furnished with stylish, high-quality pieces and appointments. The property monopolizes a third of the island with more than 600 guest units—both privately owned and otherwise—eight eateries poolside to formal, lounges, shops, a nine-hole golf course, a fitness center, a yacht harbor, 18 swimming pools, 21 tennis courts, boating, fishing, water-sports equipment rentals and lessons, excursion cruises, Fun Factory recreation program for children, and 2.5 miles of beach. A free trolley takes guests around the 330-acre property.

'TWEEN WATERS INN

General Manager: Jeff Shuff.
239-472-5161, 800-223-5865.
www.tween-waters.com.
15941 Captiva Rd., PO Box 249, Captiva Island 33924.
Price: Moderate to Expensive.*
Credit Cards: AE, D, MC, V.

'Tween Waters spans the gap between beach cottage lodging and modern super resort. Built early in the 1930s, when wildlife patron "Ding" Darling kept a cottage there, the property shows glints of Old Florida architecture (some of it rather unglamorous) and easygoing attitudes. Compact but complete, it holds 149 rooms, cottages (some of them newly restored and quite charming), efficiencies, and apartments as well as restaurants, a marina, tennis courts, and a swimming pool. Named for its location between two shores at Captiva's narrowest span, the inn lies across the road from a length of beach that is usually lightly populated because it lacks nearby public parking. Its marina, one of its best features, is the island's top water sports center, with charters, tours, boat and canoe rentals, and the Canoe & Kayak Restaurant. The Crow's Nest lounge provides the island's best nightlife. Continental breakfast is included in the rates.

Fort Myers
✪ HOLIDAY INN RIVERWALK

General Manager: Peter Demetris.
239-334-3434, 800-664-7775.
www.hiriverwalk.com.
2220 W. First St., Fort Myers 33901.
Price: Moderate to Expensive.
Credit Cards: AE, D, DC, MC, V.

This tropical riverside gem has struggled through downtown's downturns and hopefully will continue to survive as it spruces for an anticipated revival. The marble-floored lobby introduces a pineapple-plantation theme with coral-rock block walls and West Indian-style furnishings. The 147 rooms and suites, which underwent major upgrades in 2003, are lavishly furnished, some with private whirlpool baths. The lushly landscaped courtyard holds a pool, kiddie pool, playground, spa, fitness room, and waterside restaurant and outdoor bar.

✪ SANIBEL HARBOUR RESORT & SPA
Managing Director: Brian Holly.
239-466-4000, 800-767-7777.
www.sanibel-resort.com.
17260 Harbour Pointe Dr., Fort Myers 33908.
Price: Expensive to Very Expensive.
Credit Cards: AE, D, DC, MC, V.

Stunningly beautiful for a property its size, the Sanibel Harbour Resort capitalizes on Florida style and a spectacular location. Not actually on Sanibel Island as the name suggests, the resort's 401 rooms, suites, and condos are located on a chin of land across San Carlos Bay from the island, on an inlet known as Sanibel Harbour. Half the units have water views of either the bay or nearby estuaries. A boutique inn holds 107 of the rooms, decorated in European style and shiny brass and more intimate than tower accommodations. The suites feature heavy four-poster beds and oversized bathtubs. The property encompasses three restaurants, a dining yacht, five outdoor swimming pools, lit Har-Tru tennis courts, a completely made-over spa offering more than 60 services, and a small bayside beach. One of the bars has a 280-degree view of the sea, with a lovely, breezy cocktail patio. The Tarpon House, which serves family-friendly seafood, is set on a porch atop a waterside pool that brings to mind exotic Roman baths. Chez Le Bear provides a fine-dining experience. The fitness center, canoe/kayak trail, and sun sports charters and rentals provide guests a well-rounded menu of fitness and recreation options. Kids Klub takes youngsters on nature hikes and a variety of other activities.

All that's missing from Sanibel Harbour Resort's Gatsbian setting and Old Florida demeanor is the bootleg gin. Sanibel Harbour Resort & Spa

FORT MYERS BEACH
THE OUTRIGGER BEACH RESORT
General Manager: Dianne F. Major.
239-463-3131, 800-655-8997.
www.outriggerfmb.com.
6200 Estero Blvd., Fort Myers Beach 33931.
Price: Moderate to Very Expensive.
Credit Cards: AE, MC, V.

The Outrigger Beach Resort occupies the quiet south end of Fort Myers Beach, where the sand flares wide and gorgeous and is protected by a sandbar that's a bird hangout. The 30-year-old, 144-room resort boasts a casual, unstructured vacationing style that works well for families. Activity centers around its white-fenced pool and tiki bar deck area, where guests can sun and mingle. Or rent water-sports equipment through the front desk. Rooms are compact, modern, and furnished simply. Five types of accommodations range from the traditional to efficiencies with full kitchens. Prices also depend on whether they're on the first or second floor and the quality of the view. Shuffleboard, a putting green, beach volleyball, a little café, and live weekend and Wednesday night entertainment keep the place vivacious.

PINK SHELL BEACH RESORT & SPA
General Manager: John Dithmer.
239-463-6181 or 888-847-8939.
www.pinkshell.com.
275 Estero Blvd., Fort Myers Beach 33931.
Price: Moderate to Very Expensive.
Credit Cards: AE, D, DC, MC, V.

After $70 million in renovations, this resort barely resembles the longtime beach institution of its former self. Set between bay waters and 1,500 feet of beach, the 12-acre property has, in the past couple of years, gotten rid of its Old Florida cottages to build more high-rises, an Octapool fantasy water feature with an underwater theme, and a world-class spa. To the original Sanibel View Villas of 60 gulfside kitchenette suites and Beach Villas of 28 two-bedroom condos, the White Sand Villas—new in March 2004—add 92 one- and two-bedroom units with floor-to-ceiling gulf-facing windows and a central reception area with a mammoth stylized banyan tree "growing" through it. All accommodations are privately owned and decorated in tasteful Key West cottage style with a view of the wide, powdery beach and gulf. Captiva Villas, a fourth building slated for completion by 2005, will contain another 43 units, replacing two older low-rises. When completed, the property will have four pools. Three restaurants, a coffee shop/deli, boat docking, and a slew of water-sports rentals and tours complete Pink Shell's reputation as a destination resort at the northern tip of Fort Myers Beach, away from the bustle of the Times Square area.

SILVER SANDS VILLAS
Owners: Tom and Andrea Groves.
239-463-2755, 800-603-0501.
www.silversands-villas.com.
1207 Estero Blvd., Fort Myers Beach 33931.
Price: Moderate to Expensive.
Credit Cards: AE, MC, V.

In the high-rise world of Fort Myers Beach, not much can be found that one could describe as charming. I discovered this notable exception by getting lost. Its assemblage of 20 one- and two-bedroom circa 1935 cottages caught my attention from a side street. With their pale-yellow paint jobs and tin roofs, they make a strong personality statement. Inside they are simple but in character, with white wainscoting and yellow walls, full kitchens in all but two units, and Old Florida-style porches. The compact property, within beach walking distance, holds a small pool, a fountain courtyard, a huge shading banyan tree, canal-front views, tables covered by chikee thatching, and laundry facilities—all behind a picket fence and hibiscus hedge right on the happening strip of Estero Boulevard, from where you hardly notice it. Very congenial and convenient while feeling deliciously hidden away.

PINE ISLAND
BRIDGE WATER INN
Owners: Osi and Steve McCarney.
239-283-2423, 800-378-7666.
www.bridgewaterinn.com.
4331 Pine Island Rd., PO Box 457, Matlacha 33909.
Price: Inexpensive to Moderate.
Credit Cards: AE, MC, V.

In fish-frenzied Pine Island, Matlacha has its share of fishing cottages where what matters is what's biting. Fishing types will also like this tropically bright nine-unit roadside lodge because its wraparound covered deck hangs over the water. Rooms and efficiencies, decorated with distinct style and comfort, open up onto the deck, so you can step right out the door and cast. With leather furniture and eye-catching colors (check out the hanging tropical bird planters made in Colombia from old tires—on sale in the gift shop), Bridge Water is a step up from other local accommodations. Restaurants, fish markets, shops, and galleries are within walking distance.

Sanibel Island
✪ GULF BREEZE COTTAGES AND MOTEL

Owners: Sandi and Charley Hutchings.
239-472-1626, 800-388-2842.
www.gbreeze.com.
1081 Shell Basket Ln., Sanibel Island 33957.
Price: Moderate to Very Expensive (for up to 6 people).
Credit Cards: MC, V.

Pine Island's Bokeelia feels like you've arrived at the far ends of the earth.   Karen T. Bartlett

The address is Shell Basket Lane, and this place is just that charming and seashell oriented. A dozen classic cottages, efficiencies, and duplexes make for the ideal barefoot beach vacation. A basket full of beach toys sits next to the sink and table where you can clean your shells and fish. The grandma and grandpa who have owned Gulf Breeze for more than 20 years love children and treat their guests like family. This property blends old island with new, holding its ground amid low-rise, concrete neighbors. Sea grapes, bougainvillea, Bahama shades, carved balustrades, lattice, and fish-scale siding add a fairy-tale quality.

ISLAND INN

General Manager: Pegge Ford-Elsea.
239-472-1561, 800-851-5088.
www.islandinnsanibel.com.
3111 W. Gulf Dr., PO Box 659, Sanibel Island 33957.
Price: Moderate to Expensive* (two-night minimum for efficiencies and on weekends).
Credit Cards: AE, D, MC, V.

Sanibel's only historic lodging—more than 100 years old—displays all the refinement of Florida's great old inns and hotels but without the snobbery. It has the same congenial and relaxed atmosphere that Granny Matthews, a Sanibel matriarch of renown, created at the turn of the 20th century when she entertained the whole island (including guests from other resorts) at Saturday night barbecues. She also initiated the Sanibel Shell Fair as a way to keep guests busy and hosted it in the lobby, where white wicker, French doors, a lattice-edged dining room, and shell displays now give an immediate impression of immaculate spaciousness and island graciousness. During the winter season (November 15 to April 15) it's a Modified American Plan resort, including breakfast and dinner in its rates. Cottages and lodges house 57 units, all with a view of gentle gulf waves lapping at a shell-covered beach.

Cottages have one or two bedrooms; lodges contain hotel rooms, with either full kitchens or refrigerators only. They can be combined into suites. The resort doesn't pretend to furnish extravagantly; all is done in uncontrived old-island style. That does not translate into shoddiness, however. The Island Inn is owned by shareholders who reinvest profits for constant upgrading. Decor is cheerful, comfortable, and impeccably maintained. Outside each lodge room door sits a wooden table where guests display their shell finds for others to peruse and admire. It's an Island Inn tradition. The atmosphere is saturated with conviviality. Dinner, a coat-and-tie affair, is announced by the blowing of a conch shell. Outdoors, native vegetation is landscaped around tin-roofed structures. A butterfly garden frames a croquet court, a swimming pool sits squarely on the beach, and tennis and shuffleboard provide recreation.

SANIBEL'S SEASIDE INN

General Manager: Jack Reed.
www.seasideinn.com.
239-472-1400, 800-965-7772.
541 E. Gulf Dr., Sanibel Island 33957.
Price: Expensive to Very Expensive.*
Credit Cards: AE, D, DC, MC, V.

I recommend this place to visitors looking for intimacy on the beach without great extravagance. A measure of Key West—banana-yellow tints, tin roofs, and gingerbread-trimmed balconies—creates Seaside Inn's old-island charm. It's the kind of place where you kick off your shoes the first day and don't find them again until you're packing to leave. Kitchen facilities and VCRs come in every studio, beach cottage, and one-, two-, and three-bedroom suite, of which there are 32 in all. A swimming pool, brick-paved deck, complimentary continental breakfast (delivered to your door if you so desire), a video and book lending library, complimentary bike use, and tropical appointments complete the picture of seaside coziness. Use of facilities and amenities at Seaside Inn's sister resorts, including Sundial Beach Resort and Sanibel Inn, is available free of charge to guests. An inter-resort trolley provides transportation.

✪ SUNDIAL BEACH RESORT

General Manager: Pete Adania.
239-472-4151, 800-965-7772.
www.sundialresort.com.
1451 Middle Gulf Dr., Sanibel Island 33957.
Price: Expensive to Very Expensive.
Credit Cards: AE, D, DC, MC, V.

Sundial promises the perfection of a worry-free vacation. Sanibel's fine shelling beach is the focus of the 20-acre resort, which takes its name from a species of shell. In the stunning lobby, a sundial shell mosaic is inset on a marble floor. The resort provides extensive recreation, with 12 tennis courts, five heated swimming pools, bike and beach rental concessions, a fitness center, game room, children's and family programs, and an eco-center complete with touch tank. The lavish main building houses four restaurants—two overlooking the gulf, another serving Japanese food, and a fourth, casual and poolside. Less stylish, low-rise condo buildings are camouflaged by well-maintained vegetation and hold 270 fully equipped units decorated in tropical array and natural wicker. They take advantage of gulf or garden views. Given its high level of service, the Sundial is one of the area's least pretentious and most comfortable properties, especially for families.

USEPPA ISLAND

COLLIER INN & COTTAGES

Resort Manager: Michael Vanneste.
239-283-1061, 888-735-6335.
www.useppa.com.
PO Box 640, Bokeelia 33922.
Price: Expensive to Very Expensive* (minimum stay on weekends and holidays).
Credit Cards: AE, MC, V.

Elegant yet sporty digs at the Collier Inn, just the way Barron himself would have liked it. Collier Inn

Used to be that only club members could enjoy the delicious privacy and historic elitism of Useppa Island. Once an escape for turn-of-the-20th-century celebrities, the island remains exclusive and aloof from the world. Now, if you can afford the price, you can be admitted onto the carefully guarded island by checking into the Collier Inn. The 100-year-old building, the original circa 1900 home to Barron Collier's Izaak Walton Club, holds seven elegant rooms and suites individually designed for classic mood and comfort; historic cottages and the marina reception building comprise another six. Plus, there are privately owned two-bedroom cottages with kitchens available. Guests have access to the Useppa Island Club's full-service marina, Har-Tru tennis courts, swimming pool, manmade beach, croquet, outdoor chess, and fitness center. The pink-paved walkway around the island takes you past historic cottages, bounteous gardens, an ancient shell mound, and the 100-acre island's intriguing historical museum. Collier Inn Restaurant serves daily meals; continental breakfast buffet is included.

Home & Condo Rentals

Hussey Company Real Estate (239-463-3178; 2450 Estero Blvd., Fort Myers Beach 33931) Condos and homes in and around Fort Myers Beach.

1-800-SANIBEL (239-472-1800, 800-726-4235; www.1-800-sanibel.com; 13831 Vector, Fort Myers 33907) Condo, home, and cottage rentals in Sanibel and Captiva.

Sanibel Accommodations (800-237-6004; www.sanibel-captiva.com; 2341 Palm Ridge Rd., Sanibel 33957) Has available an online and print catalog of condo and home rentals on Sanibel and Captiva Islands.

RV Resorts

Fort Myers–Pine Island KOA (239-283-2415, 800-562-8505; www.pineisland koa.com; 5120 Stringfellow Rd., St. James City 33956) 371 sites, cabins, pool, saunas, hot tub, exercise room, tennis court, shuffleboard, horseshoes, lake fishing, and free bus to the beach a couple of times a week.

Groves Campground (239-466-5909; 16175 John Morris Rd., Fort Myers 33908) Close to Sanibel Island, with 298 full hookup sites and swimming pool.

Red Coconut RV Resort (239-463-7200, 888-262-6226; www.redcoconut.com; 3001 Estero Blvd., Fort Myers Beach 33931) Right on the beach but packed in a bit tightly; 250 full hookup sites, on-site trailer rentals, laundry, shuffleboard, cable TV, and car rentals. Write for reservations.

DINING

The Island Coast is home to two of the nation's shellfish capitals. Shrimp—that monarch of edible crustaceans—reigns in Fort Myers Beach, where a fleet of shrimp boats is headquartered and an annual festival pays homage to America's favorite seafood. The sweet, pink gulf shrimp is the trademark culinary delight of the town and its environs. The fish markets of Pine Island, an important commercial fishing and transshipment center, sell all sorts of fresh seafood—oysters, shrimp, scallops, snapper, catfish—but the signature seafood is the blue crab and stone crab that come from local waters.

The following listings cover the variety of Island Coast feasting in these price categories:

Inexpensive	Up to $10
Moderate	$10 to $20
Expensive	$20 to $30
Very Expensive	$30 or more

Cost categories are based on the range of dinner entrée prices, or, if dinner is not served, on lunch entrées. Many restaurants offer early-dining discounts, often called early-bird specials. These rarely are listed on the regular menu and sometimes are not publicized by tip-conscious servers. I have noted restaurants that offer them. Certain restrictions apply, such as time constraints, a specific menu, or number of people first in the door. Call the restaurant and ask about its policy. Those restaurants listed with "Healthy Selections" usually mark such on their menu.

Sizing Up a Shrimp

Gulf shrimp are graded by size and assigned all sorts of vague measurements: jumbo, large, medium-sized, boat grade, etc. The surest way to know what size shrimp you are ordering is to ask for the count-per-pound designation. This will be something like "21–25s," meaning there are 21 to 25 shrimp per pound. "Boat grade" normally designates a mixture of sizes, usually on the small side.

Note: New Florida law forbids smoking inside all restaurants and bars serving food. Smoking is permitted only in restaurants with outdoor seating.

The following abbreviations are used for credit card information and meals:

AE: American Express
D: Discover Card
DC: Diners Club
MC: MasterCard
V: Visa
B: Breakfast
L: Lunch
D: Dinner
SB: Sunday Brunch

CABBAGE KEY
✪ CABBAGE KEY INN
239-283-2278.
www.cabbagekey.com.
PO Box 200, Pineland 33945.
Price: Expensive.
Children's Menu: Yes.
Cuisine: American.
Liquor: Full.
Serving: B, L, D.
Credit Cards: MC, V.
Handicap Access: No.
Reservations: Required for dinner.
Special Features: Historic inn with walls papered in dollar bills left by visiting boaters; accessible only by boat.

Still funky after all these years, Cabbage Key has a reputation among boaters as a safe haven for a beer, a cheeseburger, and all-around friendliness. Everyone's in a good mood at Cabbage Key, particularly the bartender and wait staff. Lunch—the most popular meal—consists of shrimp, salads, stone crab in-season, burgers, sandwiches, and key lime pie. Tour boats bring in crowds, so it can get crazy, with waits for a table often a beer-sodden affair. (If you're driving the boat, you may wish to opt for a walk around the nature trail instead.) Dinner is much quieter, and the local grouper couldn't get any fresher. I recently had it with a chipotle

sauce drizzle and nearly swooned; it ruined me for grouper anywhere else. The scampi shrimp on pasta is another good bet. So are the Bloody Marys.

CAPE CORAL
IGUANA MIA
239-945-7755.
www.iguanamia.com.
1027 E. Cape Coral Pkwy., Cape Coral 33904.
Price: Inexpensive to Moderate.
Children's Menu: Yes.
Cuisine: Mexican-American.
Liquor: Full.
Serving: L, D.
Credit Cards: AE, D, MC, V.
Handicap Access: Yes.
Reservations: No.

This, the original Iguana Mia, spawned others in Fort Myers and Bonita Springs, but we like this one best, even if it means we have to cross the bridge to Cape Coral and pay a toll to get there. It's the most down-to-earth of the three. Sure, it's just as flashy, with its electric-green exterior paint job and nicely rendered interior Mexican frescos; but it retains some of the unpretentious lunchroom ambiance it started out with. Stacked cases of Mexican beer still count as decor elements. And most importantly, the food is flat-out better. Things seem more rushed at the newer places; here it's mañana paced. My husband invariably orders the sour cream chicken chimichanga, a specialty. I—usually already half full from shoveling in huge gobs of the salsa I can't resist with warm, crunchy tortilla chips—like the veggie burrito, nachos, or quesadilla. You're bound to find something you like on the menu—it's huge and lets you do some of your own meal engineering.

RUMRUNNERS
239-542-0200.
At the Cape Harbour Marina.
5848 Cape Harbour Dr., Cape Coral 33914.

Price: Inexpensive to Moderate.
Children's Menu: Yes.
Cuisine: New American.
Liquor: Full.
Serving: L, D.
Credit Cards: AE, D, MC, V.
Handicap Access: No.
Reservations: Yes.
Special Features: Waterfront setting with outdoor seating.

Cape Coral's newest restaurant happens to be one of the most enjoyable in its culinary history. Opened by the people who wow us at Bistro 41 in Fort Myers, it has its own imaginative style and overlooks a mangrove waterway in the midst of new up-market development. Even better: prices are surprisingly affordable for such specialties as seafood potpie—chockful of shrimp, scallops, and crab with a creamy lobster sauce and a flaky pastry sitting atop. We sampled a wide variety of starters, main courses, and desserts besides the potpie and had no complaints except that the calamari could be crispier. In the "loved it" category: portobello and pine nut bisque (the night's special); chicken quesadilla with blackened tomato "jam," salsa fresca, and cumin-scented crème fraîche; spinach and blue cheese salad; vodka penne; angel hair pasta generously decorated with shrimp, scallops, mussels, and torn basil; crème brûlée (totally elegant); and Rumrunners cobbler with a biscuit crust, five berries, diced mango, and vanilla ice cream (totally wonderful). Pasta dishes are available in full and half portions. The building at first seems cold and oversized, but once you're sitting in the glassed room on the water, you immediately warm to the location.

✪ SIAM HUT
239-945-4247.
4521 Del Prado Blvd., Cape Coral 33904.
Price: Inexpensive to Moderate.
Children's Menu: No.
Cuisine: Thai.
Liquor: Beer and wine.
Serving: L, D.
Closed: Sun. and lunch Sat.
Credit Cards: MC, V.
Handicap Access: Yes.
Reservations: No.

A long-standing favorite in Cape Coral, Siam Hut's affordability is matched by its versatility and authentic goodness. You basically can design your own meal from the noodles, stir fried, curry, and fried rice sections. For instance, I recently chose the pad kee mao, a stir-fried rice noodle dish of basil, colorful and crunchy veggies, and chili paste. I had a choice of tofu, beef, pork, chicken, shrimp, or squid to centerpiece that, and I chose the latter—tender, tasty rings set afire by the seasonings. (You also get to pick your degree of spiciness.) The meal was flavorful, filling, and a bargain with the inclusion of fried strips of wonton, soup, and a small iceberg and carrot salad dressed in a tasty peanut vinaigrette. House specialties include fried crispy frog legs with garlic and black pepper, fried whole fish in a variety of preparations, and Thai entrée salads. Go traditional and sit at a floor table on pillows that support your back, or choose one of the more plentiful booths or standard tables and chairs.

CAPTIVA ISLAND
THE BUBBLE ROOM
239-472-5558.
www.bubbleroomrestaurant.com.
15001 Captiva Dr., Captiva Island 33924.
Price: Moderate to Expensive.
Children's Menu: Yes.
Cuisine: American.
Liquor: Full.
Serving: L, D.
Credit Cards: AE, D, DC, MC, V.
Handicap Access: Limited.
Reservations: No.
Special Features: Museumlike displays of '30s and '40s memorabilia.

The Bubble Room is so Captiva—and something you have to experience once. It's especially fun to take kids there. The quirkiness begins outside, where bubbles bedeck the kitsch-cottage structure and lawn gnomes greet you. Inside, the tables are glass-topped showcases filled with jacks, Monopoly money, comic books, dominoes, and assorted toys from the past. A Christmas elves scene, circus plaques, Betty Boop, celebrity photos, a plaster hippo's mouth, and other nostalgic memorabilia fill every wall, phone booth, bathroom door, nook, and cranny. A toy train runs under the ceiling, and servers—Bubble Scouts—wear goofy stuff on their hats. So that's the atmosphere—and you've gotta see it for yourself. The menu continues the frivolity. At lunch, Mae's West is a charbroiled chicken breast sandwich. The Piggly Wiggly barbecued pork sandwich I ordered was delicious, from the sweet bun to the cole slaw heaped on the messy meat. Dinner's Duck Ellington is a tasty rendition of roasted duck with orange and banana sauce. Other snappily titled dishes include Beignet Goodman (crispy light grouper fingers), the Judy Garden (vegetable lasagna), and Eddie Fisherman (grouper topped with Ritz cracker crumbs and pecans, then steamed in a bag). Service is exceptional, considering the tight quarters and volume of business. Other things for which the Bubble Room is known are its basket of bubble bread (yum! cream cheesy), its sticky buns with dinner, and its fabulous desserts. You must leave room for a huge slab of moist and delicious red-velvet cake, the rich almond-studded orange crunch cake, or any of the other many tempting selections.

CAPTIVA SUNSHINE CAFÉ

239-472-6200.
Captiva Village Square, Captiva Dr., Captiva Island 33924.
Price: Moderate to Very Expensive.
Children's Menu: No.

Cuisine: New American.
Liquor: Beer and wine.
Serving: L, D.
Credit Cards: AE, D, MC, V.
Handicap Access: No.
Reservations: No.
Special Features: Outdoor patio.

With only four tables inside around the exhibit kitchen and another handful outside on the porch overlooking the parking lot, Sunshine Café's enduring reputation has nothing to do with ambiance or largesse. Even the menu is small and exacting: the famous sesame-crusted tuna salad and wood-grilled burger for lunch or dinner, other interesting salads (lump crab meat and rock shrimp, for instance) and sandwiches (wood-grilled veggies) for lunch, seven dinner entrées, and nightly specials to which you should pay close attention. The café can command a high price, positioned as it is near the gates of mammoth South Seas Resort—a captured audience, so to speak. Yet the portions are generous and well-rounded by excellent sides such as risotto with grilled half of garlic bulb, spaghetti squash, and the day's potato. The Colorado lamb chops make an elegant statement, French-boned and awash with a rich wine demi-glace. Very tender and tasty. The porcini-dusted pork tenderloin comes with olive relish and a drizzle of reduced balsamic. We recently sampled a coconut-crusted snapper special, exquisitely fresh and only lightly embellished with coconut so as to keep the fish moist and sweet. For dessert, splurge on the Sunshine Fantasia (preferably with a partner or two)—a tower of cinnamon-chocolate brownie, chocolate-chocolate chip Häagen Daz ice cream, and the finest fudge to hit your palate. The wine list, like the restaurant and its menu, is selectively small but not overpriced. Service can be a bit brisk but well-practiced—a testimony to this place's long-reigning popularity.

KEY LIME BISTRO

239-395-4000.
11509 Andy Rosse Ln., Captiva Island
33924.
Price: Moderate to Very Expensive.
Children's Menu: Yes.
Cuisine: American.
Liquor: Full.
Serving: B, L, D, SB.
Credit Cards: AE, D, MC, V.
Handicap Access: Yes.
Reservations: No.
Special Features: Outdoor patio and live
music.

Captiva's newest sensation, it evokes a
Caribbean–Key West setting with brightly
painted oversized booths indoors, a tiki hut
stage outdoors, and a prevailing sense of
whimsy. The patio overlooks historic
"downtown" Captiva, a quirky corner of the
world. As part of a small inn, the bistro
serves all meals, plus Sunday Jazz Brunch.
Musicians entertain nightly. A sax soloist

*Live island music completes the Key West attitude
at Key Lime Bistro.* Karen T. Bartlett

played the soundtrack to our most recent
dinner there. As if the 17-entrée set menu
doesn't give you enough choices, a 36-
option specials menu clouds decision-
making. Time for a key lime martini,
Midori-based, while pondering and watching life go by on the other side of the white-
picket fence. Seafood and pasta are the
clear favorites, though the menus stretch to
duck, ribs, lamb chops, and prime rib. Our
fresh mozzarella salad off the specials menu
was topped with a flavorful sun-dried
tomato and basil compote (thicker than
vinaigrette, as it was described on the
menu). We were disappointed that the red
onions were raw and not pickled as promised. Our pasta special of mussels and
asparagus was dressed in a rich and tasty
saffron cream sauce. The crab cakes, unfortunately deep-fried rather than sautéed,
came with a nice key lime aioli and julienne
of vegetables. At breakfast, there are huevos
rancheros, Monte Cristo sandwich, and
eggs Benedict with key lime hollandaise.
Interesting salads star on the lunch menu,
including a grilled red leaf lettuce salad.

FORT MYERS

BISTRO 41

239-466-4141.
13499 S. Cleveland Ave. #143, Fort Myers
33907.
At Bell Tower Mall.
Price: Moderate to Expensive.
Children's Menu: No.
Cuisine: New American.
Liquor: Full.
Serving: L, D.
Closed: Sun. lunch.
Credit Cards: AE, MC, V.
Handicap Access: Yes.
Reservations: Yes.
Special Features: Outdoor seating.

Whether you choose a sidewalk table looking
out at Saks Fifth Avenue or an indoor booth
between mustard-colored walls, Bistro 41
feels festive and chic. Divine "small plates"

and "large plates" come out of the oak-grill kitchen, visible through a showcase window with a giant fork hanging on the wall above it. The regular lunch and dinner menus highlight grilled specialties such as Yucatán Pork as an entrée or sandwich with caramelized onions-grilled pineapple chutney, marinated rotisserie chicken, and oak-grilled salmon with Mediterranean vinaigrette. Other eclectic offerings include chicken satay appetizer, seafood paella, meat loaf and roasted-garlic mashed potatoes with veal gravy, chicken pot pie, and vegetable risotto. To further complicate decision making, a tableau of specials comprise a separate menu. We come here often, usually ordering from the specials, and we've never had one complaint about our well-crafted selections. Recently, for instance, we sampled pan-seared snapper encrusted with hazelnuts and served over caramelized plantains and stir-fried vegetable, then topped with tropical fruit relish and mocha-Kahlúa butter sauce; and grilled filet mignon on garlic mashed potatoes and broccolini topped with walnut pesto and Gorgonzola crust on a port and sun-dried cherry demi-glace. Both were near-religious experiences.

✪ BLU SUSHI

239-489-1500.
13451 McGregor Blvd., Fort Myers 33919.
Cypress Square.
www.blusushi.com.
Price: Inexpensive to Moderate.
Children's Menu: No.
Cuisine: Sushi/Japanese.
Liquor: Full.
Serving: L, D.
Credit Cards: AE, MC, V.
Handicap Access: Yes.
Reservations: No.

The latest in Fort Myers chic, Blu Sushi is as blue and cutting edge as its name. Local businesspeople crowd the bar and outdoor waiting areas to score one of a dozen tables or sushi-bar chairs in the blue-walled dining room. Hydraulic bar chairs, a cool water wall, and fun martinis, sakes, and sakatinis make the wait part of the adventure. Try the mango tango martini or the Asian pear sake for something exotic. You can order from the full menu, which consists largely of sushi rolls and sashimi, in the bar. Appealing to even the less-than-enthusiastic sushi fans, the rolls fuse Japanese and American favorites for the tastiest, most creative sushi this town has ever seen. I recommend the Hurricane (eel, crab, avocado, crunchy flakes of tempura for great taste and texture, and eel sauce), the Bahama (spicy conch, cucumber, and smelt roe), and for the less daring, the Blu Special (cooked crab and cucumber topped with a seafood saladlike creamy mixture of cooked scallops, shrimp, and mayo). The seaweed salad is tasty and proportioned to share as an appetizer. Or try the tuna tataki, carpaccio-thin slices of lightly seared top-quality tuna wading in a pool of ponzu sauce. Lunch specials stray from the sushi bar with selections such as toasted shrimp taco and smoked salmon pita.

CANTINA LAREDO

239-415-4424.
5200 Big Pine Way, Fort Myers 33907.
At Bell Tower Shops.
Price: Moderate.
Children's Menu: Yes.
Cuisine: Gourmet Mexican.
Liquor: Full.
Serving: L, D.
Credit Cards: AE, D, MC, V.
Handicap Access: Yes.
Reservations: No.

Dark bead-and-board wooden booths, a suave bar, servers in black and white, and rustic arts, crafts, and artifacts decorating the walls: This place defies any loud, gaudy notion we've developed of Mexican restaurants. No bright blankets in sight. No cutesy, no kitsch. In keeping with its "gourmet

Mexican food" subtitle, Laredo is the ultimate in good taste, in all senses of the phrase. Dishes use quality ingredients and break out of the taco mold with specialties such as tequila barbecued baby back ribs, camarones Escondidos (shrimp and spinach stuffed chicken breast with chipotle-wine sauce), and marinaded, grilled rib-eye. More traditional offerings take creative curves: chicken mole enchilada; chile relleno filled with ground beef, pork, almonds, and raisins; and shrimp flautas. *Platillos* let you taste a variety of specialties. I sampled the house margarita, strong, sweet with Cointreau, and big enough to drown a cat. The two brands of salsa that came with the ubiquitous basket of chips were authentically flavored, just hot enough. The enchilada Veracruz was above standard quality with its chicken, jack, and spinach stuffing and fresh veggies side, but it was skimpy on the substantial ingredients, heavy on the fluff (rice, shredded cabbage, and tortilla strips). Tableside flourishes add to the sophistication of this new place. The top-shelf guacamole is made before your eyes. Servers shake and pour your margarita or top off the devilishly tempting Mexican brownie a la mode with brandy butter and flourish. *Olé!*

LA CASITA

239-415-1050.
15185 McGregor Blvd., Fort Myers 33908.
Price: Inexpensive to Moderate.
Children's Menu: Yes.
Cuisine: Mexican.
Liquor: Beer and wine.
Serving: B, L, D; open 11:30–9.
Credit Cards: AE, D, MC, V.
Handicap Access: Yes.
Reservations: No.

La Casita expands beyond traditional Mexican and Tex-Mex dishes to feature the cuisine of the Guanajuato region in Mexico. If you can judge a Mexican restaurant by its salsas (and I do), this one starts out on firm footing. Authentic dishes such as menudo tripe soup (said to be a good hangover remedy), spicy shrimp soup (flavored with chipotle and chockful of shrimp), Mexican beef, basil chicken, camarones a la diabla (excellent, and not too spicy hot), grilled vegetables, and shrimp ceviche intermingle with more familiar vocabulary—tacos, tamales, enchiladas, chimichangas, and huevos rancheros. These benefit from fresh ingredients and sauces, and creative finagling. Enchiladas, for instance, are dipped in chili ancho sauce, then pan sautéed and stuffed with beef, chicken, or potato, with parmesan cheese and other standard toppings. Spicy potatoes stuff corn-husk-steamed tamales. The basil chicken—shredded in a stew of onions and tomatoes and served with tortillas—is a welcome departure from tired Mexican regulars. A tasty, mild tomatillo sauce swaths the steak strips. For an added kick, ask for a side of homemade through-the-roof habanero sauce, and apply sparingly. The setting is as fresh as the food, all served in a small, brightly decorated houselike structure with fiesta colors indoors and out.

FRENCH ROAST CAFÉ

239-936-2233.
www.frenchroastcafe.com.
12995 S. Cleveland Ave., Ste. 118, Fort Myers 33907.
Pinebrook Park.
Price: Moderate to Expensive.
Cuisine: French/Vietnamese.
Liquor: Beer and wine.
Serving: B, L, D, S, SB.
Early Dining Specials: Yes.
Credit Cards: AE, D, DC, MC, V.
Handicap Access: Yes.
Reservations: Yes.

Don't write this off as a coffee shop, although uncommon brews are a specialty. The fine French food is delightfully affordable, but the best deal is the lunchtime Vietnamese specials. Recently I thoroughly enjoyed grilled beef wrapped in grape leaves (exquisitely seasoned with garlic, ginger, and lemongrass) over rice vermicelli—one of the 10 selections that day. For $8.95, I also got an excellent egg-drop chicken soup, not so impossibly salty like many renditions, and delicate spring rolls with a light sweet-sour dip along with prettily cut pickled veggies and all that the menu promised in flying flavors. The rest of the lunch menu, with the exception of its crepes, offers a typical and full complement of salads, sandwiches, and burgers. Dinner in this cozy, elegant setting of fireplace, arches, and columns is more strictly French, with such offerings as tableside flamed steak Diane, snapper provençal, breast of duck Chambord, and crepes à la Grand Marnier tableside. Despite its elevated view of a parking lot, this place exudes romance and excels at all it prepares.

✪ MANNI'S

239-277-1272.
www.mannisrestaurant.com.
1920 Boy Scout Dr., Fort Myers 33907.
Price: Moderate.
Early Dining Menu: Yes.
Children's Menu: Yes.
Cuisine: German.
Liquor: Full.
Serving: L, D.
Closed: Sun. lunch.
Credit Cards: AE, D, MC, V.
Handicap Access: Yes.
Reservations: No.
Special Features: Live polka music on weekend nights.

This corner of Highway 41 has developed into something of an international food fair, with Middle Eastern, Italian, and Oriental restaurants and groceries joining Manni's, the best around in the German genre. My litmus test: the sauerbraten, served with my favorite accoutrements, spaetzle and red cabbage. I was raised on homemade sauer-

kraut and pork hocks, so I know the real thing when I taste it. The vinegar marinated beef was just a tad tough, but its dark, rich sweet-sour gravy saved it and added zing to the properly doughy bits of noodle, flavored subtly with coriander. There was nothing subtle about the red cabbage, however, among the most flavorful I've tasted, with a thick sweet-sour beef base and a clove backbeat. German and other Continental dinners—from goulash to shrimp scampi—are available all day, including four varieties of schnitzel (pork loin cuts), the specialty of the house. For lunch, there's also beerburger, chicken wings, leberkaese (veal meat loaf), a German cold-cut platter, among others. Dinner begins with crusty bread and smooth liver pâté and should rightfully end with the very cherry Black Forest cake. The bar, right at home in this borderline tacky Bavarian setting, pours seven German drafts and serves up polka music on weekend nights.

MILLE SAPORÉ

239-437-5040.
15880 Summerlin Rd., Fort Myers 33908.
Price: Inexpensive to Expensive.
Children's Menu: Yes.
Cuisine: Mediterranean.
Liquor: Full.
Serving: L, D.
Closed: Sun. lunch.
Credit Cards: AE, D, MC, V.
Handicap Access: Yes.
Reservations: Yes.
Special Features: Outdoor seating.

The beauty of this place is you can go in and have a nice seafood or steak dinner or just an inexpensive pizza. Either way, it will surprise you. Nothing is ordinary here. Pizzas come in varieties such as the pepata, with shrimp, mussels, black peppers, and light cream; and the melanzane, with mozzarella and marinated eggplant. Order a 9-inch or a 16-inch for appetizers or entrées. Otherwise, go for the red snapper with sour oranges and red onions; pasta with shrimp, shiitake mushrooms, and arugula; or veal flank with smoked salmon green peppercorn sauce: winners all. Tucked unassumingly into a supermarket strip mall, Mille Saporé has wowed the local dining-cognizant community with a tastefully decorated bar and dining room, both feeling like mild refuges from outside bustle. The bartender is congenial and the hosts fitted with the proper accent to make this feel like an Old World experience in a thoroughly modern cadre.

UNIVERSITY GRILL

239-437-4377.
7790 Cypress Lake Dr., Fort Myers 33907.
Price: Moderate.
Children's Menu: Yes.
Cuisine: Seafood.
Liquor: Full.
Serving: L, D.
Closed: Sat. and Sun. for lunch.
Credit Cards: AE, MC, V.
Handicap Access: Yes.
Reservations: Yes, for dinner.
Special Features: Outdoor seating overlooking a fountained pond; early-dining menu.

You feel as though you've entered a privileged men's club, surrounded as you are by dark wood, a martini bar, and library shelves. But don't feel intimidated. It's neither stuffy nor overly expensive at the University Club. One of a Florida-wide string of restaurants opened by Sanibel-based folks, this one, too, concentrates on seafood with a nice sampling of pasta and meat dishes, besides. I invariably order the pasta Maria, penne whose plum tomato sauce goes multidimensional with the addition of mascarpone and smoked fresh mozzarella cheeses. Daily fresh fish specials such as crabmeat-crusted mahimahi and snapper piccata provide other tasty options. On my last visit, I decided to expand my horizons and go for the signature Crunchy Grouper, which was a little overdone for my taste; I'll

stick with Maria in the future. The daily dinner menu diversifies with char-grilled pork chops, crab cakes, and coconut shrimp with raspberry horseradish sauce. At lunch, burgers, salads, deli sandwiches, and a smattering of the entrées provide a well-rounded selection. My favorite dessert here is the Barbara B. Mann martini: Stoli vanilla vodka with a splash of amaretto.

✪ THE VERANDA

239-332-2065.
www.verandarestaurant.com.
2122 Second St., Fort Myers 33901.
Price: Moderate to Expensive.
Children's Menu: No.
Cuisine: Florida/Southern.
Liquor: Full.
Serving: L, D.
Closed: Sat. lunch, Sun. lunch and dinner.
Credit Cards: AE, MC, V.
Handicap Access: Yes.
Reservations: Recommended.
Special Features: Garden/courtyard dining; piano bar.

My husband and I had our first "big" dinner date at the Veranda, so it will always be one of my favorites—and not solely for sentimental reasons. Victorian trappings and Southern charm create an atmosphere of romance in a historic home setting. Occupying two early-20th-century houses, the Veranda is a place for business lunches and special-occasion dinners. The dining room huddles around a two-sided redbrick fireplace and looks out on a cobblestone garden courtyard, separated from traffic by showy greenery and a white fence. Historic Fort Myers photos and well-stocked wine cases line the dark-wood bar. Start with something unusual from the Veranda's appetizer board—perhaps escargots in puff pastry with Stilton cheese (a sublime rendition), artichoke fritters with blue crab and béarnaise sauce, or Southern grit cakes with pepper jack cheese and grilled andouille sausage. Entrées are traditional but exceed the ordinary. Tender medallions of filet are dressed Southern style, in a rich smoky sour-mash whiskey sauce. Rosemary merlot sauce complements the rack of New Zealand lamb. Grilled grouper is mated with a tasty blue-crab hash and caper beurre blanc. Daily specials typically include fresh seafood catches, and the menu changes to reflect the seasons. Lunches span the spectrum from specialties such as crab cakes and baked tomato pasta to fried green tomato salad and grouper sandwich. Desserts wilt willpower with such temptations as chocolate pâté on raspberry coulis, peanut-butter-fudge pie, and pecan-praline tart.

FORT MYERS BEACH
Locals go to Fort Myers Beach expecting fresh seafood and reasonable prices. It's known more for fun dining and waterfront views than for culinary innovation.

SNUG HARBOR WATERFRONT RESTAURANT
239-463-4343, 463-8077.
www.snugharborrestaurant.com.
1131 First St., Fort Myers Beach 33931.
Price: Moderate to Expensive.
Cuisine: Seafood/American.
Children's Menu: Yes.
Liquor: Full.
Serving: L, D.
Credit Cards: AE, D, MC, V.
Handicap Access: Yes.
Reservations: Yes, at dinner for parties of 4 or more after 6pm.
Special Features: Waterside view, open-air dining; early-dining menu.

Moved to a new, more sterile building in May 2003, Snug Harbor nonetheless remains a perennial favorite. The window-lined main dining room looks out on the high bridge and shrimp and other boat traf-fic. Outdoor patio and dock dining have some of the old feel and the menu remains relatively unchanged. Tableware is fancier,

and a new undersea mural pops out at you when you don the provided 3-D glasses. The menu concentrates on seafood, prepared freshly and simply, with an emphasis on grouper and shrimp. Grouper Popeye is a longtime signature dish, featuring fresh steamed spinach (of course) and a light lemon-butter sauce. The mashed sweet potato accompaniment is a wise choice. Baked garlic shrimp and the Krispy Krunchy grouper are Snug classics, but the Buffalo shrimp are gone. (I think Snug invented them.) Fried oysters, salmon cakes, fine cuts of beef, sandwiches, and pasta dishes round out the menu.

✪ TETLEY'S STEAK & STONE
239-463-1686.
1113 Estero Blvd., Fort Myers Beach 33931.
Price: Moderate to Expensive.
Cuisine: Seafood/Steaks.
Children's Menu: Yes.
Liquor: Full.
Serving: D.
Credit Cards: AE, D, MC, V.
Handicap Access: Yes.
Reservations: Yes.
Special Features: At-table cooking on hot stones.

Tetley's is the new exception to the Fort Myers Beach rule for inexpensive and frivo-lous. Not that it's overpriced or pretentious; the quality and creativity of food make this a fine dining experience that is still beach casual. The open dining room extends out onto its second-floor balcony overlooking the merry goings-on of Times Square. Indoors, red brick and a display kitchen warmly invite. Here you have the option of cooking your own dinner on a red-hot stone. Not as gimmicky as it may sound, the granite slab goes from a pizza oven to your table in a special compartmentalized tray holding a medley of sauces and side dishes. For instance, I ordered filet mignon, tuna, and jumbo scallops. If you like your meat and fish done on the rare side, as I do, the cooking takes minutes, and you can actually eat bits of it as it cooks. It's a lot of fun, given all the sauces—horseradish, mustard, and a peanut-citrus sort in my case. Other stone-cooked options include ostrich loin, chicken breast, shrimp, pork, and other steak cuts. Or, like my husband, you can order your meal kitchen cooked. His grilled veal chop stuffed with wild mushrooms and boursin was a bit rare for his taste, so he cooked chunks on my stone, which stays hot for 40 minutes. For a starter, he ordered the night's special lobster bisque, which was impressive for its lack of saltiness—a sin committed by many restaurants. In fact, I found that overwhelmingly true throughout our Tetley's experience: The natural flavors of the ingredients shone through. I can also recommend the tuna ceviche appetizer, which was more like sushi: raw ahi-grade chunks of tuna tossed with wasabi vinaigrette, throned atop a mound of cucumber shavings and served with seaweed, raw squid, pickled ginger, and wasabi. It was, like everything we tried here, as delightful to the eye as the palate.

PINE ISLAND
✪ LOBSTER SHACK
239-283-5300.
3135 Stringfellow Rd., St. James City 33956.
Price: Moderate to Expensive.
Children's Menu: Yes.
Cuisine: Seafood.
Liquor: Full.
Serving: L, D, SB.
Closed: Mon.
Credit Cards: AE, D, DC, MC, V.
Handicap Access: Yes.
Reservations: No.
Special Features: Waterfront view; early-dining menu.

This newest Pine Island sensation puts a Down East spin on this seafood headquarters. Despite the difference in weather between the two locales, the attitudes fit

together well. Eat in the funky, casual, air-conditioned interior or on one of two screened porches overlooking a canal. Besides whole live Maine lobster, the menus extol lobster fra diavolo, lobster Newburg, lobster roll, clam bake, meal-proportioned Louisiana gumbo, Dungeness crab, blackened scallops with Alfredo sauce, grouper Florentine, blackened grouper sandwich, fried platters, raw oysters, and a well-rounded selection of other entirely fresh fish selections plain to fancy. We recently arrived early to beat the in-season lunch crowd and received top service and a satisfying meal for the most part. This is a salty kind of place, and the kitchen may take that a little too literally when it comes to seasoning the food. I found it especially true of the clam chowder, which was nonetheless yummy thick and clam crammed, and the lobster roll, again lobster rich and generous—just too much sodium added to the sea's dosage. Otherwise, it serves just plain good, fresh food. We enjoyed our baked oyster sampler of Cajun, Rockefeller, and Mornay styles (the Mornay the least), baked brie en croûte with a spicy mango chutney (we think mangoes should be more prevalent on Pine Island menus), and the blackened grouper sandwich.

TARPON LODGE RESTAURANT
239-283-3999.
www.tarponlodge.com.
13771 Waterfront Dr., Pineland, FL 33945.
Price: Moderate to Expensive.
Children's Menu: Yes.
Cuisine: New Continental.
Liquor: Full.
Serving: L, D.
Credit Cards: AE, MC, V.
Handicap Access: Yes.
Reservations: Suggested.
Special Features: Historic setting.

Before there was Tarpon Lodge, Pine Island dining projected an Old-Florida-meets-the-

Midwest image. Now there's a creative, gifted force with which to reckon. Set in a 1926 fishing lodge banked with old wavy-glass windows looking out on the water, the restaurant brings on the freshness in every sense of the word. For lunch, the marinated portobello mushroom and bleu cheese sandwich, quesadilla, crab cake sandwich, or grilled Cuban-spiced pork loin with black beans, salsa, and red pepper and tomato coulis gratify. Imaginative dressings and sides make the dishes, for example, a tasty garlic mayonnaise, potato salad, and cole slaw with the crab cake sandwich, slightly heavy on breading but nicely seasoned. Try the hearty and fresh-tasting crab and roasted corn chowder for lunch or dinner. The succinct menu's eight dinner entrées include vegetarian pasta, veal piccata with wild mushrooms, and beef tenderloin medallions wrapped in bacon and finished with wild mushroom beurre rouge, plus the day's fresh catch and nightly specials. Here in this seafood kingdom with its steep fishing heritage, you can't go wrong ordering the catch, or—thanks to the chef's savvy—anything else, for that matter.

SANIBEL ISLAND

✪ DOLCE VITA

239-472-5555.
www.dolcevitaofsanibel.com.
1244 Periwinkle Way, Sanibel Island 33957.
Price: Moderate to Expensive.
Children's Menu: No.
Cuisine: Mediterranean.
Liquor: Full.
Serving: D.
Credit Cards: AE, D, MC, V.
Handicap Access: Yes.
Reservations: Recommended.
Special Features: Live music.

Newly built and opened in 2000, this has become one of Sanibel's most glamorous and popular fine-dining experiences. The large, open dining room is at the same time elegant and convivial, with a baby grand piano as centerpiece of live entertainment. The menu is extensive, yet each dish is well crafted with Mediterranean and other continental and global influences. Old-fashioned flavors infuse dishes modernized with nouveau nuances. For starters, there's everything from wok-steamed mussels to Absolut gravlax and a flavorful, soupy mariscadas—shellfish in a garlic-fish-tomato broth; you may want to ask for a spoon. The cassoulet of escargot gets an injection of individuality from mushrooms and herbs to supplement the garlic. We recently selected Angry Lobster Arrabiata and veal chop Calvados from among the dizzying choice of entrées: Indian spiced lamb shank, Texas wild-boar saddle (tamarind-honey glazed with black currant coulis), goat cheese tortelloni, jerk chicken linguine, and porterhouse béarnaise, to name a sampling. We were extremely pleased with our selections. The Florida lobster was large and so a bit tough, perhaps from being "angry"—blanketed in a spicy Tuscan pomodore sauce—not too hot, just to the point of zingy. The apple-Calvados influence on the 14-ounce chop was subtle, abetted by a lively Granny Smith salsa. Because we were eating in a place that translates as "sweet life," we decided to have dessert, which turned out to be another highlight. The Black Forest cake came with an unlikely but oddly complementary scoop of passion fruit sherbet. It was dark, rich, and delightful. For another chocolate treat, skip dessert and order the chocolate martini. You may want to sit at the bar for this one, as bartenders often do a swirling performance as they pour it in front of you.

✪ LAZY FLAMINGO

239-472-5353.
www.lazyflamingo.com.
6520-C Pine Ave., Sanibel Island 33957.
At Blind Pass.
Price: Inexpensive to Moderate.
Children's Menu: Yes.

Cuisine: Seafood/American.
Liquor: Beer and wine.
Serving: L, D.
Credit Cards: AE, D, MC, V.
Handicap Access: No.
Reservations: No.

This is the original Lazy Flamingo, which has spawned another on Sanibel's south end and others along the South Coast. Look for a Pepto Bismol–pink building at Blind Pass, just before the bridge to Captiva. Neighborhood and nautical are the concepts behind this first Flamingo, where you order and pick up your own food at the counter, eat off plastic plates in the shape of scallop shells, and wipe your hands with paper towels from a roll at the table. The menu and ambiance have an essence of the Florida Keys—the owners even lifted the idea of a popular ring-and-hook game from a bar down there. Conch fritters, clam pot, mesquite-grilled grouper, wings, prime-rib sandwich, Caesar salad, and choco-late–key lime cheesecake are some of the most popular menu items. Avoid the Dead Parrot Wings; they are inedible to all but the most callused. Most of the meals come with fries, but you can substitute a small Caesar salad, which is usually tasty. The place is small: about a dozen counter seats and a few booths. For the same food but more room, shrimp-boat decor, and table service, try the Lazy Flamingo at 1036 Periwinkle Way (239-472-6939).

MAD HATTER

239-472-0033.
6460 Sanibel-Captiva Rd., Sanibel Island 33957.
At Blind Pass.
Price: Very Expensive.
Children's Menu: No, but will accommodate.
Cuisine: New American.
Liquor: Beer and wine.
Serving: D.
Credit Cards: AE, D, MC, V.

Handicap Access: Dining room, yes; rest-rooms, no.
Reservations: Recommended.
Special Features: Sunset view.

Sanibel's finest foray into the world of adventurous cuisine, Mad Hatter set standards a decade or so ago when the island culinarily dwelled in a state of Florida cuisine Midwestern style. After a couple of changes in ownership, the quirky little restaurant with its Alice in Wonderland theme continues to satisfy diners looking for new thrills. The menu changes monthly and nightly specials keep options ever-fresh. The sea cakes are a regularly occurring favorite, blending blue crabmeat, crawfish, serona peppers and served with a chayote and jicama bouquet and mango-ginger-black sesame coulis. Ginger twangs the Gorgonzola dressing on the Bibb salad, festive with its spiral-cut carrots and beets and crisps of wonton. The last time we visited the Mad Hatter, the jumbo sea scallops were seared with a chestnut-honey and achiote glaze and served with citrus-vanilla butter sauce. Salmon was served roulade style with a Gorgonzola crust and a marvelous bed of black pepper fettuccine studded amply with morels and bits of asparagus. Each dish was masterful, to the very end when we mmm'd and ahh'd over a warm apple strudel wrapped in phyllo with vanilla ice cream and orange-ginger vanilla cream sauce. Try to hit sunset time at this gulf-front treasure. It's the golden icing on the ingenious, whimsical cake.

MATZALUNA

239-472-1998.
www.prawnbroker.com/matzaluna.
1200 Periwinkle Way, Sanibel Island 33957.
Price: Inexpensive to Expensive.
Children's Menu: Yes.
Cuisine: Italian.
Liquor: Full.
Serving: D.

Credit Cards: AE, MC, V.
Handicap Access: Yes.
Reservations: No.

Island families often head here for dependably tasty Italian specialties and seafood at a reasonable price. Big comfy booths decorated by oversized food product cutouts circle the congenial bar, where we recently pulled up some bar stools for dinner because season crowds meant a bit of a wait. We were well taken care of, nonetheless, ordering off both the specials menu, which has the most ingenious offerings for those of us who dine here often, and the regular menu. I enjoyed with pure gusto my spinach and goat cheese-stuffed salmon with red pepper coulis, which appears often on the specials menu. The regular menu covers all the Italian bases from antipasto and pizza to pasta, chicken, and veal. The crab-stuffed shrimp with creamy crab sauce is a nice departure, or try the sirloin with portobellos and marsala demi-glace for something different. For a buck you can upgrade your soup or salad course to the creamy crab bisque, a wise investment.

TRADERS STORE & CAFÉ

239-472-7242.
1551 Periwinkle Way, Sanibel Island 33957.
Price: Expensive to Very Expensive.
Children's Menu: Yes.
Cuisine: American/Bistro.
Liquor: Full liquor.
Serving: L, D.
Credit Cards: AE, D, MC, V.
Handicap Access: Yes.
Reservations: Yes.
Special Features: A restaurant embedded in the setting of a gallerylike import store.

This is the equivalent of performance art, where you become a part of the store. You sit among wooden tribal masks on import chairs, eating terrific crusty bread out of hand-woven baskets. The café occupies the front section of this unusual store, owned

by the founders of the Chico's clothing store dynasty (see "Shopping," below). The food rivals the surrounding artifact-quality furnishings and objets d'art. It's become *the* place for islanders to meet for lunch, with its succinct menu of sandwiches, pastas, and small plates. The soup of the day is usually a good bet, and the seafood gumbo, fortified with rice, could be a meal. I also can recommend the grilled marinated portobello sandwich and the pan-blackened jumbo scallops on greens with lemon-caper vinaigrette. The dinner menu describes such masterworks as salmon with avocado salsa, Asian lollipop pork chops, and horseradish-crusted swordfish. Nightly specials dazzle. We recently sampled two marvelous entrées: parmesan-crusted sea bass with avocado and dill coulis with spinach risotto, and macadamia-crusted grouper with Thai peanut sauce. Cutting edge aside, Traders is also known for its burgers and barbecue baby-back ribs.

TWILIGHT CAFÉ

239-472-8818.
751 Tarpon Bay Rd., Sanibel Island 33957.
Price: Moderate to Expensive.
Children's Menu: Yes.
Cuisine: New American.
Liquor: Beer and wine.
Serving: D, L in-season.
Credit Cards: MC, V.
Handicap Access: Yes.
Reservations: Yes.

Twilight is our favorite island dinner destination. Set back from the road, it neighbors a popular art gallery and has contracted an artistic flair by virtue of close proximity. The teeny dining room is artsy in a whimsical rather than snobbish way. The ever-changing menu presents masterpieces in design-forward cuisine where oak grilling and homemade pasta are trademarks. In the open-for-view kitchen, chefs grill seafood in such dishes as Asian shrimp with pasta in a light Thai peanut sauce (one of my favorites), and grilled scallops (perfect at medium rare) with tangerine linguine. They also grill meats for the signature cowboy steak with sweet mashed potatoes and roasted green apple glaze, and rack of lamb over spinach and vegetable orzo with three-bean ratatouille. Vegetables, too, are grilled, including greens, which lend an unusual dimension to salads and beds upon which entrées come to rest. One page of the menu is devoted to vegetarian dishes starring grilled veggies. Twilight is also known for its crawfish mashed potatoes. Remember how as a kid you sometimes shmushed all the food on your plate into your mashed potatoes? This dish, chunky with corn kernels and crawfish tidbits, takes comfort food into the new age. For a starter or light meal, try one of the pizzalike flatbread crisps. We found the Cajun crawfish with tomatoes and Gorgonzola divine. I also recommend the spinach and arugula salad with toasted pecans, Gorgonzola, and warm pancetta vinaigrette. No matter what you order, prepare yourself for novel taste sensations.

FOOD PURVEYORS

Bakeries
André's French Bakery (239-482-2011; Bridge Plaza, 12901 McGregor Blvd., Fort Myers 33919) Small but chockful of treats Français: baguettes, great olive bread, cookies, sublime tortes, and custard-filled pastries.

Bara Bread Bistro (239-334-8216; 1520 Broadway, Fort Myers 33901) A charming bistro-*boulangerie* specializing in French bread by the loaf, quiche, coffee, and luscious French pastries. There's a large seating area where you can enjoy your purchase or have French-style lunch.

Breakfast
✪ **Amy's Over Easy Café** (239-472-2625; 630-1 Tarpon Bay Rd., Sanibel Island 33957) Islanders are happy to have an alternative (and a better one at that!) to breakfast at Lighthouse Café, a tourist favorite long touted for its breakfasts. Cheerful and creative, Amy's menu does standard along with unusual dishes such as my favorites: egg Reuben sandwich, vegetarian Benedict, and portobello and spinach omelet. Breakfast, served until 2:30pm, includes regular and Atkins and Weight Watchers specials. Also lunch.

San Carlos Diner (239-454-6511; 16541 San Carlos Blvd., Fort Myers 33908) Breakfast selections, some of them served all day, are extensive and hearty. My standard: spinach and feta omelet. Also lunch and dinner.

Candies & Ice Cream
Ben & Jerry's Ice Cream & Frozen Yogurt (239-936-4155; 12995 S. Cleveland Ave, Suite 130, Fort Myers 33907)

Big Olaf Creamery (239-590-9195; 13499 S. Cleveland Ave., Fort Myers 33907; at Bell Tower Shops) Twenty-one types of sundaes, plus 36 flavors of homemade ice cream, smoothies, and a caboose kids can climb into to eat.

Captiva Garden & Gourmet (239-395-0354; 14830 Captiva Dr. #210, Captiva 33924; at Chadwick Square) Featuring Queenie's ice cream, a local brand homemade by a Captiva resident and loved by ice cream aficionados. Also try Queeniccino (espresso with Queenie's ice cream), other coffees, and treats.

Chocolate Expressions (239-472-3837; 2075 Periwinkle Way #37, Sanibel Island 33957, at Periwinkle Place) Homemade chocolates (including sugar-free varieties), hand-scooped ice cream, smoothies, nonalcoholic daiquiris, and other treats.

Kilwin's (239-463-4500; www.kilwins.com; 50 Old San Carlos Blvd., Fort Myers Beach 33931; at Times Square) Fudge, chocolates, and ice cream in many flavors.

Love Boat Ice Cream (239-466-7707; 16229 San Carlos Blvd., Fort Myers 33908) Homemade ice cream at a longtime favorite at the crossroads leading to Fort Myers Beach and Sanibel Island.

Pinocchio's Ice Cream (239-472-6566; 362 Periwinkle Way, Sanibel Island 33957) Homemade Italian ice cream and yogurt, cappuccino, espresso, and frozen coffee drinks.

Coffee

Blackhawk Fine Coffee & Provisions (239-433-7770; 13499 S. Cleveland Ave. #137, Fort Myers 33907; at Bell Tower Shops) An inviting setting of easy chairs, coffee tables, and backgammon boards where you can enjoy coffee, latte, desserts, flavored ice tea, and other goodies. Internet access available.

Brewed Awakenings (239-945-4244; 1021 Cape Coral Pkwy. E., Cape Coral 33912) Espresso and specialty coffees, with patio seating.

Cool Beans & Bottles (239-790-COOL; 2224 First St., Fort Myers 33901; downtown) It's fun to sit at the window, sip a latte, and watch the morning workaday world pass by. They also serve ice cream, sandwiches, beer, and wine.

Sanibel Bean Island Coffees (239-395-1919; www.thebeanofsanibel.com; 2240-B Periwinkle Way, Sanibel Island 33957) Sanibel's wildly popular buzz shop, it serves the usual espresso, cappuccino, and latte selections, plus fresh-squeezed juice, smoothies, ice cream, bagels, breakfast, sandwiches, and salads.

Deli & Specialty Foods

✪ **Blue Pepper Gourmet Foods & Bakery** (7091 College Pkwy., Fort Myers 33907) Fine prepared and deli meals, import cheeses, luscious desserts, and other gourmet culinary products and implements.

Cheese Nook (239-472-2666; Periwinkle Place, 2075 Periwinkle Way, Sanibel Island 33957) A longtime favorite of locals for more than cheese: wine, fresh bread, and gourmet hot sauces, preserves, and soups.

Francesco's Italian Deli and Pizzeria (239-463-5634; 7205 Estero Blvd., Fort Myers Beach 33931; at Villa Santini Plaza) New York bagels, calzones, deli sandwiches, pizza whole or by the slice, Italian dishes for reheating, gourmet cheeses and groceries.

India Bazaar (239-939-0797; 5228 Bank St., Fort Myers 33907) A shop filled with exotic smells, foods, and gifts from India, Thailand, the Middle East, and Britain. Fresh, packaged, and frozen ethnic ingredients plus premade meals.

✪ **Mario's Italian Meat Market & Deli** (239-936-7275; 12326 Cleveland Ave., Fort Myers 33907) Fresh homemade sausage, braciola, and other meats; delicious homemade Italian cheeses, sauces, pastas, soups, sandwiches, and hot and frozen prepared Italian specialties. Limited seating.

Obee's Soup Salad Subs (239-332-8802; 2117 First St., Fort Myers 33901) Deli sandwiches and three types of homemade soup daily.

Petra Middle Eastern Food (239-939-3090; 1916 Boy Scout Dr., Fort Myers 33907) Stop here for feta cheese, flat breads, and unusual processed items such as rose jam, stuffed eggplant, and exotic candies.

Wok Cuisine (239-275-8811; 1910 Boy Scout Dr., Fort Myers 33907) Part of a Chinese restaurant, this Oriental market sells fresh, packaged, and canned goods in bulk or small packages.

Fruit & Vegetable Stands

For the freshest produce, visit the plentiful roadside stands along the coast. Some feature U-Pick options, especially for tomatoes and strawberries.

Downtown Farmers Market (239-332-6813; Fort Myers; near Centennial Park under the bridge) Look for fresh fruit, vegetables, flowers, herbs and live plants, arts, and crafts every Thursday 7–2.

Mango Street Market (Estero Blvd. at Mango St., Fort Myers Beach) Roadside stand selling fresh produce.

Oakes Brothers Produce (239-466-4464, 800-413-6881; 16758 McGregor Blvd., Fort Myers 33908) My personal favorite for locally grown tomatoes, citrus, and other fresh fruit, vegetables, and preserves. They also ship fruit.

Sunburst Tropical Fruit Company (239-283-1200; 7113 Howard Rd., Bokeelia 33922) One of the oldest island groves, Sunburst specializes in mangoes but also grows carambolas, litchis, and other exotics and sells fruit products. It's best to call ahead.

Sun Harvest Citrus (239-768-2686, 800-743-1480; www.sunharvestcitrus.com; 4810 Metro Pkwy. S., Fort Myers 33912; at Six Mile Cypress) Part tourist attraction, part citrus stand, Sun Harvest offers free samples, tours, demonstrations, a playground, and a gift shop.

Vitamin C the delicious Florida way. Karen T. Bartlett

Natural Foods

Ada's Natural Foods Market (239-939-9600; 11705 S. Cleveland Ave., Fort Myers

33907) Extensive line of organic produce and other healthy food products. A deli/juice bar with seating in the back produces tasty meatless sandwiches, salads, and hot dishes.

Healthy Habits (239-278-4442; 11763 S. Cleveland Ave., Fort Myers 33907) Organic produce, dairy products, and other natural groceries.

Island Nutrition Center (239-472-4499; www.islandnutritioncenter.com; 1633C Periwinkle Way, Sanibel Island 33957) Small but well-stocked with refrigerated and packaged organic, low-fat, low-carb, and low-sodium products.

Jayne's Victorian Garden (239-482-2466; 12901-13 McGregor Blvd., Fort Myers 33919) Hard to place in one category, this establishment also qualifies as a teacup-sized restaurant and an unusual gift shop. Shelves are stocked with organic products and Jayne's homemade vinegars, oils, and preserves (nasturtium ginger lime jelly, for instance). Stay for a healthy lunch served on antique china.

Pizza & Take-out

Johnny's Pizza (239-472-3010; 2496 Palm Ridge Rd., Sanibel Island 33957) Carryout and free delivery. Regular, gourmet (the best), and deep-dish pizza, plus Italian subs and specialties.

Mama Rosa's Pizzeria (239-472-7672; Chadwick's Square, PO Box 194, Captiva Island 33924) Subs, pizzas, strombolis, calzones, and salads.

Mozella's Food Works (239-472-2555; 2330 Palm Ridge Rd., Sanibel Island 33957) Luncheon sandwiches and homemade dinners for take-out.

Plaka I on the Beach (239-463-4707; 1001 Estero Blvd., Fort Myers Beach 33931) Gyros, spinach pie, moussaka, and baklava to go or eat in a screened-in dining room near the beach.

Taste of New York Pizzeria (239-432-0990; 13499 S. Cleveland Ave., Fort Myers 33907; at Bell Tower Shops) It has sold and moved but is still declared among the best take-out or eat-in for regular or gourmet pizza—white, vegetarian, tropical, garlic—and other New York–Italian specialties. Free delivery available.

Tropical Beach Grill (239-454-0319; 17260 San Carlos Blvd., Fort Myers Beach 33931) Better-than-average drive-up take-out for burgers, chicken sandwiches, and more.

Seafood

Beach Seafood (239-463-8777, 800-771-5050; 1100 Shrimp Boat Ln., PO Box 2490, Fort Myers Beach 33932; on San Carlos Island,) Fresh seafood at its source, specializing in shrimp—fresh, frozen, steamed, and dinners. This is a local's hot spot for lunch, by the way.

Andy's Seafood Market (239-283-7100; 4330 Pine Island Rd., Matlacha 33993, on Pine Island; mail: PO Box 176, Matlacha 33993) Fresh and smoked fish and shellfish from the area's major transshipment center.

Skip One Seafood (239-482-0433; 15820 S. Tamiami Trail, Fort Myers 33908) The freshest and best-priced shrimp, stone crab (in-season), lobster tails, clams, and fish on the mainland; join the crowds who have discovered the quality of its food for lunch and dinner. Shipping service available.

Timbers Fish Market (239-472-3128; 703 Tarpon Bay Rd., Sanibel 33957) Located inside a popular seafood restaurant, Timbers has the best selection, prices, and freshness on the island for all types of seafood fresh, steamed, and smoked.

CULTURE

For many years the Island Coast was considered a cultural limbo, void of strong artistic or regional identity except for a certain retiree/Midwestern influence. Still lagging behind Sarasota and Naples in that department, the region nonetheless is making inroads toward "artsification." The population, furthermore, is diversifying in terms of ethnicity and age.

The residents of Cape Coral and North Fort Myers include many nationalities—Italian, German, Jamaican, and Hispanic—that share their customs at social clubs, restaurants, festivals, and other venues. Throughout Fort Myers, Afro-Americans, Asians, East Indians, Europeans, and other ethnic groups heighten the cosmopolitan flavor. Flashes of Southern and Cracker spirit survive in the less resortlike areas of North Fort Myers and Pine Island.

The islands along the coast have inspired their share of creativity. Singer Jimmy Buffett has frequented Cabbage Key and Captiva Island. His brand of beachy folk song is the closest thing the Gulf Coast has to homegrown music. A Sanibel musician named Danny Morgan affects that same style and has been entertaining the islands for decades.

One of the few arts that residents can truly call their own is shell art, a form that flourishes on Sanibel Island, Florida's ultimate shell island. In its highest form, shell art can be stunning and delicate; its lowest can result in some pretty tacky shell animals.

Wealthy visitors to Sanibel and Captiva have exerted an influence on the fine arts through the years. The illustrious roll call began in the 1920s with Charles and Anne Morrow Lindbergh. Edna St. Vincent Millay's original manuscript for *Conversation at Midnight* burned in a Sanibel Island hotel fire. Today Robert Rauschenberg, a maverick in the field of photographic lithography, is the Island Coast's impresario.

Architecture

Fort Myers is home to some lovely architecture downtown and along McGregor Boulevard. Thomas Edison's home was perhaps Florida's first prefab structure: Because wood and materials were scarce (most newcomers made do with palmetto huts), Edison commissioned a Maine architect to draw up plans and construct sections of the home to be shipped down and pieced together on site. Downtown, the **Richard Building**, circa 1924, boasts an Italian influence, while the courthouse annex superbly represents Mediterranean Revival. So do the Miles Building, built in 1926 by Dr. Franklin Miles, the "Father of Alka-Seltzer," and **Patio De Leon**, a restored and burgeoning entertainment and shopping complex on First Street. The newer Harborside Convention Center and other recent constructions echo the motif.

Pine Island possesses the best, most concentrated collection of preserved vernacular architecture, especially in ✪ **Matlacha**. Pineland's mound-squatting homes are also prime examples, occasionally dressed up with latticework and vivid paint jobs. In **Bokeelia**, the entire Main Street is designated a historic district. Notice especially the Captain's House, a fine example of slightly upscale folk housing of the early 1900s, with French Provincial elements. Nearby Turner Mansion represents a higher standard of living

The tropical gardens at Thomas Edison's historic winter estate in Fort Myers add color and dimension to any visit. Lee County Visitor & Convention Bureau

and is reminiscent of New England styles. The club at **Useppa Island** exhibits another prime collection of Old Florida styles, both traditional and revival.

Cinema

AMC Merchants Crossing 16 (239-995-1191; 15201 N. Cleveland Ave., North Fort Myers 33903) State-of-the-art movie complex.

Beach Theater (239-765-9000; 6425 Estero Blvd., Fort Myers Beach 33931) A new theater with four screens, serving a full-meal (and slightly overpriced) menu, beer, and wine.

Island Cinema (239-472-1701; 535 Tarpon Bay Rd., Sanibel Island 33957; at Bailey's Shopping Center) A two-screen theater showing first-run films.

Marquee Cinema Coralwood Mall (239-458-2543; 2301 Del Prado Blvd., Cape Coral 33909) Ten screens for first-run films.

Northside Drive-In (239-995-2254; 2521 N. Tamiami Trail, Fort Myers 33903) Built in 1948 when drive-ins numbered in the thousands, the Northside—now one of only about 400 outdoor theaters left—has been updated to include a second screen.

Regal Bell Tower 20 (239-590-9696; Daniels Pkwy. and U.S. 41, Fort Myers 33907) A modern megacomplex of theaters in the form of an airport hangar.

Dance

Dance City (239-275-3433; 1939 Park Meadows Dr., Suite 1, Fort Myers 33907) Adult ballroom and Latin dance instruction.

Dance Ensemble of Southwest Florida (239-768-1144; Accent on Dance, 12155 Metro Pkwy. #18, Fort Myers 33907) Classes and performance of tap, jazz, ballet, lyrical, clogging, and pointe dance for children.

Dance Theatre Academy (239-275-3131; 2084 Beacon Manor Dr., Fort Myers 33907)
Ballet, pointe, tap, jazz, and interpretative dance for adults and children.

Gulfshore Ballet (239-590-6191; 2155 Andrea Ln., Suite C 5-6, Fort Myers 33912) Ballet
instruction.

Gardens
FRAGRANCE GARDEN OF LEE COUNTY
239-432-2000.
www.leeparks.org/pdf/fragrancegardenquadfold2k2.pdf.
7330 Gladiolus Rd., Fort Myers 33908.
In Lakes Regional Park.
Open: 8am–6pm daily.
Parking: 75¢ per hour or $3 per day.

Located at the park's west end, the garden was designed primarily for the visually and physically impaired, although the general public will also enjoy this one-of-a-kind attraction.
For the visually impaired there are pungent herbs, fragrant vines, and signs in Braille.
Paved paths with vegetation planted at wheelchair height accommodate the physically handicapped. Vined arbors are built wide enough for easy wheelchair access. The gardens are
temporarily closed due to hurricane damage, but will be reopened in summer 2005.

Historic Homes & Sites
CHAPEL-BY-THE-SEA
239-472-1646.
11580 Chapin Ln., PO Box 188, Captiva Island 33924.

This quaint church is a popular spot for interdenominational Sunday services,
weddings, and seaside meditation. Many of the island's early pioneers were laid to rest
in its cemetery.

✪ EDISON & FORD WINTER ESTATES
239-334-3614, 239-334-7419.
www.edison-ford-estate.com.
2350 McGregor Blvd., Fort Myers 33901.
Open: Continuous tours 9am–4pm Mon.–Sat., 12–4 pm Sun.
Admission: For Florida residents $14 adults, $7.50 children 6–12; for nonresidents $15
adults, $8.50 children; laboratory and museum tour only $6.50 adults, $3.50 children.

Nowhere in the U.S. will you find the homes of two such important historical figures sitting
side by side. This site is so much more than just a couple of preserved houses— it's a slice of
Floridiana, Americana, and Mr. Wizard, all rolled into 17 riverside acres. The 90-minute
tour begins across the street under the nation's largest banyan tree, a gift from tire mogul
Harvey Firestone. The tree, 400 feet around, poses outside a museum that contains many of
Edison's 1,000-plus patented inventions—including the phonograph, the movie camera,
the lightbulb, children's furniture—as well as the 1907 prototype Model T Ford his friend
and wintertime neighbor, Henry Ford, gave him. Edison's late-1880s home hides in a tangle
of tropical flora which Edison experimented. (Special garden and in-depth botanical
tours are available.) Actually there are two homes, identically built and connected with an

arcade. One contained the Edisons' living quarters; the other, guest quarters and the kitchen. His laboratory, full of dusty bottles and other ancient gizmos, sits in the backyard among reflecting pools and gardens. The Friendship Gate separates Edison's estate from Ford's. "The Mangoes," as it was called in honor of the fruit orchards the car manufacturer so loved, seems humble compared to its neighbor, with furnishings true to the era and the Fords' simple tastes. On occasion, actors portraying America's geniuses circulate around the grounds. Recently a river tour has been added to the agenda aboard a replica of the electric (of course) boat Tom himself used. See "Boating" for more information.

FISHING SHACKS

Pine Island Sound at Captiva Rocks, east of North Captiva.

The last artifacts of the region's early commercial fishing enterprises have braved weather and bureaucracy to strut the shallows along the Intracoastal Waterway. The shack at the mouth of Safety Harbor on North Captiva is the most noticeable. It once served as an icehouse. If you look east, you'll spot several others where fishermen and their families used to live. Privately owned and maintained as weekend fishing homes for local enthusiasts, most are listed in the National Register of Historic Places and serve as picturesque reminders of days gone by.

✪ KORESHAN STATE HISTORIC SITE

239-992-0311.
www.floridastateparks.org/koreshan.
PO Box 7, Estero 33928.
Tamiami Trail, US 41 and Corkscrew Rd.
Open: 8am–sunset; narrated tours 10am Sat. and Sun.
Admission: $3.25 per vehicle with up to 8 passengers, $1 per cyclist, pedestrian, or extra passenger; tours $1 for adults, 50 cents for children.

Contained within a state park, this site has restored the customs and ways of a turn-of-the-last-century religious cult that settled on the banks of the Estero River. Under the leadership of Cyrus Teed, whose Hebrew name is Koresh, members of Koreshan Unity were well versed in practical Christianity, speculative metaphysics, functional and aesthetic gardening, art, occupational training, and Cellular Cosmogony. The latter, their most unusual theory, held that the earth lined the inside of a hollow globe and looked down into the solar system. Teed and his followers envisioned an academic and natural Utopia of 10,000 followers. They planted their settlement (home for only 250 at its peak) with exotic crops and vegetation. They built a theater, a communal mess hall, a store, and various workshops, all of which have been restored or reconstructed to tell the strange story of the Koreshans, who lost their momentum upon the death of their charismatic leader in 1908. Archives are kept at the library of the Koreshan Unity Foundation across the road from the park (239-992-2184). In 2003 the addition of the Planetary Court, where the seven women who governed the Koreshan society lived, was completed, along with other major renovations. Free botanical tours are available every Thursday at 1pm.

MOUND KEY STATE ARCHAEOLOGICAL SITE

239-992-0311.
www.floridastateparks.org/moundkey.

PO Box 7, Estero 33928.
c/o Koreshan State Historic Site.

The only way to reach this adjunct of the Koreshan (see above) site is by boat, and many do it by canoe or kayak from Koreshan, Lovers Key State Park (launch only, no rentals), or Estero River Tackle and Canoe Outfitters. Estero Bay Boat Tours does occasional group trips to the site, where Calusa Indians and Spanish missionaries have set up camp in eras past. A path weaves through the native shell mounds, one reaching 32 feet high, qualifying as the county's highest geologic elevation. The 133-acre island was formed from years of shellfish eating as the Calusa piled the discarded shells on a sandbar that grew to the seat of their kingdom. Farmers settled years later, and modern-day explorers can find remnants of the centuries' habitation. It is illegal to take any artifacts from the island, which is under excavation by archaeologists.

RANDELL RESEARCH CENTER
239-283-2062.
www.calusa.us.
13810 Waterfront Dr., PO Box 608, Pineland 33945.
On Pine Island.
Open: Tours 10am Sat. Jan.–Apr., other times by appointment; reservations suggested.
Admission: Suggested donation $5 adults, $3 children.

Archaeologists from Gainesville's Florida Museum of Natural History meet here at the charming village of Pineland to discover the lifestyles of the lost Calusa tribes. In 2004, a trail with interpretative signage opened. An important center of Calusa culture for more than 1,500 years, Pineland encompasses some 200 acres of shell mounds, remnants of an ancient canal system, and old Cracker shacks on the shores of Pine Island Sound, where the ancient Indians once collected shellfish for food and tools. From 53-acre Randell Research Center, tour guides reveal what they have discovered about the tall warriors on weekly walking tours. Those who wish to self-tour up the mounds and along the ancient canal that the Calusa built cross-island can obtain a guide from nearby Tarpon Lodge. On certain days archaeologists are digging at the site. Volunteers are welcome, but call in advance.

SANIBEL CEMETERY
Off the bike path on Middle Gulf Dr.; not accessible by car.

No signs direct you to it. Just follow the path, and you'll come across a fenced plot with wooden headstones announcing the names of early settlers—a wonderful, quiet place to ponder times past.

SANIBEL LIGHTHOUSE
Southeast end of Periwinkle Way, Sanibel Island.

Built in 1884, the lighthouse was the island's first permanent structure. Once vital to cattle transports from the mainland, it still functions as a beacon of warning and welcome. The lighthouse and Old Florida-style lightkeeper's cottage were renovated in 1991.

Kid's Stuff
BROADWAY PALM CHILDREN'S THEATRE
239-278-4422.
www.broadwaypalm.com.
Royal Palm Square, 1380 Colonial Blvd.,
Fort Myers 33907.

Broadway Palm Dinner Theatre puts on
three or four plays a year geared toward
families and served up with kid's-fare
lunch.

THE CHILDREN'S SCIENCE CENTER
239-997-0012.
www.childrenssciencecenter.com.
2915 NE Pine Island Rd., Cape Coral
33909.
Open: 9:30–4:30 Mon.–Fri., 12–5 Sat.
Closed: Sun.
Admission: $3 children 3–11, $5 ages 12
and older.

Encourages visitors of all ages to touch and
interact with the exhibits: mind-teaser
puzzles, hands-on electrical gadgets,
building blocks, Calusa Indian tools,
a whisper dish, and computer games.
A nature trail with bug identification, plus

*Waltz through a thunderstorm at Fort Myers's
Imaginarium.* Lee Island Coast Visitor & Convention Bureau

live captured snakes, iguanas, tarantulas, and scorpions get kids excited about nature. This
is a neighborhood science-guy kind of place without all the high-tech exhibits of the
genre's sophisticated high end, but we love it for its neighborliness and user-friendliness
(as long as you don't let the kids try to pet the iguanas).

✪ IMAGINARIUM
239-337-3332.
www.cityftmyers.com/attractions/imaginarium.htm.
2000 Cranford Ave., PO Box 2217, Fort Myers 33902.
At Dr. Martin Luther King Jr. Blvd. and Cranford Ave.
Open: 10am–5pm Mon.–Sat., Sun. 12–5pm.
Admission: $5 children 3–12 when accompanied by an adult, $7 ages 13 and up, $6.50 seniors.

I have visited many of the new-wave interactive science museums that have hit Florida in
the past decade, and I'm happy to say this is among my favorites. It is not overwhelmingly
huge, like some, but it is colorfully attractive and varied in its approach to teaching everything from the effects of chemical abuse to the world of finance. Emphasis is on weather
and water (it occupies a former city water plant). The Hurricane Experience will, as they
like to say, "blow you away." You can feel a cloud, tape yourself on location broadcasting a

tornado, and walk through a thunderstorm. Aquariums, a touch tank, a swan lagoon, and alligator feedings acquaint visitors with local water creatures. A new animal lab exhibits loveable critters such as guinea pigs, lizards, frogs, a juvenile alligator, and hermit crabs. Other displays appeal to all ages with gadgets, toys, and computers; special hands-on shows are part of the fun.

Museums
✪ BAILEY-MATTHEWS SHELL MUSEUM
239-395-2233, 888-679-6450.
www.shellmuseum.org.
3075 Sanibel-Captiva Rd., PO Box 1580, Sanibel Island 33957.
Open: 10am–4pm daily.
Admission: $3 children 5–16, $6 ages 17 and up, free 4 and under.

The only one of its kind in the U.S., this museum reinforces Sanibel's reputation as a top shell-collecting destination. It uses nature vignettes and artistically arranged displays to demonstrate the role of shells in ecology, history, art, economics, medicine, religion, and other fields. The centerpiece of the museum is a two-story globe surrounded by shells of the world. Outside is a memorial devoted to the late actor Raymond Burr, who helped establish the museum. The Children's Science Lab provides games and hands-on learning experiences in colorful reef-motif surroundings, but oddly with a touch tank you can't touch. The newest exhibit explores the role of shells in the lives of the Calusa Indians. The museum holds more than two million specimens in the showroom and catalogued upstairs, representing a third of the world's 150,000 species of living mollusks.

CAPE CORAL HISTORICAL MUSEUM
239-772-7037.
www.capecoralhistoricalmuseum.org.
544 Cultural Park Blvd., PO Box 150637, Cape Coral 33990.
Open: 1–4pm Wed., Thurs., Sun.
Closed: July and Aug.
Admission: $2 donation per adult.

A new building opened in 2003 to expand this once tiny museum by another 1,500 feet. New exhibits include a Cracker kitchen model to complement the existing Cracker house model, seashell and model boat collections, and a replicated burrowing owl nest. A new mural depicting Cape Coral's old rose gardens attraction brightens up the spot. Outside, a blossoming garden continues the link between the town and roses.

LEE COUNTY BLACK HISTORY SOCIETY WILLIAMS ACADEMY MUSEUM
239-332-8778.
http://lcbhs.ebmnet.com.
1936 Henderson Ave., Fort Myers 33916
Open: 10am–4pm Tues.–Fri., Sat. by appointment.
Admission: $3 adults, $1.50 children.

Once part of a school for the African-American population, this circa 1942 clapboard, tin-roofed building houses artifacts and exhibits illuminating the local experience for persons of African descent. Displays include a permanent audio timeline titled "A Chronology of the African American Presence in Lee County."

MUSEUM OF THE ISLANDS

239-283-1525.
www.museumoftheislands.com.
5728 Sesame Dr., Pine Island Center 33922; mail: PO Box 305, St. James City 33956.
On Pine Island.
Open: Nov.1–Apr.30, Tues.–Sat. 11am–3pm, Sun.1-4; May 1–Oct. 31, Tues.–Sat.
11am–3pm.
Admission: $2 adults, $1 children.

Occupying the old Pine Island library at Phillips Park, the museum concentrates on the area's Calusa and fishing heritage. Continue on to the settlement of Pineland to see time standing still on intact Native American mounds.

SANIBEL HISTORICAL VILLAGE & MUSEUM

239-472-4648.
950 Dunlop Rd., Sanibel Island 33957.
Near City Hall.
Open: Nov.–May, 10am–4pm Wed.–Sat.; June–mid-Aug. 10–1.
Admission: $5 donation per adult requested.

The village began with a historical Cracker-style abode, once the home of an island pioneer. The museum focuses on Sanibel's modern history of homesteading, citrus farming, steamboating, and tourism, with photos and artifacts. It recalls the Calusa era with a dugout canoe and other relics of the times. The island's original Bailey's General Store, circa 1927, was moved to the site in 1993 as a kickoff to establishing a pioneer village on the grounds. Since then a 1920s post office, a teahouse, and other vintage homes have been added. One houses a lens that outfitted the Sanibel Lighthouse in the 1960s.

SOUTHWEST FLORIDA MUSEUM OF HISTORY

239-332-5955.
2300 Peck St., Fort Myers 33901.
At Jackson St.
Open: 10am–5pm Tues.–Sat.
Closed: Sun., Mon.
Admission: $9.50 adults, $8.50 seniors, $4 children 3–12; walking tours 10am Wed.
Jan.–May, $5.

The displays in this museum—which is housed in a handsome restored railroad depot—take you back to the days of prehistoric mammals and ancient civilizations up through the eras of the Calusa Indians, Spanish exploration, fish camps, cattle driving, gladiolus farming, and World War II training. Well-arranged scale and life-sized models, graphic depictions, videos, and interactive historical games illuminate the past. Outdoors, tours examine a replica of a local early-1900s Cracker house and the world's last and longest Pullman private railcar, circa 1930. (Don't miss the Pullman tour; it's truly a highlight if you have a good guide.)

USEPPA MUSEUM
239-283-1061.
Useppa Island Club, Useppa Island 33922.
Admission: $2.50 donation requested for visitors over age 18.

The wee island of Useppa is stuffed to the gills with history, a fact that calls for a historic museum. This one is exceptionally well presented for such a small place. (It helps that wealth outmeasures square footage on the island.) Dioramas are interpreted via taped presentations you hear from small tape recorders and headsets. They describe the island's Calusa history, its fishing and resort eras, and its role in training revolutionaries for the Cuban Bay of Pigs confrontation in 1960. Since the island is owned by a private club, visitors must be island guests or guests aboard the *Lady Chadwick* luncheon cruise to the island (see Captiva Cruises under "Sightseeing & Entertainment Cruises" in this chapter).

Music and Nightlife
Downtown Fort Myers is trying to metamorphose into a hot entertainment district, featuring jazz bars, bistros, nightclubs, and street festivals. As for the islands, Fort Myers Beach is definitely the most hopping. On Sanibel and Captiva you'll find a quieter brand of partying; nightlife there is focused on theater and more highbrow forms of music. Friday's *Gulf Coasting* supplement to the *News-Press* covers the Island Coast's entertainment scene.

CAPE CORAL
Jimbob's (239-574-8100; 1431 SE 16th Place, Cape Coral 33904) Live music on weekends.

Waterford Ballroom (239-945-0034; 4646 SE 11th Place, Cape Coral 33904) Dance every Wednesday, Friday, and Sunday evening.

CAPTIVA ISLAND
✪ **Crow's Nest Lounge** (239-472-5161; www.tween-waters.com/crows.htm; 'Tween Waters Inn, 15951 Captiva Rd., Captiva Island 33924) Live contemporary dance bands Tuesday through Sunday; entertaining crab races on Monday. The islands' hottest spot.

FORT MYERS
Beat Club (239-461-9300; 1520 Hendry St., Fort Myers 33901) A high-energy club that draws a young crowd with loud music and special effects.

Club Neptunes (239-334-0245; www.clubneptunes.com; 3057 Cleveland Ave., Fort Myers 33901) Hosts name-brand bands in a club setting.

Fat Cats Drink Shack (239-226-9272; 1512 Hendry St., Fort Myers 33901) Casual and light-hearted with pool tables and occasional live music.

Fort Myers Community Concert Association (239-939-3236; PO Box 606, Fort Myers 33902) Highbrow musical entertainment—from brass ensembles to ballet—at the Barbara B. Mann Performing Arts Center (see "Theater" below).

Jazz Alliance (239-939-2787; 10091 McGregor Blvd., Fort Myers 33919; at the Lee County Alliance of the Arts headquarters) Sponsors a series of three springtime outdoor concerts featuring name artists, fine wine, and specialty foods.

Liquid Café (239-461-0444; 2236 First St., Fort Myers 33901; downtown) A sophisticated eatery with artsy entertainment, open-mike nights, and beer and wine.

Naples Jazz Society (239-332-4488, 877-787-8053; www.naplesjazzsociety.org; PO Box 1365, Naples 34106) Hosts jazz artists in winter at the Arcade Theatre (2267 First St., downtown Fort Myers) It also conducts summer jazz camp for young musicians.

Southwest Florida Jazz Society (239-945-0556; 167 S.W. 53rd St., Cape Coral 33914 or PO Box 07233, Fort Myers 33919) Sponsors a series of concerts at the Heitman House downtown Fort Myers and Friday nights at Beatniks Coffee Café (1341 SE 4th Terrace, Cape Coral, off Del Prado Blvd.).

Southwest Florida Symphony (239-418-1500; www.swflso.org ; 4560 Via Royale, Suite 2, Fort Myers 33919) Performs classical and pops series November through May at the Barbara B. Mann Hall in Fort Myers, BIG ARTS on Sanibel Island, and local churches.

Toucan Charlie's Bar & Grill (239-334-2727; www.ichotelsgroup.com/h/d/hi/1/en/hr/fmyss; 2220 W. First St., Fort Myers 33901; at the Holiday Inn Riverfront) A pleasant spot on the river, with outdoor and indoor bar and live music on certain evenings. Have dinner elsewhere if you're discriminating.

FORT MYERS BEACH

The Bridge Waterfront Restaurant (239-765-0050; www.thebridgerestaurant.com; 708 Fisherman's Wharf, Fort Myers Beach 33931) A popular spot with boat-in and drive-in barflies, featuring lively dance music outdoors on the docks, including a reggae party every Sunday afternoon and evening.

Chillers (239-463-4343; www.snugharborrestaurant.com; 1131 First St., Fort Myers Beach 33931, at Snug Harbor Waterfront Restaurant) Upstairs overlooking the bay, with live music and a typical Fort Myers Beach crowd—which is to say "rowdy."

Lani Kai Island Resort (239-463-3111; www.drfun.com/lani-kai; 1400 Estero Blvd., Fort Myers Beach 33931) *The* premier collegiate party spot on the beach, with live entertainment nightly and during the day on weekends, on the rooftop or on the beach.

Orpheus Café (239-463-1549; 1165 Estero Blvd., Fort Myers Beach 33931) A notch above other beach nightlife, offering live jazz Monday nights.

PINE ISLAND

Bert's Bar & Grill (239-282-3232; www.bertsbar.com; 4271 Pine Island Rd., Matlacha 33993) Florida funk at its finest, with a salty attitude, good munchies, waterfront stance, and live music during season (see Website for schedule).

Starboard Lounge and Grill (239-282-1131; 3421 Stringfellow Rd., St. James City 33956) Also known as the Ragged Ass Saloon, its Banana Tree Stage hosts concerts under the stars every Friday night, usually showcasing local talent.

Tarpon Lodge (239-283-3999; www.tarponlodge.com; 13771 Waterfront Dr., Pineland, FL 33945) Midweek music series February into early April features live local entertainers 6–9:30pm Tuesday–Thursday. No cover charge.

SANIBEL ISLAND

BIG ARTS (239-395-0900; www.bigarts.org; 900 Dunlop Rd., Sanibel Island 33957) Hosts classical musical quartets and trios, and orchestras November through April.

Jacaranda (239-472-1771; www.sanibelsteakhouse.org/jacaranda; 1223 Periwinkle Way, Sanibel Island 33957) Top-40 hits, reggae, and island music performed live.

Specialty Libraries

For regional reference information by phone, call 239-479-INFO.

Edison & Ford Winter Estates Research Library (239-334-7419; www.edison-ford-estate .com; 2350 McGregor Blvd., Fort Myers 33901) Open for public research and reading, the collection includes the following areas of study: Thomas Edison, Henry Ford, science, botanicals, local history and travel, and Fort Myers *New-Press* articles dating from 1885–1947 that relate to Edison and Ford. Open Tuesday and Thursday 9–noon or by appointment.

Florida Gulf Coast University Library (239-590-7610; http://library.fgcu.edu; 10501 FGCU Blvd. S, Fort Myers 33965; at Ben Hill Griffin Pkwy.) An Internet lab with 40 computer stations.

Sanibel Public Library (239-472-2483; www.sanlib.org; 770 Dunlop Rd., Sanibel Island 33957) Contains an identification collection of seashells and Internet access computers by reservation.

Talking Books Library (239-995-2665; 13240 N. Cleveland Ave., N. Fort Myers 33903) Library for the visually and physically impaired, with books on tapes or records.

Theater

The Arcade Theatre/Florida Repertory Theatre (239-332-4488, 877-787-8053; www.floridarep.org; 2267 First St., PO Drawer 2483, Fort Myers 33902; downtown) The glory of the 1920s, this Victorian playhouse has been restored and advanced to the 21st century. Home to an energetic professional company that brings new life to old boards.

✪ **Barbara B. Mann Performing Arts Center** (239-481-4849; www.bbmann pah.com; Edison Community College, 8099 College Pkwy. SW, Fort Myers 33919) Hosts major Broadway shows, musical performers, and dance troupes. Broadway season runs November to late April.

Broadway Palm Dinner Theatre (239-278-4422; www.broadwaypalm.com; 1380 Colonial Blvd., Fort Myers 33907; at Royal Palm Square) Lunch and dinner musical performances star professional actors in a made-over grocery store that seats and serves 448. Each year a few of the shows

Florida Repertory Theatre performs professional productions in a historic movie theater.

Karen T. Bartlett

are geared toward family, such as *Winnie the Pooh*. Its Off-Broadway Palm Theatre presents cabaret-style shows in an adjacent, intimate 90-seat playhouse. Lunch and dinner shows or shows only. Both closed Monday year-round and Tuesday May through October.

Claiborne & Ned Foulds Theater (239-936-3239; 10091 McGregor Blvd., Fort Myers 33919; at Lee County Alliance of the Arts headquarters) An indoor and outdoor stage for recitals, concerts, and workshops. Theatre Conspiracy, a cutting-edge professional troupe that occasionally stages family shows, performs part of its season here.

Cultural Park Community Theatre (239-772-5862; 528 Cultural Park Blvd., Cape Coral 33990) A 186-seat theater that hosts community theater.

Old Schoolhouse Theater (239-472-6862; www.oldschoolhousetheater.com; 1905 Periwinkle Way, Sanibel Island 33957) Installed in the charming setting of a circa 1896 historic one-room schoolhouse, this 96-seat theater-in-the-round has for years served as the island's cultural mainstay. In its current incarnation it hosts a lively and often hilarious professional troupe.

Periwinkle Playhouse (239-472-0324; 2200 Periwinkle Way, Sanibel Island 33957) Formerly Pirate Playhouse and J. Howard Wood Theatre. It hosts community theatre, improv comedy, music, and other various acts on a stage adaptable to proscenium, theater-in-the-round, and thrust configurations.

TECO Arena (239-948-7825; www.tecoarena.com; 11000 Everblades Pkwy., Estero 33928) Home of the Everblades hockey team, this venue also hosts touring entertainers.

Visual Art Centers

Flocks of wildlife art and other eclectic galleries make a name for Sanibel Island in cultural circles, while smaller communities support their own offbeat galleries and art associations. On Pine Island, national artists come to hide out and nourish their souls, sparking a growing art colony of sorts that's centered in Matlacha. The following entries introduce you to opportunities for experiencing art as either a viewer or a practicing artist. A listing of commercial galleries is included in the "Shopping" section.

Alliance of the Arts (239-939-2787; www.artinlee.org; 10091 McGregor Blvd., Fort Myers 33919) Operates a public gallery, members' gallery, 175-seat indoor theater, and outdoor stage and conducts classes and workshops. Home to Theatre Conspiracy troupe, Frizzell Gallery of Fine Art, and most local arts and cultural groups.

BIG Arts (239-395-0900; www.bigarts.org; 900 Dunlop Rd., Sanibel Island 33957) Home of Barrier Island Group for the Arts, an energetic multidisciplinary organization. Art shows and classes are scheduled regularly at the facility.

Cape Coral Arts Studio Rubicond Park (239-574-0802; www.capecoral.net/citydept/parks/pks_art.cfm; 4533 Coronado Pkwy., Cape Coral 33904) Classes, exhibitions, and sales.

Cultural Park Theatre Fine Arts Gallery (239-772-5862; 516 Cultural Park Blvd., Cape Coral 33990) Rotating exhibits of local art; art classes offered.

Fort Myers Beach Art Association (239-463-3909; www.fortmyersbeachart.com; Donora St. and Shell Mound Blvd., PO Box 2359, Fort Myers Beach 33932) Member and other exhibits.

Gallery of Fine Art (239-489-9313, Edison Community College, 8099 College Pkwy. SW, Fort Myers 33919) Exhibits works of nationally and internationally renowned artists.

RECREATION

Shelling, island-hopping, fishing, sailboarding, and warming chilled bones on hospitable beaches: These are a few of the favorite things to do along the Island Coast.

Beaches

The Island Coast's 50 miles of local beaches are known for their natural state and abundance of shells. *Family Fun* magazine recently rated this stretch of beach the "#1 beach in the southeast U.S." Most charge for parking. Sanibel Island beach stickers can be purchased and allow you to park for free at most accesses. Along the Gulf Drives you'll see signs at beach accesses designating resident sticker-only parking. Cyclists and walk-ins, however, can take advantage of these accesses without stickers. For more information about beach stickers, call 239-472-9075.

BONITA BEACH

BAREFOOT BEACH PRESERVE

Collier County Parks and Recreation Dept.
239-498-4364.
www.colliergov.net/parks/colliercountyp/beach/beachparks/bbpreserve.html.
3300 Santa Barbara Blvd., Naples 34116.
Entrance at Hickory Blvd. and Bonita Beach Rd., south end of Little Hickory Island.
Facilities: Restrooms, showers; nature learning center, aquatic butterfly garden; snack bar.
Parking: $4 per day.

Actually within neighboring Collier County but accessible from Bonita Beach, the 342 acres in this preserve contain a coastal hammock and 8,200 feet of beach and low dunes. Sea grapes, cabbage palms, and other native vegetation landscape the grounds. Gopher tortoises often lumber across the road and footpaths. Rangers give nature walks and shell talks at the chikee learning center.

✪ BONITA BEACH PARK

239-229-0459.
www.fortmyers-sanibel.com.
27954 Hickory Blvd., south end of Little Hickory Island.
Facilities: Picnic table shelters, restrooms, lifeguard, water-sports and beach rentals, volleyball, nearby restaurants.
Parking: 75¢ per hour.

The only true public park on Bonita Beach, it becomes lively during high season and on weekends. Water sports and volleyball, plus a hamburger and bar joint, create a

Happy-go-lucky on Bonita Beach. Karen T. Bartlett

youthful spirit. Vegetation is sparse; there's nothing hidden about this beach. Parking fills up early in-season and on weekends year-round. About 10 other accesses with free but limited parking line Hickory Boulevard to the north.

CAPE CORAL
CAPE CORAL YACHT CLUB COMMUNITY PARK
239-574-0806.
www.capecoral.net/citydept/parks/pks_yachtclub.cfm.
5819 Driftwood Pkwy., Cape Coral 33904.
Facilities: Restrooms, showers, picnic shelters, swimming pool, marina, shuffleboard, outdoor racquetball courts, fishing pier.
Open: Swimming pool (239-542-3903) 10am–5pm daily.
Admission: Free. Pool admission $3.50 ages 18 and up, $2.50 for 10–17, and $1.50 for 9 and younger.

The manmade beach on the Caloosahatchee River is part of a large park that sponsors recreational and other programs and exudes a true sense of community. The groomed beach is better for sunning than swimming, for which the pool fills the void.

CAPTIVA ISLAND
CAPTIVA BEACH
North end Captiva Rd., Captiva Island.
Parking: 75¢ per hour.

Only early arrivals get the parking spots for this prime spread of deep, shelly sand. It's also a good place to watch a sunset.

FORT MYERS
LAKES REGIONAL PARK
239-432-2000.
7330 Gladiolus Dr., Fort Myers 33908.
Facilities: Picnic areas, restrooms, showers; playgrounds, model railroad ride, fitness trail, bike path; water-sports rentals; restaurant.
Parking: 75¢ per hour or $3 per day.

This land of 158 acres of freshwater lakes features a small sand beach with a roped-off swimming area. Though the quality of the water might be questionable since the lakes—erstwhile quarries—are stagnant, this is a great place for the family to spend the day. The 279-acre park offers a new water playground, canoeing, paddleboating, fishing, nature and bike trails, an exercise course, an observation tower, a miniature train ride (admission), and terrific playground facilities. The new wet playground, Florida Cypress Swamp, provides 17 squirting, spraying, and splashing frogs, snakes, and birds.

FORT MYERS BEACH
BOWDITCH POINT REGIONAL PARK
239-463-1116.
www.leeparks.org/facility_info.cfm?project_num=0111.
50 Estero Blvd., Fort Myers Beach 33931.
At the north end.

Facilities: Picnic shelters, restrooms, showers; hiking paths.
Parking: 75¢ per hour metered parking.

This pretty, green, 17-acre park fronts Estero Bay and the gulf. It's a nice, quiet beach, underutilized and unspoiled, and a favorite of boat-ins.

✪ LYNN HALL MEMORIAL PARK
239-463-1116.
www.fmbeach.org/parks/lynn_hall.htm.
950 Estero Blvd., Fort Myers Beach.
In the Times Square vicinity.
Facilities: Picnic areas, restrooms, showers; playground, fishing pier, water-sports rentals; nearby restaurants, bars, and shops.
Admission: Metered parking. (Warning: Park only in designated areas, or your car will be towed at great expense.)

Part of the new pedestrian Times Square plaza, this park attracts college students in the spring and families the rest of the year. A rocking, rollicking place, it appeals to beach bar hoppers, crowd watchers, and those interested in water sports, with volleyball, a fishing pier, beachwear stores, restaurants, ice cream shops, beachside drinks, parties, parasailing, jet skiing. For thinner crowds, hit public accesses on the south end of Estero Boulevard.

✪ LOVERS KEY STATE PARK
239-463-4588.
www.floridastateparks.org/loverskey.
8700 Estero Blvd., Fort Myers Beach 33931.
Route 865 between Fort Myers Beach and Bonita Beach.
Facilities: Picnic area, restrooms, showers; boat ramps, fishing; food concession, beach shop.
Parking: $4 per vehicle with up to 8 passengers, $2 for single passengers, $1 for extra passengers, bicyclists, and pedestrians.

Ride a truck-pulled tram through the natural mangrove environment to South Beach. Or you can walk to secluded North Beach. The area between Estero and Little Hickory Island consists of natural island habitat populated by birds, dolphins, and crabs. On the barrier island of Lovers Key, Australian pines provide shaded picnicking along a narrow, natural stretch of sand that is due for renourishing in coming years. South of the park entrance, Dog Beach is the county's only designated off-leash dog beach. (Most beaches on Sanibel Island allow pets on leash.) A gazebo provides a picnic shelter and a popular wedding venue. Away from the beach, shaded picnic grounds line estuarine inlets with a launch for canoes and kayaks, and a path accommodates hikers and cyclists.

SANIBEL ISLAND
✪ BOWMAN'S BEACH
Bowman's Beach Rd. off Sanibel-Captiva Rd., Sanibel Island.
Facilities: Picnic area, restrooms, fitness trail.
Parking: $2 per hour.

Aptly named Lovers Key. Karen T. Bartlett

Bowman's is Sanibel's most natural beach—long, coved, and edged by an Australian pine forest—on an island all its own. It can be reached by footbridges from the parking lot (a rather long walk, so go lightly on the beach paraphernalia). Shells are plentiful here—in some places a foot or more deep along the high-tide mark.

LIGHTHOUSE PARK BEACH
239-472-6477 (Sanibel Parks and Recreation Dept.).
South end of Periwinkle Way, Sanibel Island.
Facilities: Picnic area, restrooms, nature trail, fishing pier, mobile food concession in-season.
Parking: $2 per hour.

Skirting Sanibel Island's historic lighthouse is an arc of natural beach fronting both the gulf and San Carlos Bay. One of Sanibel's most populated beaches, its highlights include a nature trail and a fishing pier. Strong currents forbid swimming off the point. The wide beach gives way to sea oats, sea grapes, and Australian pine edging. I like the neighborhood around it—historic and more laid-back than other parts of the island.

SANIBEL CAUSEWAY BEACH
Sanibel Causeway Rd.
Facilities: Picnic area, restrooms.

Windsurfers and fishermen especially favor this packed-sand roadside beach. It's been dressed up with palms and pines, but it's noisy and typically jammed. Beach lovers in RVs and campers often pull up here to picnic and spend the day in the sun.

TARPON BEACH
239-472-6477.
Middle Gulf Dr. at Tarpon Bay Rd., Sanibel Island.
Facilities: Restrooms, mobile food concession in-season.
Parking: $2 per hour.

Another popular beach, this one is characterized by sugar sand and a nice spread of shells. It's a bit of a hike from the parking lot to the beach, and the area gets congested on busy days. RVs can park here. Great for swimming.

TURNER BEACH
239-472-6397.
South end Captiva Rd., Captiva Island.
Facilities: Restrooms, nearby restaurants, water sports, and store.
Parking: $2 per day.

A pretty beach with wide, powdery sand, Turner tends to get crowded, and parking is limited. The entrance is on a blind curve, which can be dangerous. More bad news: Riptides coming through the pass make this taboo for swimming. Park your beach towel far north or south of the pass for calmer, swimmable waters. We like to come here in the evening to watch the sunset and walk the beach. Surfers like the waters to the north in certain weather. It's also a hot spot for fishermen, who line bayside shores and the bridge between Sanibel and Captiva.

Sanibel's 23 miles of paved bike paths take you past wildlife habitat and historic sites such as this theater, once a school for pioneer children. Karen T. Bartlett

✪ CAYO COSTA ISLAND STATE PARK

941-964-0375.
www.floridastateparks.org/cayocosta.
La Costa Island, accessible only by boat.
Facilities: Picnic ground, restrooms, showers.
Admission: $1 per person.

The Island Coast is blessed with some true getaway beaches, untamed by connection to the mainland. On these, one can actually realize that romantic fantasy common to beach connoisseurs: sands all your own. Cayo Costa stretches for 7 miles and is most secluded at its southern extremes. A larger population of beachgoers congregates at the north end, where docks and a picnic and camping ground attract those who seek creature comforts with their sun and sand. Shelling is superb in these parts, particularly at Johnson Shoals, which surfaces at the island's north end during low tide.

NORTH CAPTIVA

Across Redfish Pass from South Seas Resort and Captiva Island; accessible only by boat.

Like Cayo Costa, here's a place to go for private beaching. Though it's narrow at the south end, the sand is like gold dust. You'll find no facilities unless you venture across the island to the bay, where restaurants and civilization inhabit the north end.

Bicycling

The bikeways of the Island Coast come in two varieties. Bicycle paths, the most common, are separated from traffic by distance and, ideally, a vegetation buffer. Bicycle lanes are a designated part of the roadway. Cyclists also take to the road in rural areas, where no bikeways exist but traffic is light. By law they must abide by the same rules as motor vehicles. Children under age 16 are required to wear a helmet.

Best Biking

Bike trails run through **Lakes Park,** where bike rentals are also available. Long stretches of bike path in **Fort Myers** follow **Daniels Parkway, Metro Parkway, Colonial Boulevard,** and **Summerlin Road.** The **Summerlin path** leads to the Sanibel causeway (cyclists cross for $1), to connect with island paths. **McGregor Boulevard**'s sidewalk provides another popular and scenic circuit. Design is under way for Ten Mile Linear Park, which will follow Ten Mile Canal from downtown Fort Myers to Estero. Far-reaching plans could eventually hook up the system with a West Coast Greenway extending from Tampa to Naples. More than 2 miles of bike paths also wind through **Lovers Key State Park,** and a ranger leads a guided bike tour the first Friday of each month beginning at 10am.

Many of **Cape Coral**'s city streets designate bike lanes. Serious bikers favor **Burnt Store Marina Road,** which goes to Charlotte County from the northwest side of town.

✪ **Sanibel**'s 23-mile path covers most of the island and occasionally leaves the roadside to plunge you into serene backwoods scenery. Segments along busy Periwinkle Way have recently been widened and moved away from roadside. The Sanibel Historical Society (239-472-4648) distributes brochures on Pedaling Periwinkle Way and exploring by bike or foot Old Sanibel around the lighthouse at the east end. Cyclists also pedal 5-mile paved Wildlife Drive through "Ding" Darling National Wildlife Refuge and its unpaved but hard-packed Indigo Trail.

A growing bike path/route travels from **Pine Island Center to St. James City** on Pine Island. Work is under way to extend it northward to Bokeelia.

BMX bikers can use the **Sanctuary Skate Park** (see "Kid's Stuff," below) on Monday evenings. Cape Coral also has a dedicated BMX park.

Rental/Sales

Billy's Rentals (239-472-5248; 1470 Periwinkle Way, Sanibel Island 33957) Bicycles, surrey bikes, and equipment for family biking. Also scooters and beach gear. Rentals by hour, day, or week.

Fun Rentals (239-463-8844; 1901 Estero Blvd., Fort Myers Beach 33931) Rentals and repairs.

Jim's Rentals (239-472-1296; www.yolo-jims.com; 11534 Andy Rosse Ln., Captiva Island 33924) Rentals by the half-day, full-day, and 24 hours. Also in-line skates.

Paradise Bicycles (239-772-2453; 1712 Del Prado Blvd., Cape Coral 33990) Rentals and sales.

Boats & Boating

With its procession of unbridged islands and wide bay, the Island Coast begs for outdoor types to explore her waters. Island-hopping constitutes a favorite pastime of adventurers.

Canoeing & Kayaking

Many resorts and parks rent canoes, in addition to those outlets listed below.

Adventure in Paradise (239-472-8443, 239-437-1660; www.adventureinparadiseinc .com; 14341 Port Comfort Rd., Fort Myers 33908; at Port Sanibel Marina, east of Sanibel toll booth) Naturalist- or self-guided tours through a marked mangrove trail. Rentals available. Free pickup from hotels and condos on Sanibel.

Adventure Sea Kayaking (239-437-0956; sanibelkayaking@compuserve.com; 'Tween Waters Marina, 15951 Captiva Rd., Captiva Island 33924; 1641 S. Fountain-head Rd., Fort Myers 33919) Owner Brian Houston is well-known for his kayaking enthusiasm and nationwide promotion. He offers instruction in kayak operation and informed guided tours in local waters.

Captiva Kayaks & Wildside Adventures (239-395-2925; McCarthy's Marina, 15041 Captiva Dr., Captiva Island 33924) Sea-kayaking tours focus on natural history and sea life; sunrise, sunset, starlight, full moon, and children's adventures. Kayak and canoe rentals are available; delivery and pickup.

Estero River Tackle and Canoe Outfitters (239-992-4050; opposite Koreshan Historic Site, 20991 S. Tamiami Trail, Estero 33928) Rents and outfits canoes for a four-mile adventure down the natural Estero River to Estero Bay.

Try canoeing as a form of fun—and environmentally sensitive—recreation. Karen T. Bartlett

GAEA Guides (239-694-5513, 866-256-6388; www.gaeaguides.com; mail only: 340 Kingston Dr. W., Fort Myers 33905) Guides kayaking tours at Lovers Key State Park, Estero Bay, and up the Caloosahatchee River for birding. Also teaches kayak clinics at Manatee Park and conducts archaeological tours for Randell Research Center from Pine Island.

✪ **Great Calusa Blueway** (239-461-7400; www.thegreatcalusablueway.com) Completed in spring 2005, this new paddling trail along the island Intracoastal Waters extends more than 80 miles, from Boca Grande to Bonita Springs. Using GPS technology, it takes paddlers to Mound Key, Lovers Key State Park, Bunche Beach, Cayo Costa, and other dynamic birding, archaeological, and beaching destinations. You can view maps or request a free map at the site or phone number listed above.

Gulf Coast Kayak Company (239-283-1125; 4530 Pine Island Rd., Matlacha 33993; Pine Island) Morning nature and sunset trips in ✪ Matlacha Aquatic Preserve and other local natural areas; full moon and manatee nature (Thanksgiving through St. Patrick's Day only) ventures. All guides are naturalists and kayak instructors. Rentals available for self-guided tours.

Lakes Park (239-432-2000; 7330 Gladiolus Dr., Fort Myers 33908) Canoe rentals for paddling on freshwater lakes.

Manatee Park (239-432-2038, 239-694-3537; 10901 Route 80, Fort Myers 33905) Kayak among the manatees with a double kayak rental (November–March only).

✪ **Tarpon Bay Explorers** (239-472-8900; www.tarponbay.com; 900 Tarpon Bay Rd., Sanibel Island 33957) Rents canoes and kayaks for use in the bay and through "Ding" Darling Refuge's Commodore Creek Canoe Trail. Also, guided canoe/kayak tours. *Canoe & Kayak* magazine has rated Tarpon Bay among the top ten places to paddle in the U.S.

Tropic Star Cruises (239-283-0015; www.tropicstarcruises.com; 16499 Porto Bello St., Bokeelia 33922; on Pine Island) Rent single and double kayaks for half- and full-day trips from Bokeelia and Cayo Costa.

Dining Cruises

Big M Casino (239-765-7529, 888-373-3521; www.bigmcasino.com; Moss Marine, 450 Harbor Ct., Fort Myers Beach 33931) Gambling cruise with live entertainment and buffet and à la carte dining.

Fort Myers Beach Cruises (800-238-1776; www.fortmyersbeachcruises.com; 18400 San Carlos Blvd., Fort Myers Beach 33931) New to the Beach, its lunch and dinner sunset cruises run daily.

J. C. Cruises (239-334-7474; www.modernsurf.com/jccruises; Fort Myers Yacht Basin, PO Box 1688, Fort Myers, FL 33902; downtown) Lunch, dinner, Sunday brunch, and sightseeing cruises up the Caloosahatchee River aboard the *Capt. J.P.*, a three-deck paddle wheeler.

Sanibel Harbour Princess (239-466-2128; 17260 Harbour Pointe Dr., Fort Myers, FL 33908; at Sanibel Harbour Resort, off Summerlin Rd. before Sanibel Island causeway) Sunset dinner buffet and hors d'oeuvre cruises aboard a sleek, elegant 100-foot luxury yacht.

Personal Watercraft Rentals/Tours

Holiday Water Sports (www.holidaywatersports.net; 239-765-4386; Pink Shell Beach Resort, 250 Estero Blvd. Fort Myers Beach 33931; and 239-463-6778, Best Western Beach Resort, 684 Estero Blvd., Fort Myers Beach 33931) Waverunner rentals, lessons, and dolphin-spotting/heritage tours.

Powerboat Rentals

Adventure in Paradise (239-472-8443 , 239-437-1660; www.adventureinparadiseinc .com; 14341 Port Comfort Rd., Fort Myers 33908; at Port Sanibel Marina, east of Sanibel toll booth) Rent Grady White bow riders and center consoles or deck boats by half day, day, and week.

Bluewater Vacations (239-839-7368; www.bluewatervacations.com; 217 E. Cape Coral Pkwy., Cape Coral 33904) Rent 41-foot air-conditioned houseboats for one- to seven-day cruises out of Cape Harbour Marina. Full galley and fishing gear included.

The Boat House (239-472-2531; Sanibel Marina, 634 N. Yachtsman Dr., Sanibel Island 33957) Powerboats for trips into intracoastal waters only.

Fish-Tale Marina (239-463-3600; 7225 Estero Blvd., Fort Myers Beach 33931) Rents Grady Whites, pontoons, and skiffs.

Four Winds Marina (239-283-0250; www.fourwindsmarina.com; 16501 Stringfellow Rd., Bokeelia 33922; Pine Island) Rent 19- to 21-foot fishing and deck boats.

Southwest Florida Yachts (239-656-1339, 800-262-SWFY; www.swfyachts.com; 3444 Marinatown Ln., Suite 19, North Fort Myers 33903) Offers power-yachting lessons and rentals in the 32- to 43-foot range. Courses include offshore navigation, electronic navigation, overnight anchoring, advanced marlinspike, and others.

SweetWater Boat Rentals (239-472-6336; www.tween-waters.com/sweet%20water.htm; 15951 Captiva Dr., Captiva 33924; at 'Tween Waters Inn Marina) Rents 19-foot center-console boats that hold up to six passengers.

Public Boat Ramps
Cape Coral Yacht Club (239-574-0815; 5819 Driftwood Pkwy., Cape Coral 33904) Two free public ramps on the Caloosahatchee River, with recreational facilities.

Lovers Key State Park (239-463-4588; www.floridastateparks.org/loverskey; 8700 Estero Blvd., Fort Myers Beach 33931; at Route 865 between Fort Myers Beach and Bonita Beach) Access to Estero Bay and the gulf, with picnicking.

Matlacha Park (Matlacha, Pine Island) Playground and fishing pier.

Punta Rassa (Summerlin Rd., Fort Myers, before the Sanibel causeway) Picnic facilities and restrooms.

Sanibel (Causeway Rd.) Two ramps at the west end of the Sanibel causeway.

Sailboat Charters
New Moon (239-395-1782 or 888-472-7245; www.newmoonsailing.com; 'Tween Waters Inn Marina, 15951 Captiva Dr., PO Box 352, Captiva Island 33924) Up to six passengers aboard a 40-foot sloop. Sailing classes for kids and adults, three-hour cruises, and extended custom sails.

Sailboat Rentals & Instruction
✪ **Offshore Sailing School** (239-454-1700, 888-454-1700; www.offshore-sailing.com; 16731 McGregor Blvd., Fort Myers 33908; at South Seas Resort Marina on Captiva Island) Week-long and three-day certification (US SAILING) instruction offered, from beginning women's-only or kids-only and mixed sailing courses to advanced racing and bareboat cruising preparation; operated by an Olympic and America's Cup veteran. Course instructors are knowledgeable, experienced, and easygoing ("no yelling" is the rule). Accommodation packages with South Seas Resort available.

✪ **Southwest Florida Yachts/Florida Sailing & Cruising School** (239-656-1339, 800-262-SWFY; www.flsailandcruise school.com; 3444 Marinatown Ln. NW, Suite 19, N. Fort Myers 33903) American Sailing Association (ASA)

Set sail for an adventure on a chartered sailboat.
Karen T. Bartlett

certification courses and bareboat charters provide excellent adventures into Charlotte Harbor for live-aboard experiences. Also powerboat courses.

Shuttles

Sea Bridge (239-878-8990, www.seabridge.info; Tarpon Point Marina, 1430 Rose Garden Road, Cape Coral, at the southernmost end of Pelican Blvd.) Daily shuttle service to Bowditch Point Regional Park on Fort Myers Beach, it departs daily from Cape Coral every two hours from 9am to 3pm and makes returns every two hours from 10am to 4pm. Between June 1 and November 15 the boat runs Tuesday through Sunday only.

Sightseeing & Entertainment Cruises

✪ **Captiva Cruises** (239-472-5300; www.captivacruises.com; PO Box 580, Captiva Island 33924; at South Seas Resort) A complete menu of upper island sightseeing, beach, and luncheon trips is offered aboard the finely fitted 150-passenger *Lady Chadwick* and the 48-passenger *Playtime,* with history and lore lessons along the way. As a nonguest, it's the only way to see private Useppa Island, where you can enjoy lunch at the Collier Inn restaurant.

Edison & Ford Winter Estates (239-334-7419; www.edison-ford-estate.com; 2350 McGregor Blvd., Fort Myers 33901) Tour the Caloosahatchee River the way Thomas Edison did, aboard a replica of his circa 1900 electric launch. Narration relates some of Edison's favorite "fish tales" and other historic background. Tours depart every half-hour 9–3, Monday through Friday, weather permitting. Estate-touring and boat tour packages are available.

J. C. Cruises (239-334-7474, 239-334-2743; www.modernsurf.com/jccruises; PO Box 1688, Fort Myers 33902; at Fort Myers Yacht Basin) Sightseeing jungle/manatee cruises and dinner-boat tours.

Stars & Stripes (239-472-2531; www.sanibelmarina.com/stars.htm; Sanibel Marina, 634 N. Yachtsman Dr., Sanibel Island 33957) Ninety-minute sightseeing and wildlife tours depart three times daily, plus one sunset cruise with complimentary beverages.

Sun Princess (239-466-4000, ext. 2991; 17260 Harbour Pointe Dr., Fort Myers 33908; at Sanibel Harbour Resort) Beach and lunch tour that takes you to the upper islands for eco-tours, family fishing, dolphin spotting, and lunch in a restaurant on an unbridged island. Certified naturalists conduct the eco-tours.

Tropic Star Cruises (239-283-0015; www.tropicstarcruises.com; 16499 Porto Bello St., Bokeelia 33922; on Pine Island at Knight's Landing) Full-day nature cruises and ferry service to Cayo Costa (ferry/kayak package available) and Boca Grande.

Fishing

Snook and tarpon are the prized catch of local anglers. Snook, which is a game fish and can't be sold commercially, is valued for its sweet taste.

Redfish is another sought-after food fish. More common catches in back bays and waters close to shore include mangrove snapper, spotted sea trout, shark, sheepshead, pompano, and ladyfish. Deeper waters offshore yield grouper, red snapper, amberjack, mackerel, and dolphinfish. Most fish are released in these days of environmental consciousness. Check local regulations for season, size, and catch restrictions.

Nonresidents age 16 and over must obtain a license unless fishing from a vessel or pier covered by its own license. Inexpensive, temporary nonresident licenses are available at county tax collectors' offices and most Kmarts, marinas, and bait shops.

Deep-Sea Party Boats
Getaway Deep Sea Fishing (239-466-3600; Getaway Marina, 18400 San Carlos Blvd., Fort Myers Beach 33931) All-day or half-day excursions.

Fishing Charters/Outfitters
Competent fishing guides work out of the region's major marinas. If it's your first time fishing these waters, I recommend hiring someone with local knowledge.

Backwater Fishing School (941-753-7811, 800-755-1099 ext. 490; www.genmar.com/pr; **Tarpon Lodge,** (Pine Island; mailing address: 1651 Whitfield Ave., Sarasota 34243) This intensive three-day school debuted in 2003. The curriculum—taught by fishing instructors, charter boat captains, and an ecologist—introduces newcomers and enhances existing skills. Basic through advanced fly fishing and light-tackle sportfishing skills are part of the program, as is instruction in basic boat operation, maintenance and trip preparation, and boating safety. Other subjects include bait rigging, live bait and artificial techniques, fish habits, electronics, cast netting, knots, trailering, light tackle, fly casting, and the environment. Cost includes lodging package at historic Tarpon Lodge.

Captain Mike Fuery (239-466-3649; www.sanibel-online.com/fuery; PO Box 1302, Captiva Island 33924) Located at 'Tween Waters Inn Marina, he has a good reputation for finding fish.

Capt. Pat Hagle Charters (239-283-5991; e-mail: captpathagle@aol.com; PO Box 245, Pineland 33945) Fish excursions into Pine Island Sound; also nature, history, shelling, beachcombing, and water-taxi cruises.

Sanibel Marina (239-472-2723; www.sanibelmarina.com; 634 N. Yachtsman Dr., Sanibel Island 33957) Several experienced fishing guides operate out of the marina. Captain Dave Case (home phone 239-472-2798) has been at it a long time.

Fishing Piers
Cape Coral Yacht Club (239-574-0815; www.captiva.com/boat%20ramps/capecoral yachtclub_boatramp.htm; 5819 Driftwood Pkwy., Cape Coral 33904) The 620-foot lit fishing pier is part of a boating/recreational complex. Bait and tackle shop.

Centennial Park (www.coastlinememories.com/fort.myers.florida.centennial.park.html; Edwards Dr. near Yacht Basin, downtown Fort Myers) Complete park, with playgrounds and other facilities.

✪ **Fort Myers Beach Pier** (www.captiva.com/fishing/piers/fortmyersbeachpier.htm; 1000 Estero Blvd., Fort Myers Beach 33931; at Lynn Hall Memorial Park, Times Square) The pier holds a bait shop (239-765-9700), which also rents rods and offers lots of casting room and hungry pelicans.

Lee County Manatee Park (239-432-2038, 239-694-3537; www.captiva.com/stateparks/ leecountymanatee.htm; 10901 Route 80, Fort Myers 33905) A great place for visitors to learn more about the endangered West Indian manatee native to the region. On the Orange River.

Matlacha Park (Matlacha, Pine Island) Playground and boat ramps.

Sanibel Lighthouse Park Beach (Southeast end of Periwinkle Way, Sanibel Island) A T-dock into San Carlos Bay.

Golf

Home of such golfing greats as Patty Berg and Nolan Henke, the Island Coast keeps pace with the growing popularity of golf.

Public Golf Courses

Alden Pines (239-283-2179; 14261 Clubhouse Dr., Bokeelia 33922; on Pine Island) Semiprivate 18 holes, par 71 course, with affordable rates year-round. Snack bar.

Bay Beach Golf Club (239-463-2064; 4200 Bay Beach Ln., Fort Myers Beach 33931, off Estero Blvd.) 18 holes, par 60. Affordable rates.

Dunes Golf & Tennis Club (239-472-2535; www.dunesgolfsanibel.com; 949 Sandcastle Rd., Sanibel Island 33957) Semiprivate 18-hole, par 70 course. Restaurant and bar. Lush, Audubon-preserve links. High rates, especially in-season.

Eastwood Country Club (239-275-4848; www.cityftmyers.com/attractions/golf/eastwood .htm; 4600 Bruce Heard Ln., Fort Myers 33994) One of the region's favorites; 18 holes located away from traffic.

Fort Myers Country Club (239-936-2457; www.cityftmyers.com/attractions/golf/fmcc .htm; 3591 McGregor Blvd., Fort Myers 33901) Fort Myers's oldest; 18 holes, par 71. Restaurant and lounge.

The Golf Club (239-542-7879; 4003 Palm Tree Blvd., Cape Coral 33909) Semiprivate course with 18 holes, par 72. Restaurant and bar.

Summerlin Ridge Golf Course (239-432-0000; 16750 Pine Ridge Rd., Fort Myers 33908) Lit 18-hole executive course, popular during hot summer days. Driving range and snack bar.

Health & Fitness Clubs

Gold's Gym (239-549-3354; 1013 Cape Coral Pkwy. E, Cape Coral 33904) Classes in spinning, step aerobics, body flex, yoga, and karate. Personal training.

Sanibel Fitness Center (239-395-2639; 975 Rabbit Rd., Sanibel Island 33957) Newly expanded with full cardiovascular and weight-training studios, aerobic classes, personal training, and seniors program. Short-term memberships (one to six days) available.

Sanibel Recreation Center (239-472-0345; 3840 Sanibel-Captiva Rd., Sanibel Island 33957; at Sanibel School) Outdoor lap pool, weight room, basketball courts. City owned and operated. No admission fees.

South Seas Resort (239-472-SLIM, www.south-seas-resort.com; PO Box 194, Captiva Island 33924; at Chadwick Square) Open to the public for use of weight-training and cardiovascular equipment, sauna, exercise classes, and personal training.

Hiking

Cayo Costa State Park (941-964-0375; www.floridastateparks.org/cayocosta; PO Box 1150, Boca Grande 33921; at Barrier Islands GEO Park, Cayo Costa) Six miles of trail take you through barrier island ecology, a pioneer cemetery, and remnants of a circa 1904 quarantine station.

Corkscrew Regional Ecosystem Watershed (CREW) Marsh (239-657-2253; mailing address: 2301 McGregor Blvd., Fort Myers 33901; 23998 Corkscrew Rd., Estero 33928, 18 miles east of Interstate 75 exit 123) Five miles of hiking trails through peri-Everglades environment—pine flatwoods, oak and palm hammock, and sawgrass marsh—to a 12-foot observation tower. Free guided tours the second Saturday of every month, Oct.–May.

✪ **J. N. "Ding" Darling National Wildlife Refuge** (239-472-1100; www.dingdarling.fws.gov, www.dingdarlingsociety.org; 1 Wildlife Dr., Sanibel Island 33957, off Sanibel-Captiva Rd.) Its longest hike, the Indigo Trail, travels for more than 4 miles from the refuge education center, across a boardwalk, and along bird-rich ponds. Plans are to extend it with a new loop in 2004. A shorter trail takes you to a protected Calusa shell mound.

Sanibel-Captiva Conservation Foundation (239-472-2329; www.sccf.org; 3333 Sanibel-Captiva Rd., PO Box 839, Sanibel Island 33957) Nearly 5 miles of trails through natural habitat along the Sanibel River. The majority of wildlife consists of birds, lizards, and insects.

Kid's Stuff

Fort Myers Beach Pool (239-463-5759; 2600 Oak St., Fort Myers Beach 33931) Not your ordinary city pool, this one has a two-story slide and the toddler Tad Pool. Admission is $3 for ages 12 and older, $1 for ages 3–11.

Fort Myers Skatium (239-461-3145; www.fmskatium.com; 2250 Broadway, Fort Myers 33901) Open indoor ice skating plus hockey and figure skating. There's also a laser tag game. Hours vary. Cost for public ice skating sessions is $4 for children ages 12 and under, $5 for adults, $2 for skate rental.

Greenwell's Bat-A-Ball and Family Fun Park (239-574-4386; 35 NE Pine Island Rd., Cape Coral 33909) Named after the city's favorite sports son, Red Sox player Mike Greenwell, this facility contains batting cages, a miniature golf course, a small playground, a maze, a video arcade, four go-cart tracks, and snack concessions. Kids really love it here, but be prepared to lay out a lot of money if you spend much time—especially in the arcade room.

Periwinkle Park (239-472-1433; 1119 Periwinkle Way, Sanibel Island 33957) The owner of this trailer park raises and breeds exotic birds and waterfowl. He daddies roughly 600 birds of 133 species, specializing in African and Asian hornbills. flamingoes, parakeets, cockatiels, cockatoos, and others occupy the park and 15 aviaries. During the off-season, visitors can drive through; in-season, biking is recommended. A few of the birds raised here can be seen more easily at Jerry's Shopping Center (1700 Periwinkle Way). Take the children in the evening, when the birds are most talkative.

Sanctuary Skate Park (239-337-5297; www.sanctuaryskateparks.com; 2277 Grand Ave., Fort Myers 33901; downtown behind the Skatium) Skateboarders and in-line skaters love this city-owned outdoor facility with its cool ramps and half-pipes. Skate and pad rentals available. Admission: $7 for a two-hour session. On Monday evenings the park is open for BMX riders.

The Shell Factory (239-995-2141, 800-282-5805; www.shellfactory.com; 2787 N. Tamiami Trail, N. Fort Myers 33903) A shell shop on steroids, this longtime attraction has grown into a megacomplex—still old-fashioned, with restaurants, a fun park, a small wild animal zoo, Waltzing Waters lit fountain show, stuffed African animal collection, aquariums, video games, and lots of souvenir shops carrying gifts from fine to tacky. Local kids can sign up for the free Kids Club for special family events. Admission to the Shell Factory is free; zoo $8 for adults and $3 for children ages 4–16, Waltzing Waters $4, bumper boat rides and miniature golf $4, water wars $2.50, pitching cage $1 for three balls. Fun park hours are 11–7 Monday–Thursday, 11–8 Friday–Sunday.

Strausser BMX Sports Complex (239-458-1943; www.capecoralbmx.org; 1410 SW Sixth Pl., Cape Coral 33991) A bicycle motocross track is provided for practice and weekly races, along with picnic grounds, a playground, a softball field, and a sand volleyball court.

Sun Splash Family Waterpark (239-574-0557; www.sunsplashwaterpark.com; 400 Santa Barbara Blvd, Cape Coral 33991) This spot offers wet fun in a dozen varieties, with pools, slides, flumes, a log roll, cable drops, a river ride, volleyball, food, lockers, and special events. Admission is $10.95 for guests 48 inches or taller, $8.95 for shorter children, $5.95 for senior citizens, and $2.95 for children ages 2 and younger (plus tax). Parking is $1. The park is open early March through September, but schedule varies according to time of year and day; open daily late May–mid-August.

Germain Arena (239-948-7825; www.tecoarena.com; 11000 Everblades Pkwy., Estero 33928; exit 123 off Interstate 75, at Corkscrew Rd.) The public can ice or in-line skate at one of the three indoor NHL-sized rinks daily (times vary) for $6 for a regular session. Skate rental is $3. Sunday family skating is $3 each, including rentals, plus there are special late skate and pizza and pop sessions. Learn-to-skate classes, ice-hockey league, in-line teams, and figure-skating club.

Racquet Sports

Cape Coral Yacht Club Community Park (239-574-0806; www.capecoral.net/citydept /parks/pks_yachtclub.cfm; 5819 Driftwood Pkwy., Cape Coral 33904) Five lit tennis courts and two outdoor racquetball courts.

Fort Myers Racquet Club (239-278-7277; 4900 DeLeon St., Fort Myers 33907) Eight clay courts and two hard courts (eight lit), lessons, and tournaments. Admission.

Hancock Bridge Community Park (239-565-7748; 2211 Hancock Bridge Pkwy., Cape Coral 33990) The Lee County Community Tennis Association (www.leecountytennis.com) conducts classes and league play on five lit courts.

Rutenberg Community Park (6500 S. Pointe Blvd., Fort Myers 33907)

Signal Inn Resort (239-472-4690; www.signalinn.com; 1811 Olde Middle Gulf Dr., Sanibel Island 33957) Two racquetball courts. Admission.

STARS Complex (239-332-6671; www.cityftmyers.com/departments/recreation/stars .htm; 2980 Edison Ave., Fort Myers 33916; downtown Fort Myers) Two tennis courts.

A wealth of whelks. Karen T. Bartlett

Shelling

Welcome to shelling heaven. Sanibel Island, in particular, is known for its great pickings. Be aware that a state of Florida law prohibits the collection of live shells on Sanibel Island, to preclude the possibility of dwindling populations. Collecting live shells is also prohibited in state and national parks. Elsewhere in the county, live collecting is also discouraged. Any shell with a creature still inside is considered a live shell. Shellers who find live shells washed up on the beach—a common occurrence after storms—are urged to gently return (no flinging!) the shell to deep water.

Hot Shelling Spots

Big Hickory Island (northwest of Little Hickory Island, accessible only by boat) An unhitched crook of beach favored by local boaters and shellers.

Bonita Beach (Little Hickory Island) Look north of the public beach.

✪ **La Costa Island** (between North Captiva and Boca Grande, accessible only by boat) Because it takes a boat ride to get there, these sands hold caches of shells merely by virtue of their remoteness. North-end Johnson Shoals provides a thin strip of sandbar for good low-tide pickings.

Sanibel Island Known as the Shelling Capital of the Western Hemisphere, the island even has its own name for the peculiar, shell-bent stance of the beach collector: Sanibel Stoop. Unlike the other Gulf Coast barrier islands, Sanibel takes an east-west heading. Its perpendicular position and lack of offshore reefs allow it to intercept shells that arrive from southern seas. Its fame as a world-class shelling area has made Sanibel a prime destination for shell collectors for decades. With shell-named streets, store shelves awash in shells and shell crafts, an annual shell fair, and a shell museum, one risks suffering shell shock just by visiting there. Best gulf-side shelling spot: Bowman's Beach, midisland, away from the paths leading to the parking lot.

Shelling Charters

Adventure in Paradise (239-472-8443 , 239-437-1660; www.adventureinparadiseinc
.com; 14341 Port Comfort Rd., Fort Myers 33908; at Port Sanibel Marina, east of
Sanibel toll booth) Shelling and snorkeling excursions to Cayo Costa aboard power
catamarans.

Capt. Mike Fuery's Shelling Charters (239-466-3649; www.sanibel-online.com/fuery;
PO 1302, Captiva Island 33924) A local shelling expert, who authors a how-to column for
the *Sanibel-Captiva Islander* newspaper, takes small groups to Cayo Costa, Johnson Shoals,
and other shelling hot spots.

The Playtime (239-472-5300; www.captivacruises.com; PO Box 580, Captiva Island 33924;
at Captiva Cruises, South Seas Resort) Three-hour shelling trips to Cayo Costa and North
Captiva with experienced instruction.

Spas

Sanibel Day Spa (239-395-2220; www.sanibeldayspa.com; 2075 Periwinkle Way #27,
Sanibel Island 33957; at Periwinkle Place, upstairs) Long-established and well-reputed
place of pampering offering extensive à la carte and spa package services, including hair
care, manicures, pedicures, men's treatments, facials, oxygen therapy, steam therapy,
scrubs, and massage.

Sanibel Harbour Resort & Spa (239-466-4000, 800-767-7777; www.sanibel-resort.com;
17260 Harbour Pointe Dr., Fort Myers 33908; directly before the Sanibel causeway)
Sanibel Harbour was a spa before it became a resort (see "Lodging"). Guests, members,
and day visitors can take advantage of the swimming pool, whirlpools, training room, aerobics and tai chi classes, saunas, steam rooms, and racquetball courts. Renovated in 2003,
the spa's special services capitalize on the resort's important archaeological Calusa location with a living wishing-shell mound, interactive couples treatments, herbal wraps, aromatherapy massage, a new flexibility studio and relaxation bistro, personal training,
facials, and the unique BETAR musical and sound relaxation system.

Spectator Sports

Crab Races

'Tween Waters Inn Crow's Nest (239-472-5161; 15951 Captiva Dr., Captiva Island 33924)
Held at 6 and 9 every Monday night. Participate or watch. The early session is geared
toward families.

Pro Baseball

City of Palms Park (239-334-4700, 877-RED-SOX9; www.redsox.com; 2201 Edison Ave.,
Fort Myers; 33901; downtown at Jackson St) Home of the Boston Red Sox's spring exhibition games, starting in March and played into April.

Hammond Stadium (239-768-4210; 14100 Six Mile Cypress Rd., Fort Myers 33912) Hosts
the Minnesota Twins (239-768-4270, 800-33TWINS; www.mntwins.com) for spring
training in March and early April. From April through August, the Miracle Professional
Baseball team (239-768-4210; www.miraclebaseball.com), a member of the Florida State
League, competes here.

Pro Football

Florida Firecats (239-390-CATS; www.floridafirecats.com; TECO Arena, off Interstate 75, exit 123, at Corkscrew Rd., 11000 Everblades Pkwy., Estero 33928) Part of the arenafootball2 league, they play April through July.

Pro Hockey

Florida Everblades (239-948-7825; www.floridaeverblades.com; TECO Arena, off Interstate 75, exit 123, at Corkscrew Rd., 11000 Everblades Pkwy., Estero 33928) Southwest Florida's professional ice hockey team plays its October–April season at TECO Arena. The public can skate at the rink daily (times vary) for a fee. (See "Kid's Stuff," above.)

City of Palms Park hosts Red Sox spring training games. |Julie Cordeiro/Boston Red Sox

Waterskiing

Southern Extreme Waterski Show Team (239-571-4957; www.southernextremewater ski.com) Puts on two free shows every Sunday at Miromar Outlets (see "Shopping").

Water Sports

Dive Shops & Charters

Underwater Explorers (239-481-4733; 12600 McGregor Blvd., Fort Myers 33919) Certification courses and equipment, plus dive trips out of the region. This operation has been around for years. Others come and go throughout the region, but this is most dependable.

Parasailing & Waterskiing

Holiday Water Sports (239-765-4FUN; 250 Estero Blvd.; at Pink Shell Beach Resort; also 239-463-6778; 684 Estero Blvd., Fort Myers Beach 33931; at Best Western Beach Resort) Sun Cat, kayak, aquacycle, parasailing, and Waverunner rentals available, with lessons.

Ranalli Parasail (239-542-5511; www.ranalliparasail.com; 2000 Estero Blvd., Fort Myers Beach 33931) Rides along Fort Myers Beach and Waverunner rentals.

Rebel Watersports (239-463-3351; 1028 Estero Blvd., Fort Myers Beach 33931) Waverunner rentals and dolphin tours.

YOLO Watersports (239-472-YOLO; www.yolo-jims.com; 11534 Andy Rosse Ln., PO Box 1150, Captiva Island 33924) Parasailing rides from 600 to 1,200 feet high; double and triple rides available.

Sailboarding & Surfing

Winter and summer storms bring the sort of waves that surfers crave, but in general gulf waves are too wimpy for serious wave riders. Strong winds, however, provide excellent conditions for sailboarders in several locations throughout the region. Sanibel Causeway is the most popular windsurfing spot.

Ace Performer (239-489-3513; www.ace performer.com; 16842 McGregor Blvd., Fort Myers 33908) Rents and gives lessons for windsurfers, kite boards, and kayaks. Free delivery to the Sanibel causeway.

Snorkeling & Scuba

Florida's west coast has no natural reefs, but several have been built to provide a home for marine life and make divers and fishermen happy. Nearly 20 of these artificial reefs lie along the Sanibel Island–area coast. The Edison Reef, one of the largest, was created from the sinking of a former Fort Myers bridge in 42 feet of water 15 nautical miles off the Sanibel Lighthouse. The Belton Johnson Reef, constructed of concrete culvert, lies about 5 nautical miles off Bowman's Beach on Sanibel. Other popular sites include the Redfish Pass Barge, in 25 feet of water less than a nautical mile from Redfish Pass between Captiva and North Captiva, and the Doc Kline Reef, a popular tarpon hole less than 8 nautical miles from the Sanibel Lighthouse. Cayo Costa State Island Preserve offers snorkelers nice ledges in 2 to 5 feet of water, alive with fish, sponges, and shells.

Soaring views and elevated heart rates: the thrill of parasailing. Karen T. Bartlett

Wilderness Camping

Cayo Costa State Park (941-964-0375; www.floridastateparks.org/cayocosta; PO Box 1150, Boca Grande 33921; at Barrier Islands GEO Park, La Costa Island) You'll need boat transportation to reach this unbridged island, home to wild pigs and myriad birds. Bring your own fresh drinking water and lots of bug spray. And don't expect to plug in the camcorder. There are showers, picnic grounds, boat docks, nature trails, a tram that runs cross-island, and tent sites. Call ahead to reserve the latter. Camping was once allowed anywhere on the 2,225-acre island, but today it's restricted to a specific area.

Koreshan State Historic Site (239-992-0311; www.floridastateparks.org/koreshan; PO Box 7, Estero 33928) Koreshan's 60 campsites circle a volleyball court and are built fairly close together. The park contains a nature trail, canoe trail, boat ramp, and 12 buildings in the historic compound. For reservations call 800-326-3521 or visit www.reserve america.com.

Wildlife Spotting

Loggerhead turtles lumber up on local beaches each summer to lay their cache of eggs. (Only vigilant night owls actually see them, but you can find their tracks and see their nests, which patrols stake off.) Brown pelicans swarm fishing piers for handouts. Black skimmers nest on uninhabited sandy islands, while hundreds of other birds visit or stay in local habitats. The Island Coast is a vital area for wildlife, and many opportunities exist to spy on them in their natural setting.

Alligators

Once endangered, the alligator population has sprung back in recent decades, thanks to organizations and laws that fought to protect the prehistoric reptiles. Sanibel Island paved the way by pioneering a no-feeding regulation that later became state law. (Hand-fed alligators lose their fear of man.)

Innate homebodies, alligators usually leave their home ponds only during spring and summer mating. Spotting them is easiest then. You will often hear the bellow of the bull gator in the night and see both males and females roaming from pond to pond in search of midsummer night's romance. They can do serious damage to a car, so be alert. And never approach one on foot.

When it's cold, alligators stay submerged to keep warm. When they're in the water, you first spot their snouts, then their prickly tire-tread profiles. Once your eye becomes trained to distinguish them from logs and background, you'll notice them more readily. On sunny days throughout the year you can spot them soaking up rays on the banks of freshwater rivers and streams.

Serious gator searchers should try Sanibel Island's J. N. "Ding" Darling National Wildlife Refuge.

Birds

Roseate spoonbills are the stars of the "Ding" Darling National Wildlife Refuge, but hundreds of other species live among the sanctuary's wiry mangrove limbs and shallow estuarine waters, including ibises, brown and white pelicans, tri-color herons, red-shouldered hawks, snowy egrets, anhingas, and ospreys. In 2002 *Birder's World* magazine listed "Ding" Darling as third among the Top 15 Birding Hot Spots.

Dolphins

Playful bottle-nosed dolphins cruise the sea, performing impromptu acrobatic shows that it's hard to believe aren't staged. When the next performance will be is anybody's guess, but if you learn their feeding schedules, you have a better chance of catching their act. They often like to leap out of the wake of large boats. Out in the gulf I've been surrounded by their antics to the point where I suffered minor whiplash from spinning around to keep track of them all. Don't expect them to get too close—take some binoculars—and forget seeing them in captivity around here. Locals once staged a protest in Pine Island Sound when collectors tried to take some of their dolphins. And when a swim-with-the-dolphins facility was proposed near Sanibel Island, citizens again rose up in arms against animal exploitation.

Manatees

In east Fort Myers—where warm waters discharged from the Florida Power & Light Company have always attracted the warm-blooded manatees in the winter months to so-called Yankee Canal—Manatee Park (see below) has opened to provide a manatee viewing

Local sightseeing tours hold the promise of sighting bottlenose dolphins, which love to play in a boat's wake.
Karen T. Bartlett

area, exhibits, and other recreational and educational assets on the wild and natural Orange River.

Pine Island's backwaters offer a good venue for manatee spotting. Check out the bay behind Island Décor & More, a popular sea-watch site, just before the Matlacha Bridge. If you're around South Seas Resort on Captiva Island, watch the marina waters for surfacing manatees.

Nature Preserves & Eco-Attractions
CALUSA NATURE CENTER & PLANETARIUM
239-275-3435.
www.calusanature.com.
3450 Ortiz Ave., Fort Myers 33905.
Open: 9am–5pm Mon.–Sat., 11am–5pm Sun. Call for astronomy and laser show times.
Admission: Museum, trails, and planetarium: $7 adults, $4 children 3–12, free under 3.

This multifaceted environmental center offers a free 2-mile wildlife trail, with a Seminole Amerindian village, a butterfly aviary, a native plant garden, a caged bobcat and albino raccoon, 100 other live animals, and an injured-bird aviary. Join a guided walk of the Cypress Swamp Boardwalk every Tuesday and Friday at 9:30am. Indoors you can see live animal exhibits—snakes, tarantulas, alligators, and bees—and demonstrations. Daily programs allow visitors to get up close and personal with some of the fascinating creatures of Southwest Florida. Snakes are fed every Sunday at 11:15am. The planetarium uses telescopes, laser lights, and astronomy lessons in its presentations.

CAYO COSTA STATE PARK
941-964-0375.
www.floridastateparks.org/cayocosta.
PO Box 1150, Boca Grande 33921.
Barrier Islands GEO Park, Cayo Costa Island, accessible only by boat.
Admission: $1 per person.

A wildlife refuge occupies about 90 percent of this 2,225-acre island. Cayo Costa preserves the Florida that the Native Americans tried to protect against European invasion. Besides the occasional wild hog that survives on the island, egrets, white pelicans, raccoons, osprey, and black skimmers frequent the area. The path across the island's northern end features a side trip to a pioneer cemetery. Blooming cacti and other flora festoon the walk, which is sometimes a run when the weather turns warm and uncontrolled mosquito populations remind us of the hardships of eras gone by.

C.R.O.W.
239-472-3644.
www.crowclinic.org.
3883 Sanibel-Captiva Rd., Sanibel Island 33957.
Open: Tours at 11am Mon.–Fri. and 1pm Sun., Nov.–Apr. only.
Admission: $5 adults, free for children 12 and under.

C.R.O.W. is the acronym for Clinic for the Rehabilitation of Wildlife. This hospital complex duplicates natural habitats and tends to sick and injured wildlife: birds, bobcats, raccoons, rabbits, and otters. The facility cares for more than 3,000 patients a year. You can visit animals on the mend by tour.

FOUR MILE COVE ECOLOGICAL PRESERVE
239-549-4606.
At the end of SE 23rd Terrace, north of Midpoint Memorial Bridge in Cape Coral (follow the signs off Del Prado Blvd. north of Coralwood Mall at SE 21st Ln.).
Open: Dawn to dusk daily.
Admission: Free.

An urban preserve runs parallel to the bridge and allows exploration of 365 acres of wetlands along a 4,500-foot boardwalk and nature trails that take you away from the bustle of traffic. Interpretive center, restrooms, picnicking, guided nature walks, and kayak rentals on the weekends (October–May only).

✪ J. N. "DING" DARLING WILDLIFE REFUGE
239-472-1100.
http://dingdarling.fws.gov, www.dingdarlingsociety.org.
1 Wildlife Dr., Sanibel Island 33957.
Off Sanibel-Captiva Rd.
Open: Refuge, sunrise to sunset (closed Fri.); education center, 9am–5pm, 9am–4pm May–Oct.
Admission: Free to education center; $5 per car for refuge, $1 per cyclist or pedestrian.

More than 6,000 acres of pristine wetlands and wildlife are protected by the federal government, thanks to the efforts of Pulitzer Prize–winning cartoonist and politically active conservationist J. N. "Ding" Darling, a regular Captiva visitor in the 1930s. A 5-mile drive takes you through the refuge, once a satellite of the original Everglades National Wildlife Refuge. To really experience "Ding," get out of the car. At the very least follow the easy trails into mangrove, bird, and alligator territory. Look for roseate spoonbills, yellow-crowned night herons, white pelicans, painted buntings, and dozens of other life-list prizes. Narrated tram and guided canoe tours are available (239-472-8900). The new education center holds hands-on wildlife displays, realistic habitat vignettes, bird sculptures, a birders' room, and a peek into the world of the refuge's namesake. Naturalist programs take place throughout the week in-season.

✪ MANATEE PARK

239-432-2038.
www.leeparks.org/manatee.htm.
10901 Route 80 (Palm Beach Blvd.), Fort Myers 33905.
Open: 8am–8pm daily Apr.–Sept.; 8am–5pm daily Oct.–Mar.
Parking: 75¢ per hour, $3 per day.

A well-kept, 16-acre recreational park feeds our fascination for the loveable manatee, teddy bear of the water world. In addition to a manatee viewing area, it provides hydrophones (in-season) so visitors can eavesdrop on the marine mammals, polarized filters for peeping underwater, habitat exhibits, a nature boardwalk, a

Fort Myers's new Manatee Park overlooks the sea cow's favorite winter vacation spot.
Lee County Visitor & Convention Bureau

canoe and kayak launch (and rentals and clinics in winter and on summer weekends), nature programs (in winter), wildlife habitat areas, an information center, and picnic facilities. The park also serves as a rescue and release site for injured and rehabilitated manatees. For manatee viewing updates, call 239-694-3537.

MATANZAS PASS PRESERVE

239-765-4222.
www.leeparks.org.
119 Bay Rd., Fort Myers Beach.
At School St.
Open: Dawn to dusk.
Admission: Free.

A quiet respite from vacationland action, this 56-acre preserve provides a 1.25-mile loop trail and boardwalks through mangroves and maritime hammocks to out-of-the-way bay waters.

OSTEGO BAY FOUNDATION'S MARINE SCIENCE CENTER

239-765-8101.
www.ecotrail.com/ostego_bay.htm.
718 Fisherman Wharf, Fort Myers Beach 33931.
Open: 10am–4pm Wed.– Fri., 10am–1pm Sat.
Admission: By donation.

Primarily a marine-science education and research facility, Ostego Bay maintains a showroom of local sea life for visitors to tour. Aquariums hold local species in various habitats, such as sea grass, estuarine, and gulf. Manatee, loggerhead, and other kiosks explain the plight of endangered species and the workings of the local shrimping industry. Interactive displays include a dry-touch table, microscopes, and a touchable shark's skin and blue marlin's bill. The Foundation has built a boardwalk along the bay where the shrimp boats dock off Main Street. Here you can learn yet more about shrimping, estuaries, and local maritime heritage. A three-hour Wednesday Working Waterfront Tour takes you along the boardwalk beginning at 9am; cost is $10 each.

SANIBEL-CAPTIVA CONSERVATION FOUNDATION CENTER
239-472-2329.
www.sccf.org.
3333 Sanibel-Captiva Rd., PO Box 839, Sanibel Island 33957.
Open: 8:30am–3pm Mon.–Fri. during summer; 8:30am–4pm Mon. mid-Oct.–mid-May; 10–2 Sat. between Thanksgiving and Easter; closed Sun. and most Sat.
Admission: Nature Center admission is $3 for visitors 17 and older.

This research and preservation facility encompasses more than 1,800 acres. A guided or self-guided tour introduces you to indigenous flora and natural bird habitats. Indoor displays and dioramas further educate and include a touch tank. Guest lecturers, seminars, and workshops address environmental issues during the winter season. The weekly beach walk is fun and informative. Native plant nursery and butterfly house also on the premises.

SIX MILE CYPRESS SLOUGH PRESERVE
239-432-2040.
www.leeparks.org/sixmile.
7751 Penzance Crossing, Fort Myers.
On Six Mile Cypress Pkwy.
Open: 8–5 daily Oct.–Mar.; 8–8 daily Apr.–Sept.
Admission: Free; parking 75 cents an hour (maximum $3).

Egrets, herons, ibises, and cormorants come to feed at this shallow waterway. Take a guided or self-guided tour around the more than one-mile-long boardwalk through cypress stands and wetland. Guided walks are at 9:30am daily (Wednesdays only May–October), with an extra 1:30 tour January–March.

Wildlife Tours & Charters
Adventure in Paradise (239-472-8443, 239-437-1660; www.adventureinparadiseinc .com; 14341 Port Comfort Rd., Fort Myers 33908; at Port Sanibel Marina off Summerlin Rd. before the Sanibel causeway) Sea-life-encounter excursions led by a marine biologist aboard a 40-foot power catamaran; also, shelling snorkel quests.

Canoe Adventures (239-472-5218; Sanibel Island 33957) Guided tours with a noted island naturalist in "Ding" Darling National Wildlife Refuge, on the Sanibel River, and in other natural areas.

Manatee World (239-693-1434; www.manateeworld.com; 5605 Palm Beach Blvd., Fort Myers 33905; on Route 80 at Interstate 75 exit 141, Coastal Marine Mart, East Fort Myers) Specializes in one-hour tours up the Orange River to spot manatees. Educational video viewing and canoe and kayak rentals.

Sanibel-Captiva Conservation Foundation Center (239-472-2329; www.sccf.org; 3333 Sanibel-Captiva Rd., Sanibel Island 33957) Hosts guided nature-trail, beach-walk, and island-boat tours.

Tarpon Bay Explorers (239-472-8900; www.tarponbayexplorers.com; 900 Tarpon Bay Rd., Sanibel Island 33957) Naturalist-guided kayak, pontoon boat, and tram tours through "Ding" Darling National Wildlife Refuge. Also aquarium talks, canoe and kayak rentals, bike and boat rentals, beach walks, and free lunchtime wildlife talks.

Shopping

Shopping Centers & Malls

Two new mega shopping-entertainment malls are being planned for the fast-growing Estero-San Carlos Park area south of Fort Myers. One will include a Bass Pro Shops Outdoor World sportsman shopping attraction.

Bell Tower Shops (239-489-1221; www.thebelltowershops.com; 13499 S. Cleveland Ave., Fort Myers 33907) Saks Fifth Avenue anchors this alfresco, Mediterranean-style plaza of one-of-a-kind shops, upscale chains (Victoria's Secret, Brookstone, Williams-Sonoma), restaurants, and movie theaters.

Captiva Island Like Captiva in general, the shopping scene here is quirky and beach oriented. Chadwick's Square, near the entrance to the South Seas Resort, provides the best (if somewhat pricey) concentration of gifts and fashion, but is under renovation after hurricane damage.

Coralwood Mall (2301 Del Prado Blvd., Cape Coral 33909) An outdoor mall of restaurants and chain stores, including Bealls Department Store.

Downtown Fort Myers (First Street) Downtown is slowly looking up. More business- and government-minded than commercial, it does harbor some interesting book and cigar stores and unusual antique and what-not shops. Urban renewal emphasis is on entertainment and dining, so most shops are utilitarian.

Edison Mall (239-939-5464; www.simon.com; 4125 Cleveland Ave., Fort Myers 33901) An entirely commercial, enclosed, and air-conditioned mall with major department stores such as Burdines, Dillard's, JC Penney, and Sears, plus about 150 smaller clothing and gift shops and a food court.

Fort Myers Beach Shop in your bikini, if you wish, at Times Square, a hub of ultracasual island activity. You'll find a profusion of swimsuit boutiques, surf shops, and food outlets at this pedestrian mall. At the island's south end, Villa Santini Plaza has some interesting shops and food stops.

Matlacha (Pine Island) Sagging old fish houses, cracker-box shops, quirky art galleries, and fishing motels heavily salt the flavor of this island village. Knickknack historic structures painted in candy-store colors give the town an artistic, Hansel and Gretel feel. Sea-themed gifts, art, and jewelry comprise the majority of merchandise.

McGregor Antiques District (Fort Myers) A nucleus of 17 shops spread around five small strip centers at College Parkway.

Page Field Commons (www.pagefieldcommons.com; Cleveland Ave. at Fowler Ave., Fort Myers) A conglomeration of mega-marts such as Old Navy, Toys "R" Us, Best Buy, Books-A-Million, and Michael's Crafts.

Sanibel Island Periwinkle Way and Palm Ridge Road constitute the shopper's routes on Sanibel, which is known for its galleries (specializing in wildlife art), shell shops, and resort-wear stores. These are clustered in tastefully landscaped, nature-compatible outdoor centers, the largest being Periwinkle Place on Periwinkle Way. One of the most interesting, both architecturally and in terms of merchandise, is The Village on Periwinkle Way.

Antiques & Collectibles

Albert Meadow Antiques (239-472-8442; 15000 Captiva Dr., Captiva Island 33924) Turn-of-the-20th-century decorative arts by Tiffany, Gorham, and Steuben; antique jewelry, Navajo weavings, and Art Deco and Art Nouveau.

Judy's Antiques (239-481-9600; 12710 McGregor Blvd., Fort Myers 33919) One of the oldest in the McGregor Antiques District, this establishment is well-organized and sells quality merchandise: furniture, jewelry, clothes, and decorative items.

McGregor Antique Mall (239-433-0200; 12720 McGregor Blvd., Fort Myers 33919) In the same neighborhood as Judy's but more folksy and nostalgic in its considerable offerings—household goods, books, toys, country-style furnishings, and more.

Books

Beach Book Nook (239-463-3999; 7205 Estero Blvd., Fort Myers Beach 33931; at Villa Santini Plaza) New and used paperback exchange; a nice selection of local guides and books.

The Island Book Nook (239-472-6777; 2330 Palm Ridge Rd., Sanibel Island 33957; at Palm Ridge Place) Paperback exchange, hardbacks for sale and rent, complete collection of local books.

✪ **MacIntosh Books** (239-472-1447; www.sanibelbooks.com; 2365 Periwinkle Way, Sanibel Island 33957) A tiny shop packed full of books of local and general interest.

Clothing

Anna's Distinctive Moroccan Clothing (239-482-5600; 13499 Cleveland Ave., Fort Myers 33907; at Bell Tower Shops; and 2055 Periwinkle Way, Sanibel 33957, at Forever Green Shops) Comfortable hand-woven fashions of natural fibers from Morocco. Women's garments, shoes, jewelry, and other accessories.

Candace's at Frangi-Pani (239-472-3777; PO Box 425, Captiva Island 33924; unit #110 at Chadwick's Square) Stylish and casual women's resort fashions, Fresh Produce label, and lots of swimsuits.

Chico's (239-472-3773; 2330 Palm Ridge Rd., Sanibel Island 33957; at Palm Ridge Place) I prefer this Chico's store to the original because it's more low-key, with less hustle and bustle.

Dockside (239-472-9098; 2075 Periwinkle Way, Sanibel Island 33957; at Periwinkle Place) Shirts and sportswear for men with a fishing, marine, and tropical sensibility; also shoes and sandals.

H2o Outfitters and Footloose of Captiva (239-472-7507; PO Box 665, Captiva Island 33924; at Chadwick's Square) Name-brand men's and women's beach and marina fashions, shoes, quality souvenir T-shirts and sweatshirts.

Mr. Pants and Michelle's Resortwear (239-463-1515; 7205 Estero Blvd., Fort Myers Beach 33931) Fine casual, Florida-fit fashions for men and women.

Nanny's (239-472-0304; 2340 Periwinkle Way, Sanibel 33957, at The Village) Adorable outfits, shoes, books, and gifts for the little people.

Peach Republic (239-472-8444; 2075 Periwinkle Way #16, Sanibel Island 33957; at Periwinkle Place) Stylish cotton and other tropical resort wear for women, plus shoes and jewelry.

Trader Rick's (239-489-2240; 13499 US 41 #217, Fort Myers 33907; at Bell Tower Shops; and 239-472-9191, 2075 Periwinkle Way #38, Sanibel 33957, at Periwinkle Place) Creative casual Florida wear for women plus unusual and handmade jewelry, toiletries, and other accessories.

T-Shirt Hut (239-472-1415; 1504 Periwinkle Way, Sanibel Island 33957) The best T-shirts on the island; also other clothing, gifts, and beach supplies.

Consignment
Buying secondhand on the Island Coast is not the embarrassment it is in some places. Because of the wealthy and transient nature of its residents, the area offers the possibility of great discoveries in its consignment shops.

Classy Exchange (239-278-1123; 12791 Kenwood Ln. #B1, Fort Myers 33907) Designer women's fashions and housewares.

Designer Consigner (239-472-1266; 2460 Palm Ridge Rd., Sanibel Island 33957; at Tarpon Bay Center) Clothing, furniture, and household items.

Elite Repeat (239-936-1001; 12955 Cleveland Ave. #156, Fort Myers 33907; at Pinebrook Park) Formal, career, and casual wear for women.

Perennials (239-275-8838; 7051 Crystal Dr., Fort Myers 33907) Baby furniture, toys, and children's and women's clothes.

Sarah's Consignments (239-283-3302; 5990 Mackerel Rd., Bokeelia 33922; on Pine Island) Stuffed full with housewares, decorative items, and women's clothing.

Second Hand Rose (239-574-6919; 1532 SE 14th St., Cape Coral 33990; at Del Prado Mall) Extensive selection of fashion, jewelry, household items, furniture, and collectibles.

Factory Outlet Centers
Miromar Outlets (239-948-3766; www.miromar.com/florida.html; 10801 Corkscrew Rd., Estero 33928; at exit 123 off Interstate 75) An above-average assortment of factory shops, designer outlets, and eateries, including Adidas, Nike, Reebok, Harry and David, Nautica,

Coach, and Pottery Row. Watch the Southern Extreme Waterski Show Team (239-571-4957; www.southernextremewaterski.com) on Sunday, or replenish (so you don't drop) at one of several restaurants.

Sanibel Tanger Factory Outlets (239-454-1974, 888-471-3939; www.tangeroutlet.com; 20350 Summerlin Rd., Fort Myers 33908; at McGregor Blvd.) Sitting at Sanibel's doorstep are outlets for Samsonite, Maidenform, Gap, Reebok, OshKosh, and Bass Shoes.

Flea Markets & Bazaars

Fleamasters Fleamarket (239-334-7001; www.fleamall.com; 4135 Dr. Martin Luther King Jr. Blvd., Fort Myers 33916) Some 300,000 indoor square feet of produce, souvenirs, and novelties; open Friday through Sunday.

McGregor Boulevard Garage Sales (Fort Myers) Drive the boulevard early—the earlier you go, the better the pickings—every Friday and Saturday morning, and watch for garage sale signs directing you to private sales.

Ortiz Fleamarket (239-694-5019; 1501 Ortiz Ave., Fort Myers 33905) Smaller than Fleamasters, this market convenes every Saturday and Sunday, 6am to 4pm.

Galleries

During season, hit Pine Island's Matlacha, a thriving artists' community, for Art Night the second Friday of the month. Besides gallery tours, visitors get entertainment, food, and Pine Island's special brand of fun.

Aboriginals: Art of the First Person (239-395-2200; www.tribalworks.com; 2340 Periwinkle Way, Sanibel Island 33957; at The Village) More of a museum than a store, this gallery focuses on Native American, African, and Australian tribal art.

Captiva's Finest (239-472-8222; 110 Chadwick's Square #340, Captiva Island 33924) Local artists' renditions of birds and other wildlife, framed decorative prints, animal sculptures—all in an affordable price range.

Crossed Palms Gallery (239-283-2283; www.crossedpalmsgallery.com; 8315 Main St., Bokeelia 33922; Pine Island) A delightful gallery facing the sea, it occupies

Captiva's Jungle Drums Gallery fits right in with the historic district's whimsical idiosyncrasies.
Karen T. Bartlett

two restored 1950s fishermen's cottages built around a cistern, which becomes part of the gallery. Its rooms are filled with original fine arts, glasswork, pottery, and jewelry by local and national artists.

Island Gallery (239-463-7100; 6151 Estero Blvd. #5, Fort Myers Beach 33931) Affordable framed art and prints by local artists, nice paintings by a Seminole Indian, statues, wall hangings, and other decorative items.

Jungle Drums (239-395-2266; www.jungledrumsgallery.com; 11532 Andy Rosse Ln., PO Box 368, Captiva Island 33924) On the outside, dolphins and birds are carved into the stair rail and floor studs. Inside, local and national artists depict wildlife themes in various media, much of it whimsical, all of it delightfully creative.

Matlacha Art Gallery (239-283-6453; 4637 Pine Island Rd., Matlacha 33993) Too much fun to be taken seriously as a gallery, it does sell the work of local sculptors, painters, and the owner, who specializes in colorized photographs and painted coconut postcards. Look for the trademark mannequins, dressed for the weather, outside. Stay for a cup of coffee in the waterfront Oz gallery garden in back.

Matsumoto Gallery (239-472-2941; www.ikkimatsumoto.com; 2340 Periwinkle Way, B-3, Sanibel 33957; at The Village) Besides the wildlife graphics of its locally popular Japanese-born owner, this affordable gallery carries the unusual in pottery, textiles, sculptures, and framed art.

Seaweed Gallery (239-472-1167; www.seaweedgallery.com; 11509 Andy Rosse Ln., Captiva Island 33924; 239-472-2585, 2340 Periwinkle Way, Sanibel Island 33957; at The Village) Fun and colorful painted furniture, tropical oil paintings, fused glass jewelry, palm-pattern pottery, and other works with a sense of place.

Sistarz (239-283-7370; www.sistarz.com; 4643 Pine Island Rd. NW, Matlacha 33993) Part of Pine Island's quirky art scene, it's as fishy and fun as you'd expect. Anything that stands still gets hand-painted here: toilet seat covers, floor candleholders, shoes, earrings, bags—you name it.

Tower Gallery (239-472-4557; www.towergallery-sanibel.com; 751 Tarpon Bay Rd., Sanibel Island 33957) In its charming Caribbean-motif old-beach-house digs, this artist's cooperative specializes in fine tropical art by area artists: masterful black-and-white photography by Charles McCullough, Sanibel scenes, batik, pottery, and baskets.

General Stores

Bailey's General Store (239-472-1516; 2477 Periwinkle Way, Sanibel Island 33957; at Bailey's Shopping Center, corner Tarpon Bay Rd.) An island fixture for ages, it stocks mostly hardware and fishing and kitchen supplies, with an attached grocery, bakery, and deli.

Island Store (239-472-2374; 11500 Andy Rosse Ln., PO Box 907, Captiva Island 33924) Here's where you can buy those necessities you forgot—but try not to forget too much because the prices reflect the location, here at the end of the earth.

Gifts

Cheshire Cat Toys (239-482-8697; 13499 S. Cleveland Ave., Fort Myers 33907; at Bell Tower Shops) Lamaze, Playmobil, stuffed animals, puppets, fine dolls, books, CDs, and learning toys.

Discovery Bay (239-463-4715; 7205 Estero Blvd., Fort Myers Beach 33931; at Villa Santini Plaza) "Your [sic] never too old to have a happy childhood," reads the owners' business card. Nice thought, although the gifts here are mostly grown-up, if somewhat whimsical: tasteful nautical and tropical gifts and home accessories, art class, and crystal.

Jerry's Bazaar (239-472-8185; 1700 Periwinkle Way, Sanibel Island 33957; at Jerry's Shopping Center) Collection of T-shirts, beach toys, jewelry, and shells all under one roof, selling affordable mementos of the island.

Lady Bugs & Dragonflies (239-332-3382; 2214 First St., Fort Myers 33901; downtown) Fun gifts especially for women (a little on the naughty side) and kids.

Pandora's Box (239-472-6263; 2075 Periwinkle Way #1, Sanibel Island 33957; at Periwinkle Place) Delightful decorative items, creative jewelry, potpourri, specialty children's gifts, soaps, yard art, and art greeting cards.

A Swedish Affair (239-275-8004; 1400 Colonial Blvd., Fort Myers 33907; at Royal Palm Square) Scandinavian gifts from funny to fine: Swedish joke books, lingonberry preserves, folk art, candles, glassware, Christmas ornaments, and fine pewter serving pieces.

Toys Ahoy (239-472-4800; 2075 Periwinkle Way, Sanibel Island 33957; at Periwinkle Place) Old-fashioned and learning-focused toys, puppets, books, stuffed toys, and more.

Jewelry
✪ **Congress Jewelers** (239-472-4177, 800-882-6624; www.congressjewelers.com; 2075 Periwinkle Way, Sanibel Island 33957; at Periwinkle Place) Dolphin, mermaid, bird, sandals, sand bucket, and shell gold pendants, plus other fine jewelry.

Friday's (239-472-1454, 800-850-6605; www.sanibeldiamond.com; 1700 Periwinkle Way, Sanibel 33957, in Jerry's Shopping Center) Specializes in diamonds as home of the "Sanibel diamond."

Mayors (239-590-6166; 13499 S. Cleveland Ave., Fort Myers 33907) Swiss watches and pens, rings, and elegant baubles of all sorts in a spacious setting.

Sanibel Silver & Pewter Company (239-395-2002; www.sanibelsilver.com; 1989 Periwinkle Way, Sanibel 33957; at Tahitian Gardens) For affordable island-theme pendants, bracelets, and earrings, browse the sterling silver and pewter selections here.

Scruples (239-463-0500; 7205 Estero Blvd., Fort Myers Beach 33931; at Villa Santini Plaza) I like this shop for its interesting heirloom-style pieces and its affordable jewelry along with the fine.

Kitchenware & Home Decor
Cheese Nook (239-472-2666; 2075 Periwinkle Way, Sanibel Island 33957; at Periwinkle Place) Fun and tropical placemats, towels, and dishware; also gourmet food items, including a wide selection of hot-pepper sauces.

Island Decor & More (239-283-8080; 4206 Pine Island Road, Matlacha 33993) Long known for its shells and trinkets, it has recently evolved into an emphasis on affordable decorative home art and accessories with an islandy appeal.

Island Style (239-472-6657; www.islandstylegallery.com; 2075 Periwinkle Way, Sanibel Island 33957; at Periwinkle Place) Whimsical, artistic, and one-of-a-kind decorative elements with a Sun Belt motif: hand-painted chairs, carved wooden mobiles and stabiles, brightly colored dishware, Caribbean-inspired pieces.

Sanibel Home Furnishings (239-472-5552; www.sanibelhomefurnishings.com; 1618 Periwinkle Way, Sanibel 33957) Sophisticated and tasteful island-style furnishings and decoration ideas.

Traders (239-395-3151; www.tradersstoreandcafe.com; 1551 Periwinkle Way, Sanibel Island 33957) This restaurant-and-store combo excels at both (see "Dining"). Warehouse-sized, the shop brims with furniture, objets d'art, candles, and gifts from distant, exotic lands.

Wilford & Lee (239-395-9295; 2009 Periwinkle Way, Sanibel 33957; at Tahitian Gardens) Affordable (for Sanibel) and distinct home decorations, including lamps, marine life wall sculptures, and tableware.

Shell Shops

Island Decor & More (239-283-8080; 4206 Pine Island Road, Matlacha 33993) The focus at this longtime shell shop has changed to home decor (see above), but it still carries an aisle of specimen shells. Bonus: a good location for spotting dolphin and manatees.

Sanibel Seashell Industries (239-472-1603; www.seashells.com; 905 Fitzhugh St., Sanibel 33957; just off Periwinkle Way) Serious shell junkies and shell artisans should head here for the best specimens at the best price in a warehouse setting.

She Sells Seashells (239-472-6991; 1157 Periwinkle Way, Sanibel 33957; and 239-472-8080; 2422 Periwinkle Way, Sanibel 33957) The island's oldest shell dealer has everything you need for shell crafts and displays.

The Shell Factory (239-995-2141, 800-282-5805; 2787 N. Tamiami Tr., North Fort Myers 33903) A palace of Florida funk and junk, the Shell Factory is built like a bazaar, with dozens of minishops within its 65,500 square feet. The main part displays specimen shells and shell-craft items of every variety. Jewelry, art, clothes, and knickknacks fill other nooks. Also at the complex (can't miss it; look for the giant conch shell on the sign) are restaurants, an arcade, a stuffed exotic animal collection, a small nature park, and bumper-boat rides.

Showcase Shells (239-472-1971; www.molluscs.net/Showcase_Shells; 1614 Periwinkle Way, Sanibel Island 33957; at

Big on shells: North Fort Myers's Shell Factory sells seashells plus fun games and attractions for the whole family. Karen T. Bartlett

Heart of the Islands Center) As elegant as a jewelry store, this boutique adds a touch of class to sifting through specimen shells by putting them under glass and into artistic displays.

Tarpon Bay Shell Shop (239-454-1111; 17711 San Carlos Blvd., Fort Myers Beach 33931) Loads of shells and other souvenirs, inexpensive to fine.

Sporting Goods
Note: For supplies and equipment for specific sports, please refer to "Recreation."

Sports Authority (239-418-0281; 2317 Colonial Blvd., Fort Myers 33907) Full line of equipment, sportswear, and shoes.

CALENDAR OF EVENTS

January
Medieval Faire (239-693-8036; Lakes Park, Fort Myers) Two weekends of flashback fun, including jousting, live chess, period food, kids' activities, live entertainment, jugglers, artisans, and antiques.

February
Black History Celebration (239-332-8778; Clemente Park, 1936 Henderson St., Fort Myers) A month of special events kicks off with a Saturday party early in the month.

Celebrate Cape Coral (239-549-6900; Cape Coral) Ball, antique car show, parade, music, and art exhibits. Month-long into March.

✪ **Edison Pageant of Light Festival** (239-334-2999; www.edisonfestival.org; Fort Myers) Commemorates the birthday of Thomas Edison, culminating in a spectacular lighted night parade. Two weeks early in the month.

Greek Fest (239-481-2099; Greek Orthodox Church, 8210 Cypress Lake Dr., Fort Myers 33907) Ethnic food and music. Three days midmonth.

Sanibel Music Festival (239-336-7999; www.sanibelmusicfestival.org; Sanibel Island) Features concerts by classical artists from across the nation. Most events held at Sanibel Congregational Church, 2050 Periwinkle Way. Month-long.

March
Fort Myers Beach Lions Club Shrimp Festival (239-463-9738; Lynn Hall Memorial Park, Fort Myers Beach) Blessing of the fleet, 5K run, parade, and shrimp boil. Two days mid-month.

Lee County Reading Festival (239-461-2914; www.lee-county.com/library/reading festival home.htm; Centennial Park, downtown Fort Myers) One day to celebrate literacy with prominent authors and related activities.

Sanibel Shell Fair and Show (239-472-2155; www.leeislandcoast.com/everything_to_do/ beach/sanibelshellfair.php; Sanibel Community House, 2173 Periwinkle Way, Sanibel Island 33957) Showcases sea life, specimen shells, and shell art. Four days in early March. Admission to show.

Sounds of Jazz (239-573-3121; Jaycee Park, 4125 SE 20th Place, Cape Coral) An outdoor concert midmonth featuring popular contemporary jazz artists.

April

Earth Day (239-472-2329; Sanibel-Captiva Conservation Foundation, 3333 Sanibel-Captiva Rd., Sanibel Island 33957) Participants ride free rental bikes to this midmonth homage to Mother Earth.

River & Blues Festival (239-338-3500; Centennial Park, Fort Myers) One day midmonth of live music, local food, and activities for kids.

May

Cinco de Mayo (239-573-3125; Iguana Mia restaurant, Cape Coral) A celebration of Cape Coral's Latin population with food and live entertainment.

Israelfest (239-481-4449; Patio de Leon, downtown Fort Myers) One day early in the month devoted to Jewish culture and ethnic foods of the Middle East and Eastern Europe.

Taste of the Islands (239-472-3644; Sanibel Island) About 20 Captiva and Sanibel restaurants participate, with live music and competitions to benefit wildlife. One day; admission.

June

Caloosa Catch & Release Fishing Tournament (941-479-7916; South Seas Resort, Captiva Island) Four-day event.

Taste of the Beach (239-454-7500; Fort Myers Beach) A gathering of restaurateurs and sun-loving gourmets (and gourmands).

July

✪ **MangoMania** (239-283-4842; www.mangomaniafl.com; German-American Social Club, 2101 SW Pine Island Road, Cape Coral) Celebrates Pine Island's favorite fruit with music and a stand selling mangos, mango trees, mango drinks, mango cookies, and other local delicacies. Good, honest community fun, one weekend in early July. Admission.

August

Cape In-Shore Redfish Challenge (239-573-3121; Yacht Club Community Park, Cape Coral) A fishing tournament for all anglers with cash prizes totaling $10,000 and other awards. Two days at the beginning of the month.

Summer Slam (239-479-7916; South Seas Resort, Captiva) Two days of slam-bang fishing competition limited to 75 boats and awarding more than $15,000 in cash and prizes.

October

Calusa Nature Center Haunted Walk (239-275-3435; www.calusanature.com; Calusa Nature Center, 3450 Ortiz Ave., Fort Myers 33905) The great-granddaddy (dead and molding) of all local haunted walks. Takes place nightly for a couple of weeks around Halloween.

"Ding" Darling Days (239-472-1100; J. N. "Ding" Darling National Wildlife Refuge, Sanibel Island) One week in October is devoted to exploring the refuge and celebrating the birthday of its namesake.

Jazz on the Green (239-477-4683; www.jazzonthegreen.com; Florida Gulf Coast University, Fort Myers) One day of soothing al fresco jazz by well-known artists. Admission.

Oktoberfest (239-281-1400; www.gasc -capecoral.com; German-American Social Club, Cape Coral) Cape Coral celebrates its strong German heritage with Oktoberfest music, food, and activities. Two weekends.

November
American Sandsculpting Contest (239-454-7500; www.sultansofsand.com; Outrigger Beach and Holiday Inn Gulfside Resorts, Fort Myers Beach) Amateur and masters divisions. One weekend in early November.

BIG ARTS Fair (239-395-0900; www.bigarts.org; Sanibel Community House, Sanibel Island) Juried arts and crafts exhibits. Thanksgiving weekend.

Fort Myers Beach is known for its bar-hopping scene and sand castles. Karen T. Bartlett

Fiesta Latino (239-418-1441; Fort Myers Toyota, Colonial Blvd. and Fowler St., Fort Myers) Local salsa, merengue, and other Latin musicians entertain while guests enjoy Latino food, talent shows, and children's activities. One day midmonth.

Taste of the Town (239-277-1197; Centennial Park, downtown Fort Myers) About 40 restaurants sell their specialties; live entertainment and children's games. One Sunday early in the month. Admission.

December
Christmas Luminary Trail (239-472-1080; Sanibel and Captiva Islands) More than 3 miles of luminary candles line the main roads of Sanibel's and Captiva's commercial areas, where businesses stay open and dole out free drinks and food. One weekend early in the month.

Edison/Ford Homes Holiday House (239-332-6680; www.edison-ford-estate.com/hh .asp; Edison/Ford complex, 2350 McGregor Blvd., Fort Myers) Period and seasonal exhibits and miles of light strings draw crowds to this popular attraction. Admission.

Holiday Boat-a-Long (239-573-3125; Four Freedoms Park, Cape Coral) Decorated boat parade with live entertainment, Santa, Christmas crafts, food, and more.

6

Naples & The South Coast

Precious Commodities

Perched on alabaster sands at the edge of Florida's Everglades, meticulous Naples transcends its wild setting like a diamond in the rough. Settled by land developers late in its life, this cultural oasis historically has appealed to the rich and the sporting. Today the state's final frontier is known for its million-dollar homes, great golfing, art galleries, posh resorts, world-class shopping, and fine dining. In the spirit of its Italian namesake, Naples has in the past decade undergone a sort of renaissance that has included a highly successful urban renewal project on Fifth Avenue South, a developing residential-shopping community nearby at Bayfront Center, and various new cultural venues, including Sugden Community Theatre, von Liebig Art Center, and the world-class Naples Museum of Art. In 2005 watch for the opening of an exciting new and progressively planned botanical garden. In its northern reaches the city spreads into the quiet residential district of **North Naples**, seaside **Vanderbilt Beach**, and the town of **Bonita Springs.**

The latter still adheres to an early agricultural heritage with a reputation for tomatoes, citrus, and other cash crops. Citrus freeze-outs farther north, plus the town's navigable Imperial River, created the community first called Survey in 1893. Here Henry Ford maintained a hunting lodge to which he and his Fort Myers friends traveled by horseback. Today, where the tomato fields end, upscale golfing communities begin, all surrounding a neighborly little town left frozen in time by dint of Tamiami Trail's rerouting. These days Bonita Springs starts to blend in with north Naples, both physically and in its character. New residential, hotel, and shopping developments boost it upward like an overachieving tomato vine climbing above its stake.

At the South Coast's southern and eastern extremes, the civility is balanced with swamp-buggy mud races, agriculture, Native American villages, fishing lodges, vanishing Florida panthers, and the unvarnished wilderness of the Everglades.

Neighboring **Marco Island** introduces the labyrinthine, mysterious land of Ten Thousand Islands. It was once an important center of the ancient Calusa culture, and the carved Key Marco Cat archaeological find (now exhibited at the Smithsonian Institution) has become an island icon. Tempered in a rough-and-tumble history, the island also boasts contemporary upscale resorts and good manners. Ancient Indian mounds, clam canneries, and pineapple plantations color the past of its three communities: **Isles of**

The architecture of the Village on Venetian Bay shopping district contributes to the Italian flavor of America's Naples. Karen T. Bartlett

Capri, Marco, and ✪ **Goodland.** First settled by the clan of William Collier (no relation to Barron Collier) in 1871, Marco Island has done most of its growing in the past few decades. Between 1960, when plans for a modern bridge were being formed, and 1980, the population increased by 755 percent. Goodland, so named because its land provided fertile soil for avocado farming, has purposely kept itself behind the times, giddily stuck in a good-time, catch-fish mode.

✪ **Everglades City**—the county seat until Naples took over—languishes in its wilderness setting at the doorstep to Big Cypress Swamp and Ten Thousand Islands. Its settlers have always kept a step ahead of the law, doing what they must to survive, whether it was fishing, alligator poaching, or pot smuggling. Today commercial fishing restrictions have channeled the town's orientation toward stone crabbing and tourism. A new coat of paint on the town and the mowing down of the forest of billboards that once welcomed visitors has meant a surge in growth and property values. There's talk of a spiffy new 58-acre resort and marina in town. Across a long, narrow causeway, Chokoloskee Island remains relatively untouched by change. It's a haven for RV campers and fishermen.

All contained within Collier County, this fast-growing region recently voted on a development moratorium in encroaching rural areas to preserve the sensitive Everglades environment that spreads before Naples' doorstep.

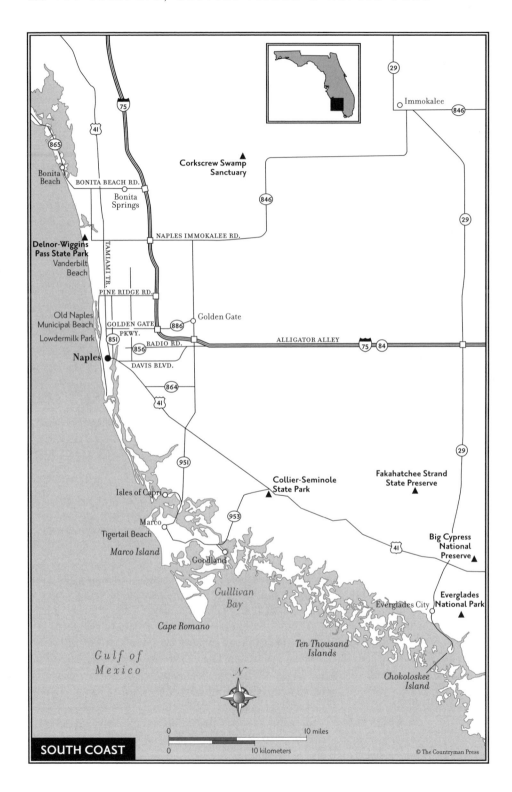

Immokalee

Corkscrew Swamp
Sanctuary

846

29

Bonita
Beach

BONITA BEACH RD.

Bonita
Springs

NAPLES IMMOKALEE RD.

Delnor-Wiggins
Pass State Park
Vanderbilt
Beach

TAMIAMI TR.

PINE RIDGE RD.

Golden Gate

Old Naples
Municipal Beach

GOLDEN GATE
PKWY.

Lowdermilk Park

851

856

RADIO RD.

886

ALLIGATOR ALLEY

75 84

Naples

DAVIS BLVD.

864

41

951

29

Collier-Seminole
State Park

Fakahatchee Strand
State Preserve

Isles of Capri

953

Marco

Big Cypress
National
Preserve

41

Tigertail Beach

Marco Island

Goodland

Everglades
National Park

Gulllivan
Bay

Everglades City

Cape Romano

Ten Thousand
Islands

Gulf of
Mexico

Chokoloskee
Island

N

0   10 miles

0   10 kilometers

SOUTH COAST

© The Countryman Press

LODGING

The South Coast was once a place for roughing it and low-key vacationing. The old wooden Naples Hotel, built in the 1880s by town developers, was as posh as it got. In 1946 Naples became a forerunner in the golf resort game when the Naples Hotel was bought and converted. In 1985, the Ritz-Carlton came to town and set a new tone. Naples changed forever. The Registry and other smaller luxury hotels followed the Ritz. As Naples renovates its downtown, new properties continue to rise, tending toward intimacy and European style, giving Naples a well-rounded menu of options from cottages and inns to golf meccas and grandes dames. Bonita Springs, to the north, is growing into its own as a destination with fine lodging, including a Hyatt Regency that opened in fall 2001. Nearby Marco Island lines up high-rise after high-rise resort and condo community along its coveted beaches. Privately owned second homes and condominiums provide another source of upscale accommodations along the South Coast. (Vacation brokers who match visitors with such properties are listed under "Home & Condo Rentals" at the end of this section.) Away from the metropolitan airs of Naples and Marco, lodging options reflect the simple, primitive nature of the Florida Everglades.

The highlights of South Coast hospitality listed here include the best and freshest in the local industry. Toll-free 800, 877, 866, or 888 reservation numbers, where available, are listed after local numbers.

Pricing codes are explained below. They are normally per person/double occupancy for hotel rooms and per unit for efficiencies, apartments, cottages, suites, and villas. The range spans low- and high-season rates. Many resorts offer packages at special rates. Prices do not include the 6 percent Florida sales tax, and some large resorts add service gratuities or maid charges. Collier County imposes a tourist bed tax, as well, proceeds from which are applied to beach and environmental maintenance.

Rate Categories

Inexpensive	Up to $75
Moderate	$75 to $150
Expensive	$150 to $200
Very Expensive	$200 and up

(An asterisk after the pricing designation indicates that at least a continental breakfast is included in the lodging rate.)

The following abbreviations are used for credit card information:

AE: American Express
MC: MasterCard
D: Discover Card
V: Visa
DC: Diners Club

Accommodations

BONITA SPRINGS
❂ **HYATT REGENCY COCONUT POINT RESORT & SPA**
Managing Director: Carlos Cabrera. 239-444-1234, 800-55-HYATT. www.coconutpoint.hyatt.com. 5001 Coconut Rd., Bonita Springs 34134. Price: Moderate to Very Expensive. Credit Cards: AE, D, DC, MC, V.

Opened defiantly soon after 9/11, this new tower of luxury has succeeded against the odds to make a glamour statement on shores where fish camps and pristine estuary formerly dominated. Despite its high-rise contrast to the surrounding low-key landscape, the resort strives to blend with its Florida setting wherever possible. The elegant Italian marble and mahogany lobby is localized with Florida-look terrazzo, and colors reflect the sea, sand, and verdure throughout the public spaces and 450 rooms and suites, all outfitted with minifridges, CD and DVD players, data ports, robes, safes, and coffeemakers. The Tarpon Bay restaurant resembles the old fish-shack architecture down the road and serves local seafood. To make up for the lack of readily available beach (guests must take a boat shuttle to a private island for sand), Hyatt's signature water features fill in with a waterslide kiddie pool, an adult pool, and stunning fountains and a reflecting pool. Many guests are more interested in golfing, anyway, and the Hyatt pleases them with 18 top-notch holes, with 9 more still to come. Kids camp, a spa with one of Florida's few Watsu (water + shiatsu) pools, tennis, fine-dining in the Tanglewood restaurant, and a medley of bars and casual eateries make this a full destination resort for those who don't mind being away from the beach, shopping, and nightlife that's getting the Bonita-Naples area noticed.

✪ TRIANON BONITA BAY

General Manager: Darren Robertshaw.
239-948-4400, 800-859-3939.
www.trianon.com.
3401 Bay Commons Dr., Bonita Springs 34134.
Price: Moderate to Very Expensive.*
Credit Cards: AE, D, DC, MC, V.

The name implies "a special place," in the spirit of the Grand Trianon and Petit Trianon on the grounds of Versailles near Paris. Heavy on European influence, the hotel's lobby displays both elegance and intimacy, with an inviting fireplace, polished marble, and high-arched ceilings. The dramatic entryway segues into a cozy lounge-breakfast nook where tropical iced tea and fruit are on hand to refresh guests. Attention to detail is a hallmark of Trianon, which is a spin-off of a Naples Fifth Avenue South prototype. In its 100 spacious guest rooms and suites you'll find the same refinement previewed in the lobby: dark-wood armoires, sliding French doors to a balcony, gourmet European coffee service, roomy all-white bath, and space enough to dance. Continental breakfast, served in the lounge, is included in the rates. A small pool lies in the backyard of the four-story chateaulike structure. Shoppers will like its proximity to the fine stores and restaurants of walking-distance Promenade.

EVERGLADES CITY
✪ THE IVEY HOUSE

General Manager: Sandee Harraden.
239-695-3299.
www.iveyhouse.com.
107 Camellia St., Everglades City 34139.
Price: Inexpensive to Expensive.*
Credit Cards: MC, V.

For outdoor enthusiasts, the family-run Ivey House is tailor-made. The original Ivy House Lodge, a born-again boardinghouse from the 1920s, offers 10 simple B&B rooms. The new 17-room Ivy House Inn opened in 2001, plus there's the Ivey House Cottage (two-night minimum stay) that has two small bedrooms. Smoking or alcohol is not allowed in the rooms. In the original B&B, men's and women's bathrooms are separate from the rooms, dorm style. The new inn rooms, which encircle the courtyard swimming pool, have private baths and offer added comfort and style, including TVs and phones. Breakfast is included in all room rates. Lunch and dinner, served in the inn's Italian seafood restaurant, are extra. Ivey's main attraction is its proximity to Everglades waterways and partnership with North American Canoe Tours. You could call this a BB&B: bed, breakfast, and back country. It leads tours into the Ten Thousand Islands by canoe, kayak, or boat, rents equipment, and provides shuttle service. Sightseeing, birding, and other excursions are available. Bike use is complimentary.

PORT OF THE ISLANDS RESORT & MARINA

General Manager: John "Robby" Robinson.
239-394-3101.
www.poiresort.com.
25000 Tamiami Trail E., Naples 34114.
Price: Inexpensive to Very Expensive.
Credit Cards: AE, D, MC, V.

This resort has seen its share of instability, having experienced many owners over the past years and now another new one who took over early 2004. It's a lovely canal-front property, nonetheless—one that deserves to survive. Its 80 rooms—some privately owned; 65 are on the rental program—are housed within the handsome Mediterranean-style main building and in groups of eight clustered in one-story, red barrel-roofed stucco structures. A two-story building holds some of the privately owned units. Located between the national park and Naples, it's something of a water- and nature-lovers outpost, with a marina that it shares with a residential community by the same name. The grand lobby sets a tone that speaks of creature comforts despite the remoteness, with high raftered ceiling, saltillo tiles, fetching rattan furniture, and a glazed-tile-trimmed fireplace. It also holds a fitness room and men's and women's saunas. The attractive brick-paved pool area lies outside a bar and grill through French doors. Most of the rooms have a private screened patio. All are suite-like, with a divider between the bed and living areas, and include a pull-out couch, small refrigerator and sink, coffeemaker, stovetop, and microwave.

ROD & GUN CLUB

Innkeeper: Marcella Bowen.
239-695-2101.
200 Broadway, PO Box 190, Everglades City 34139.
Price: Inexpensive to Moderate.
Credit Cards: No.
Handicap Access: No.

Steeped in both history and outdoorsmanship, this circa 1850 lodge crowns a modest town that serves as the South Coast's gateway to the Everglades. The club's main building was built as luxury pioneer housing; the Old South-style mansion came under the ownership of the county's developer and namesake, Barron Collier, who turned it into a fishermen's and hunters' haven during the 1920s. A sportsman's lodge in the finest sense, its cypress walls are still decorated with mounted tarpon, a gator hide, and tools of the fishing trade. Seventeen rooms in tin-roofed cottages scatter around the white-clapboard lodge, which has a wraparound veranda and yellow-striped awnings. The rooms are furnished for function rather than pampering—TV and air-conditioning are the extent of luxury. The club's restaurant, which has a screened porch facing the river, specializes in local delicacies and

The lodge at Everglades City's Rod & Gun Club blends southern charm with wilderness sportsmanship. Karen T. Bartlett

will cook your catch for a nominal fee. The swimming pool lies off the dining room and is decorated with banana trees, lattice, and rock waterfalls.

MARCO ISLAND
THE BOAT HOUSE
General Manager: Desiree and Nick Buhelos. 239-642-2400, 800-528-6345. www.theboathousemotel.com. 1180 Edington Place, Marco Island 34145. Price: Inexpensive to Very Expensive. Credit Cards: MC, V.

At Marco Island's north end, known as Olde Marco, things are a-changing. Once quiet and immune to the resort activity along the beach, the area now sees the completion of a large, fancy resort and spa adjunct to the historic Marco Inn. If you're seeking something less upscale and expensive than Marco's trademark resort scene, drive past the new Olde Marco Inn and turn the corner to this waterfront gem. Twenty rooms, studios, condos, and the two-bedroom gazebo house (expensive to very expensive) line boat docks and a small pool in a two-story strip among the giants. The rooms are nicely appointed and designed for easy, breezy waterfront living.

✪ MARCO ISLAND MARRIOTT RESORT & GOLF CLUB
General Manager: Bob Dictor. 239-394-2511, 800-438-4373. www.marcomarriottresort.com. 400 S. Collier Blvd., Marco Island 34145. Price: Very Expensive. Credit Cards: AE, D, DC, MC, V.

Marriott was still in the midst of a facelift when I visited in January 2004. The crux of its upgrade is a magnificent new spa with an outdoor Watsu therapy pool. Restaurants have changed, and the lobby area was being modernized, but it remains a sprawling complex on the beach—an extra-wide, shell-cluttered, sandbar-sheltered beach—

providing a fantasy playground for vacationers of all ages. For children there are a pool with slide, a wading pool, and yet another pool for good measure; watersports rentals; a pizza parlor; a game room and Ping-Pong tables; and a remarkable kids' program. Adults can shop in the marble-floored arcade, golf at an off-site Marriott course, dine grandly or beach style, and act like a kid when the mood strikes. The 735 rooms and 62 suites—which all got a new palm/plantation look—each provide a minifridge, coffeemaker, hair dryer, and minibar. Historic photography and beach sculptures adorn the walls; blond-wood furniture pieces are carved with palm fronds. In the new spa building, which replaces the 18-hole miniature golf course, a state-of-the-art fitness center extracts a fee from guests; or they can use the original fitness room for free.

RADISSON SUITE BEACH RESORT
General Manager: Alan Brand. 239-394-4100, 800-333-3333. www.radisson.com/marcoislandfl. 600 S. Collier Blvd., Marco Island 34145. Price: Expensive to Very Expensive. Credit Cards: AE, D, DC, MC, V.

Along the island's stretch of shell-strewn beach, the Radisson accommodates guests in typical Marco high-rise style, with 268 spacious suites and rooms. The 207 suites—all with private balconies and comfortable furniture—are of the one- or two-bedroom variety and offer a completely equipped kitchen. Microwaves, refrigerators, and coffeemakers provide all guests with in-room dining options. Off the impressive marble lobby you'll find a game room as well as the gulfside dining room; both take advantage of the sea view. Active guests enjoy a heated free-form pool, tennis courts, whirlpool, exercise room, volleyball, kayaking, sailing, tubing, jet skiing, fishing, cruising, biking, and golf on three nearby courses. Families are attracted to the Radisson, where kids can enroll in a staffed recreational program or just have fun in the splashy pool area or on the beach.

NAPLES
COVE INN ON NAPLES BAY
General Manager: Carol Nerone.
239-262-7161, 800-255-4365.
www.coveinnnaples.com.
900 Broad Ave. S., Naples 34102.
Price: Inexpensive to Expensive.
Credit Cards: AE, D, DC, MC, V.

Back before the Ritz-Carlton and the Registry, Naples was about water, boating, and fishing. Cove Inn persists in the old tradition, with a focus on the harbor it edges: Naples's original circa 1915 settlement of fishermen and builders of Tamiami Trail. Accommodations range from hotel rooms to efficiencies to one- and two-bedroom units with separate living/dining area. The 85 balconied units are individually owned and decorated, most with a view of the harbor, and even the hotel rooms come equipped with a refrigerator, coffeemaker, microwave, and ironing board and iron. An old-fashioned coffeehouse serves breakfast and lunch, and the marina-side chikee bar slaps down cold ones for sunbathers around the pool. Part of the Crayton Cove and city docks community, Cove Inn is close to casual waterfront restaurants, shops, and marina services.

THE EDGEWATER BEACH HOTEL
General Manager: William R. Doyle.
239-403-2000, 800-821-0196.
www.edgewaternaples.com.
1901 Gulf Shore Blvd. N., Naples 34102.
Price: Expensive to Very Expensive.
Credit Cards: AE, D, DC, MC, V.

The Edgewater hints at New Orleans style with lacy white-iron balustrades on two of its three buildings, all of which face the gulf-lapped beach. You can't stay much closer to the sand than at this appropriately named hotel. Its 124 one- and two-bedroom suites are spacious, convenient, and handsomely appointed with clay tile, designer furnishings, and thick bedspreads. The floor plan of each includes a full kitchen with microwave, living/dining area, and private patio or balcony. Guests can dine in the newly made-over sixth-floor dining room or poolside under stylish market umbrellas. There's an on-site exercise room, spa services, and opportunities for other recreation nearby, including golf at the hotel's new Naples Grande Golf Club. Guests have privileges at The Registry sister resort.

INN BY THE SEA
Innkeepers: Maas and Connie van den Top.
239-649-4124, 800-584-1268.
www.innbythesea-bb.com.
287 11th Ave. S., Naples 34102.
Price: Moderate to Expensive.*
Credit Cards: AE, D, MC, V.

Here is a taste of all that's special about Naples—its shopping, its beach, and its history. The 1937 tin-roofed bungalow, listed on the National Register of Historic Places, was one of Naples's first guesthouses. Its new owners (Maas from the Netherlands and Connie from the U.S.) have retained the charm built into the six guest rooms by former owners. Named for local islands, each room exudes its own personality, with individual touches such as handmade quilts, Roman shades, a four-poster bed, and seaside motif. The three rooms downstairs claim private, attached baths. Upstairs, two suites have an adjoining room with daybed and detached baths. One also has a separate spare bedroom, making it perfect for families. Antiques adorn the downstairs parlor with its fireplace, heart-pine floors, leather sofa, and the inn's only television and telephone. Maas and Connie serve fruit and fresh-baked goodies in the breakfast room each morning. Guests have complimentary use of bicycles, beach chairs, and beach towels.

✪ INN ON FIFTH
Owner: Philip McCabe.
239-403-8777, 888-403-8778.
www.naplesinn.com.
699 Fifth Ave. S., Naples 34102.
Price: Moderate to Very Expensive.
Credit Cards: AE, DC, MC, V.

Modeled after Europe's intimate city hotels, the Inn on Fifth marks a crescendo in the burgeoning renaissance of Naples's historic downtown main street. A staid, ugly bank building was transformed into an ocher-colored eye-opener with Mediterranean archways and flourishes. Smack dab in the middle of downtown's lively dining, shopping, and entertainment scene, the hotel fronts Fifth Avenue South and edges the Sugden Theatre. Its greatest sensation is an Irish pub originally from near Dublin that was reassembled on site here. It spills out into the plaza and serves guests and the local community alike. The inn's magnificent marble lobby foreshadows the rich European style carried out in the rooms. The 102 rooms and suites overlook the street, the plaza, or the hotel's courtyard. Thick-paned French doors and careful soundproofing ensure that the town's bustle does not interfere with privacy and relaxation. All rooms come with bathrobes, hair dryers, irons, and other deluxe amenities. Guests have access to a small rooftop pool, a small fitness room, and a spa with sauna, steam room, and massage services. This is a lovely city retreat in terms of architecture, decor, and convenience.

LEMON TREE INN
General Manager: Steve Sbertoli.
239-262-1414, 888-800-LEMON.
www.lemontreeinn.com.
250 Ninth St. S., Naples 34102.
Price: Inexpensive to Expensive.*
Credit Cards: AE, D, MC, V.

Despite its lemon-pulp-yellow paint job and free lemonade in the lobby, this property is anything but a lemon. At the edge of downtown's fashionable drags, it retains a humble charm, dressed in white-tin roofs and flowering plants. The 35 rooms with porches (most are screened) are named Periwinkle, Plumosa, Poinciana, and such, after local flowers. Spacious, simple, and clean, they are outfitted with a tiled kitchen containing a microwave, toaster, coffeemaker, and minifridge. Around the pool and a gazebo in the courtyard, thick foliage and stylish globe streetlamps create character. At the breakfast nook you can help yourself to continental goodies. Shopping is steps away and the beach, a short drive.

NAPLES BEACH HOTEL & GOLF CLUB
Owners: The Watkins Family.
General Manager: Jim Gunderson.
239-261-2222, 800-237-7600.
www.naplesbeachhotel.com.
851 Gulf Shore Blvd. N., Naples 34102.
Price: Moderate to Very Expensive.
Credit Cards: AE, D, DC, MC, V.

The doyenne of Naples resorts, this combines the best of the area—its beaches and its golf—into a three-generation tradition in the heart of town. The 18-hole golf course hosts the Florida State PGA Seniors Open and other major golf tournaments. In 2000 the resort rolled out its new spa and clubhouse complex overlooking the greens. The spacious facility also holds meeting rooms, a fitness center, and Broadwell's, an elegant dining room. Har-Tru tennis courts, a heated pool, Beach Klub 4 Kids, and water-sports equipment rentals vie for off-the-course recreational hours. The hotel's spacious lobby and Everglades Room, where a breakfast buffet is served, communicate Florida vacationing ease. Its

329 guest rooms, efficiencies, and suites are done in Florida decor, with some lingering classic trademarks of yesteryear. Accommodations overlook the wide palm-studded beach or the lush golf course. Golf, tennis, and other packages are available.

✪ THE REGISTRY RESORT

Resort Manager: Ron Albeit.
239-597-3232, 800-247-9810.
www.registryresort.com.
475 Seagate Dr., Naples 34103.
Price: Very Expensive.
Credit Cards: AE, D, DC, MC, V.

The Registry fits Naples like a gold lamé wetsuit. Its distinctive red-capped tower, villas, and 15 Har-Tru tennis courts dominate north Naples's pristine, mangrove-fringed estuaries. Luxury with beach casualness, the resort's style impresses from the moment you walk through the front door into a marble-and-crystal lobby with soothing fountains. Outside on the second-floor level, a boardwalk leads around shops and restaurants, and downstairs the family pool has a Flintstones feel with a 100-foot on-the-rocks waterslide and private cabanas. Also for families is a fine kids' program. A 0.6-mile bridge leads to the beach. Tram service is available along the boardwalk that traverses estuaries to Clam Pass Recreation Area, a 3-mile stretch of plush sands with all manner of watersports rentals. Fifty tennis villas edge the courts; another 424 rooms and suites overlook the gulf, each spacious and furnished with a wet bar, marble vanity, and class. The Registry owns a nearby 18-hole golf course and provides a golf concierge. Five heated pools include Jacuzzis; the health club contains a sauna and steam baths plus a fitness room with a view of mangrove wilderness. Five restaurants range from poolside casual to world-class (Lafite). Don't miss Sunday brunch at Café Chablis. Covered parking is free to guests.

✪ THE RITZ-CARLTON GOLF RESORT

Hotel Manager: Bradley N. Cance.
239-593-2000, 800-241-3333.
www.ritzcarlton.com/resorts/naples_golf_resort.
2600 Tiburon Dr., Naples 34109.
Price: Very Expensive.
Credit Cards: AE, D, DC, MC, V.

Making Naples the only city in the world with two Ritz-Carltons on the same street, the golf resort opened amid 27 holes of lush, Greg Norman-designed greens in 2002. The Rick Smith Golf Academy, a putting course and practice area, and a clubhouse with pro shop make this a complete golf resort. Its sybaritic relationship with its elder sister out on the beach gives both properties the most complete menu of leisure activities possible. Guests at the golf resort have access via shuttle to the beach resort's spa, beach, kids' program, and fine restaurants. Its own Lemonia restaurant gives guests a reason to stay right on property for a fabulous Tuscan feast overlooking the links. A gourmet pastry shop, pool grill, cigar bar, room service, and other lounges help fill the dining-entertainment bill. The golf resort also has an on-property fitness center, four lit tennis courses, and a pool. Kids from both resorts learn golf and golf etiquette at the newer resort. Overlooking the greens with private balconies, 295 rooms and suites have it all, from cuddly robes and oversized marble bathrooms to high-speed Internet access and safes designed large enough to hold laptop computers.

✪ THE RITZ-CARLTON NAPLES

Hotel Manager: John Tolbert.
239-598-3300, 800-241-3333.
www.ritzcarlton.com/resorts/naples.
280 Vanderbilt Beach Rd., Naples 34108.
Price: Very Expensive.
Credit Cards: AE, D, DC, MC, V.

The gold standard for regal accommodations,

An entourage of royal palms hints at the regal, Old World elegance of the Ritz-Carlton in Naples. Karen T. Bartlett

the Ritz-Carlton molds Old World elegance to Old Florida environment. The hotel's facade looms majestically classic. Inside, oversized vases of fresh flowers, massive chandeliers, cabinets filled with priceless china, 19th-century oil paintings, vaulted ceilings, and crystal lamps detail Ritz extravagance. Each of the 463 units in the U-shaped configuration faces the gulf. Guest rooms and suites are dressed in fine furniture, plush carpeting, and marble bath areas. Accommodations include honor bar, refrigerator, bathrobes, hypoallergenic pillows, telephones in the bathroom, clothes steamers, and private balconies overlooking the hotel's backyard, where wilderness and civility meet. In the courtyard, fountains and groomed gardens exude European character. Classic arches, stone balustrades, and majestic palm-lined stairways lead to a boardwalk that takes you through mangroves, at the end of which lie golden sands where two beach restaurants serve refreshments and water-sports rentals are available. Other amenities and services that earn the Ritz its five stars include a formal dining room, afternoon tea service, grill, café, lap pool and free-form family pool, outdoor poolside café, lounge, ballroom, tennis courts, sister-property golf facilities, fitness center, beauty salon, children's programs, nature center, bicycle rental, shops, transportation services, and twice-daily maid service. A new full-service spa occupies its own separate wing at the resort's entrance, behind the rose garden, and it recently added air-brush bronzing to its list of services.

VANDERBILT BEACH

✪ LAPLAYA BEACH & GOLF RESORT

General Manager: Scott Shoenberger.
239-597-3123, 800-237-6883.
www.laplayaresort.com.
9891 Gulf Shore Dr., Naples 34108.
Price: Very Expensive.
Credit Cards: AE, D, DC, MC, V.

The new beauty on Vanderbilt Beach, LaPlaya was buffed up in 2002 to the tune of $51 million, with a new Thai spa, exercise room, rocky waterfall pool, pool bar, and restaurant menu that showcases the talent of Miami darling Chef Robin Haas (see **Baleen** under "Dining" below). Rooms show meticulous attention to detail, some sporting Jacuzzis with sea views, all luxurious with netted four poster beds, Frette linens, goose down pillows, private balconies, and marble baths. Of its 189 units, 141 are beachfront with private balconies. The "golf" part of the name refers to course privileges 15 minutes away. The "beach" part is obvious—a delicious slice of sands that gives way to the property's lush tropical garden and Colonial-style public areas.

VANDERBILT INN

General Manager: Brian Schomacker.
239-597-3151, 800-643-8654.
www.vanderbiltinn.com.
11000 Gulf Shore Dr., Naples 34108.
Price: Moderate to Very Expensive.
Credit Cards: AE, D, DC, MC, V.

Informal and beachy, this longtime Vanderbilt Beach fixture focuses on poolside and water sports along a well-populated stretch of sand. Anyone who's been around for a while knows that its chikee bar is a place of vitality and fun, day or night. It stands between the white sand beach and the pool and serves food as well as libations. An indoor café serves slightly more formal fare. Kids ages 12 and under eat free with their parents. Like its lobby, restaurant, and grounds, the hotel's 147 rooms and efficiencies—stacked

Recent renovations have enhanced LaPlaya Beach Resort's watery world. Karen T. Bartlett

up two high—let you know with cool, breezy lushness that you're in the subtropics.

Home & Condo Rentals

Florida Vacation Accommodations (239-261-7577, 800-462-4403; www.vacationinfl.com; 3757 Tamiami Trail N., Naples 34103) Visit the Website for photos and description of vacation homes, condos, and resorts for rent in the area.

Resort Quest Southwest Florida (239-597-1102, 800-237-2010; www.resortquest.com; 26201 Hickory Blvd., Bonita Springs 34134) Rentals from Fort Myers Beach to Marco Island.

RV Resorts

Chokoloskee Island Park (239-695-2414; www.chokoloskee.com; PO Box 430, Chokoloskee, 34138) Rustic fisherman's paradise with easy access to the Everglades and the gulf. Full-service marina, tackle shop, guide service, boat rentals, ramps, and docks. Overnight or seasonal RV sites with complete hookups.

Mar-Good Resort (239-394-6383; 321 Peartree Ave., PO Box 248, Goodland 34140) Site on the waterfront, with a restaurant, store, small museum, boat docking, laundry, rec room, and cottages.

Outdoor Resorts of Chokoloskee Island (239-695-3788; 150 Smallwood Dr., PO Box 39, Chokoloskee 34138). Marina, boat rentals, a bait and tackle shop, and guide service for fishing and touring. Pull into one of 283 full-service sites, or stay in the motel. Either way you can take advantage of the resort's three pools, health spa, lit tennis and shuffleboard courts, and restaurant.

Rock Creek RV Resort (239-643-3100; www.rockcreekrv.com; 3100 North Rd. at Airport Rd., Naples 34104) Full hookups for 221 RVs, pool, laundry, and shade trees. No pets.

DINING

Everglades City considers itself a fishing and stone-crab capital, so figure you can expect some highly fresh seafood in these parts. Stone crab, in fact, was discovered as a food source in the Everglades—at least that's the way some of the old-timers tell it. Before a couple of locals began trapping stone crabs and selling them to a Miami restaurant, the delicate, meaty flavor of these crustaceans went unappreciated. Along with stone crab, alligator, frog legs, and other local delicacies make up the substance of Everglades cookery.

Marco Island, too, is known as a good market for buying stone crab, which gets quite expensive the farther from the source. With more than 100 restaurants on the island, Marco covers every genre of cuisine. Its trademark is its Old Florida style of no-nonsense, trend-resistant seafood preparation. German cuisine also surfaces repeatedly.

Naples's dining reputation is staked on hauteur and creativity. Even the old fish houses dress up their catches in the latest fashion, which ranges from redesigned home cooking and continental nouvelle to Floribbean, Pacific Rim, and fusion styles. Naples is a dining-out kind of place. The renovation of downtown's Fifth Avenue South has brought restaurants out into the street and sparked the genesis of what has been termed Naples's "café society."

The following listings sample all the variety of South Coast feasting in these price categories:

Inexpensive	Up to $10
Moderate	$10 to $20
Expensive	$20 to $30
Very Expensive	$30 or more

Cost categories are based on the range of dinner entrée prices, or, if dinner is not served, on lunch entrées. Many restaurants offer early-dining discounts, often called early-bird specials. These rarely are listed on the regular menu and sometimes are not publicized by tip-conscious servers. I have noted those restaurants that offer them. Certain restrictions apply, such as time constraints, a specific menu, or number of people first in the door. Call the restaurant and ask about its policy.

The following abbreviations are used for credit card information and meals:

AE: American Express
D: Discover Card
DC: Diners Club
MC: MasterCard
V: Visa
B: Breakfast
L: Lunch
D: Dinner
SB: Sunday Brunch

Note: New Florida law forbids smoking inside all restaurants and bars serving food. Smoking is permitted only in restaurants with outdoor seating.

BONITA BEACH
DOC'S BEACH HOUSE

239-992-6444.
www.docsbeachhouse.com.
27980 Hickory Blvd., Bonita Beach 34134.
Price: Inexpensive to Moderate.
Cuisine: American.
Liquor: Beer and wine.
Serving: B, L, D.
Credit Cards: None.
Handicap Access: Yes.
Reservations: No.
Special Features: On the beach, with outdoor and indoor seating.

This is the kind of place where Gidget and Moondoggie would hang out (if there were surfable waves, that is). It's all about being on the beach—Bonita's colorful, action-packed beach. If you can't bear leaving the sands, you can just grab a quick burger or dog and get back to it. If you need a break from the sun, duck inside. Downstairs is open and barefoot casual. Upstairs is blessedly air-conditioned, with huge

picture windows so you won't miss any of the beach action. Both levels have bars and sports TVs. The menu makes no pretense of fine dining, but the food is solidly good. Grab-and-go items include Sand Dollar Burgers, Chicago-style pizza, tacos, chili, and sandwiches of all sorts. For dinner or a heartier lunch, add a choice of grilled seafood, strip steak, and a fried seafood combo basket.

TOUCAN GRILLE

239-495-9464.
www.toucangrille.com.
4480 Bonita Beach Rd., Bonita Beach 34134.
Price: Inexpensive to Moderate.
Cuisine: Floribbean.
Children's Menu: Yes.
Liquor: Full.
Serving: L, D.
Credit Cards: MC, V.
Handicap Access: Yes.
Reservations: No.

Rattan paddle fans spin lazily from tall ceilings, swirling the cool air and hot reggae around sand-toned rattan, wicker, and bamboo splashed bright with toucan colors. The menu is just as colorful and Caribbean inspired. Some of its trademark items include pineapple pork sandwich, chili rum glazed salmon, mahimahi and shrimp with banana chutney, jerk chicken, and barbecued baby back ribs. The salmon specialty is sticky sweet and grilled; I prefer it as part of a salad to cut the sugary glaze and add an element of fresh health to the meaty salmon flavor. A bamboo bar is the centerpiece of Toucan, small but not packed tightly with tables. It's known for its tropical sweet drinks with names such as Island Sunset, Gilligan's Island, and BonitaRita. This is a fun place for a lunch that feels deliciously away, a light dinner, or happy hour with complimentary plantain chips and black bean salsa.

BONITA SPRINGS
✪ CHOPS CITY GRILL
239-992-4677.
www.chopsbonita.com.
8200 Health Center Blvd., Bonita Springs
34134.
Hwy. 41 and Coconut Rd. at Brooks Grand
Plaza.
Price: Expensive to Very Expensive.
Children's Menu: No.
Cuisine: Steaks, Asian.
Liquor: Full.
Serving: D.
Credit Cards: AE, D, MC, V.
Handicap Access: Yes.
Reservations: Yes.

A spin-off from its original downtown
Naples success, Chops's name is a double
entendre for the food it does unerringly
well: steaks and Pacific Rim-style dishes.
Seriously fashionable with a burnished
copper bar and modern kitchen theater
dining room, Chops's ambience sets a tone
for nouvelle sophistication that the food
follows. The menu rhapsodized my pan-
seared grouper's sauce, for instance, as
"screaming hot rock shrimp with tomatoes,
garlic, and white wine." The "screaming
hot" was overstated, but certainly not the
garlic, apparent in crunchy slices throughout the sauce and the gooey-good risotto.
We discovered a clear penchant for garlic
here, for in my husband's mound of arugula
whipped potatoes, the chef had buried
treasures of whole roasted garlic cloves.
The arugula was there in color but not so
much in flavor, which we found also true of
the ginger in the ginger-Grand Marnier
sauce accompanying his Roquefort-and-
ricotta-crusted grilled veal chop. Still
another great sauce, deeply sweet and rich,
it paid excellent service to the thick, juicy
chop, grilled just to the brink of medium.
Creative sushi rolls and other Asian inspi-
rations (big eye tuna tartare, beef satay,
Hawaiian duck pot stickers) start the meal

out right. Meat lovers can order the
unadulterated finest in steaks, while more
adventurous palates will choose from day's
specials and a selection of imaginative
entrées and fine wines. For dessert, the
banana coconut spring rolls wrap up the
meal in proper motif and exotic sweetness.

SOUTH BAY BISTRO
239-949-6030.
26821 South Bay Dr., Ste. 114, Bonita
Springs 34134.
The Promenade at Bonita Bay.
Price: Inexpensive to Expensive.
Early Dining Menu: Yes.
Children's Menu: Yes.
Cuisine: American Fusion.
Liquor: Full.
Serving: D.
Closed: Sat. and Sun. for lunch.
Credit Cards: AE, D, MC, V.
Handicap Access: Yes.
Reservations: Yes.
Special Features: Courtyard seating; early-
dining specials.

South Bay made a big sensation with its
retro-futuristic decor and daring menu
when it opened a few years back. I've noticed
the boldness of the recipes has toned down
somewhat, probably to the satisfaction of
most, but I preferred its original spunk. Still,
rolls arrived in a spiral funnel, and many of
the favorites remain the same, just less
spicy and inventive. Take, for instance, the
mussels provençal I ordered. Tiny but tasty
and swimming in a light broth with angel
hair pasta, the mussels needed more of the
bits of tomato, garlic, and basil that gave it
flavor. The panko breaded oysters with prosciutto, garlic spinach, and smoked tomato
hollandaise have survived the cut, as did the
blackened tuna ahi. The preparations and
accompaniments change somewhat according to the season; when I last visited, the
summer menu had the tuna matched with
cucumber slaw, wild-rice pilaf, and sweet

coconut-curry sauce. The best values are the sandwiches served all night on the dinner menu and the early-dining specials from 4:30 to 6pm (5:30 on weekends). For $12 you get a soup or salad and a smaller portion of one of several favorites from the regular menu. Come dessert time, the pastry chef wows with a dandy selection, ranging from something called "Chocolate Explosion" to Florida citrus crème brûlée and a marvelously tart key lime tart with white chocolate sauce.

✪ TARPON BAY RESTAURANT

239-444-1234.
www.coconutpoint.hyatt.com.
5001 Coconut Rd., Bonita Springs 34134.
At the Hyatt Regency Coconut Point.
Price: Expensive.
Children's Menu: Yes.
Cuisine: Seafood.
Liquor: Full.
Serving: L, D.
Credit Cards: AE, D, MC, V.
Handicap Access: Yes.
Reservations: Yes.
Special Features: Patio seating overlooking fountain pond.

White-clapboard fish houses were once the architectural icon of this just-lately developed area. The Hyatt Regency designed its casual resort restaurant to pay homage to the old Florida it replaced. Considerably more well-dressed than the real thing, the ambiance nonetheless feels cottage comfortable. (Outdoor seating overlooks a pond containing a fountain and a floating golf hole, which can provide its share of entertainment.) Local and imported seafood get a tropical zing. My favorite reason for dining there is the ceviche raw bar. Besides the typical shellfish, you can sample one of seven types of raw seafood "cooked" in various citric marinades. Can't make up your mind? Try the sampler for $15. On the lunch menu, creative salads make eating

healthy more exciting than you've ever imagined. Try the peppered tuna with greens, snow peas, and wasabi orange dressing or the beef tips with blue cheese and shallot vinaigrette. At the dinner table, crispy fried red snapper is a visual and gastronomic masterpiece. Unusual ingredients and exquisite freshness make the meal: strawberry grouper with glazed kohlrabi, chicken Reuben sandwich with jalapeño jack cheese, and passion fruit glazed shrimp are just some examples. Dessert specialties include key lime curd with coconut sorbet and warm pear tart with ginger ice cream.

CHOKOLOSKEE ISLAND

✪ JT'S ISLAND GRILL & GALLERY

239-695-3633.
www.chokoloskee-island.com.
238 Mamie St., Chokoloskee 34138.
Price: Moderate.
Cuisine: Floribbean.
Liquor: No.
Serving: L, D.
Closed: Dinner Mon.–Wed., all of Oct.
Credit Cards: No.
Handicap Access: No.
Reservations: No.
Special Features: Historic building; live dinner music.

It started as a homey little neighborhood place for breakfast, deli sandwiches, and a little light shopping. Well, to be accurate, it actually all began in 1890, when pioneer C. G. McKinney opened his store and served hungry neighbors. I was surprised to find that today it has grown into a respectable kitchen that opens the window on Everglades dining to let in the imagination. Just a smidgen of a place, it sets up a few tables outside in the sun and another dozen mismatched sets inside among shelves of local paintings, health food products, and other interesting buys. Start with a sweet glass of key limeade, and move on to a selection that reflects the chef's island persuasion. You can't go wrong with fish down here where they're practically jumping on your plate. I tried the fresh catch (happily, grouper that day) rojo style, after struggling between it and the triple crab—stone, snow, and blue—cakes with pineapple tartare. Don't know if I made the best decision, but I made a good one. Rojo meant a tasty tomato and cucumber salsa with authentic black beans and rice. The grouper had been marinated in lime juice and couldn't have tasted fresher. I also tried a cup of the day's soup, tomato bisque, that was anything but ordinary. Finely minced onions and peppers had settled to the bottom of a heartwarming brew that dared to stand on its own without all the salt and gummy thickness that often defines bisque. Lunch is most popular, and the selections are as varied as they are inventive: avocado BLT, reggae-grilled veggie wrap, shrimp and scallops sautéed with pineapple in a rum butter ginger sauce, cheeseburgers, pulled pork, and stone crab. At night the culinary, visual, and performance arts merge as local musicians accompany such masterpieces as yellowfin tuna in flambé vanilla rum and jerk shrimp and scallops.

EVERGLADES CITY
ROD AND GUN CLUB
239-695-2101.
200 Broadway, PO Box 190, Everglades City 34139.
Price: Moderate to Expensive.
Children's Menu: Sometimes, dinner only.
Cuisine: Florida.
Liquor: Full.
Serving: L, D.
Credit Cards: No.
Handicap Access: Yes.
Reservations: No.
Special Features: Historic waterfront setting.

Dining here on a screened porch overlooking the Barron River with the mangroves on the other side always triggers the relaxation

mechanism in my body, mind, and spirit. It goes deeper than the serenity of the scene, for there's a time-reversion effect here. Paddle fans twirl from pressed-tin ceilings, and white columns, a rounded portico, a porch with wicker chairs, and yellow-and-white striped awnings at the lodge's entrance evoke plantation manors of the Old South. The inside dining room, the antithesis of the patio's lightness, is all dark pecky-cypress wood, polished wood floors, and mounted fish and fowl—remnants of the lodge's sporting past. From the 1890s to 1960 the club hosted presidents, movie stars, and other intrepid Everglades hunters and fishermen. Back then guests dined on frog legs, alligator tail, and fresh fish. They still do. Menus also offer more conventional fare—Reubens, burgers, New York strip steak, and shrimp linguine—but the ultimate Everglades City experience requires sitting back, taking in the view, enjoying local hospitality, and dining on Everglades specialties. The frog legs are incredibly tasty; the onion rings, the crunchiest and lightest imaginable; the gator nuggets, well tenderized but salty and a tad greasy; and the peanut butter pie and key lime pie, simply divine.

GOODLAND
✪ OLD MARCO LODGE CRAB HOUSE
239-64-CRABS.
1 Papaya St., Goodland 34140.
Price: Inexpensive to Expensive.
Children's Menu: Yes.
Cuisine: Seafood/Florida.
Liquor: Full.
Serving: L, D.
Closed: Mon. during off-season, Sept.
Credit Cards: AE, MC, V.
Handicap Access: Yes.
Reservations: Yes, for dinner.
Special Features: Waterfront dining, salad bar.

Goodland is a town where a more modest pace of tourism has allowed folks to remain

Boaters have been docking at Old Marco Lodge Crab House to satisfy seafood cravings for 135 years. Karen T. Bartlett

proudly hometown. A long-ingrained fishing tradition means you'll find both the freshest catches and people who know how to prepare them. Old Marco Lodge has been doing it longer than anyone, in a waterfront restaurant built in 1869. Specialty of the house is—no surprise—crab. In soft-crab sandwiches, in the incredibly full-flavored vegetable-crab soup, and most popularly steamed and served simply with a hammer or nutcracker. Hammer away at a bowl of signature garlic crabs—blue crabs in butter and garlic—or try stone, king, or snow crab. The extensive all-day menu embraces everything seafood-lovers and landlubbers want: mussels marinara, oyster po'boy sandwich, cheeseburger, seafood pasta, grouper Oscar, stuffed shrimp, and much, much more. The key lime pie makes you pucker, just like it should, and the Bloody Marys are among the best I've tasted.

ISLES OF CAPRI

NICK'S BACKWATER CAFÉ

239-642-5700.
231 Capri Blvd., Isles of Capri 34113.
Price: Inexpensive to Expensive.
Children's Menu: Yes.
Cuisine: Seafood/American.
Liquor: Full.
Serving: L, D.
Credit Cards: AE, MC, V.
Handicap Access: Dining area, yes; restrooms, no.
Reservations: No.
Special Features: Waterfront dining.

Tucked away in the less-traveled Isles of Capri, Nick's overlooks Johnson Bay from beneath an authentic chikee (Indian thatched roof) open structure. When it's chilly, clear plastic sheathing rolls down, and space heaters ignite around the massive wood bar that dominates the scene. In any weather, many of the patrons arrive by boat and hitch up at the docks, then settle in for a grab-and-go meal served on Styrofoam and plastic. The all-day menu has lost some of its bravado of the past and now concentrates mostly on sandwiches and fried-seafood baskets, which it still perks up with sassy condiments such as mango Thai chili ketchup, Tabasco mayo, and brandy cocktail sauce. The crab cakes are a delight, served as a dinner or a sandwich. The crab wins in this contest of shellfish versus breading. Instead of a deep fryer, it meets a light sauté pan, just enough that it's brown and falling apart at the touch of a fork. Recently I tried the Southwest chicken wrap with jalapeño cheese and salsa: nicely done. Try the red potato salad as a side, excited with a bit of turmeric. In the past I've sampled the chicken, black bean, and cheese quesadilla, also a winner. Other popular selections include baby back ribs, conch fritters, coconut shrimp, and oyster or shrimp po'boys. Skip the coffee drinks; they're served unspectacularly in Styrofoam sans whipped cream and lukewarm. What I like best are the view and laid-back atmosphere. In short, be in a casual mood, or don't be here.

MARCO ISLAND (SEE ALSO GOODLAND AND ISLES OF CAPRI)

✪ SALE E PEPE

239-393-1600.
www.sale-e-pepe.com.
480 S. Collier Blvd., Marco Island 34145.
At Marco Beach Ocean Resort.
Price: Expensive to Very Expensive.
Cuisine: Tuscan Italian.
Liquor: Full.
Serving: B, L, D.
Credit Cards: AE, D, DC, MC, V.
Handicap Access: Yes.
Reservations: Yes.
Special Features: View of beach and gulf; terrace dining.

Whether it's your fantasy to dine under the Tuscan sun or the Florida moon, Sale e Pepe brings it to reality in a replicated palace-proportioned Italian villa setting with an outdoor terrace. Perched on the second floor, it affords an elevated perspective of sand and sea. Sinatra is on the audio and Frette linens are on the table. Inside, you can choose a formal frescoed dining setting (jackets required) or a more casual lounge setting, all serving the same finely crafted, award-winning Tuscan-based creations. Everything's made fresh, from the crusty olive and rustic herb breads to the pasta, soups, sausage, and tiramisu. The menu adapts to the seasons, always paying tribute to the main Tuscan food groups: beans, fish, meat, and pasta. You may find the peppery green lentil soup I once savored, drizzled with olive oil and studded with substantial bits of prosciutto, or a chestnut and porcini mushroom soup. In the pasta department I can recommend the addicting agnolotti stuffed with spinach and ricotta cheese topped with silky mascarpone and parmesan cream or the Maine lobster over linguine, entire meaty tail and claw sections atop a subtly spicy tomato sauce flavor-bolstered by strips of dried tomato. I've also raved about the seared yellowfin tuna, masterfully complemented with a tangle of caramelized onions and whole-grain mustard sauce. The marinated pork tenderloin with port wine reduction and braised cabbage is a specialty. Roast pork also stars in the four-course tasting menu ($65, $100 including wine pairings). The lunch offers lighter versions of some of the dinner entrées, along with focaccia sandwiches and pizza. Stop in the huge gas-lit lounge, a shrine to artist Toulouse-Lautrec, for an after-dinner drink. Or take the staircase down to walk off the dinner in which you've undoubtedly overindulged on the beach.

TIDE BEACHFRONT BAR & GRILL

239-393-8433.

900 S. Collier Blvd., Marco Island 34145.

At Apollo Condominiums.

Price: Inexpensive to Moderate.

Children's Menu: No, but appropriate
items on regular menu.

Cuisine: American.

Liquor: Full.

Serving: L, D.

Credit Cards: AE, V, MC.

Handicap Access: Yes.

Reservations: No.

Special Features: Outdoor beachfront seating; sports bar.

Get the best view for your buck at this
favorite watering and feeding hole just next
to the south-end public access. Sit on the
open porch, but guard your food from hungry birds. There's also indoor seating in a
sports bar arena, where you'll also find a
soup-and-salad bar that's typical in its
offerings. Let's face it, nothing on the
menu is going to win any awards for ingenuity, but the selection is varied and
affordable, everything from grilled cheese
to seafood marinara. In between, find
beach food the likes of wings, fried finger
baskets, burgers, fajitas, shrimp Caesar
salad, and baby back ribs—in short, something to please everyone. Dinners tend
toward seafood or Italian persuasion. For
finger food try the appetizer sampler of
clams casino, conch fritters, grouper fingers, oysters Rockefeller, and fried shrimp.
For sandwich or dinner, grouper is always a
sure bet, grilled, blackened, or fried. I like
the grouper club, a twist on the traditional.
Wash it down with any in a wide selection of
beers or tropical cocktails.

NAPLES

✪ BHA! BHA!

239-594-5557.

847 Vanderbilt Rd., Naples 34108.

At Pavilion Shopping Center.

Price: Moderate to Expensive.

Children's Menu: No.

Cuisine: Middle Eastern.

Liquor: Beer and wine.

Serving: L, D, SB.

Credit Cards: AE, MC, V.

Handicap Access: Yes.

Reservations: Yes, for dinner.

An Iranian chef and an American artist
(recently deceased) partnered in this deliciously exotic enterprise. The merger of
creativities results in a sleek, bright, and
sunny setting of ocher and key-lime-green
walls, ottomans, a fountain, and Turkish
tapestries. They call it a Persian bistro. In
an Iranian dialect the name means Yum!
Yum! And that's where Chef Michael Mir
comes in. He fuses his native background
with his experience in fine American
kitchens to present an intriguing menu that
maintains the authenticity and boldness of
Middle Eastern cuisine while employing a
few tricks of classic continental and experimental new American styles. Prepare your
palate for a magic carpet ride. Aash, a
peasant-style herbed bean soup, starts out
simple but, as you nibble into the center
garnish of pickled onions, becomes more
and more complex and extraordinary. In
the appetizer of eggplant and artichoke, we
could discern an orchestra of flavors: distinctive Bulgarian feta, dill and a hint of
sweetness in the mustard sauce, and the
peanut oil in which the eggplant was
sautéed. Yum, yum. From the lunch menu,
the marinated portobello mushroom
stuffed with tender braised lamb and feta is
divine. The dinner menu is divided
between classic and innovative Persian cuisine and *khoreshes* (specialties). I recommend the spicy kermani beef, its dark
saffron sauce enlivened by pepperoncini
and cucumber yogurt; char-broiled lamb
(incredibly beautiful and tasty); garlic eggplant chicken (wonderful!); and duck fesenjune—braised in orange saffron stock

and served with pomegranate walnut sauce (a bit heavy-sweet). Turkish coffee comes served in a delicate espresso service with an ornamental wooden box full of rock candy and sugar. Try the unusual rose-flavored ice cream or gooey baklava for dessert.

BISTRO 821
239-261-5821.
www.bistro821.com.
821 Fifth Ave. S., Naples 34102.
Price: Moderate to Expensive.
Children's Menu: No.
Cuisine: American Bistro.
Liquor: Full.
Serving: D.
Credit Cards: AE, D, DC, MC, V.
Handicap Access: Yes.
Reservations: No.
Special Features: Sidewalk dining.

Bistro 821, the maverick of Fifth Avenue South and trendsetter in the local bistro craze, still leads today, despite a swell of competition in its wake. The menu benefits from an injection of fearless creativity. Small plates range from the familiar escargot, calamari, lobster bisque (yummy but a bit salty), and black bean soup to the inventive duck ravioli, rock lobster satay, and portobello "fries" with melted Maytag bleu cheese and onion jam. Salads come in appetizer and full portions (be sure to indicate "appetizer" even if you order it as a first course). One menu section is devoted to pasta and risotto, also as appetizer and full options, with such tempters as grilled vegetable and wild mushroom pasta with goat-cheese cream, and artichoke and asparagus risotto. Entrées, too, wax from such traditional bistro fare as chicken pot pie and bouillabaisse to house specialties: sugarcane-skewered prawns, prosciutto-wrapped filet mignon, seafood paella, and more. The coconut, ginger, and lemon-grass-encrusted snapper with coconut-ginger jasmine rice and coconut butter sauce

will dazzle any sweet tooth. On the specials menu, chefs flex even further with such adventures as the elk rib chop crusted with maple caramelized pistachio nuts that I recently relished. A robust wine list and intriguing dessert menu (try the wonderfully complex opera cake) round out the reasons Bistro 821 will always remain at the Fifth Avenue forefront.

BLEU PROVENCE
239-261-8239.
www.bleuprovence-naples.com.
1234 Eighth St. S., Naples 34102.
Price: Moderate to Very Expensive.
Children's Menu: No.
Cuisine: French.
Liquor: Beer and wine.
Serving: D.
Credit Cards: AE, D, MC, V.
Handicap Access: Yes.
Reservations: Recommended.

Sipping a French Bordeaux and dipping chunks of steaming French baguette into a salty tapenade while sultry French lyrics were wafting in the background, I felt quite like I was dining in a small provincial village in the south of France. So truly French, there's seating on a side patio when weather allows—but as summer had turned up the thermostat, I was cooling off among the impossibly blue walls, at once rustic and celestial, of Bleu Provence. Here, the setting is provincial, but the food sophisticated as Paris itself. From the menu—signed by Tom Hanks, Chuck Norris, and Madonna—I chose a cooling appetizer of cold tomato and basil soup. It came served in a martini glass with a measure of avocado cream at the base and then swirled on top in a fetching cobweb pattern. The flavors meshed marvelously, and the silky textures made this a highlight of the meal, although the salmon filet brightened with caper butter sauce was also top-notch. Other selections demonstrate Bleu Provence's winning

Un petit peu de France in Naples. Karen T. Bartlett

way with styles both classic and nouvelle: provençal fish soup, warm goat cheese salad, black truffles and foie gras in puff pastry, short ribs bourguignon, grilled bison tenderloin, and bourbon vanilla crème jalapeño. Six- and four-course dégustation menus offer well-rounded samplings of the restaurant's charm.

✪ CILANTRO TAMALES
239-597-5855.
10823 Tamiami Trail N., Naples, 34108.
Price: Inexpensive to Moderate.
Children's Menu: Yes.
Cuisine: Mexican.
Liquor: Beer and wine.
Serving: L, D.
Credit Cards: MC, V.
Handicap Access: Yes.
Reservations: No.

Cilantro Tamales touts "modern Mexican food" in a bright bistro setting. With a slab

of clay tile for a placemat and two bottles of chili sauce on the table, you're ready to dip into a Mexican dining experience that's as authentic as it is creative. I knew this the minute the cursory presentation of chips and salsa hit the table. Or the earthenware throne holding two types of sauces: a fresh pico de gallo and a spicier red tomatillo sauce, its recipe straight from Mexican country, our server said. Full of flavor, its heat played backup to the first burst of flavor. This is how Mexican food is supposed to be: zest, then zing. We ordered a side of guacamole—my barometer for truth in Mexican—and a cup of sopa de tortilla to get things rolling. The guac passed the litmus test with flying colors, neither pureed nor mashed and dressed lightly in a garlic-seasoned tomato sauce. We ended up eating it out of its flowerpot dish with a spoon. The tortilla soup also carried off that homemade flavor, full of the goodness of chicken, tortilla pieces, and cilantro. For entrées try the house specialty: cilantro tamales, what else? Their smoked Gouda cheese stuffing lends an unusual, worldly quality to the bell pepper and onions inside. Tamales also come in pork and chicken varieties, plus the menu carries many other Tex-Mex standards. The stuffed poblano pepper dish triumphed with a tomatillo-based salsa verde, but we would have preferred that the chili had been deseeded before stuffing it with the cheddar, which was still hard in the center. (It could have used a bit longer in the heating process.) All in all, Cilantro Tamales lives up to its menu promise: "cooked with Old World know-how seasoned and plated with modern imagination."

✪ THE DOCK AT CRAYTON COVE
239-263-9940.
www.dockcraytoncove.com.
845 12th Ave. S., Naples 34102.
Price: Moderate to Expensive.
Children's Menu: Yes.

Cuisine: Seafood/American.
Liquor: Full.
Serving: L, D.
Credit Cards: AE, D, MC, V.
Handicap Access: Yes.
Reservations: No.
Special Features: Open-air view of the marina.

The Dock remembers what Naples is about —clear down to its roots—while keeping up with what Naples has become. The roots part reflects in the fun, casual, waterlogged atmosphere it exudes from its breeze-through setup and location along Naples's original circa 1915 fishing harbor. Opened in 1976, the fish-house-style eatery has kept abreast of Naples's sophistication with remakes and menu upgrades. Once a pur-veyor of typical fried seafood fare, today it makes a serious stance among the town's tough culinary standards. Seafood still reigns, but island and Cajun influences have washed in to give us such offerings as Red Stripe lager-steamed shrimp, conch fritters, Cuban roasted-pork sandwich, Jamaican jerk-barbecued baby-back ribs, and black bean soup with smoked shrimp and jalapeño cream. Chefs execute the creative offerings with complexity. For instance, I recently ordered the blackened grouper, but no ordinary dish was this. The slappy-fresh grouper wasn't exactly black-ened but seasoned with a salty-kicky blend. The real stars of the plate were the tangy-crunchy crawfish-shrimp salsa and a grainy mustard sauce that enhanced the fish with texture, color, and multidimensional flavor. Crafty salads, sandwiches, and luncheon specials complete the midday offerings. Want something simpler? The menu offers six fresh catches prepared just with olive oil and an assortment of deep-fried seafood that hearkens back to its old-Florida past. Or choose from a select menu of oysters imported from several seasonal locations.

DOLCE & BANANA

239-649-6556.
4910 Tamiami Trail N., Naples 34120.
At Tanglewood Plaza.
Price: Moderate.
Children's Menu: Yes.
Cuisine: Caribbean, Mediterranean.
Liquor: Beer and wine.
Serving: L, D.
Credit Cards: AE, D, MC, V.
Handicap Access: Yes.
Reservations: Yes.

Dolce & Banana scored its share of "bests" in our mental book of dining memories: best bean soup for the spicy garbanzo and chorizo puree soup with a curry kick on the night's special menu; best scallops for the succulent sea scallops dusted with cumin and coriander and bathed in a sweet, creamy, tangy mango sauce; and even best bread basket for the assorted breads featur-ing sunflower seeds, sun-dried tomatoes, and a cruet of olive oil infused by a fat chili pepper. That cruet exemplifies the coming together of two cooking styles, Mediter-ranean and Caribbean—the best of regional cuisines in my book. A "tropical bistro" in an intimate redbrick, wood-floor setting, it's all about daring—but without the daunt-ing price tags one finds in downtown Naples. Other most honorable mentions from the menu: Mediterranean cioppino, escargot with lemon garlic sauce, wasabi and sesame crusted ahi tuna, port flan under a sweet citrus sauce, and crème brûlée flavored with—what else?—banana.

LEMONIA

239-593-2000.
www.ritzcarlton.com/resorts/naples_golf_resort/dining/venues/lemonia.
2600 Tiburon Dr., Naples 34109.
At Ritz-Carlton Golf Resort, off Airport-Pulling Rd.
Price: Expensive to Very Expensive.
Children's Menu: Yes.

Cuisine: Tuscan Italian.
Liquor: Full.
Serving: B, L, D, SB.
Credit Cards: AE, D, DC, MC, V.
Handicap Access: Yes.
Reservations: Strongly advised.
Special Features: Golf course view.

Our server poured our wines-by-the-glass from the bottle tableside while a guitarist strummed classics. And so began the impeccably mannered experience of a Ritz dining room. With the business of ordering, we received a bread basket and two tapenades, one of black olives and one of green. For starters, the Caesar salad redefined the classic dish with the addition of red leaf lettuce, a poached quail egg, and fractions of prosciutto among the romaine lettuce and exquisitely blended dressing. From the seasonally changing menu, the pumpkin risotto spilled out of a baked miniature pumpkin with a ghost of Halloween flavors rising from the creamy, cheesy richness. One can taste the Old World traditions and the patience of simmering pots in each bite at Lemonia. The seared duck breast was cooked medium rare for exquisite moistness and tenderness while trumpet mushrooms and a rich stock reduction escalated the pronounced meaty flavor. The roasted salmon was fine simplicity manifest: The thick, perfectly done filet was unadorned but for a single, elegant foie gras ravioli and a bed of orzo. Capers, olives, baby fennel, and confetti of tomato and cucumber lent texture and taste to the pasta. The tightly strung menu samples other Tuscan classics and twists: seared gnocchi and calamari, veal and prosciutto ragout, wild striped bass, and grilled veal chop with petite osso buco. For a grand finale, indulge in the Grand Marnier soufflé, served with a tiny pitcher of vanilla sauce and fluffily divine. To complete the experience, we received a *digestif* of lemon cello, the house liqueur, with a saucer of

biscotti and candied lemon rind. Minding *our* good manners, we polished it off.

USS NEMO

239-261-6366.
3745 Tamiami Trail N., Naples 34103.
Parkshore Centre.
Price: Moderate to Expensive.
Children's Menu: Yes.
Cuisine: Seafood.
Liquor: Beer and wine.
Serving: L, D.
Credit Cards: AE, D, MC, V.
Handicap Access: Yes.
Reservations: Yes.

Finding USS Nemo, tucked into an inconspicuous strip of offices, isn't easy, but it's worth the effort. Look for the porthole windows, a clue (if the name didn't give it away) to the theme. The decor has a decided submarine chic about it—nothing gimmicky or forced. The dinner menu, attached to a metal clipboard, is cleverly divided between "below sea level" and "above sea level." Nemo starts you off with bread and a taste-teaser of raw zucchini sticks, pickled ginger, seaweed, and an Oriental-flavored hummus-type concoction. Pacific Rim flavors and ingredients surface throughout Nemo's dinner menu. Its signature dish, for instance, is miso-broiled sea bass, and the menu gives you a choice of Eastern or Western preparation on the tuna and filet mignon. Tempura is done with a surprising light, crisp touch. We sampled it in the fried calamari appetizer. We also tried the seafood ceviche starter, a spicy ginger-infused "lime-cooked" marinade of raw shrimp, sea bass, and squid topped with salty strands of seaweed. The textures and seasonings balanced applaudably. From the entrée menu I can strongly recommend the ahi tuna and duck liver, an intriguing combination, and the Volcano Yellowtail Snapper, grilled and topped with a creamy Asian aioli. In the dessert department the grilled Asian chocolate fondue for two looks particularly tempting. At lunchtime USS Nemo and its outdoor tables fill with the business crowd ordering such selections as Japanese bento box, honey-ginger chicken, Pacific Rim salad, grilled mahi teriyaki sandwich, and tataki tuna salad.

ZOE'S
239-261-1221.
www.zoesnaples.com.
720 Fifth Ave. S, Naples 34102.
Price: Moderate to Very Expensive.
Children's Menu: No.
Cuisine: New American.
Liquor: Full.
Serving: D.
Credit Cards: AE, D, MC, V.
Handicap Access: Yes.
Reservations: Yes.

Here, the menu is created for the wine instead of vice versa, and so we made wine the prime factor in our Zoe's decision making. For our starter course, for instance, we ordered the Stilton and pear salad special and the wild mushroom strudel with a stout, full-flavored port sauce to complement two chardonnays from the extensive by-the-glass selection. The special seared ostrich filet with portobello mushrooms and red wine truffle demi-glace and the regular menu's pecan-crusted sea bass with mashed sweet potatoes and yellow pepper coulis went well with the pinot noirs we selected. The crusting on the sea bass was ever so light to add a pleasant crunch to the tender, creamy fish it had so effectively sealed. The ostrich, which makes regular appearances on the specials menu, came perfectly medium rare as ordered. Menu selections demonstrate a solid foundation of American cuisine with continental and Oriental influences: duck spring rolls, oysters Rockefeller, veal meat loaf, wild mushroom risotto, shrimp and scallops black-pepper fettuccine, macadamia nut and mustard-seed-crusted grouper, and rack of lamb; for dessert, tiramisu and warm chocolate cake. The food is marvelous here, but the service can be spotty.

BALEEN
239-597-3123.
www.laplayaresort.com.
9891 Gulf Shore Dr., Naples 34108.
At LaPlaya Beach & Golf Resort.
Price: Expensive to Very Expensive.
Children's Menu: Yes.
Cuisine: Seafood.
Liquor: Full.
Serving: B, L, D.
Credit Cards: AE, D, DC, MC, V.
Handicap Access: Yes.
Reservations: Yes.
Special Features: Indoor and outdoor seating with gulf view.

Monkeys have become the motif of fashion these days in Florida, and here you see their likeness hanging from chandeliers and poking their noses out of the earthy tropical decor. The round crusty loaf of bread is even called "monkey bread," why I'm not sure. (I'm also a bit confused by the whale reference in the restaurant's name.) Outdoors, heavy teak tables and chairs provide a front-row seat to sunset and the percussion of surf. The brainchild of Miami's highly hailed Chef Robin Haas, the menu allows you to order your seafood simple—roasted, grilled, or sautéed—or dressed in all the trappings of creative New World cuisine on which Haas has based his reputation. My roasted grouper was elevated to gourmet status with an excellent garlic-caper sauce and superb accompaniment of artichoke-bacon mashed potatoes. A couple of meat dishes round out the menu, and the Roquefort-crusted filet mignon we sampled demonstrated the kitchen's expert handling in that department. It was done to the perfect degree of wellness as ordered, and its red wine sauce anointed it like a blessing. For lunch try the chopped BLT salad or seared shrimp burger with avocado tomato relish.

FOOD PURVEYORS

Bakeries
Bakeries today are often combined with delis, grocery stores, and even wine shops.

Doughmonkey (239-389-9380; 588 Bald Eagle Dr., Marco Island 34145; at Island Plaza Shopping Center) Breakfast breads, cakes, tortes, brownies, pie, pastries, and other desserts from scratch. Cake and pie by the slice.

Naples Cheesecake Co. (239-598-9070, 800-325-6554; 8050 Trail Blvd., Naples 34108) Eight to twelve different flavors, including key lime, amaretto, and peanut butter.

Tony's Off Third (239-262-7999; 1300 Third Ave. S., Naples 34102) European bakery featuring legendary desserts, pastries, and breads, and a well-respected selection of wine and coffee, plus deli items and sandwiches.

Breakfast
First Watch (239-434-0005; 225 Banyan Blvd., Naples 34102; at Charleston Square; also: 239-566-7395; 1000 Immokalee Rd., Naples 34110) A popular upscale chain that has rein-vented breakfast with such terminology such as "crepeggs" and the "bacado" (bacon and avocado) omelette. Also lunch.

✪ **Manna from Heaven** (239-593-4948; 835 Vanderbilt Beach Road; at Pavilion Shopping Center) European-style breakfast offering crepes, interesting eggs Benedict varieties, and specialties such as "Moo and Cluck"—bacon-wrapped filet mignon with sautéed mushrooms and poached eggs.

Skillets Sunrise Café (239-566-1999; 5461 Airport Rd., Naples 34109) Sunny as its name with an award-winning menu-full of Belgian waffles, pancake platters, Irish oats, Benedicts, frittatas, and healthy options. Also lunch. There's also a Skillets in Bonita Springs (239-992-9333; 9174 Bonita Beach Rd., Bonita Springs 34135, at Sunshine Plaza).

Candy & Ice Cream
The Chocolate Strawberry (239-394-5999; 135 S. Barfield Dr., Marco Island 34145; at the Shops of Marco) The specialty is strawberries hand dipped in various types of chocolate; also seahorse lollipops, ice cream, smoothies, chocolate turtles, shells, dolphin, other local critters, and coffee.

Everglades Scoop (239-695-0375; 203 S. Copeland, Everglades City 34139) Cheerful, bright ice cream parlor serving 16 flavors of hand-dipped ice cream.

Regina's Ice Cream (239-434-8181; 824 Fifth Ave. S., Naples 34102) An old-fashioned soda fountain with modern frozen yogurts, sorbets, and sugar-free and name-brand ice cream.

The Serious Cookie Company (239-263-3382, 877-263-3383; 1200 Fifth Ave. S., Naples 34102; at Tin City) Just try to pass this place by without succumbing. Besides their trade-mark half-pound cookies, they make brownies, saltwater taffy, chocolates, turtles, choco-late pretzels, cordial creams, rugelach, and other irresistible goodies.

Coffee

Fifth Avenue Coffee Company (239-261-5757; 599 Fifth Ave. S., Naples 34102) Hot and iced coffee and tea, cappuccino, café latte, macchata, bakery goods. Seating indoors and out.

Java-ol'-o-gy (239-389-JAVA; 599 S. Collier Blvd. #302, Marco Island 34145) Stop in for the barista's special brews, light breakfast or lunch, and some online time. Also: smoothies, freezies, tea, cake, and other desserts.

L'Alouette (239-643-5993; 4350 Gulf Shore Blvd. N., Suite #506, Naples 34103; at the Village on Venetian Bay) Espresso, cappuccino, latte, chai tea, frozen yogurt, smoothies, shakes, salads, and sandwiches.

Roberto's (239-394-8388; 1031 N. Collier Blvd., Marco Island 34145; at Marco Town Center Mall) Espresso bar, fresh bagels and other bakery goods, light breakfast and lunch, ice cream, key lime pie, and other desserts. Seating indoors and out.

Deli & Specialty Foods

Artichoke & Co. (239-263-6979; 4370 Gulf Shore Blvd. N., Naples 34103; at the Village on Venetian Bay) Gourmet take-out, soups, breads, cheeses, pastries, salads, and wines.

Crayton Cove Gourmet (239-262-4362, 800-678-4362; www.craytoncovegourmet.com; 800 12th Ave. S., Naples 34102) Old-fashioned purveyor of Florida goodies, specializing in citrus shipping, fresh orange juice, homemade fudge, key lime pie and other citrus sweets, and orange-blossom honey. Closed mid-May to October.

Fantozzi's (239-262-4808; 1148 Third St. S., Naples 34102) In a historic Naples building, Fantozzi's is a popular place to grab a specialty or deli sandwich to enjoy at the tables outside. It also sells fine cheeses, wine, premade dinners such as lamb pie and beef Wellington, salmon, and herbed vinegars.

Mel's New York Deli (239-642-6206; 591 S. Collier Blvd., Marco 34145) Deli sandwiches, subs hot and cold, bagels, knishes, muffins, pastries, homemade desserts.

Ródes Fresh & Fancy (239-992-4040; 3756 Bonita Beach Rd. SW, Bonita Beach 34134) Fresh produce and local seafood market, also sells fresh breads and gourmet groceries.

Tony's Off Third (239-262-7999; 1300 Third St. S., Naples 34102) Build your own sandwich, plus prepackaged deli salads.

✪ **Wynn's on Fifth** (239-261-0901; 745 Fifth Ave. S., Naples 34102) Since 1945 the Wynn family has operated this Fifth Avenue landmark, most famous for its fine selection of wine, fresh bakery goodies, desserts, and hot-and-cold prepared deli foods.

Fruit & Vegetable Stands

Third Street South Farmers' Market (Parking lot at Third St. S. and 13th Ave., Old Naples) Every Saturday 7:30–11:30am, November through Easter.

Natural Foods

For Goodness Sake (239-992-5838; 9118 Bonita Beach Rd. E., Bonita Springs 34135; at Sunshine Plaza) Full line of health groceries, including food for low-carb and diabetic diets; also dietary supplements.

European-style market convenes Saturdays during the winter in Old Naples. Karen T. Bartlett

JT's Island Grill & Gallery (239-695-3633; www.chokoloskee-island.com; 238 Mamie St., Chokoloskee 34138) Organic refrigerated, frozen, and dry goods; homemade breads, fresh salsa, and deli items.

Summer Day Market and Café (239-394-8361; 1027-1/2 N. Collier Blvd., Marco Island 34145; in Marco Town Center) Inviting market with full line of fresh, bulk, and processed organic and low-carb products, including baby food. Sandwich and smoothie-juice bar with outdoor tables.

Pizza & Take-out
Aurelio's (239-403-8882; 590 N. Tamiami Trail, Naples 34102) Since 1959 pizza, pasta, and other Italian specialties to eat in or to go.

Cilantro Tamales (239-597-5855; 10823 Tamiami Trail, Naples 34108) Modern Mexican food for take-out and delivery. See listing above.

JT's Island Grill & Gallery (239-695-3633; www.chokoloskee-island.com; 238 Mamie St., Chokoloskee 34138) An island-style grocery store with sandwich take-out (cooler-proof on request) and healthy foods.

Seafood
Captain Jerry's Seafood (239-262-7337; 141 9th St. N., Naples 34102; inside Wynn's Market) Shrimp, stone crab, fish, and live Maine lobster.

Everglades Fish Company (239-695-3241; 208 Camillia St., Everglades City 34139) Located right next to the stone crab docks in Everglades City, it has to sell the freshest. You can also buy shrimp, Florida lobster tails, frog legs, and fish.

Kirk's Fresh Seafood Market (239-394-8616; 417 Papaya Dr., Goodland 34140) Right on the fish docks, with crab traps piled around it, selling wholesale and retail.

Ródes Fresh & Fancy (239-992-4040; 3756 Bonita Beach Rd. SW, Bonita Springs 34134) Fresh produce and local seafood market.

CULTURE

The affluent residents of Naples—many of them transplanted CEOs and captains of industry from lands to the north—share their county with impoverished migrants who work in Immokalee, the nearby agricultural center. The influences of Haitian, Puerto Rican, Jamaican, and other Caribbean cultures are finding their way into the mainstream, while flashes of southern spirit and Cracker charm surface in Goodland, Everglades City, and Chokoloskee.

The Miccosukee and Seminole Indians inhabit reservations in the Everglades. They celebrate their culture each year at the Green Corn Ceremony, during the first new moon in June. They contribute the South Coast's only authentic, indigenous art: colorful weaving, stitching, jewelry, and other age-old handicrafts.

Highbrow art has become a trademark of Naples and its long roll of galleries and performance spaces.

Architecture

In **Naples,** commercial architecture is marked by style and panache, not to mention the architectural beauty of homes and resorts. Banks and insurance companies seem to compete for virtuosity. It's truly a land of visual allure. **Pelican Bay** developments provide examples of a new residential style and provide a contrast with old-money **Port Royal.**

Old Naples, that neighborhood in the vicinity of the pier and Fifth Avenue South, has held on to some real treasures, including the tabby-mortar **Palm Cottage,** the old **Mercantile,** and the **Old Naples building** at Broad and Third. In the same neighborhood, on **Gordon Drive,** pay attention to the charming board-and-batten Cracker survivors.

In **Everglades City** and **Chokoloskee Island,** recreational vehicles and cement-block boxes typify the fishing-oriented community's style. The **Rod & Gun Club,** built in 1850, stands out and dresses the town in southern flair. The style of thatch housing, perfected by the Indians, known as chikee (pronounced *chi-KEY*) prevails in the Everglades and serves as a trendy beach-bar motif at the ritziest resorts throughout the coastal region.

Cinema

Bonita Springs 12 Regal Cinemas (239-949-2600; Hwy. 41 and Pelicans Nest Dr., Bonita Springs 34134)

Hollywood Cinema 20 Cinemas (239-597-9494; 6006 Airport Pulling Rd., Naples 34109; at Pine Ridge Rd.)

Marco Movies (239-642-1111; www.marcomovies.com; 599 S. Collier Blvd., Marco Island 34245; at Marco Walk) Four screens with first-run movies, food, beer, and wine service.

The humble (at left) and lavish (above) extremes of South Coast architecture. Karen T. Bartlett

Naples Twin Drive-In (239-774-6661; 7700 E. Davis Blvd., Naples 34104) Shows nightly, double features on weekends.

Pavilion Cinema (239-596-0008; Vanderbilt Beach Rd., Naples 34108, at Pavilion shopping center)

Dance
Southwest Florida Swing Club (239-774-0651; www.swfsc.com; 7100 Airport Pulling Rd., Naples 34109; at St. Katherine Greek Orthodox Church Fellowship Hall) Dance lessons every Wednesday 7:30–8:45 for cha-cha, swing, and other genres.

Gardens
CARIBBEAN GARDENS: THE ZOO IN NAPLES
239-262-5409.
www.napleszoo.com.
1590 Goodlette-Frank Rd., Naples 34102.
Open: 9:30am–5:30pm daily (last ticket sold at 4:30).
Admission: $15.95 adults; $9.95 children 4–15.

These tropical gardens, today the setting for a nicely proportioned zoo (see "Kid's Stuff" in this section), were planted in 1919 by Dr. Henry Nehrling, a botanist who brought his private collection to Naples. After he died, Julius Fleischmann, a developer, restored and expanded the doctor's 3,000-plus specimens and opened the gardens to the public in 1954. Besides native vegetation, exotics such as magnificent creeping figs, birds of paradise, and monkey-puzzle, calabash, mango, and kapok trees flourish in wetlands and on hammocks.

NAPLES BOTANICAL GARDEN
239-643-7275.
www.naplesgarden.org.
4820 Bayshore Dr., Naples 34112.
Open: Garden open 9–4 Mon.–Fri.; extended weekend hours for special exhibits.
Admission: Free.

Developing in phases 160 acres of subtropical and tropical gardens with plants from many warm lands, it currently has 1.5 acres open to the public. It also holds botanical workshops, seminars, lectures, and special exhibits. Over the next 20 years, other gardens will be developed that will reflect Naples's location at the 26th latitude north.

Historic Homes & Sites
INDIAN HILL
Scott Drive, Goodland.

Though rich in natural and historic heritage, Marco Island hides it well among 20th-century trappings. Witness Indian Hill. On your own you'll have to search to find it, and when you do, only a barely noticeable plaque marks the spot. (Or take a trolley tour—**Marco Island Trolley**, 239-394-1600—to get there.) Southwest Florida's highest elevation at 58 feet above sea level, built up by ancient Calusa Indian shell mounds, it now holds a ritzy neighborhood called the Heights, which feels a little like San Francisco.

PALM COTTAGE

239-261-8164.
137 12th Ave. S., Naples 34102.
Open: 1–4pm Sun.–Fri.; Wed. and Sat. in summer.
Admission: Donation of $6 each requested; children ages 10 and under free.

Land was selling for $10 a lot when Naples founder Walter N. Haldeman (no relation to H. R. Haldeman of Watergate fame) built a winter home for fellow worker Henry Watterson. Haldeman, publisher of the *Louisville Courier Journal,* had discovered the exotic beaches and jungles of Naples in 1887 and proceeded to buy up land and sing its praises. His enthusiasm persuaded winter escapees from Kentucky and Ohio to visit, including Watterson, his star editorial writer. The cottage Haldeman built for his friend was made of Florida pine, tidewater cypress, and a certain type of tabby mortar made by burning seashells over a buttonwood fire. It was one of the first buildings in southwest Florida to be constructed of local materials. Before reaching its present museum status, the cottage—rather spartan by modern standards—knew many lives. If the walls could talk at Palm Cottage, as it eventually came to be known, they would tell of wild parties with the likes of Gary Cooper and Hedy Lamarr in attendance. The cottage, which recently underwent a $400,000 renovation, is now the headquarters of the Collier County Historical Society. It leads 90-minute bimonthly walking tours departing from Palm Cottage Jan.–Apr.; cost is $15 each.

SMALLWOOD STORE

239-695-2989.
360 Mamie St., Chokoloskee Island 34138.
South of Everglades City.
Open: 10am–5pm Dec.–May; 11am–5pm May–Nov.
Admission: $2.50 adults, $2 seniors, children under 12 free.

A historic throwback to frontier days in the 'Glades, this museum preserves a Native American trading post of the early 1900s. Splintery shelves hold ointment containers, FlyDed insect killer, livestock spray, and hordes of memorabilia. Rooms recall life in the pioneer days. The best feature is the view from the back porch. This was the site of a Jesse James–era murder immortalized in Peter Matthiessen's novel *Killing Mr. Watson.*

Kid's Stuff
CARIBBEAN GARDENS: THE ZOO IN NAPLES

239-262-5409.
www.napleszoo.com.
1590 Goodlette-Frank Rd., Naples 34102.
Open: 9:30am–5:30pm daily (last ticket sold at 4:30).
Admission: $15.95 adults, $9.95 children 4–15 (plus tax).

Big cats are the specialty of this zoo. Not just your lions and Bengal tigers but such rarities as the Indochinese tiger (the only zoo in Florida to have this rarest of cats), white tiger, ocelot, jungle cat, serval, and caracal. Panther Glade, the newest exhibit, gets to know America's big kitties. They are the stars of "Meet the Keeper" programs and the multimedia Planet Predator show. (This is Florida's only zoo exhibiting all four of Africa's top predators—lions, spotted hyenas, leopards, and the endangered African wild dogs.)

"Serpents: Fangs & Fiction" explores native venomous snakes and other reptiles. A free boat ride takes a close-up look at the zoo's primate population, which is sequestered on nine islands. Three separate play areas amuse toddlers and older children. Shaded, meandering, chirp-orchestrated paths take you past other fenced animals. The 52-acre grounds are attractively maintained with the lush vegetation of the zoo's so-called Caribbean Gardens (see "Gardens" in this section).

Museums
✪ COLLIER COUNTY MUSEUM
239-774-8476.
www.colliermuseum.com.
3301 Tamiami Trail E., Naples 34112.
Open: 9am–5pm Mon.-Fri.
Closed: Weekends, except during special winter exhibits.
Admission: Donations accepted.

The unique aspects at this village of history include typical Seminole chikee huts, a vintage swamp buggy that kids can climb into, the skeleton of an Ice Age giant ground sloth, a working archaeological lab, a replicated Seminole war fort, and a 1910 steam locomotive from the county's cypress-logging era. Exhibits of prehistoric fossils and Native American artifacts, housed in pretty vintage structures and nicely landscaped, take you back 10,000 years. More recent historical reminders include a recreated 19th-century trading post, 1920s furnishings, period vignettes, and a native plant garden. One exhibit likens the opening of Tamiami Trail to the Panama Canal.

KEY MARCO MUSEUM
239-389-6447.
Marco Island Realtors Office, 140 Waterway Ct., Marco Island 34145, at Bald Eagle Dr.
Also: Shops at Old Marco, 100 Palm Dr., PO Box 2282, Naples 34146.
Open: 9am–4pm Mon.–Fri.
Closed: Weekends.
Admission: Free.

Through photographs, artifacts, replicas, and memorabilia, this fledgling museum (for the time being in two commercial locations) depicts the past of Key Marco, as it was once known. It concentrates on the island's rich Calusa Indian culture, displaying a life-size diorama, shell tools, masks, wood carvings, and other artifacts unearthed in the 1895 archeological expedition that established Marco as an important center of the Calusa kingdom. The dig's most important find, the Calusa Cat, has become an island icon and is replicated here (at the Old Marco branch). The original resides at the Smithsonian Institution. Modern times are also represented by displays exploring pineapple farming, clam canning, and residential development (at the Bald Eagle branch). Plans are underway for Collier County Museum to build its fourth branch on the island and replace the two smaller museums.

MUSEUM OF THE EVERGLADES
239-695-0008.
www.colliermuseum.com.
105 W. Broadway, PO Box 8, Everglades City 34139.

Hours: 10am–4pm Tues.–Sat.

Closed: Sun. and Mon.

Admission: $2 suggested donation.

The museum takes over a renovated historic laundry started by developer Barron Collier to serve the community of road builders during the construction of the Tamiami Trail in the 1920s. The museum concentrates on the tremendous feat of blazing a trail through the swampy, buggy Everglades, plus the region's Calusa Indian and fishing heritage.

NAPLES DEPOT/LIONEL TRAIN MUSEUM

239-262-1776.

1051 Fifth Ave. S., Naples 34102.

Corner Tamiami Trail and 10th St. S.

Hours: 12–4 Thurs.–Sat.

Admission: $5 for adults, $3 for children.

Gary Cooper, Hedy Lamarr, and other illuminati of yore once arrived at this circa 1927 depot. Recently, Lionel has set up an elaborate display of eight operating model trains inside, and a small railroad outside for kiddie rides. The attractions are staffed by volunteers, and so hours vary according to their availability.

✪ TEDDY BEAR MUSEUM OF NAPLES

239-598-2711, 866-365-2327.

www.teddymuseum.com.

2511 Pine Ridge Rd., Naples 34109.

Open: 10am–5pm Tues.–Sat.

Closed: Sun., Mon.

Admission: $8 adults, $6 seniors, $3 children 4–12.

Home to more than 5,000 teddies, this cuddly museum showcases collector, antique, and limited-edition bears and includes a signed first edition of A. A. Milne's *Winnie the Pooh*. The collection began as one woman's penchant for the stuffed animals and is whimsically displayed: bears at clown school, bears on parade, etc. New: a train running overhead bearing – what else? – bears. Tots will have fun in the Three Bears House. A gift shop sells bears and fine gifts. Saturday morning story hour for kids.

Music and Nightlife

✪ **Bimini's Beach Club** (239-394-7111; 657 S. Collier Blvd., Marco Island 34145) A lively resort-scene, indoor/outdoor venue for live dance music—pop, jazz, reggae, and Motown—nightly. Serves a full food menu until midnight.

Little Bar (239-394-5663; 205 Harbor Dr., Goodland 34140) Hosts live music on Friday and Saturday nights.

✪ **Luna** (239-514-3777; 475 Seagate Dr., Naples 34108; at The Registry Resort) Multi-level music and dancing in one of Naples's most fashionable locales.

Mamie Street Music Hall at JT's (239-695-3633; www.chokoloskee-island.com; 238 Mamie St., Chokoloskee 34138) Local musicians play jazz, folk, bluegrass, blues, island, country, and rock music 5–9pm.

✪ **McCabe's Irish Pub** (239-403-8777; 699 Fifth Ave. S., Naples 34102) Authentic Irish music and rowdy camaraderie in a Dublin-built pub.

Naples Concert Band (239-263-9521; Naples) For 32 years its 90 volunteer musicians have been performing free Sunday concerts once a month at Cambier Park in Old Naples and once a year at Mackle Park on Marco Island.

Naples Jazz Society (239-566-1997; www.naplesjazzsociety.org; PO Box 1365, Naples 34106) Hosts jazz artists in winter at Norris Center (Cambier Park, 755 Eighth Ave., Naples). It also conducts summer jazz camp for young musicians.

The Naples Concert Band performs Sunday afternoons at Cambier Park. Karen T. Bartlett

The Nightclub at The Ritz-Carlton (239-598-3300; 280 Vanderbilt Beach Rd., Naples 34108) Live contemporary music every night.

Snook Inn (239-394-3313; 1215 Bald Eagle Dr., Marco Island 34145) Live local bands, contemporary and island music.

Tommy Bahama's Tropical Café (239-643-6889; 1220 Third St. S., Naples 34102) Lively island music in the evenings with outdoor seating.

Vanderbilt Inn (239-597-3151; 11000 Gulf Shore Dr. N., Naples 34108) Live music and karaoke indoors and at the chikee bar on the beach.

Zoe's (239-261-1221; 720 Fifth Ave. S., Naples 34102) One of Fifth Avenue's liveliest spots, it hosts live jazz on select evenings during season.

Theater
Marco Players (239-642-7270; 1083 N. Collier Blvd., Marco Island, FL, 34145; at Marco Town Center Mall) Nonprofit community theater that produces comedies and musicals January–April.

Naples Dinner Theatre (239-514-STAR; 877-519-STAR; www.naplesdinnertheatre.com; 1025 Piper Blvd., Naples 34110) Top Broadway hit musicals as you dine, including ice cream matinees for families.

✪ **Philharmonic Center for the Arts** (239-597-1900, 800-597-1900; www.thephil.org; 5833 Pelican Bay Blvd., Naples 34108) "The Phil," as locals call it, is home to the 85-piece Naples Philharmonic. It hosts audiences of up to 1,473 for Broadway shows, touring orchestras, opera, comedians, modern dance, and the Miami City Ballet.

Sugden Community Theatre (239-263-7990; 701 Fifth Ave. S., Naples 34102) The home of the **Naples Players**, a community theater troupe that has been entertaining October–

May for 50 years. The complex features a main stage plus a more experimental black-box theater, and plays host to Naples Jazz Society, ballet, opera, and other performance art.

Visual Art Centers & Resources

Like its Italian namesake, Naples serves as the region's aesthetic pacesetter. Gallery-lined streets host artists of local, national, and international stature. The following entries introduce you to opportunities for experiencing art as either a viewer or a practicing artist. A listing for commercial galleries is included in the "Shopping" section.

Art League of Bonita Springs Center for the Arts (239-495-8989; www.artcenterbonita .org; 26100 Old 41 Rd., Bonita Springs 34135) Classes, children's programs, exhibitions, and national art festivals in January and March (see "Events").

Art League of Marco Island (239-394-4221; www.marcoislandart.com; 1010 Winterberry Dr., Marco Island 34145) Workshops, lectures, two galleries with monthly changing exhibits, and gift shop. It sponsors Marco Outdoor Artists, which schedules paint-ins at local scenic venues. Call 239-642-7649 for details.

Naples Museum of Art (239-597-1900, 800-597-1900; www.thephil.org; Philharmonic Center for the Arts, 5833 Pelican Bay Blvd., Naples 34108) Opened in 2000, Naples's latest cultural showpiece is as stunning as you'd expect. Permanent exhibits include a collection of modern American masters 1900–1955, including Alexander Calder, Jackson Pollock, and Stuart Davis. The museum also holds a priceless collection of Chinese artifacts, scrolls, sculptures, pottery, and other pieces dating back to the Han Dynasty (206 BC–220 AD). World-renowned glass sculptor Dale Chihuly created two magnificent chandeliers for the museum: one that hangs from its dome glass conservatory and another suspended in the three-story stairwell. The $10.6 million museum's 15 galleries elegantly showcase world-class traveling exhibitions. Open Tuesday–Saturday 10am–4pm, Sunday 12–4pm; closed Monday. Admission: $6 adults, $3 students, free for children under 5. Free docent tours Tuesday–Saturday at 11 and 2 October–May.

Philharmonic Galleries (239-597-1111; www.thephil.org; Philharmonic Center for the Arts, 5833 Pelican Bay Blvd., Naples 34108) Exhibitions of well-known works. Open one hour before Philharmonic Center performances, postperformances, and during intermission for patrons only.

United Arts Council (239-263-8242; www.uaccollier.com; 501 Goodlette Rd. N. #A210, Naples 34102) A central clearinghouse for culture, music, dance, theater, and visual arts in the Naples area.

✪ **The von Liebig Art Center** (239-262-6517; www.naplesartcenter.org; 585 Park St., Naples 34102) Home of the Naples Art Association, the art center holds classes, workshops, and showings for children and its members and other special exhibitions. The skylighted library contains arts information.

RECREATION

The Ten Thousand Islands are the meat of the South Coast's recreational banquet. Here, the old-fashioned sports—fishing, canoeing, hiking—are most in style. The beaches of

Naples and Marco Island serve up the newer, exhilarating side dishes, everything from parasailing to jet skiing.

Beaches

In 2003, a poll conducted by Yahoo! Travel Web site and *National Geographic Traveler* magazine ranked Naples as number 10 for "Top Sands" in the nation.

Parking fees are levied at most beaches; county residents can purchase stickers that allow them to park free. For information on county beaches, contact Department of Collier County Parks & Recreation (239-353-0404; www.colliergov.net; 3300 Santa Barbara Blvd., Naples 34116).

CLAM PASS RECREATION AREA

239-353-0404.
Registry Resort of Seagate Dr., 410 Seagate Dr., Naples 34103.
Facilities: Restrooms, showers, food and beach concessions.
Parking: $4 per day.

This beach used by guests of Registry Resort but open to the public is reached by a tram that follows a nearly 1-mile boardwalk over a tidal bay and through mangroves. Boat and cabana rentals are available at this county facility. The sand is fine and fluffy. You can kayak or sail into the sea, or canoe along a trail among the mangroves, which are frequented by ospreys, hawks, and a variety of other feathered creatures.

DELNOR-WIGGINS PASS STATE PARK

239-597-6196.
www.floridastateparks.org/delnor-wiggins.
11100 Gulf Shore Dr. N., Naples 34108.
At Route 846, Vanderbilt Beach.
Facilities: Picnic areas, grills, pavilion, restrooms, showers, boat ramp, volleyball, lifeguard.
Admission: $5 per car, up to 8 passengers; $1 pedestrians, cyclists, or extra passengers.

This highly natural, low-key beach, named among America's 40 Certified Healthy Beaches, extends for 1 mile south from the mouth of the Cocohatchee River. The lush white sands are protected during loggerhead turtle nesting season (summer) and support stands of natural maritime vegetation such as cactus, sea grape, nickerbean, and yucca. A nature trail leads to an observation tower at the beach's north end. This is a popular park, but you can usually find parking in one of the many lots. Restrict your swimming to south of the pass's fast-moving waters, which are a boon to fishermen.

✪ LOWDERMILK PARK

239-263-6078.
257 Banyan Blvd. at Gulf Shore Blvd., Naples.
Facilities: Picnic area, restrooms, showers, volleyball, playground, concessions, special handicap access, and wheeled surf chairs.
Parking: Metered, 75¢ per hour.

Beach headquarters for the South Coast: There are lots of special activities at this gulfside

Naples pier: the heart of Old Naples. Karen T. Bartlett

party spot with its 1,000 feet of sandy beach. Across the street, a deli and restaurant fuel your beach day.

NAPLES MUNICIPAL BEACHES
239-213-3062.
Gulf Shore Blvd. south of Doctors Pass, Naples.
Facilities: Restrooms, shower, concessions, fishing pier.
Parking: Metered, 75¢ per hour.

The historic pier on 12th Avenue South, where facilities and a parking lot are located, anchors stretches of natural beach.

SOUTH MARCO BEACH
S. Collier Blvd. at Swallow Ave., south end of Marco Island.
Parking: $4 per vehicle.

Parking is on the other side of Collier Blvd. a half block away. A paved brick path beneath palm trees leads to this patch of public beach between giant high-rises. No facilities, but there's a restaurant next door.

TIGERTAIL BEACH
Hernando Dr., north end of Marco Island.
Facilities: Picnic area, restrooms, showers, water-sports rentals, restaurant, playground volleyball.
Parking: $4 per vehicle.

This county-owned beach is a good place for shelling and sunning. In season, arrive early to find a parking spot. Wooden ramps cross dunes to 31 acres of wide, marvelous beach. The south end fronts high-rises, but the north end stretches into wilderness. The fun playground is divided for two different age groups. Tidal pools separate the main beach and a fronting sandbar known as Sand Dollar Island, which attracts feeding and nesting birds and shellers.

VANDERBILT BEACH
239-353-0404.
280 Vanderbilt Dr., Vanderbilt Beach, north of Naples.
Facilities: Restrooms, showers, food; water-sports rentals available at nearby resorts.
Parking: $4 per vehicle at nearby lot on Vanderbilt Dr.; metered on the street.

This recently refurbished stretch of sand runs alongside resorts and is well suited to those who like sharing the beach with a lot of people as well as bar- and restaurant-hopping along the beach.

Bicycling
City and country biking are available to those who prefer this slow, intimate mode of exploration. Sidewalks, bike paths (marked with white diamonds), and roadsides accommodate cyclists. By state law, cyclists must conduct themselves as pedestrians when using sidewalks. Avoid cycling on crowded downtown walks. Where they share the road with other vehicles, cyclists must follow all the rules of the road. Children under age 16 must wear a helmet.

Best Biking
Naples has laid out a sporadic system of metropolitan bike paths. A favorite route of local cyclists loops through 10 miles of pathway in the north-end Pelican Bay development. Within it, a 580-acre nature preserve provides a change of scenery from upscale suburbia.

A bike path runs the length of **Bonita Beach**, nearly 3 miles long, and connects to another at its south end, which leads to **Vanderbilt Beach.**

Bike paths traverse **Everglades City** and cross the causeway to **Chokoloskee Island.** Back-road bikers take to the 12-mile (one-way) ✪ **W. J. Janes Memorial Scenic Drive** through Fakahatchee Strand State Preserve, off Highway 29 north of Everglades City. Royal palms, cypress trees, and air plants provide pristine scenery and bird habitat (10 miles in you'll find a popular bird feeding pond). Morning or sunset riders may spot wild turkeys, alligators, raccoons, snakes, otters, bobcats, and deer. A 5.5-mile mountain bike trail at **Collier-Seminole State Park** travels through cabbage palm hammock.

Rentals/Sales
Many resorts rent bikes or provide bike use to guests.

Bonita Bike & Baby (239-947-6377; 27241 Bay Landing Dr. #19, Bonita Beach, FL 34135) A variety of bikes including kids', trailers for kids, and beach and jogging strollers.

Bonita Cyclery (239-949-0026; 27820 S. Tamiami Trail, Bonita Springs 34134) Delivery available for all sizes and styles of bicycles and gear, including helmets, locks, and kid carriers.

Vanderbilt Beach cyclist Karen T. Bartlett

Ivey House B&B (239-695-3299; www.iveyhouse.com; 107 Camellia St., Everglades City 34139) Rents bikes to the public.

Naples Cyclery (239-566-0600; www.naplescyclery.com; 813 Vanderbilt Beach Rd., Naples FL 34108; at Pavilion Shopping Center) Rents a wide variety of speed bikes, recumbent bikes, surreys, and equipment for kids.

Scootertown (239-394-8400; www.islandbikeshop.com; 845 Bald Eagle Dr., Marco Island 34145) Rents scooters and bikes in various sizes and styles; also skates and strollers. Rates by the day, week, and month. Delivery available.

Boats & Boating
Naples, Marco Island, and Everglades City are lousy with marinas. These are headquarters for boat rentals, tours, and charters to serve every interest, from shelling and fishing to gaping at mansions.

Canoeing & Kayaking
The ultimate paddling experience, Everglades National Park has marked a ✪ 99-mile Wilderness Waterway trail that extends from Everglades City to Flamingo, the park's main eastern access. Chikee hut campsites accommodate overnighters. There are also good canoeing trails near the Oasis Visitors Center in **Big Cypress National Preserve**. Outfitters in Everglades City provide rentals, supplies, tours, and shuttle service. In addition to the outlets listed below, many resorts and parks rent canoes and kayaks.

Cocohatchee Nature Center (239-592-1200; www.cocohatchee.org; 12345 Tamiami Trail N., Naples 34110) Rents kayaks and canoes for self-guided or guided tours into the estuary wilderness of the Cocohatchee River, which empties into the gulf.

Collier-Seminole State Park (239-394-3397; www.floridastateparks.org/collier-
seminole; 20200 E. Tamiami Trail, Naples 34114; between Naples and Everglades City)
Rents canoes for use on the park's 13.5-mile canoe trail into mangrove wilderness preserve. Guided tours available Sundays in-season by reservation.

Conservancy of Southwest Florida (239-262-0304; www.conservancy.org; 1450 Merrihue
Dr., Naples 34102; 239-775-8569; 401 Shell Island Rd., Naples 34133) Canoes are available to rent at Naples and Briggs Nature Center (respective addresses above). Guided
canoe trips from the latter include birding, sunset, and full-moon excursions.

✪ **Everglades National Park Boat Tours** (239-695-2591, 800-445-7724 in Florida;
www.nps.gov/ever; Everglades Ranger Station, PO Box 119, Everglades City 34139) Free
ranger-led canoe trips in season (mid-December through Easter) every Saturday and
Sunday 10-2; must bring your own canoe or kayak.

Get Wet Sports (239-394-9557; 11369 E. Tamiami Trail, Naples; mail: PO Box 226, Marco
34146) Sales, rentals, free delivery to Marco (with advance notice), and nature tours that
depart from Backwater Nick's on Isles of Capri.

G.R. Boating (239-947-4889; 4892 Bonita Beach Rd., Bonita Springs, FL 34134; near the
public beach) Rents canoes and kayaks.

North American Canoe Tours (239-695-4666; www.evergladesadventures.com; 107
Camellia St., PO Box 5038, Everglades City 34139) Rents 17- to 19-foot aluminum canoes,
high-quality kayaks, and equipment with complete outfitting and shuttle service. Guided
excursions into the Everglades range from one day to seven nights.

Dining Cruises

Marco Island Princess (239-642-5415; www.sunshinetoursmarcoisland.com; 951 Bald
Eagle Dr., Marco Island 34145; at Marco River Marina) Daily narrated eco-sightseeing
cruises, lunch and dinner cruises, and sunset excursions.

Naples Princess (239-649-2275; www.naplesprincesscruises.com; Port-O-Call Marina, 550
Port-O-Call Way, Naples 34102; on Hwy. 41 across the river from Tin City) Excursions include a buffet lunch, sunset hors d'oeuvres, and sunset buffet dinner. Full-service cash bar.

Marine Supplies

Boat/US Marine Center (239-774-3233; 3360 E. Tamiami Trail, Naples FL 34104) All
boating, yachting, and fishing needs. Discounts and emergency service available with
membership.

Personal Watercraft Rentals/Tours

Marco Island Ski & Water Sports (239-642-2359; www.marcoislandwatersports.com; 400
S. Collier Blvd., Marco Island 34145; at Marriott's Marco Island Resort) Rents Waverunners
and conducts Waverunner excursions into Ten Thousand Islands. Also parasailing.

Powerboat Rentals

Back Bay Marina of Southwest Florida (239-992-2608; 4751 Bonita Beach Rd., Bonita
Springs 34134) Pontoon boats by the half and full day.

Cedar Bay Marina (239-642-6717; www.cedarbaymarina.com; 705 E. Elkcam Circle,
Marco Island 34145) Top-of-the-line, fully equipped fishing and pleasure boats.

G. R. Boating (239-947-4889; 4892 Bonita Beach Rd., Bonita Beach 34134; near the public beach) Rents skiffs, pontoon, and deck boats.

Port-O-Call Marina (239-774-0479; off Hwy. 41 E., 550 Port-O-Call Way, Naples 34102) Rents deck boats and powerboats 17 to 23 feet in length, to accommodate 6 to 12 people.

Walker's Coon Cay Marina (239-394-2797; 604 E. Palm Ave., Goodland 34140) 24-by-24-foot pontoons and 19-foot center consoles with VHF radios.

Public Boat Ramps
Caxambas Park (239-642-0004; www.co.collier.fl.us; 909 S. Collier Ct., Marco Island 34145) Restrooms, bait, fuel, and access to Roberts Bay.

Cocohatchee River Park (239-591-8596; www.co.collier.fl.us/parks/colliercountyp /beach/boatramps/cocohatchee.html; 13531 Vanderbilt Dr., Naples 34108; at Vanderbilt Beach) Park with three ramps onto the river (which runs to the gulf), restrooms, picnic tables, and boat rentals. Parking fee.

Delnor–Wiggins Pass State Park (239-597-6196; www.floridastateparks.org/delnor -wiggins; 11100 Gulf Shore Dr. N., Naples 34108) The boat ramp allows access to the back bays, the Cocohatchee River, and the Gulf of Mexico, providing visitors with excellent fishing opportunities. Admission.

Marco Island approach (1 mile before the bridge on Route 951)

Naples Landing (239-213-1819; 1101 Ninth St. S., Naples 34102, off Ninth St. S.)

Sailboat Charters
Sea Excursions (239-642-7704; www.seaexcursions.com; Marco River Marina, 951 Bald Eagle Dr., Marco Island 34145) Shelling, beaching, luau, sunset, and dolphin-watch tours about the *Kahuna* 42-passenger catamaran. Rental, racing, and ASA instruction.

Sightseeing & Entertainment Cruises
Collier-Seminole State Park Boat Tours (239-642-8898; www.floridaeverglades tours.com; 20200 E. Tamiami Trail, Naples 34114; at Collier-Seminole State Park, 17 miles south of Naples on Hwy. 41) One-hour tours narrate human and natural history along the Blackwater River. Bonus for traveling pets: Dogs under 50 pounds are allowed on the pontoon boats.

Speedy Johnson's Airboat Tours (239-695-4448, 800-998-4448; www.florida -everglades.com/speedy; Everglades City 34139) You'll find any number of airboat

Setting sail through the maze of Ten Thousand Islands. Karen T. Bartlett

tour operators in and around Everglades City. Most are equal in that they despicably feed wildlife to attract it to the boat. This one is better than others for its accessibility to grass-lands and its elevated seats.

Sweet Liberty (239-793-3525; www.sweet liberty.com; 4,620 Gail Blvd., Naples 34104; at the Boat Haven off Hwy. 41 at Davis Blvd.) Daily shelling, sightseeing, and sunset trips aboard a 53-foot catamaran.

Fishing

Many visiting sports folk arrive at the South Coast eager to fight the big fish and brave the deep waters of the Gulf of Mexico. They come equipped with their 50-pound test line, heavy tackle, and tall fish tales. Yet closer to home, in the back bays and shallow waters of Ten Thousand Islands, experienced fishermen find what's best about the region. Sea trout, snook, redfish, sheepshead, mangrove snapper, and pompano abound in the brackish creeks, grass flats, and channels.

Nonresidents age 16 and over must obtain a license unless fishing from a vessel or pier covered by its own license. You can buy inexpensive temporary nonresident licenses at county tax collectors' offices and most Kmarts and bait shops. Check local regulations for season, size, and catch restrictions.

Fishing Charters/Outfitters

Check the large marinas for fishing guides. Experienced guides can take the intimidation and guesswork out of open-water fishing.

Captain Lee Quick (239-695-0032; www.florida-southwest.com/quick/guide.htm; PO Box 804, Chokoloskee 34138) Fly and light tackle fishing in Ten Thousand Islands and Everglades.

Captain Max Miller (239-695-2420; Everglades City 34139) Specializes in light-tackle back-bay fishing.

Captain Paul (239-263-4949; 1200 Fifth Ave. S., Naples 34102; Tin City) Half-day back-country fishing trips into Ten Thousand Islands.

Chokoloskee Island Outfitters (239-695-2286; www.cyberangler.com/guides/prickett; Chokoloskee Island 34138) Capt. Dave Prickett takes you out for half and full days.

Estero Bay Boat Tours (239-992-2200; 5231 Mamie St., Bonita Springs 34134; at Weeks Fish Camp, next to The Hyatt Regency) The Weeks family has been fishing these backwa-ters for generations.

Everglades Angler (239-262-8228, 800-57-FISHY; www.evergladesangler.com; 810 Twelfth Ave. S., Naples 34102) Half and full-day backcountry fishing expeditions for up to three fishermen to the Everglades and Ten Thousand Islands, Marco Island, and Estero Bay for snook, redfish, and tarpon. One-day fly-tying and fly-casting clinics.

Lady Brett 45 (239-263-4949; 1200 Fifth Ave. S., Naples 34102; Tin City) Half-day off-shore trips aboard a 45-foot powerboat with head on board.

Mangrove Outfitters (239-793-3370; www.mangrove-outfitters.com; 4111 E. Tamiami Trail, Naples 34112) Guides charters and, in-season, teaches classes on casting.

Peg Leg Charters (239-642-4333 or 250-0625; PO Box 171, Goodland 34140; at Stan's Idle Hour Restaurant in Goodland) Capt. Ron Kennedy takes anglers offshore for half- and full-day trips.

Puddlejumper II (239-992-6752; e-mail: puddlejumper2@mindspring.com; 26107 Hickory Blvd., Bonita Springs 34134; at Big Hickory Marina) Captain Bruce Clark takes you out on four-hour near-shore and half- and full-day offshore excursions. Maximum six people.

Sunshine Tours (239-642-5415; www.sunshinetoursmarcoisland.com; 951 Bald Eagle Dr., Marco Island 34145; at Marco River Marina) Takes small parties aboard a 32-foot boat with bathroom for offshore excursions, half to full day. Also does backcountry fishing trips.

Fishing Piers
✪ **Naples Fishing Pier** (239-213-3062; www.explorenaples.com/naples_municipal _beach_fishing_pier.phtml; 25 12th Ave. S., Naples 34102) Extends a thousand feet into the gulf, with bait shop, snack bar, restrooms, and showers.

Golf
Naples earns its title as Golf Capital of the World with more golf holes per capita than any other statistically tracked metropolitan area.

Public Golf Courses
Bonita Fairways Country Club (239-947-9100; www.thegolfcourses.net/golfcourses/ FL/2904.htm; 9751 W. Terry St., Bonita Springs 34135) Play 18 holes at a reasonable price. Restaurant.

Lely Resort Flamingo Island Club (239-793-2223, 800-388-GOLF; http://naples-golf -courses.tee-times-usa.com/flamingo-island-club.htm; 8004 Lely Resort Blvd., Naples 34113; off Route 951 east of Naples) Public course designed by Robert Trent Jones Sr. Offers 18 holes, par 72, and a golf school.

The Links of Naples (239-417-1313; 16161 E. Tamiami Trail, Naples 34110) Lit 18-hole course with driving range, PGA lessons, and rentals.

Naples Beach Golf Club (239-434-7007; www.naplesbeachhotel.com; 851 Gulf Shore Blvd. N., Naples 34102) An 18-hole, par 72 resort course that is host to many pro and amateur tournaments. Restaurant and lounge.

Pelican's Nest Golf Club (239-947-4600, 800-952-6378; 4450 Pelican's Nest Dr., Bonita Springs 34134) A 36-hole course, par 72.

Tiburón Golf Club (239-594-2040; www.wcigolf.com/courses/new_tiburon.htm; 2600 Tiburón Dr., Naples 34109; at the Ritz-Carlton Golf Resort) One of Naples's newest and most exclusive golfing venues; semiprivate with two 18-hole courses—the Black and the Gold—and a golf academy.

Golf Centers
David Leadbetter Golf Academy (239-592-1444, 800-424-3542; www.leadbetter.com; LaPlaya Beach & Golf Resort, 333 Palm River Blvd., Naples 34110) Offers golf school at LaPlaya Golf Course. Lessons, classes, and golf retreats can last anywhere from one hour to three days.

Naples Golf Center (239-775-4242; 7700 E. Davis Blvd., Naples 34104) Lit driving range with putting and chipping greens and sand traps. Home to Naples Golf Academy (239-732-9944; www.learninggolf.com): video, single, series, and group lessons.

The Rick Smith Golf Academy (239-594-2040; www.wcigolf.com/ricksmithacademy; 2600 Tiburón Dr., Naples 34109; at the Ritz-Carlton Golf Resort) Features individualized instruction, computerized swing analysis, private video viewing rooms.

Golf Shops

World of Golf (239-263-4999, 800-505-9998; www.worldofgolf.com; 4500 N. Tamiami Trail, Naples 34103) From tees to clubs, this shop carries all name-brand equipment and apparel.

Health & Fitness Clubs

Fitness Quest (239-643-7546; 2975 S. Horseshoe Dr., Naples 34104) Complete fitness center, aerobics, karate, heart-healthy café, nursery.

Golden Gate Fitness Center (239-353-3636; Golden Gate Community Park, 3300 Santa Barbara Blvd., Naples 34116) Full range of Cybex and Keiser equipment, cardio machines, and free weights. Personal training and assessment available.

Gold's Gym (239-598-4455; 2151 Trade Center Way, Naples 34109; 239-498-3339; 9110 Bonita Beach Rd., Bonita Springs 34135) Weight- and cardio-training equipment, fitness classes, physical therapists, child care, boxing room, climbing wall, and tanning with sur-round sound.

Marco Fitness Club (239-394-3705; 871 E. Elkcam Circle, Marco Island 34145) Top-of-the-line cardiovascular and weight machines, free weights, personal trainers, massage therapist.

Hiking

✪ **Big Cypress National Preserve** (239-695-4111, ext. 0; www.nps.gov/bicy; HCR 61, Box 110, Ochopee 33141) East of Rte. 29, short hiking trails lead off Rte. 839; longer trails begin about 15 miles away at the Oasis Visitor Center and join up with the Florida Trail, a national scenic trail that will eventually traverse the state's length.

✪ **Collier-Seminole State Park** (239-394-3397; www.floridastateparks.org/collier -seminole; 20200 E. Tamiami Trail, Naples 34114) A 7-mile trail winds through pine flat-woods and cypress swamp with primitive campsite, and a self-guided boardwalk leads into a salt marsh.

Conservancy of Southwest Florida (239-262-0304; 1450 Merrihue Dr., Naples 34102) Guided and unguided nature hikes through a subtropical hammock. Also hosts day-trip safaris, some of which involve hiking.

✪ **Fakahatchee Strand State Preserve** (239-695-4593; www.floridastateparks.org/ fakahatcheestrand; W. J. Janes Memorial Scenic Dr. in Copeland, SR 29, north of Hwy. 41) Several trails—actually, old logging tramways—traverse the strand off 12-mile (one-way) Janes Drive from the gates on either side of the road. They range in length from 1 to 2 miles. Summer flooding can make your hike a slosh. Adjacent **Picayune Strand State**

Forest (at the end of Janes Drive) introduces access to 3.2-mile Sabal Palm Hiking Trail through cypress forest, habitat for a variety of birds.

Hunting

The Everglades provides some of Florida's best shots at hunting. You must obtain a state license and a Wildlife Management Area stamp. Permits are required for early-season hunting and special types of hunting. For information on seasons and bag limits, request a copy of *Florida Hunting Handbook & Regulations Summary* when you buy your license. Skeet shooting is available at Port of the Islands development between Naples and Everglades City.

Kid's Stuff

Coral Cay Adventure Golf (239-793-4999; www.funspotrentals.com; 2205 E. Tamiami Trail, Naples 34112) Two 18-hole courses with a tropical island theme. Admission.

Golden Gate Aquatic Complex (239-353-7128; Golden Gate Community Park, 3300 Santa Barbara Blvd., Naples 34116) Swimming fun for all ages, with water slides, wading pool and fountain, and competition pool with low and high dives. Admission.

Golf Safari (239-947-1377; 3775 Bonita Beach Rd., Bonita Springs 34134) Jungle-themed miniature golf.

✪ **King Richard's Family Fun Park** (239-598-1666; 6780 N. Airport Rd., Naples 34109) Merlin's Moat interactive water attraction (bring your swimsuit), roller coaster, bumper boats, batting cages, a castle full of video and other electronic games, go-carts, a kiddie train, and two 18-hole miniature golf courses. No admission; you buy tickets per attraction. Age restrictions apply for some of the rides.

Naples Go-Cart Center (239-774-7776; 11402 Tamiami Trail E., Naples 34113) Video games, pinball, and a snack center. Closed Tuesday.

Racquet Sports

Cambier Park (239-434-4694; www.cambiertennis.com; between Eighth and Park Streets, Naples) Twelve lit tennis courts. Fee.

Collier County Racquet Center (239-394-5454; 1275 San Marco Rd., Marco Island 34145) County facility with five deco-turf courts, two racquetball courts, pro shop, and lessons.

Fleischmann Park (239-434-4692; 1600 Fleischmann Blvd., Naples 33940) Lit racquetball courts.

Golden Gate Community Park (239-353-0404; 3300 Santa Barbara Blvd., Naples 34116) Lit tennis and racquetball courts.

Naples Park Elementary (111th Ave. N., Naples) Two lit courts.

Pelican Bay Community Park (239-353-0404; 764 Vanderbilt Rd., Naples 34108) Lit tennis and racquetball courts.

Tommie Barfield Elementary (101 Kirkwood St., Goodland, Marco Island 34140) Two lit courts.

Shelling

It is illegal to collect live shells in state and national parks. Collier County discourages the collection of live shells.

Hot Shelling Spots

Coconut Island (north of Marco Island) A destination for most Marco Island shelling expeditions.

✪ **Key Island** (south of Naples, accessible only by boat) A partly private, partly state-owned unbridged island, Key holds a great many shell prizes that are not as picked over as on beaches that are accessible by car. **Naples Nature Center** (see "Nature Preserves") conducts a beachcombing-shelling tour of the island by a pontoon boat in-season (December through April).

Ten Thousand Islands Shell Island, Kingston Key, and Mormon Key provide lots of empty shells to collect.

Shelling Charters

Captain Paul (239-263-4949; 1200 Fifth Ave. S., Naples 34102; in Tin City) Daily trips to Keewaydin Island.

Sail Marco/Sea Excursions (239-642-7704; Marco River Marina, 951 Bald Eagle Dr., Marco Island 34145; mailing address 821A Palm St., Marco Island 34145) Go to unbridged barrier islands for shelling aboard a powered or sailing boat.

Spas

Danielle (239-947-5900; www.daniellespa.com; 27160 Bay Landing Dr., Bonita Springs 34135) An elegant spa that designs wellness programs—including Pilates, personal consultations and training, and wellness classes—and makes you feel pampered with massage, body treatments, hydrotherapy, facials, and the works.

La Piel Spa (239-352-5554; www.la-piel.com; 6370 Pine Ridge Rd., Ste. 101, Naples 34119) A full-service day spa incorporated into a cosmetic-surgery practice. It offers facials, peels, body treatments, massages, manicures, and other services.

Naples Beach Hotel & Golf Club (239-261-2222, 800-237-7600; www.naplesbeachhotel. com/resort/spa; 851 Gulf Shore Blvd. N., Naples 34102) This recent addition to a landmark Naples hotel brings full-service spa facilities, from extensive massage services (aromatherapy, reiki, shiatsu, neuro-muscular, etc.) to body treatments (wraps, gommage, scrubs) and facials. A hair salon and fitness center enhance the wellness experience here.

SeaSide Day Spa (239-393-2288, 888-393-4SPA; www.seasidedayspa.com; 651 S. Collier Blvd., Marco Island 34145) Conveniently located across the street from the Radisson resort, this spa administers a full line of massage, body, and skin treatments, with a focus on facials and face treatments: classic European facial, LaStone facial, oxygen treatments, microdermabrasion, and peels.

Spa-Fari (239-695-1006; www.spa-fari.com; 201 W. Broadway, Everglades City 34139) Above and beyond pampering spas, this adjunct to a local inn performs services such as colonics, ear candling, and polar alignment as well as massage, scrubs, and wraps.

And they're off! "Going to the dogs" is a favorite pastime in Bonita Springs. Karen T. Bartlett

Spectator Sports
Greyhound Racing
Naples-Fort Myers Greyhound Track (239-992-2411; 10601 Bonita Beach Rd. SE; Bonita Springs 34134) Matinees, night races, simulcasting, and trackside dining. Admission.

Waterskiing
Gulf Coast Skimmers (239-732-0570; www.gulfcoastskimmers.com; mailing address: 4002 Cindy Ave., Naples 34112; Lake Avalon at Sugden Regional Park, Outer Drive, Naples) This group stages live shows every Sunday at 3pm October–April and Saturday at 6:30pm May–September.

Water Sports
Parasailing & Waterskiing
Gulf Sea Adventures (239-594-2464; 11000 Gulf Shore Dr. N., Vanderbilt Beach 34108; at Vanderbilt Inn) Go parasailing, kayaking, Waverunning, sailing, sea-cycling, snorkeling, or windsurfing.

Marco Island Ski & Water Sports (239-394-6589; www.marcoislandwatersports.com; 400 S. Collier Blvd., Marco Island 34145; at Marriott's Marco Beach Resort) Parasailing; Waverunner and other water-sport rentals.

Sky Scraper Parasailing (239-949-1649; www.floridaparasail.com; Eagle's Nest, 500 S. Collier Blvd., Marco 34145) Single, tandem, and triple rides; photos available on request.

Snorkeling & Scuba
Murky waters here send most divers to Florida's east coast and the Keys, although some charters take you out into deep local waters.

The subtle majesty of the Everglades. Karen T. Bartlett

SCUBAdventures (239-434-7477; www.scubadventureslc.com, 971 Creech Rd., Naples 34103) Supplies, instruction, and diving arrangements.

Wilderness Camping

Big Cypress National Preserve (239-695-4111; www.nps.gov/bicy; HCR 61, Box 110, Ochopee 33141) Eight primitive campgrounds lie off loop road, about 18 miles east of Rte. 29. Some are closed in summer.

Big Cypress Trail Lakes Campground (239-695-2275; 40904 Hwy. 41 E., Ochopee 34141; Highway 41, 5 miles east of Route 29) Tent or RV camping in Big Cypress National Preserve, a 729,000-acre sanctuary adjacent to Everglades National Park.

Collier-Seminole State Park (239-394-3397; www.floridastateparks.org/collier -seminole; 20200 E. Tamiami Trail, Naples 34114; 17 miles south of Naples) This 6,470-acre park straddles Big Cypress Swamp and Ten Thousand Islands Mangrove Wilderness and provides the least primitive camping in Everglades Country. There are RV hookups and tent sites; the first loop is more conducive to tenters, while the second has sites close together, a laundry, dump station, and recreational facilities for RVers. The park is full of possibilities for exploring nature and history, but no swimming is allowed.

Everglades National Park (239-695-2591; www.nps.gov/ever) Backcountry camping along the Everglades canoe trails requires a permit, available from the Everglades City Ranger Station on Route 29. Most sites provide chickee huts on pilings with chemical toilets. Take mosquito repellent—gallons in summer.

Wildlife Spotting

The Florida Everglades, Big Cypress National Preserve, and Ten Thousand Islands are home to the reclusive golden Florida panther, along with bobcats, manatees, wood storks, brown pelicans, black skimmers, roseate spoonbills, and ibises. Some creatures, such as the panther and bobcat, are rarely seen out of captivity. Others, especially the brown pelican, live side by side with residents. I've driven along Route 29 between the interstate and Tamiami Trail and spotted flocks of ibises and herds of white-tailed deer. Deep in the 'Glades birds flock like a blizzard. Optimum wildlife viewing is December through March, when birds migrate and dry weather concentrates them in diminished ponds and other waterways.

Alligators

The Everglades is the New York City of Florida's alligator population. They thrive in the freshwater ponds and brackish creeks of the River of Grass. When the sun is shining along Alligator Alley (Interstate 75) and Tamiami Trail, you can see hundreds of these prehistoric reptiles on the banks, sunning themselves. Crocodiles also live in the 'Glades, but they are rare on this side.

Birds

The South Coast is a bird-watcher's haven—especially in winter, when migrating species add to the vast variety of the coast's residential avifauna. Rare visitors and locals include roseate spoonbills, black skimmers, yellow-crowned night herons, wood storks, white pelicans, lumpkins, and bald eagles (in smaller version than you see up north). More commonly seen are frigates, ospreys, Louisiana herons, great blue herons, ibises, snowy egrets, brown pelicans, anhingas, cormorants, terns, seagulls, plovers, oystercatchers, pileated woodpeckers, owls, and hawks.

In its October 2002 issue, *Birder's World* magazine named two of the South Coast's sanctuaries among its Top 15 Birding Hot Spots. For the best bird-watching, try Everglades National Park (rated #4); Naples's Corkscrew Swamp Sanctuary (rated #5), home to the largest nesting colony of wood storks in the U.S.; Rookery Bay National Estuarine Reserve near Marco Island; and Ten Thousand Islands, a haven for birds of all sorts. Marco Island is a proclaimed sanctuary for bald eagles. Barfield Bay in Goodland is one of their favorite locales. At the beach, the threatened piping plover gets support and protection from local environmentalists.

Nature Preserves & Eco-Attractions
BIG CYPRESS NATIONAL PRESERVE

239-695-2000.
www.nps.gov/bicy.
HCR 61, Box 110, Ochopee 34141.
Adjacent to Everglades National Park. Oasis Visitor Center about 20 miles east of SR 29 on Hwy. 41.

This 729,000-acre preserve abuts Everglades National Park to the north and Fakahatchee Strand Preserve to the east. From the Oasis Visitor Center you can depart on wilderness hikes to sample its Everglades environment. In summer the trails—which connect to the Florida National Scenic Trail—can be very wet. You'll see the grasslands and bald cypress stands for which Big Cypress is known as well as profuse birds and an alligator nursery.

The preserve boasts the state's major population of the reclusive, endangered Florida panther. A small museum at the visitor center contains Indian artifacts and wildlife exhibits. Rangers lead swamp walks, bike and canoe trips, and campfire programs in season. A 26-mile scenic loop road, with several primitive campgrounds, is open to vehicles when road conditions allow. Closer to Everglades City, Birdon Road (Route 841) takes a 17-mile trip through sawgrass prairie habitat. It connects to Route 837 and then Route 839, which leads to two 2.5-mile hiking trails, one to the north and the other to the south of the intersection.

✪ COLLIER-SEMINOLE STATE PARK

239-394-3397.
www.floridastateparks.org/collier-seminole.
20200 E. Tamiami Trail, Naples 34114.
Open: Daily, dawn to dusk.
Admission: $4 per car, up to 8 passengers; $2 per car, single occupant; $1 cyclists or pedestrians.

Here, Naples meets the Everglades. One of the region's prettiest state parks, it encompasses manicured lawns in contrast to jungle wilderness. Besides its historic attractions—a garden memorial to developer Barron Collier, the only remaining dredge used to build Tamiami Trail across the Everglades, and a replicated Civil War blockhouse—it harbors the wealth of birds, otters, cats, manatees, and other critters who seek shelter in the outlying Everglades. Learn about them at the little visitors center in the blockhouse; then take to the nature, bike, and canoe trails. Ranger activities and a boat tour on the Blackwater River will provide biological background. Camping available.

Pelicans gather on a "Florida snow cap"—otherwise known as a sandbar. Karen T. Bartlett

✪ CORKSCREW SWAMP SANCTUARY

239-348-9151.
www.audubon.org/local/sanctuary/corkscrew.
375 Sanctuary Rd., Naples 34120.
Off Naples-Immokalee Rd., 21 miles east of N. Tamiami Trail.
Open: Daily 7am–5:30pm Dec.–mid-April, 8am–7:30pm mid-April–Nov.
Admission: $10 adults, $6 college students, $4 children 6–18.

This 11,000-acre sanctuary, operated by the National Audubon Society, protects one of the largest stands of mature bald cypress trees in the country. Some of the towering specimens date back nearly 500 years. The threatened wood stork once came to nest here in great numbers. Diminished populations still do, at which time the nesting area is roped off to protect them. A 2.25-mile-long boardwalk takes you over swampland inhabited by rich plant and marine life. You can usually spot an alligator or two. In 2000 the new state-of-the-art Blair Audubon Center, a national prototype, opened at the sanctuary in a "stealth" building that blends with the pristine environment. Its Swamp Theater dramatically recreates seasons and times of day on the boardwalk, plus there are hands-on opportunities for kids.

DELNOR-WIGGINS PASS STATE PARK

239-597-6196.
www.floridastateparks.org/delnor-wiggins.
11100 Gulf Shore Dr. N., Naples 34108.
At Vanderbilt Beach.
Admission: $4 per car, up to 8 passengers; $2 per car, single occupant; $1 cyclists or pedestrians.

Prehistoric loggerhead turtles lumber ashore to lay and bury their eggs every summer, away from the lights and crowds of other area beaches. Fifty-six days later the baby turtles emerge and scurry to the sea—hopefully before birds can snatch them up. Beach turtle talks are available during the loggerhead season.

✪ EVERGLADES NATIONAL PARK /GULF COAST VISITOR CENTER

239-695-3311.
www.nps.gov/ever.
PO Box 120, Everglades City 34139.
Tamiami Trail south of Naples; ranger station and visitors center on SR 29, before the Chokoloskee Causeway in Everglades City.

This massive wetland—home to the endangered Florida panther and other rare animals—covers 2,200 square miles and shelters more than 600 types of fish and 347 bird species. It stretches from here to the Florida Keys on the east coast. Along with Ten Thousand Islands, it also contains the largest mangrove forest in the world. So what's the best way to see this seemingly overwhelming expanse of wildlife? Take your pick. From this end, you really can't drive through it, but you can from the eastern access, two hours away. Highway 41 skirts the edge of the park and Big Cypress, which is part of the same ecosystem. Closest access to Naples is Route 29 and Everglades City. Canoe trips from 8 to 99 miles long put you in closer range of birds, manatees, dolphins, and alligators. There's also a variety of

other options. The park offers boat tours, and other private sightseeing cruises exist.
During the winter, ranger programs and canoe tours from the Gulf Coast Visitor Center
teach about the unique environment. You can rent a pontoon boat or hire a charter captain
in Everglades City for sightseeing and fishing. Get advice at the welcome center or visitors
center, or see "Wildlife Tours & Charters," below. The visitor center holds a few wildlife
and hands-on exhibits. Tables and a chikee hut accommodate picnickers.

FAKAHATCHEE STRAND STATE PARK PRESERVE
239-695-4593.
www.floridastateparks.org/fakahatcheestrand.
PO Box 548, Copeland 34137.
W. J. Janes Memorial Scenic Dr. (SR 29) in Copeland, north of Hwy. 41.
Open: Preserve Administration Office open 9–4 weekdays.
Admission: Free; donations accepted.

Rangers lead swamp walks the third Saturday of the month November–February. You can
also hike on your own. Park at the gates on either side of the road and follow the short
pathways into the strand. In summer the trails are often muddy and submerged. You can
also access the strand (a linear swamp forest that snakes along ancient sloughs) via the
2,000-foot Big Cypress Bend boardwalk, west of Everglades City on Highway 41. The
ecosystem is known for its orchids, including 31 varieties of threatened and endangered
species, 14 native varieties of bromeliads, and stately stands of native royal palm. Florida
panthers, black bears, mangrove fox squirrels, and Everglades minks have all been docu-
mented along the 20-mile-long strand. You're more likely to spot alligators, white-tailed
deer, ospreys, ibises, and egrets. A ranger office on Janes Scenic Drive, past the old fire
tower, has displays and information on the preserve. Next to the boardwalk you'll find an
Indian village with a gift shop.

✪ NAPLES NATURE CENTER
239-262-0304.
www.conservancy.org.
1450 Merrihue Dr., Naples 34102.
One block east of Goodlette Rd.
Open: 9am–4:30pm Mon.–Sat.
Admission: Nature Center, $7.50 adults and $2 children 3–12. Nature trails and wildlife
rehabilitation facility are free. Kids admitted free the first Sat. of the month.

This tucked-away nature complex on the Gordon River was built by the Conservancy of
Southwest Florida to educate the public about the environment. Within its 13.5 acres it
encompasses a nature store; trail walks; free boat tours of the river; a rehabilitation center
for birds, deer, turtles, and other injured animals; and a beautiful nature center with live
Florida snakes, an offshore tank (where you'll often find a loggerhead turtle swimming),
fascinating touch tables, interactive games, and habitat vignettes. Friendly and chattily
informative guides conduct special programs throughout the day as they feed their live critters. The Conservancy also hosts interpretative nature field trips. Canoes and kayak rentals
are available for use on the Gordon River and the Conservancy's canoe rental facility in
Rookery Bay National Estuarine Reserve (See "Canoeing & Kayaking"). Special kids' day
programs and activities take place the first Saturday of each month at the Naples Center.

Stealing a Peek at Orchids

Susan Orleans's true account of orchid lust, *The Orchid Thief*, inspired the outlandish 2003 movie *Adaptation* starring Nicholas Cage, Chris Cooper, and Meryl Streep. The setting: Florida's steamy corners—specifically, Fakahatchee Strand Preserve State Park.

It was here that Orleans sloshed through the swamps with her unlikely hero searching for the coveted ghost orchid. You can, too, through ranger slough walk programs held in season. The Strand—approximately 20 miles long and 3 to 5 miles wide—has enjoyed a surge in popularity since the book and movie. As the orchid capital of the U.S., it harbors 31 species of native wild orchids listed as threatened or endangered, among them the ghost orchid. In fact biologist Mike Owen reports spotting six specimens on a recent winter trip in 2004.

That's the good news. The bad news is, you have to get wet to see them, and the best time to view the most species a-bloom are the buggiest, hottest months, particularly September and October.

THE NAPLES PRESERVE

239-213-7120.
1690 Tamiami Trail N., Naples 34102.
Open: Daily, dawn to dusk.
Admission: Free.

Newly developing, this 9.5-acre patch of ancient ecology along the highway was recently cleaned up and fitted with a 0.4-mile boardwalk that crosses scrub oak, grassy meadow, and pine-flatwoods communities. Gopher tortoises, deer, bobcat, and birds occupy the habitat. A visitors center will eventually house dioramas depicting the preserve's fauna and flora.

✪ ROOKERY BAY ENVIRONMENTAL LEARNING CENTER

239-417-6310.
www.rookerybay.org.
300 Tower Rd., Naples 34113.
Off Rt. 951 toward Marco Island.
Open: 9–4 Tues.–Sun.
Closed: Mon.
Admission: $5 for adults, $3 for children ages 6–12.

Rookery Bay National Estuarine Research Reserve, the Gulf Coast's largest and most pristine wildlife sanctuary, occupies more than 110,000 acres at the gateway to Ten Thousand Islands. It's "Ding" Darling without the crowds and a favorite for fishermen and birdwatchers. Rare creatures such as the American crocodile, manatee, Atlantic green and Ridley sea turtles, bald eagle, and roseate spoonbill inhabit its backwaters. For an introduction to this vast, largely inaccessible land, stop at this Department of Environmental Protection laboratory facility, newly opened in March 2004. The mangrove estuary is the star of high-tech, interactive exhibits. The centerpiece, a 2,000-gallon aquarium, has a 15-foot tall mangrove "growing" out of it and spaces into which kids can crawl and get to know the crucial habitat. Forming a backdrop to the aquarium, a curved wall holds various habitat dioramas, three-dimensional tactile displays of local creatures, local wildlife artist murals, Crab Condo, a touch tank, Mosquito Landing, and other fun and original learning tools. The unusual polka dot batfish is the center's mascot and has been replicated in huge proportion. Kids can play with puppets and read books in the mangrove forest play area. In time the center will encompass nature trails, a footbridge and boardwalk, kayaking in the canals out back, educational programs, and a second story of exhibits.

Wildlife Tours & Charters

Cocohatchee Nature Center (239-592-1200; www.cocohatchee.org; 12345 Tamiami Trail N., Naples 34110) Nature and sunset boat tours dip into the pristine, bird-rich waters of the Cocohatchee River and onto the gulf, where passengers often spot dolphin.

The polka dot batfish is the mascot and centerpiece of the habitat display at Rookery Bay Reserve's new environmental learning center.
Rookery Bay National Estuarine Research Reserve

Conservancy of Southwest Florida (239-262-0304; www.conservancy.org; 1450 Merrihue Dr., Naples 34102; one block east of Goodlette Rd.) Boat tours of the mangrove waterway are included in admission. It also hosts wildlife cruises of Rookery Bay Reserve, Key Island shelling expeditions, and sunset bird-watching tours aboard the pontoon boat *Good Fortune*.

Double Sunshine (239-263-4949; 1200 Fifth Ave. S., Naples 34102; Tin City on Hwy. 41) Departs five times daily for 1.5-hour narrated nature and dolphin-sighting cruises.

Estero Bay Boat Tours (239-992-2200; 5231 Mamie St., Bonita Springs 34134; at Weeks Fish Camp, end of Coconut Rd.) The best sightseeing tour of Mound Key's Calusa history, Estero Bay wildlife, and Big Hickory Island's shells is conducted by a local native and his staff, who know these islands and waters like family.

Everglades National Park Boat Tours (239-695-2591, 800-445-7724; www.nps.gov/ever/visit/tours.htm; Gulf Coast Visitor Center, PO Box 119, Everglades City 34139) Naturalist-narrated tours through the maze of Ten Thousand Islands and its teeming bird and water life.

Manatee Sightseeing Adventure (239-642-8818, 800-379-7440; www.see-manatees.com; 25000 Tamiami Trail E., Naples 34114) Captains Barry and Carol take up to six passengers on a 90-minute sightseeing charter into manatee sanctuary by appointment. The boat departs from Port of the Islands development.

SHOPPING

Custom-designed jewelry, exclusive top-designer fashion lines, original masterpiece art, and the world's first street concierge make the experience of browsing, buying, and window-yearning in Naples entirely unique. Naples ranks among Florida's most chic arenas for spending, including Palm Beach's Worth Avenue and Sarasota's St. Armands Circle. Downtown's renaissance concentrates the shopping frenzy in the Old Naples districts of Fifth Avenue South and Third Street Plaza, but a number of other fashionable shopping centers are found throughout town. Downtown shops are known for their individually owned, one-of-a-kind, and designer outlets.

Shopping Centers & Malls

Bayfront (239-263-6884; Goodlette Rd. at Tamiami Trail, Naples) This new high-style apartment-shopping-dining complex does its bit to earn Naples its Italian nomenclature. Quite handsome, it has a higher ratio of eateries than shops, which are very high-end and include the likes of Cerruti and Valentino.

Coastland Center (239-262-2323; www.coastlandcenter.com; Tamiami Trail N. and Golden Gate Pkwy., Naples) Naples's largest and only enclosed, climate-controlled shopping center, its 150 stores include a full array of shopping options, from major department stores to small specialty shops. Chain names include Burdines, Sears, Old Navy, GAP, Victoria's Secret, and Bath & Body Works.

✪ **Fifth Avenue South** (www.fifthavenuesouth.com; Naples) Once upon a time, members of the Seminole Indian tribe sold their crafts from a stand on Fifth Avenue. Today it's one of Naples's most fashionable addresses. In 1996 a movement started to update the historic district, which had begun to look run-down. Famed Florida planner Andre Duany was hired to breathe new life into the district. Besides cosmetic improvements, he brought a new bustle to the street. Tony hotels, new shops, and 20-plus restaurants and sidewalk cafés attract Naples's new "café society." Live entertainment and special events are regularly scheduled.

Marco Town Center Mall (www.marcotowncentermall.com; Collier Blvd. and Bald Eagle Dr., Marco Island) A popular cluster of more than 10 distinctive eateries and 40 shopperies. During season there's live entertainment Tuesday and Thursday evenings 6–9pm.

The Promenade (239-430-1670; www.bonitasprings.com/promenade; at Bonita Bay on Hwy. 41) Bonita's latest sprint to keep up with neighbor Naples, this fashionable plaza even looks like Naples, with Mediterranean style, fine restaurants, galleries, and name shops.

Shops of Marco (San Marco Rd. and Barfield Dr., Marco Island) One-of-a-kind clothing and gift shops.

Third Street South Plaza and the Avenues (239-434-6533; www.thirdstreetsouth.com; Naples) Visit this upscale shopping quarter in Old Naples, the heart of the arts scene, and view fine outdoor sculptures on loan from local galleries. This is window-shopping (on my budget, anyway) at its best: exquisite clothes, art, jewelry, and home decorations and furnishings. Thursday nights bring live entertainment.

Tin City (239-262-4200; www.tin-city.com; 1200 Fifth Ave. S., Naples 34102; Hwy. 41 at Goodlette Rd.) I love the structure of this mall, which resurrected old tin-roofed docks. Comprised of two buildings, its 30 shops tend to be touristy, selling mainly nautical gifts and resort wear. But it also offers enjoyable waterfront restaurants, and it's a good place to catch a fishing or sightseeing tour.

✪ **The Village on Venetian Bay** (239-261-0030; www.naples.com/village; 4200 Gulf Shore Blvd., Naples 34103; at Park Shore Dr.) Upscale, Mediterranean-style domain of fashion, jewelry, and art located on the waterfront.

Waterside Shops at Pelican Bay (239-598-1605; www.watersideshops.com; 5415 Tamiami Trail #320, Naples 34108; Seagate Dr. and Tamiami Trail N., Pelican Bay) This shopping enclave features Saks Fifth Avenue, Victoria's Secret, Williams-Sonoma, Ann Taylor, and some one-of-a-kind shops, all located amidst cascading waters and lush foliage. A summer Friday concert series is held here May through August.

Antiques & Collectibles

Ashely Adams Arts & Antiques (239-435-7273; www.free-limoges-box.com; 795 Fifth Ave. S., Naples 34102) Literally packed with large European, Oriental, and American bronze, silver, and porcelain sculptures; clocks, furniture, and more, both new and old.

The Englishman (239-649-8088; www.theenglishmanusa.com; 1170 Third St. S., Naples 34102; at The Plaza on Third Street) For top-shelf European furniture, oil paintings, and sculpture from the 19th and 20th centuries, browse the fine treasures here.

Naples Antiques Mall (239-591-8182; 5430 Yahl St., Naples 34109) A collection of 40 dealers selling lamps, golf clubs, books, jewelry—everything!—warehouse style.

Shirley Street Antique Mall (239-592-9882; 5510 Shirley St., Naples 34109) One of Naples's largest antiques malls, containing 40 sellers and antiques of every kind.

Wisteria (239-948-0266; 3634 Bonita Beach Rd. SW, Bonita Springs 34134) Specializes in country-cottage style; antiques and collectibles.

Books

✪ **The Bookstore at The Pavilion** (239-598-2220; 857 Vanderbilt Beach Rd., Naples 34108; at Tamiami Trail N.) An old-fashioned bookstore crowded with the printed word—the antithesis of the new generation of megabookstores. Wide selection of specialty periodicals, Florida books, and new and used volumes.

Sunshine Booksellers (239-393-0353; 677 S. Collier Blvd., Marco Island 34145) Large, modern store with a complete line of books—and coffee always brewing.

Clothing

Casablanca (239-394-2511; 400 S. Collier Blvd., Marco Island 34145; at Marco Island Marriott Resort) Fashionable and colorful women's resort apparel such as Jam's World and Tommy Bahama.

Island Woman (239-642-6116; www.islandwoman.com; 1 Harbor Pl., Goodland 34146) Hand-painted silk fashions, gemstone jewelry, T-shirts, sarongs, tropical art, crafts, wild wigs, and other crazy stuff.

Shopping in high style at Naples's Waterside Shops. Karen T. Bartlett

JIKI Monte Carlo Creations (239-430-0080; www.jiki.net; 453 Bayfront Place, Naples 34102) Top elegance with a European flair.

Kirsten's Boutique (239-598-3233; www.kirstensboutique.com; 5535 Tamiami Trail N., Naples 34108; at Waterside Shops) Subtitled "A Gallery of Fine Art to Wear," this unique shop sells Moroccan and African-inspired clothes, jewelry, and art.

Marco Island Clothing Co. (239-642-7277; 117 S. Barfield Dr., Marco Island 34145; at Shops of Marco) Stylish name-brand women's swimsuits, shoes, tropical resort fashions, and accessories.

Marissa Collections (239-263-4333; 1167 Third St. S., Naples 34102) Carries prestige designer labels such as Gianni Versace, Jill Sanders, and Oscar de la Renta.

McFarland's of Marco (239-394-6464; 117 S. Barfield Dr., Marco Island 34145; at Shops of Marco) Specializing in tropically appropriate menswear: casual, golf, suits, and resort.

Mondo Uomo (239-434-9484; 4200 Gulf Shore Blvd., Naples 34103; at The Village on Venetian Bay) Fine, tasteful fashion and European styles for men: tropical wool, German cotton, sweaters, and distinctive casual and dress wear for Gulf Coast climes.

Outback T's (239-261-7869; 1200 Fifth Ave. S., Naples 34102; Tin City, Hwy. 41 E. and Goodlette Rd.) The best in souvenir T-shirts, with wildlife and local themes.

Simply Natural (239-643-5571; 4330 Gulf Shore Blvd. N., Ste. 302, Naples 34103; at the Village on Venetian Bay) High-end youthful women's fashions in lace, denim, and other contemporary fabrics and styles.

Weekends (239-949-4163; 26841 South Bay Dr., Bonita Springs 34134; at The Promenade) Sporty casual threads for Florida men and women.

Wildflower (239-643-6776; 4222 Gulf Shore Blvd. N., Naples 34103; at The Village on Venetian Bay) Distinct fun and formal women's wear with Florida flair and style.

Consignment

Naples is a secondhand shopper's paradise. In many of the clothing consignment shops you can find designer fashions with the price tags still attached. Oh, the joys of hunting down the castoffs of the well-to-do!

Act II (239-495-6647; 8951 Bonita Beach Rd. #605, Bonita Springs 34135; at Springs Plaza, Hwy. 41) Women's clothing and accessories.

Encore Shop (239-775-0032; 3105 Davis Blvd., Naples 34104) Designer furniture, paintings, decorative items, and collectibles.

New to You Consignments (239-262-6869; 933 Creech Rd., Naples 34103; at Hwy. 41) Women's designer clothing, furniture, and decorative items.

Factory Outlet Centers

Naples Prime Outlets (239-775-8083, 888-545-7196; www.primeoutlets.com; 1920 Isle of Capri Rd., mail: 6060 Collier Blvd. #121, Naples 34114; on Route 951 toward Marco Island) Factory outlet discounts of up to 65 percent off for Dansk housewares; Mikasa crystal; and Liz Claiborne, Geoffrey Beene, and Izod clothing, among other name brands.

Flea Markets & Bazaars

Flamingo Island Flea Market (239-948-7799; www.flamingoisland.com; 11902 Bonita Beach Rd., Bonita Springs 34135) Open Friday through Sunday, 8–4.

Naples Drive-In Flea Market (239-774-2900; 7700 Davis Blvd., Naples 34104) Open Friday through Sunday.

Galleries

Naples has earned a reputation as a mecca for fine art. **Gallery Row** (239-513-3888), along Broad Avenue South at Third Street South, is a good place to begin in your art quest. About a dozen galleries line the street selling a wide spectrum of art. Several more lie in the immediate vicinity. Fifth Avenue South is another arena, although the galleries are more spread out, less concentrated. **Trade Center,** off Pine Ridge Road in north Naples, is the latest to make the art scene, bringing galleries to an area known for its home decor and design outlets.

Art Sellers (239-389-5269; www.artsellers.biz; 1035 N. Collier Blvd. #310, Marco Island 34145; at Marco Town Center Mall) Pop art, jewelry, photo gifts (including tiles), and Mel Fisher antique silver.

The Darvish Collection (239-261-7581; www.artnet.com/darvish.html; 1199 Third St. S., Naples 34102) Features the work of North American and European masters within its seven wood-lined clublike galleries. Most works in the four- to six-figure range.

Gallery Matisse (239-649-7114; www.gallerymatisse.com; 1170 Third St. S., Naples 34102) Picasso pieces, fine oils, art jewelry, and a bit of whimsy.

Guess-Fisher Gallery, Etc. (239-659-2787; 824 Fifth Ave. S., Naples 34102) Delightful works by namesake artists Natalie Guess and Phil Fisher, plus other locals.

Knox Galleries (239-263-7994; www.knoxgalleries.com; 375 Broad Ave. S., Naples 34102) One of the Gallery Row collection, it specializes in large and small realistic bronze sculptures of people and animals, showcasing the work of George Lundeen.

Kokopelli Contemporary Gallery (239-261-7229; www.kokopelligallery.com; 4320 Gulf Shore Blvd. N., Naples 34103; at The Village on Venetian Bay) Look for lizards, fish, cats, and floral motifs in jewelry, art glass, and other decorative wares.

Native Visions Gallery (239-643-3785; www.callofafrica.com; 737 Fifth Ave. S., Naples 34102) Remarkable works themed around Africa, the sea, and the environment.

New River Fine Art (239-435-4515; www.newriverfineart.com; 604 Fifth Ave. S., Naples 34102) Truly fine art, pieces here range from contemporary paintings to the etchings of Salvador Dali and exquisite glass sculptures by Frederick Hart.

Rick Moore Fine Art (239-592-5455; www.rickmooregallery.com; 5415 Tamiami Trail N., Naples 34108; at Waterside Shops; and 239-434-6464; 4230 Gulf Shore Blvd., Naples 34103; at The Village on Venetian Bay) A pleasing selection of glass, contemporary paintings, and ceramics bowls and sculptures.

Silver Eagle (239-403-3033; www.silvereaglegallery.com; 651 Fifth Ave. S., Naples 34102) Decorative Native American skin drums, blankets, and candles; paintings and beautiful silver and turquoise jewelry.

Sweet Art (239-597-2110; www.steetartsstudios.com; 2054 Trade Center Way, Naples 34109) Affordable tropical decorative art and home accessories.

Trudy Labell Fine Art (239-593-0211; 1610 Trade Center Way #3, Naples 34109) This is one of my favorite Naples galleries. Spacious and airy, its collection is extraordinary, with a subtle Florida bent. Find sculptures, fine abstracts and landscapes, and glasswork.

Gifts

Some of Naples's best souvenirs are found in the gift shops at nature and other attractions.

Conch Shelf (239-394-2511; 400 S. Collier Blvd., Marco Island 34145; at Marco Island Marriott Resort) Fine sea-themed gifts and art.

Holiday House Gifts (239-642-7113; 133 S. Barfield Dr., Marco Island 34145; at Shops of Marco) Yankee Candles, country- and tropical-style items, Christmas ornaments and decorations.

JT's Island Grill & Gallery (239-695-3633; www.chokoloskee-island.com; 238 Mamie St.,Chokoloskee 34138) Great selection of Everglades art, books, charts, jewelry, and other lore.

Julie's of Naples (239-434-9761, 888-793-9894; www.dockside-boardwalk.com/ boardwalk_info.phtml?store_id=2; 1100 Sixth Ave. S., Naples 34102; at The Boardwalk) A bit of everything: clothing, home accessories, candles, and jewelry, including a fun variety of flip-flop jewelry.

Karisma (239-389-0955; www.karismagalleries.com; 599 S. Collier Blvd. #315, Marco Island 34145) Colorful and whimsical island-style furnishings, art, and decorations at a high price.

Regatta Resort (239-262-3929; 760 Fifth Ave. S., Naples 34102) Its subtitle describes it best: "gifts, gadgets & gorgeous stuff." Clothes, toys, and things for the home, all in a fun and whimsical tone.

Thirsty Mouse (239-261-4148; 1200 Fifth Ave. S., Naples 34102; Tin City, Hwy. 41 E. and Goodlette Rd.) Florida food (smoked alligator) and gifts, sea-themed tableware, and other inexpensive decorative items.

Jewelry

Cleopatra's Barge (239-261-7952, 800-678-7934; www.cleopatrasbarge.com; 1197 Third St. S., Naples 34102) Home of "Naples Medallion" jewelry and other fine and estate pieces. Certified jewelers and diamond setters.

DuFrane Jewelers (239-495-9005, 888-DUFRANE; www.dufranejewelers.com; 26841 South Bay Dr. #152; Bonita Springs 34134; at The Promenade) Besides gorgeous jewelry and watches, this large outlet sells fine china and crystal and other elegant table and bar wares.

Marco Island Fine Jewelry (239-394-3377; www.marcoislandfinejewelry.com; 1089 N. Collier Blvd., Marco Island 34145; in Marco Town Center) The Marco Cat, an ancient Calusa artifact found during local excavating, is an island icon. Wear it around your neck as a gold pendant available here, or buy the crystal figurine version. Also unusual Italian charm bracelets, gemstone pieces, and lovely home accessorizing gifts.

✪ **Port Royal Jewelers** (239-263-3071; 623 Fifth Ave. S., Naples 34102) This place is like a museum: 18th-century royal jewels, and antique pieces in Art Deco, Edwardian, Georgian, and Victorian styles. Also custom-designed and estate jewelry. So exclusive you have to ring a doorbell to get in, and there's a special vault containing the real treasures.

Schilling Jewelers (239-642-3001; 121 S. Barfield Dr., Marco 34145; at Shops of Marco) Custom design and manufacturing; cloisonné turtles and fish jewelry; extraordinary sea-themed pieces.

✪ **Thalheimers Fine Jewelers** (239-261-8422, 800-998-8423; www.thalheimers.com; 3200 Tamiami Trail N. #100, Naples 34103) The most respected name in jewelers, carrying quality watches, diamond jewelry, gems, crystal, and porcelain. Watchmaker, designer, and appraiser on premises.

✪ **Wm. Phelps, Custom Jeweler** (239-434-2233; www.phelpsjewelers.com; 4200 Gulf Shore Blvd., Naples 34103; at The Village on Venetian Bay) Fine-crafted pendants, rings, earrings, and pins on display, plus colored stones and diamonds for customizing.

Yamron Jewelers (239-592-7707; 5415 Tamiami Trail N., Naples 34108; at Waterside Shops) A select stock of exquisite jewelry and Swiss watches.

Kitchenware & Home Decor

Catherine's Home Collections (239-594-1300; 5435 Tamiami Trail N., Naples 34108; at Waterside Shops) Fine bed and bath wares including elegant linens, silver plates, picture frames, and personal nightwear.

El Condor Imports (239-732-5855; www.elcondornaplesfl.com; 6060 Collier Blvd. #123, Naples 34114; at Prime Outlets) Rustic pine furniture, pottery, and decorative crafts from Mexico.

Fabec-Young & Company (239-649-5501; 4360 Gulf Shore Blvd., Ste. 604, Naples 34103; at The Village on Venetian Bay) Unusual table settings from napkins and candles to glassware, silver, and ceramics.

Gattle's (239-262-4791, 800-344-4552; 1250 Third St. S., Naples 34102) Linens for bed, bath, and table; fine home accessories and nursery items.

The Good Life (239-262-4355, 800-846-2540; 1170 Third St. S., Ste. A101, Naples 34102) Gourmet cookware, tabletops, serving pieces, imported Portmeiron and colorful beach-theme tableware, quality implements, unusual gadgets, and gourmet food products.

A Horse of a Different Color (239-261-1252; 4200 Gulf Shore Blvd., Naples 34103; at the Village on Venetian Bay) Pricey one-of-a-kind, highly contemporary gifts, lamps, clocks, and other home accents.

Huggs (239-435-7555; www.huggsgifts.com; 469 Fifth Ave. S., Naples 34102) Painted Florida furniture, candles, soaps, gifts, and home accessories.

Jennings (239-430-4321, 866-857-8152; www.jenningsofnaples.com; 449 Bayfront Place, Naples 34102; 800-562-6616; 3652 9th St. N., Naples 34103) Fine china, crystal, silver, and other ultra-elegant home accessories.

Lady from Haiti (239-649-8607; 476 Fifth Ave. S., Naples 34102) Steel-drum sculptures, hand-painted wooden items, fine Haitian art. Enjoy the sand on the floor and Caribbean music while you shop.

Tribal Findings Wholesale (239-593-5811; www.tribalfindings.com; 5974 Taylor Rd. #2, Naples 34109) In Naples's Trade Center, this shop sells an intriguing collection of masks, carvings, pottery, ceramics, and other folk art and decorative items from West Africa, Mexico, and Haiti at reasonable prices.

Shell Shops

Marco Craft & Shell Company (239-394-7020; 1089 N. Collier Blvd., Marco Island 34145, at Marco Town Center Mall) Craft and specimen shells, locally handcrafted gifts, craft classes.

Shells by Emily (239-394-5575; www.shellsbyemily.com; 651 S. Collier Blvd. 2C, Marco Island 34145) Walk or take the elevator to the second floor to find this award-winning shell crafter, who sells specimen shells and crafting supplies.

Sporting Goods

Note: For supplies and equipment for specific sports, please refer to "Recreation" in this chapter.

Sports Authority (239-598-5054; 2505 Pine Ridge Rd., Naples 34109) Complete line of sports and outdoor equipment and clothing.

CALENDAR OF EVENTS

January

Bonita Springs National Art Festival (239-495-8989; www.artinusa.com/Bonita; the Promenade, Bonita Springs) A top-rated two-day show midmonth, featuring fine artists from around the world. Also in March.

Mullet Festival (239-394-3041; www.stansidlehour.com, Stan's Idle Hour restaurant, Goodland) Celebrating Goodland's fishing heritage and an extravaganza of music and tomfoolery. Three days midmonth.

Naples Invitational Art Fest (239-263-1667; Fleischmann Park, Naples) One of the nation's top-rated juried arts festivals, with select 220 artists and artisans, and gourmet food. Last weekend of the month.

Swamp Buggy Races (239-774-2701, 800-897-2701; www.swampbuggy.com; Florida Sports Park, Route 951, east Naples) Nationally televised event; the Everglades equivalent of tractor pulls or monster truck racing.

February

ACE Group Classic (877-FORE-TIX PGA; The Club at Twin Eagles, Naples) Nationally televised Senior Tour golf tournament one week early in the month.

Collier County Fair (239-455-1444; www.home.earthlink.net/~countyfair; Collier County Fairgrounds, Immokalee Rd., Naples) A good old-fashioned fair with rides and exhibits. End of January and early February.

Everglades Seafood Festival (239-695-3941; www.evergladesseafoodfestival.com; Everglades City) Three days of music, arts and crafts, and fresh seafood. Early in the month.

Grecian Festival (239-591-3430; St. Katherine's Greek Orthodox Church, Airport-Pulling Rd., Naples) Greek food specialties, music, costumed dancers, and exhibits. First weekend.

Naples National Art Festival (239-513-2492; www.naplesartcenter.org/nnartfestival.htm; Cambier Park, downtown Naples) This prime art festival event takes place over two days late in the month.

Native American and Pioneer Heritage Festival (239-394-3397; Collier-Seminole State Park) Honoring local heritage. Third weekend of the month.

March

Bonita Springs National Art Festival (239-495-8989; www.artinusa.com/Bonita; the Promenade, Bonita Springs) Two days midmonth, featuring fine artists from around the world. Also in January.

Country Jam (239-353-0404; www.countryjamnaples.com; Vineyards Community Park, Naples) Top national country entertainers, local country acts, carnival rides, and carnival games, a petting zoo, pony rides, a rock wall, a mechanical bull, and plenty of food for a midmonth weekend.

Wacky costumes are as important as rowing skills in Naples's annual Great Dock Canoe Race. Karen T. Bartlett

Dig the Arts Festival (239-263-8242; Lowdermilk Park, Naples) Art meets the beach in true Naples style. United Arts Council hosts a day of free music, art, sand sculpture, and kids' games. One day late in the month.

Downtown Festival of the Arts (239-435-3742; www.artfestival.com/events /naples 0304/index.cfm; Fifth Ave. S., Naples) Works by area artists and other talented folks from around the country, musical entertainment, food court. One weekend late in the month.

Seminole Indian Day (239-695-2989; Smallwood Store Museum, Chokoloskee Island) Reenactments, period clothing competition, and entertainment and food of the Seminole nation.

Swamp Buggy Races (239-774-2701, 800-897-2701; www.swampbuggy.com; Florida Sports Park, Route 951, east Naples) See above, under January.

May

A Taste of Collier (www.tasteofcollier.com; Fifth Ave. S., Naples) Naples's renowned restaurants serve samples of their culinary specialties. Live music. One day.

Great Dock Canoe Race (239-263-9940; www.greatdockcanoerace.com; The Dock at Crayton Cove restaurant, 12th Ave. S., Naples) More than 200 teams, many in festive cos-tumes, paddle across Naples Bay in good-spirited competition one Saturday.

SummerJazz (239-261-2222; Naples Beach Hotel & Golf Club, Naples) A series of sunset concerts under the stars on the third Saturday of every month, May through September.

Teddy Bears Tea Party (866-365-BEAR; www.teddymuseum.com; Teddy Bear Museum, Naples) Wear your finest Easter bonnet, and enjoy a full English tea party with the bears. Three sittings one day near Easter, 10:30, 12:30, and 2:30. Reservations required.

June

South Florida PGA Open (239-261-2222; Naples Beach Hotel & Golf Club, 851 Gulf Shore Blvd. N., Naples) Golf enthusiasts can qualify to play side-by-side with PGA pros in the four-day competition.

July

Fourth of July (Fifth Avenue South and Naples Pier, Naples) Fireworks at the pier follow a Main Street parade.

October

Swamp Buggy Races See above, under January.

November

Marco Island Film Festival (239-642-FEST; www.marcoislandfilmfest.com; Marco Movies, Mission Plaza, Marco Island) Five days early in the month, featuring more than 50 short, documentary, and feature independent films.

Old Florida Festival (239-774-8476; www.colliermuseum.com; Collier County Museum, Naples) Living history from the Stone Age to World War II, with food, crafts, games, and demonstrations the first weekend.

A parade precedes October's Swamp Buggy Races, featuring the crowning of the year's queen—who then gets initiated with a dunk in the mud.

Karen T. Bartlett

December

Christmas Walk and Avenue of Lights (239-435-3742; Fifth Avenue South, Naples) Holiday street- and tree-lighting festivities, open houses at shops and other merchants. Early December.

Naples Bay Christmas Boat Parade (239-261-0882; Naples City Dock) An annual holiday maritime event midmonth.

New Year's Eve Art Festival (239-435-3742; Fifth Ave. S., Naples) Fine artisans fill the street the weekend after Christmas.

7

INFORMATION

Practical Matters

We hope that you never need a hospital or a policeman, but in case you should, we offer that information here as well as information on other topics:

Heed this warning sign at Pine Island's "World's Fishingest Bridge." Karen T. Bartlett

AMBULANCE/FIRE/POLICE

All five southwest coast counties have adopted the 911 emergency phone number system. Dial it for ambulance, fire, sheriff, and police. Listed below are non-emergency numbers for individual communities.

Town	Ambulance	Fire	Police/Sheriff
FOR EMERGENCY	911	911	911
Anywhere in the region	Florida Highway Patrol		800-483-5912
CHARLOTTE COUNTY			
Boca Grande		941-964-2908	
Punta Gorda		941-575-5529	941-639-4111
Charlotte County	941-964-0256	941-743-1367	941-639-2101
			941-474-3233
Florida Highway Patrol (Venice)			941-483-5911

Town	Ambulance	Fire	Police/Sheriff
COLLIER COUNTY			
Everglades City		239-695-2902	239-695-2301
Isles of Capri		239-394-8770	
Naples			239-213-4844
Collier County Sheriff			239-793-9300
Florida Highway Patrol (Naples)			239-354-2377
LEE COUNTY			
Bonita Springs	239-992-3320		
Cape Coral	239-574-0501	239-574-3223	
Captiva	239-472-9494		
Fort Myers	239-338-2000	239-334-6222	239-338-2111
Fort Myers Beach	239-463-6163	239-765-2300	
Pine Island (Matlacha)	239-283-0030		
Sanibel	239-472-5525	239-472-3111	
Lee County Sheriff			239-477-1200
Florida Highway Patrol (Fort Myers)			239-278-7100
SARASOTA/BRADENTON COUNTIES			
Anna Maria	941-741-3900	941-778-4711	
Bradenton		941-747-1161	941-746-4111
Bradenton Beach	941-741-3900	941-778-6311	
Holmes Beach	941-741-3900	941-778-7875	
Longboat	941-316-1944	941-316-1977	
Sarasota	941-951-4211	941-316-1199	
Venice	941-488-6711		
Manatee County	941-747-3011		
Sarasota County	941-951-4211	941-951-5800	
Florida Highway Patrol (Bradenton)			941-751-7647

AREA CODE/TOWN GOVERNMENT

Area Code
The area code for the Sarasota Bay area and the Charlotte Harbor Coast is 941. The 239 code covers the entire Island Coast and South Coast.

Government
All incorporated cities within the region are self-governing, with councilmen, commissioners, mayors, and city managers in various roles. The unincorporated towns and communities are county-ruled.

The incorporated cities of the Sarasota Bay coast include Bradenton, Anna Maria, Holmes Beach, Bradenton Beach, Sarasota, Longboat Key, and Venice. Bradenton is the county seat for Manatee County; Sarasota for Sarasota County. On the Charlotte Harbor coast, Punta Gorda (county seat) is incorporated. Cape Coral, Fort Myers (county seat), Fort Myers Beach, and Sanibel make up the Island Coast's incorporated cities. Naples is Collier County's seat; Naples, Marco Island, and Everglades City are incorporated.

Banks

Several old and established banks have branches located throughout Florida's Gulf Coast.
Some are listed below with toll-free information numbers.

Bank	Number
AmSouth	800-267-6884
Bank of America	800-299-2265
NationsBank	800-299-2265
South Trust	800-225-5782
SunTrust	800-732-9487

BIBLIOGRAPHY

Books about the region are available in bookstores and online outlets.

Biography & Reminiscence

Brown, Loren G. "Totch." *Totch: A Life in the Everglades*. Gainesville: University Press of
Florida, 1993. 279 pp., photos. Paper. $16.05. A folksy, firsthand adventure tour of Ten
Thousand Islands through the words of a former native.

Lindbergh, Anne Morrow. *Gift from the Sea*. New York: Pantheon, 1955. 142 pp., illus.
Hardcover $16. New York: Vintage Books, 1955. 138 pp., illus. Paper, $7. A small book
packed with sea-inspired wisdom from Charles Lindbergh's wife, who died in 2001.
Strong evidence points to Captiva as the book's inspiration.

Salty and serene on Captiva Island. Karen T. Bartlett

Newton, James. *Uncommon Friends*. New York: Harcourt, Brace, Jovanovich, 1987. 368 pp. $16. Local man's memories of his friendships with Fort Myers's illustrious winterers: Thomas Edison, Henry Ford, Harvey Firestone, and Charles Lindbergh.

Orlean, Susan. *The Orchid Thief: A True Story of Beauty and Obsession*. New York: Random House, 1998. 284 pp. $25. Paperback: New York: Ballantine, 1998. 297 pp. $14. Set in Fakahatchee Strand Preserve, Naples, and other local venues, Orlean tells a bizarre nonfiction tale about the elusive ghost orchid and the people who sought it.

Weeks, David C. *Ringling: The Florida Years, 1911–1936*. Gainesville: University Press of Florida, 1993. 350 pp., photos, annotations, index. $24.95.

Cookbooks

Junior League of Fort Myers. *Gulfshore Delights*. Fort Myers, Fla., 1984. 286 pp., illus., index. $14.95.

——. *Tropical Settings*. Fort Myers, Fla., 1995. 254 pp., illus., index. $19.95.

Reynolds, Doris. *When Peacocks Were Roasted and Mullet Was Fried*. Naples, Fla.: Enterprise Publishing, 1993. 175 pp., photos. $23.95. Naples history flavored with recipes.

Fiction

Dever, Sean Michael. *Blind Pass*. Kearney, Neb.: Morris Publishing, 1996. 244 pp. $7.99. Mystery set in Sanibel and Captiva.

MacDonald, John D. Many of his Travis McGee and other mysteries take place in a Sarasota Bay coast setting, where he had a home.

Matthiessen, Peter. *Killing Mr. Watson*. New York: Random House, 1990. Hardcover, 372 pp. $14. The parents of this award-winning author live on Sanibel Island. The subject of his historical trilogy is the posse killing of a murderer who hid out in the frontier of Ten Thousand Islands.

——. *Lost Man's River*. New York: Random House, 1997. Hardcover, 539 pp. $15. Second in the trilogy.

——. *Bone by Bone*. New York: Random House: 1999. Hardcover, 410 pp. $14. Final book in the trilogy, told in Ed Watson's own voice.

White, Randy. *Sanibel Flats*. New York: St. Martin's Press, 1990. 307 pp. $3.95. Mystery by a local fishing guide/journalist in local setting. He has written several books in this series that take place mostly along the Gulf Coast.

History

Anholt, Betty. *Sanibel's Story: Voices & Images from Calusa to Incorporation*. Virginia Beach, Va.: Donning, 1998. 191 pp., illus., maps. Written by a longtime island resident and historian.

Beater, Jack. *Pirates & Buried Treasure*. St. Petersburg: Great Outdoors Publishing, 1959. 118 pp., illus. $2.95. Somewhat factual, ever-colorful account of José Gaspar and his cohorts, by the area's foremost legendaire.

Board, Prudy Taylor, and Esther B. Colcord. *Historic Fort Myers*. Virginia Beach, Va.: Donning, 1992. 96 pp., photos, index. $15.95. Largely photographic treatment, written by two of the area's leading historians today.

——. *Pages from the Past*. Virginia Beach, Va.: Donning, 1990. 192 pp., photos, index. $29.95. Largely photographic treatment of Fort Myers's history.

Dormer, Elinore M. *The Sea Shell Islands: A History of Sanibel and Captiva.* Tallahassee: Rose Printing, 1987. 274 pp., illus., index. $16. The definitive work on island and regional history.

Jordan, Elaine Blohm. *Pine Island, the Forgotten Island.* Pine Island, Fla.: 1982. 186 pp., photos.

———. *Tales of Pine Island.* Ellijay, Ga.: Jordan Ink Publishing, 1985. 142 pp. $12.

Matthews, Janet Snyder. *Edge of Wilderness: A Settlement History of Manatee River and Sarasota Bay.* Sarasota: Coastal Press, 1983. 464 pp., photos, index. $21.50.

———. *Journey to Centennial Sarasota.* Sarasota: Pine Level Press, 1989. 224 pp., photos, index. $29.95.

———. *Venice: Journey to Horse and Chaise.* Sarasota: Pine Level Press, 1989. 394 pp., photos, index.

Zeiss, Betsy. *The Other Side of the River: Historical Cape Coral.* Cape Coral: 1986. 215 pp., photos, index. $8.95.

Natural History

Campbell, George R. *The Nature of Things on Sanibel.* Fort Myers: Press Printing, 1978. 174 pp., illus., index. $14.95. Factual yet entertaining background on native fauna and flora.

Douglas, Marjory Stoneman. *The Everglades: River of Grass.* St. Simons, Ga.: Mockingbird Books, 1947. 308 pp., $4.95. The book that focused the nation's attention on the developing plight of the pristine Everglades.

Ripple, Jeff. *Southwest Florida's Wetland Wilderness: Big Cypress Swamp and the Ten Thousand Islands.* Gainesville: University Press of Florida, 1992. Paperback, 112 pp., $16.95. This book celebrates the natural history of one of the most diverse, endangered, and beautiful ecosystems in the world. Stunning black and white photography by Clyde Butcher.

Toops, Connie. *The Florida Everglades.* Stillwater, Minn.: Voyageur Press, 1998. Paperback, 112 pp., color photography. Written by a former national park ranger.

Pictorial

Butcher, Clyde. *Clyde Butcher: Portfolio I.* Fort Myers: Shade Tree Press, 1994. 64 plates. The master of natural landscape photography collects his haunting black-and-white large-format images in a coffee-table edition.

Capes, Richard. *Richard Capes' Drawings Capture Siesta Key.* Sarasota: Capes Studio of Florida, 1992. 175 pp. An artistic tour of the island in pen and ink, with handwritten descriptions.

Stone, Lynn. *Sanibel Island.* Stillwater, Minn.: Voyageur Press, Inc., 1991. 96 pp., photos. $16.95. Sanibel's natural treasures in words and striking pictures.

Travel

MacPerry, I. *Indian Mounds You Can Visit.* St. Petersburg: Great Outdoors Publishing, 1993. 319 pp., photos, index. $12.95. Covers the entire west coast of Florida, arranged by county.

Walton, Chelle Koster. *Adventure Guide to Tampa Bay and Florida's West Coast.* 3rd ed. Edison, N.J.: Hunter Publishing, 2004. Paperback, 308 pp., maps, index. $18.99. Covers Tampa to the western Everglades.

Check It Out

Out-of-print books you can find in local libraries when you're visiting.

Bickel, Karl A. *The Mangrove Coast: The Story of the West Coast of Florida*. 4th ed. New York: Coward-McCann, 1989. 332 pp., photos, index. Vintage regional history of the area from Tampa Bay to Ten Thousand Islands, from the time of Ponce de León to 1885, spiced with romantic embellishments.

Briggs, Mildred. *Pioneers of Bonita Springs (Facts and Folklore)*. Bonita Springs, 1976. 100 pp., photos. Pirates, Indian healers, outlaws, and more.

Fritz, Florence. *Unknown Florida*. Coral Gables: University of Miami Press, 1963. 213 pp., photos, index. Focuses on southernmost Gulf Coast.

Gonzales, Thomas A. *The Caloosahatchee: History of the Caloosahatchee River and the City of Fort Myers, Florida*. Fort Myers Beach: Island Press, 1982. 134 pp. Memories of a native son, descendant of city's first settler.

Grismer, Karl H. *The Story of Fort Myers*. Fort Myers Beach: Island Press, 1982. 348 pp., photos, index.

——. *The Story of Sarasota*. Tampa: The Florida G Press, 1946. 376 pp., photos, index.

Hann, John H., ed. *Missions to the Calusa*. Gainesville: University of Florida Press, 1991. 460 pp., historic documents, index.

Marth, Del. *Yesterday's Sarasota*. Miami: E. A. Seemann Publishing, 1977. Updated. 160 pp., photos. Primarily pictorial history.

Matthews, Kenneth, and Robert McDevitt. *The Unlikely Legacy*. Sarasota: Aaron Publishers, 1980. 64 pp., illus. The story of John Ringling, the circus, and Sarasota.

Peeples, Vernon. *Punta Gorda and the Charlotte Harbor Area*. Virginia Beach, Va.: Donning, 1986. 208 pp., photos, index. Pictorial history authored by local politician.

Romans, Bernard. *A Concise Natural History of East and West Florida*. Gainesville: University of Florida Press, 1962. 342 pp., index. A facsimile reproduction of the 1775 edition.

Schell, Rolfe F. *De Soto Didn't Land at Tampa*. Fort Myers Beach: Island Press, 1966. 96 pp., illus.

——. *History of Fort Myers Beach*. Fort Myers Beach: Island Press, 1980. 96 pp., photos, index.

Tebeau, Charlton W. *Florida's Last Frontier: The History of Collier County*. Coral Gables: University of Miami Press, 1966. 278 pp., photos, index.

Widmer, Randolph J. *The Evolution of the Calusa*. Tuscaloosa: University of Alabama Press, 1988. 334 pp., index. Very technical discussion of the "nonagricultural chiefdom on the Southwest Florida Coast."

CLIMATE, SEASONS, AND WHAT TO WEAR

The tropics brush the Mangrove Coast but do not overwhelm it.
—Karl Bickel, The Mangrove Coast, 1942

Florida's nickname, the Sunshine State, was once as fresh as it was apt. Although overuse has tended to cloud the once-perfect image, Florida still remains the ultimate state of sunshine through the sheer power of statistics. The sun beams down on the Gulf Coast for nearly 75 percent of all daylight hours and constitutes the one asset on which locals can bank.

To residents, the sun's smile can seem more like a sneer as they await fall's begrudging permission to turn off air conditioners and open windows. They suffer their own brand of cabin fever during the summer months, which often seem to linger as long as a Canadian winter. Although visitors revel in the warmth and sunlight, they often wonder how residents endure the monotony of seasonal sameness.

The seasons *do* change along the southern Gulf Coast —although more subtly than "up north." Weather patterns vary within the region. The Sarasota Bay and Charlotte Harbor areas often get more rain.

Predictions call for flurries of ibises in the Everglades. Karen T. Bartlett

However, weather can be very localized—it may rain on the southern end of 12-mile-long Sanibel Island while the north end remains dry. Islands generally stay cooler than the mainland in summer and warmer in winter, thanks to their insulating jacket of gulf water. This is especially true where Charlotte Harbor runs wide and deep, creating a small pocket of tropical climate.

Winter is everyone's favorite time of year weatherwise, with temperatures along the coast reaching generally into the 70s during the day and dropping into the low 50s at night. Visitors find green, balmy relief from snow blindness and frostbite. Floridians enjoy the relative coolness that brings with it a reprieve from sweltering days, steamy nights, and bloodthirsty insects. The fragrance of oranges, grapefruits, and key limes fill the air. It's a time for activity; one can safely schedule a tee time past noon. Resort areas fill up, and migratory houseguests from the north arrive.

Spring comes on tiptoe to the coast. No thaw-and-puddle barometer alerts us; the sense of spring giddiness affects only longtime residents. Floridians emerge from hibernation raring to leap and frolic—and perhaps do a little mischief. Gardenias, Hong Kong orchids, and jasmine bloom, and everything that already looks green and alive bursts forth with an extra reserve of color. It's a time to celebrate the end of another season and to greedily enjoy the domain that's been shared with visitors during the winter months.

Summers used to be reserved for die-hard Floridians. All but the most devoted residents boarded up their homes and businesses and headed somewhere—*anywhere*—cooler. Now there's a summer trade, composed of Floridians, Europeans, and northern families —enough to keep the resort communities alive through temperatures that snuggle up to 100 degrees. Although technically classified as subtropical, starting in June, the region feels the bristles of that tropical brush. The pace of life slows, and late-afternoon rains suddenly and unpredictably revolt against the sun's constancy. Mangoes and guavas blush sweet temptation. Moonlit nights bring magic to the cereus vine, with its white starburst blooms the size of Frisbees.

Fall appears in October as a sharpening of vision after a blur of humidity. Residents don't exactly go out and buy wool plaids, but they do break out sweatshirts. Many build fires in hearths that have held dried floral arrangements for eight months. The leathery leaves of the sea grape tree turn as red as the northern oak, and the gumbo-limbo coaxes out rakes. The best part about a Gulf Coast fall, for those residents who once endured northern winters, is that it doesn't bode of snow-proof boots and long underwear.

Green Flash

The sun is setting, melting, golden, into the sea like a round pat of butter balanced on its edge in a sauté pan. Just as the final crescent of light disappears, it sends up a green farewell flare on the horizon.

What you've just witnessed is a tropical phenomenon called a green flash. It occurs infrequently, and most people miss it—or only realize what they've seen after the fact.

Skeptics will tell you that green flashes are just a good excuse to sit on the beach at sunset, perhaps with a celebratory glass of champagne or rum punch. The drinking part of the sunset ritual, they further theorize, may be more responsible for green flash sightings than reality.

Physics, however, backs up the notion that the sun emits a split-second green explosion as it winks below the sea's surface. It all has to do with spectrum, wavelengths, refraction, and other terms you may remember from school science experiments. In short, it takes conditions such as those we enjoy on the Gulf Coast—sunsets over the sea and near-tropical climes—to make the green flash happen. Cloudless evening skies are also required, which occur more regularly during the cool months. Binoculars or a small telescope will help widen the band of refracted green light so that it lasts longer.

Patience and persistence are crucial. Once you've seen a green flash, some say, your now-trained eye is apt to spot more. With or without rum.

Winter temperatures dip, albeit rarely, into the freezing range, so be prepared for just about any weather between December and February. Fortunately swimsuits take up little room, so pack more than one (Florida's high humidity often prevents anything from ever really drying out). Loose-fitting togs and cotton work best in any season. Long sleeves are welcome in the evenings during winter. Summer showers require rain gear, especially if you plan on boating or playing outdoors.

Don't worry about dress codes in most restaurants. Ties and pantyhose are strictly for the office and (possibly) the theater. Worry more about comfort, particularly if your skin burns easily. Pack hats and lots of sunscreen. Bring insect repellent, too, especially if you plan on venturing into the jungle—or simply watching an island sunset, for that matter. Counties do spray for mosquitoes, but it has little effect on the tiny but prolific no-see-um (sand flea). Any DEET product repels mosquitoes. The best protection against both pests is sitting under a ceiling fan—practically standard equipment in homes and hotels.

On the cloudier side, Florida weather includes a high incidence of lightning, summer squalls, tornadoes, waterspouts, and the dreaded H-word. Hurricane season begins in June, but activity concentrates toward season's end in November. Watches and warnings alert you in plenty of time to head inland or north; to be safest, do so at first mention, especially if you are staying on an island.

Florida's celebrated sunshine is at its best on the Gulf Coast. Ol' Sol visits practically every day, and it's also where he slips into bed. Gulf Coast Florida boasts the most spectacular sunsets in the continental United States. (OK, so I'm a little biased.)

Average Gulf Coast Air Temperatures

Month	Avg. Max.	Avg. Min.
Jan.	72.8°	52.8°
Feb.	73.8°	53.8°
Mar.	78.3°	57.8°
Apr.	82.5°	61.6°
May	87.7°	67.1°
June	89.7°	72.1°
July	90.5°	73.7°
Aug.	90.9°	73.8°
Sept.	89.1°	72.7°
Oct.	84.9°	66.8°
Nov.	77.9°	59.4°
Dec.	74.1°	53.8°

Gulf Coast Water Temperatures

Annual average	77.5°
Fall/winter average	70.8°
Spring/summer average	84.1°
Winter low	66.0°
Summer high	87.0°

SERVICES FOR THE PHYSICALLY IMPAIRED

Regulations concerning disabled access vary, depending on locale. In general, most restaurants, parks, attractions, and resorts provide physically impaired visitors with special ramps, bathroom stalls, and hotel rooms. Some beaches, particularly in the Naples area, provide fat-wheeled beach chairs for the handicapped.

HOSPITALS & CLINICS

Charlotte Harbor Coast

ENGLEWOOD

Englewood Community Hospital (941-475-6571; www.englewoodcommunityhospital.com; 700 Medical Blvd., Englewood 34223) Emergency room open 24 hours.

PORT CHARLOTTE

Bon Secours-St. Joseph Hospital (941-766-4122; www.bonsecours.org/portcharlotte; 2500 Harbor Blvd., Port Charlotte 33952) Emergency room open 24 hours.

Englewood Community Hospital (941-475-6571; www.englewoodcommhospital.com; 700 Medical Blvd., Englewood 34223) Emergency room open 24 hours. For 24-hour Consult A Nurse line, call 473-3919 or toll free 888-685-1598.

Fawcett Memorial Hospital (941-629-1181; www.fawcetthospital.com; 21298 Olean Blvd., Port Charlotte 33952) Emergency room open 24 hours.

Fort Myers's stylish HealthPark Medical Center continues to grow. Karen T. Bartlett

Charlotte Regional Medical Center (941-639-3131; www.charlotteregional.com; 809 E. Marion Ave., Punta Gorda 33950) Emergency room open 24 hours.

Island Coast
Cape Coral
Cape Coral Hospital (239-574-2323; 636 Del Prado Blvd, Cape Coral 33990) Emergency room open 24 hours.

Gulf Coast Hospital (239-768-5000; www.gulfcoasthospital.com; 13681 Doctor's Way, Fort Myers 33912)

HealthPark Medical Center (239-433-7799; 9981 HealthPark Circle, Fort Myers 33908) Home of Children's Hospital of Southwest Florida. Emergency room open 24 hours. Twenty-four-hour medical information HealthLine, 800-936-5321.

Lee Memorial Hospital (239-332-1111; www.leememorial.org; 2776 Cleveland Ave., Fort Myers 33901) Emergency room open 24 hours.

Southwest Florida Regional Medical Center (239-939-1147; www.swrfmc.com; 2727 Winkler Ave., Fort Myers 33901) Acute care and outpatient surgery. Emergency room open 24 hours. For 24-hour Consult-a-Nurse Healthcare Referral, call 800-257-0944.

Sarasota Bay Coast
Bradenton
HCA L.W. Blake Medical Center (941-792-6611; www.blakemedicalcenter.com; 2020 59th St. W., Bradenton 34209) Emergency room open 24 hours.

Manatee Memorial Hospital (941-746-5111; www.manateememorial.com; 206 Second St. E., Bradenton 34208) Emergency room open 24 hours.

SARASOTA
Doctors Hospital of Sarasota (941-342-1100; www.doctorsofsarasota.com; 5731 Bee Ridge Rd., Sarasota 34233) Emergency room open 24 hours.

Sarasota Memorial Hospital (941-917-9000; www.smh.com; 1700 S. Tamiami Trail, Sarasota 34239) Emergency room open 24 hours.

VENICE
Bon Secours Venice Hospital (941-485-7711; www.bonsecours.org/venice; 540 The Rialto, Venice 34292) Emergency room open 24 hours.

South Coast
BONITA SPRINGS
Bonita Bay Surgery Center (239-947-7776; www.bonita.icu.ehc.com; 26800 Tamiami Trail, Bonita Bay 34134) Outpatient surgery; open Monday–Friday, no ER.

MARCO ISLAND
Marco Healthcare Center (239-394-8234; www.nchhcs.org; 40 Heathwood Dr., Marco Island 34145) Twenty-four-hour medical care and rehab on out-patient basis.

NAPLES
Naples Community Hospital (239-436-5000; www.nchmd.org; 350 Seventh St. N., Naples 34102) Heart and cancer institutes; emergency room open 24 hours.

North Collier Hospital (239-513-7000; www.nchhcs.org; 11190 Healthpark Blvd., Naples 34101, off Immokalee Rd.) Emergency room open 24 hours.

LATE-NIGHT FOOD AND FUEL

Certain categories of Florida liquor licensing require bars to serve food, which provides a good source for late-night eating. Many chain restaurants located along major thorough-fares—such as Grandma's Kitchen, Denny's, and Perkins—stay open late or all night.

Chain convenience stores, gas stations, and fuel/food marts also are open around the clock. These include 7-Eleven, Starvin' Marvin, Mobil Mart, and Circle K.

MEDIA

Media flood the Gulf Coast like high tide. Many publications are directed toward tourists, and some are only as permanent as the shoreline during a tidal surge. Magazines come and go, and radio stations often shift formats.

Four daily newspapers stand out for their endurance and dependability: the *Bradenton Herald,* the *Sarasota Herald-Tribune,* the *Fort Myers News-Press,* and the *Naples Daily News.* Weeklies are also firmly established in their respective communities, primarily because many are owned collectively by one corporation. Specialty tabloids address seniors, shop-pers, fishermen, women, and other groups.

Magazines show the most fluctuation. Traditionally they were created to appeal to the region's upscale, mature population, which is concentrated in Sarasota and Naples. *Sarasota Magazine, Naples Illustrated,* and *Gulfshore Life* have been the stalwarts of regional lifestyle glossies, but even they shift focus to address changing populations and economic trends.

Fort Myers carries the majority of the region's broadcast media, which reach to the Charlotte Harbor and the South Coast. Much of the Sarasota Bay coast's TV comes from Tampa.

Charlotte Harbor Coast
Newspapers
Boca Beacon (941-964-2995, 800-749-2995; www.bocabeacon.com; PO Box 313, Boca Grande 33921) Weekly.

Charlotte Sun-Herald (941-629-2855; www.sun-herald.com; PO Box 2390, Port Charlotte 33949)

Englewood Sun-Herald (941-474-5521; www.sun-herald.com; 167 W. Dearborn St., Englewood 34223) Weekly.

Gasparilla Gazette (941-964-2728; www.flguide.com; PO Box 929, Boca Grande 33921)

Island Coast
Newspapers
Cape Coral Breeze (239-574-1110; www.flguide.com; 2510 Del Prado Blvd., Cape Coral 33904) Daily.

Fort Myers Beach Bulletin (239-463-4421; www.flguide.com; 19260 San Carlos Blvd., Fort Myers Beach 33931)

Island Reporter (239-472-1587; www.flguide.com; PO Box 809, 2340 Periwinkle Way, Sanibel Island 33957) Weekly.

News-Press (239-335-0200; www.news-press.com; PO Box 10, 2442 Dr. Martin Luther King Jr. Blvd., Fort Myers 33901) The 10th-largest newspaper in the state in terms of circulation, it publishes editions for Charlotte County and Bonita Springs.

Observer Papers (239-765-0400; www.flguide.com; 17274 San Carlos Blvd., Fort Myers Beach 33931) Publishes weekly editions for Fort Myers Beach and other neighborhoods.

Pine Island Eagle (239-283-2022; www.flguide.com; 10700 Stringfellow Rd., Suite 60, Bokeelia 33922) Weekly.

Sanibel-Captiva Islander (239-472-5185; PO Box 56, 395 Tarpon Bay Rd. #13, Sanibel Island 33957) Weekly; free subscription.

Magazines
Florida Journal (239-481-7511; www.floridajournal.com; 6249 Presidential Ct., Fort Myers 33919) A travel and relocation magazine published in both English and German.

Television
WBBH-TV Fort Myers. NBC.
WFTX-TV Cape Coral. Fox.
WINK-TV Fort Myers. CBS.
WZVN-TV Fort Myers. ABC.

Sarasota Bay Coast
Newspapers
Bradenton Herald (941-748-0411; www.bradenton.com; 102 Manatee Ave. W., Bradenton 34205) Daily.

Herald-Tribune (941-953-7755; www.newscoast.com; 801 S. Tamiami Trail, Sarasota 34236) Florida's eighth largest daily in terms of circulation.

Longboat Observer (941-383-5509; www.longboatobserver.com; 5570 Gulf of Mexico Dr., Longboat Key 34228) Weekly.

Pelican Press (941-349-4949; 230 Avenida Madera, Sarasota 34242) Weekly covering Siesta Key and Sarasota.

Venice Gondolier (941-484-2611; www.venicegondolier.com; 200 E. Venice Ave., Venice 34285) Published semiweekly.

Weekly (941-923-2544; www.sarasotaweekly.com; 3755 S. Tuttle Ave., Sarasota 34239) Heavy on entertainment.

Weekly Planet (941-365-6776; www.weeklyplanet.com; 1383 Fifth St., Sarasota 34236) Giveaway entertainment weekly with a youthful, irreverent voice.

Magazines
Sarasota Magazine (941-366-8225, 800-881-2394; www.sarasotamagazine.com; 601 S. Osprey Ave., Sarasota 34236) Lifestyle for upscale Sarasotans.

Sarasota Scene (941-365-1119; www.scenesarasota.com; 2015 S. Tuttle Ave., PO Box 1418, Sarasota 34230) Weekly covering the Sarasota-Bradenton area.

West Coast Woman (941-954-3300; PO Box 819, Sarasota 34230) Monthly free publication.

Television
BLAB-TV Sarasota.
SNN-TV Sarasota News Now.
WWSB-TV Sarasota. ABC.

South Coast
Newspapers
Bonita Banner (239-992-2110; www.bonitabanner.com; 9102 Bonita Beach Rd., Bonita Springs 34135) Semiweekly.

Marco Island Sun Times (239-394-7592; www.marcoislandflorida.com; 317 N. Collier Blvd. Ste. 202, Marco Island 34145) Free distribution paper.

Naples Daily News (239-262-3161; www.naplesnews.com; 1075 Central Ave., Naples 34102) Daily; publisher of all the newspapers listed above.

Magazines
Gulfshore Business (239-594-9980, 800-220-4853; www.gulfshorebusiness.com; 9051 N. Tamiami Trail, Suite 202, Naples 34108)

Gulfshore Life (239-594-9980, 800-220-4853; www.gulfshorebusiness.com; 9051 N. Tamiami Trail, Suite 202, Naples 34108) Longtime slick lifestyle and news guide to the southwest coast.

N, The Magazine of Naples (239-594-9404; www.nmagazine.com; 4500 Executive Dr., Suite 1, Naples 34119) Fashion and society oriented.

Naples Illustrated (239-434-6966; www.naplesillustrated.com; 3066 Tamiami Trail N., Ste.102, Naples 34103) Haute lifestyles glossy.

Television
WTVK-TV Bonita Springs. UPN.

REAL ESTATE

Real-estate prices run the gamut from reasonable to ultraexpensive. In parts of Bradenton, Sarasota, and Fort Myers, planned communities cater to young families. Exclusive areas such as Longboat Key, Casey Key, Manasota Key, Sanibel Island, Captiva Island, and Naples are known for their pricey waterfront homes and golfing developments. Florida's $25,000 homestead exemption gives residents a tax break on primary home purchases.

Real-estate publications can be found on the newsstands, or check local newspapers. Otherwise, contact the agencies listed below.

Florida Association of Realtors (407-438-1400; PO Box 725025, Orlando 32872)

Fort Myers Association of Realtors, Inc. (239-936-3537; 2840 Winkler Ave., Fort Myers 33916)

Naples Area Board of Realtors, Inc. (239-597-1666; 1455 Pine Ridge Rd., Naples 34109)

Sanibel & Captiva Islands Association of Realtors, Inc. (239-472-9353; 1648 Periwinkle Way, Ste. F, Sanibel Island 33957)

Sarasota Association of Realtors (941-923-2315; 3590 Tuttle Ave. S., Sarasota 34239)

Fly-fishing is "catching on" in the Everglades area. Karen T. Bartlett

ROAD SERVICE

AAA Auto Club

941-362-2220; www.aaa.com; 3844 Bee Ridge Rd., Sarasota; 24-hour emergency road service

941-362-2500; www.aaa.com; 258 Ringling Shopping Center, Sarasota; 24-hour emergency road service

239-939-6500; www.aaa.com; 2516 Colonial Blvd., Fort Myers; 24-hour emergency road service

239-594-5006; www.aaa.com; 4910 N. Tamiami Trail, Suite 120, Naples; 24-hour emergency road service

TOURIST INFORMATION

Visit Florida (888-7FLA-USA; www.flausa.com; 661 E. Jefferson St., Ste. 300, Tallahassee 32301)

Charlotte Harbor Coast

Boca Grande Chamber of Commerce (941-964-0568; www.bocagrandechamber.com; 5800 Gasparilla Rd., Suite A1; PO Box 704, Boca Grande 33921) Information center located in Courtyard Plaza at the island's north end.

Charlotte Harbor & the Gulf Islands Visitor's Bureau (941-743-1900, 888-4PUREFLA; www.pureflorida.com; 18501 Murdock Circle, Port Charlotte 33948)

Englewood–Cape Haze Area Chamber of Commerce (941-474-5511, 800-603-7198; www.englewoodchamber.com; 601 S. Indiana Ave., Englewood 34223)

Island Coast

Cape Coral Chamber of Commerce (239-549-6900, 800-226-9609; www.capecoralchamber .com; PO Box 747, Cape Coral 33910) Information center at 2051 Cape Coral Pkwy. E.

Estero Chamber of Commerce (239-948-7990; www.esterochamber.org; PO Box 508; Estero 33928)

Greater Fort Myers Beach Chamber of Commerce (239-454-7500, 800-782-9283; www.fmbchamber.com; 17200 San Carlos Blvd., Fort Myers Beach 33931)

Greater Fort Myers Chamber of Commerce (239-332-3624, 800-366-3622; www.fort myers.org; PO Box 9289, Fort Myers 33902) Welcome center located downtown at 2310 Edwards Dr.

Greater Pine Island Chamber of Commerce (239-283-0888; www.pineislandchamber .org; PO Box 525, Matlacha 33909) Information center located before the bridge to Matlacha on Pine Island Road.

Lee County Visitor & Convention Bureau (239-338-3500, 800-237-6444; www.fort myers-sanibel.com; University Park, 12800 University Drive, Suite 550, Fort Meyers 33907-5337)

North Fort Myers Chamber of Commerce (239-997-9111; www.northfortmyerschamber .org; 3323 N. Key Dr., Ste. #1, North Fort Myers 33903)

Sanibel-Captiva Islands Chamber of Commerce (239-472-1080; www.sanibel-captiva .org; 1159 Causeway Rd., Sanibel Island 33957) Information center located shortly after the causeway approach to Sanibel.

Southwest Florida Hispanic Chamber of Commerce (239-418-1441; www.swflhispanic chamber.org; 10051 McGregor Blvd., Suite 204, Fort Myers 33919)

Sarasota Bay Coast

Anna Maria Island Chamber of Commerce (941-778-1541; www.amichamber.org; 5313 Gulf Dr., Holmes Beach 34217)

Bradenton Area Convention & Visitors Bureau (941-729-9177, 800-4-MANATEE; www.flagulfislands.com; PO Box 1000, Bradenton 34206)

Downtown Partnership of Sarasota (941-951-2656; www.downtownsarasota.com; 1818 Main Street, Sarasota 34236)

Longboat Key Chamber of Commerce (941-383-2466; www.longboatkeychamber.com; Whitney Beach Plaza, 6854 Gulf of Mexico Dr., Longboat Key 34228)

Manatee Chamber of Commerce (941-748-3411; www.manateechamber.com; 222 Tenth St. W., Bradenton 34206)

Sarasota Convention & Visitors Bureau (941-957-1877, 800-522-9799; www.sarasotafl .org; 655 N. Tamiami Trail, Sarasota 34236)

Siesta Key Chamber of Commerce (941-349-3800, 888-837-3969; www.siestakey chamber.com; 5118 Ocean Blvd., Siesta Key 34242)

Gulf Coast Florida time is kept by tides and the sun.
Karen T. Bartlett

Venice Area Chamber of Commerce (941-488-2236; www.venicechamber .com; 597 S. Tamiami Trail, Venice 34285)

South Coast

Bonita Springs Area Chamber of Commerce (239-992-2943, 800-226-2943; www.bonitaspringschamber.com; 25071 Chamber of Commerce Dr., Bonita Springs 34135)

Everglades Area Chamber of Commerce (239-695-3941, 800-914-6355; www.florida-everglades.com; 32016 E. Tamiami Trail, PO Box 130, Everglades City 34139) Welcome center corner of Hwy. 41 and Rte. 29.

Greater Naples Marco Everglades Convention & Visitors Bureau (239-403-2379, 800 688 3600; www.paradisecoast .com; 3050 N. Horseshoe Blvd. #218, Naples 34104)

Marco Island Area Chamber of Commerce (239-394-7549, 800-788-MARCO; www.marcoislandchamber.org; 1102 North Collier Blvd., PO Box 913, Marco Island 34145)

Naples Chamber of Commerce (239-262-6141; www.napleschamber.org; 895 5th Ave. S., Naples 34102-6605) At the corner of Hwy. 41.

IF TIME IS SHORT

Not enough time to do it all on this trip to southwest Florida? Here are some highlights that I suggest to weekenders and short-term vacationers who wonder how they can best spend their precious time. Beach time, of course, is a high priority for those with only a few days to spend in the sun. I list must-see beaches as well as other attractions, adventures, restaurants, and lodgings you should not miss.

Sarasota Bay Coast

Siesta Key County Beach (239-346-3310; Midnight Pass Rd. at Beach Way Dr., Siesta Key), despite its weekend and high-season crowds, is the area's ultimate beach, with sands whiter and fluffier than a down quilt.

Downtown Sarasota is a happening place. Take in a play and circle the galleries of the Theatre and Arts District. Don't miss the shops of **Palm Avenue** and the galleries of **Towles Court Artist Colony** (941-365-9146; www.towlescourt.com; 1943 Morrill St., Sarasota 34239).

The **John and Mable Ringling Museum of Art**, the **Ringling Estate**, and its various circus and Gilded Age attractions (941-359-5700; www.ringling.org; 5401 Bay Shore Rd., Sarasota 34243) crown in glory Sarasota's famed cultural scene. **Longboat Key** provides a drive on the coast's wealthy side. Depending on your budget, dine in high style at **Euphemia Haye** (941-383-3633; www.euphemiahaye.com; 5540 Gulf of Mexico Dr., Sarasota 34228) or in the spirit of maritime fun at **Mar-Vista Dockside Restaurant & Pub** (941-383-2391; 760 Broadway St., Sarasota 34228).

Stop at **Mote Marine Aquarium** (941-388-2451, 800-691-MOTE; www.mote.org; 1600 Ken Thompson Pkwy., Sarasota 34236) to check out the new giant squid and other fishy stuff.

Charlotte Harbor Coast

The best of Charlotte Harbor lies in its hidden-from-the-spotlight barrier islands. **Manasota Key** and **Englewood Beach** boast sunny beaches flecked with sharks' teeth. For a unique and nature-intensive lodging experience, book at **Manasota Beach Club** (941-474-2614; www.manasotabeachclub.com; 7660 Manasota Key Rd., Englewood 34223), a longstanding beach resort with accommodations from rustic to lavish.

On Gasparilla Island, **Boca Grande** supplies a full day of beaching, shopping, and dining. Have lunch or dinner at **PJ's Seagrille** (239-964-0806; 312 Park Ave., Boca Grande 33921) and savor something from the sea, inventive and well crafted. For a different flavor of island life, take a room at the old, gracious **Gasparilla Inn** (239-964-2201; 5th St. & Palm St., PO Box 1088, Boca Grande 33921), as the Vanderbilts and Du Ponts have since 1912.

Explore the extensive aquatic preserves of Charlotte Harbor aboard a catamaran or kayak with **Grande Tours** (239-697-8825 from Boca Grande; 941-697-8825; www.grande tours.com; 12575 Placida Rd., PO Box 281, Placida 33946). For an island wilderness adventure that returns you to the days of Florida cow-hunting, ride the bouncy swamp buggy through a modern-day cattle and alligator ranch at **Babcock Wilderness Adventures** (941-637-0551, 800-500-5583; www.babcockwilderness.com; Rte. 31, Punta Gorda 33950).

Island Coast

Fort Myers's finest attraction, the **Edison & Ford Winter Estates** (239-334-3614; www. edison-ford-estate.com; 2350-2400 McGregor Blvd., Fort Myers 33902), peeks into the times and genius of America's greatest inventors, who lived side by side in winter months. Dine Victorian in the two historic homes that make up **The Veranda** (239-332-2065; 2122 Second St., Fort Myers 33902), which specializes in southern charm and fine cuisine.

Much of what's special about the Island Coast has to do with what's wild. Half of Sanibel Island is devoted to the **J. N. "Ding" Darling National Wildlife Refuge** (239-472-1100; http://dingdarling.fws.gov; 1 Wildlife Dr., Sanibel Island 33957; off Sanibel-Captiva Rd.), home to alligators, roseate spoonbills, manatees, river otters, and bobcats. The best way to see it is by tram or kayak tour from **Tarpon Bay Explorers** (239-472-8900; www.tarpon bayexplorers.com; 900 Tarpon Bay Rd., Sanibel Island 33957).

Sanibel's beaches are renowned for their bountiful shells and minimal impact on nature's birthright beauty. Most natural and secluded is **Bowman's Beach** (Bowman's Beach Rd. off Sanibel-Captiva Rd.). To find the utmost in remote beaches, rent a boat or hop a charter to unbridged **LaCosta Island** and **Upper Captiva Island**, where state parks preserve slices of Old Florida.

For lively beaching, follow **Route 865** through Estero Island's **Fort Myers Beach** and down along lovely, undeveloped Lovers Key en route to **Bonita Beach**. On the way you'll pass bustling resort scenes and quiet island vistas.

South Coast

To explore the highbrow face of Naples and its environs, stop for afternoon tea at **The Ritz-Carlton** (239-598-3300; 800-241-3333; www.ritzcarlton.com/resorts/naples; 2 Vanderbilt Beach Rd., Naples 34108) and take in a concert and art stroll at the **Naples Philharmonic** (239-597-1900, 800-597-1900; www.thephil.org; 5833 Pelican Bay Blvd., Naples 34104) and the new **Naples Museum of Art** next door (239-597-1900; www.naples philcenter.org; 5833 Pelican Bay Blvd., Naples 34104). Downtown's **Fifth Avenue South** has evolved into a fashionable shopping and sidewalk dining district. Try **Bistro 821** (239-261-5821; www.bistro821.com; 821 Fifth Ave. S, Naples 34102) for an example of the latest in Naples's cutting-edge chic.

To really have experienced Naples, you must do sunset at the **Naples Pier** (www.discover naples.com/Naples_Pier_Sunset.htm; 12th.Ave. S.). It's a nightly ritual for fishermen, strollers, lovers, and pelicans. By day the pier is the center of activity along a beach that stretches for miles.

My favorite part of Marco Island is **Goodland**. A little fishing village "on pause," it serves fresh seafood and country fun in its restaurants and introduces the unruly flavor of Ten Thousand Islands and the Florida Everglades.

Everglades City is headquarters for tours that explore this labyrinthine land down under. **Everglades National Park** (239-695-2591, 800-445-7724 (in Florida); www.nps.gov/ever; Everglades Ranger Station, Everglades City) has a base here, conducts boat tours, and rents canoes for launching into the 98-mile **Wilderness Trail.**

CHELLE'S HIGH FIVES

Here, I give a "high five" to my top picks in a number of offbeat categories. These are the crème de la crème of Southwest Florida, whether you're looking for the best martini or the swankiest jewelry store. Within the chapters, look for starred entries to indicate the High Fivers.

Beachy Keen Resorts
1. Palm Island Resort, Cape Haze
2. Manasota Beach Club, Manasota Key
3. Colony Beach and Tennis Resort, Longboat Key
4. Marco Island Marriott Resort & Golf Club, Marco Island
5. LaPlaya Beach & Golf Resort, Vanderbilt Beach

Family-Loving Resorts
1. Sundial Beach Resort, Sanibel Island
2. Colony Beach and Tennis Resort, Longboat Key
3. Sanibel Harbour Resort & Spa, Fort Myers
4. Palm Island Resort, Cape Haze
5. Marco Island Marriott Resort, Marco Island

City-Smart Hotels
1. The Ritz-Carlton Sarasota
2. Trianon, Bonita Springs
3. Inn on Fifth, Naples
4. Holiday Inn Riverfront, Bradenton
5. Holiday Inn Riverwalk, Fort Myers

Inns & B&Bs
1. Harrington House B&B, Sarasota
2. Collier Inn, Useppa Island
3. Gasparilla Inn, Boca Grande
4. The Cypress B&B, Sarasota
5. Ivey House B&B, Everglades City

Cottage by the Sea
1. Rolling Waves Cottages, Longboat Key
2. Cabbage Key Inn, Cabbage Key
3. Jensen's Twin Palms Cottages & Marina, Captiva Island
4. Gulf Breeze Cottages, Sanibel Island
5. Collier Inn & Cottages, Useppa Island

Splurge Accommodations
1. The Ritz-Carlton Naples
2. Sanibel Harbour Resort & Spa, Fort Myers
3. The Registry Resort, Naples
4. The Ritz-Carlton Golf Resort, Naples
5. Hyatt Regency Coconut Point Resort & Spa, Bonita Springs

Raw Bars

1. Tarpon Bay Restaurant, Hyatt Regency Coconut Point, Estero
2. Phillippi Creek Village Oyster Bar, Sarasota
3. Lobster Shack, St. James City
4. The Dock at Crayton Cove, Naples
5. Lazy Flamingo, Sanibel Island

Martini Meccas

1. Blu Sushi, Fort Myers
2. Dolce Vita, Sanibel Island
3. Monkey Room, Colony Beach and Tennis Resort, Longboat Key
4. Cà d'Zan Lounge, The Ritz-Carlton Sarasota
5. Beach Bistro, Holmes Beach

Tables with a Water View

1. Sale e Pepe, Marco Island
2. Old Salty Dog, Lido Key
3. Mar-Vista Dockside Restaurant & Pub, Longboat Key
4. The Crow's Nest, Venice
5. The Dock at Crayton Cove, Naples

Seafood Noshing

1. PJ's Seagrille, Boca Grande
2. Captain Brian's Seafood Market Restaurant, Sarasota
3. Star Fish Company, Cortez
4. Captain Eddie's Seafood Restaurant, Nokomis
5. Everglades Seafood Company, Everglades City

Romantic Restaurants

1. Beach Bistro, Holmes Beach
2. Sale e Pepe, Marco Island
3. The Summerhouse, Siesta Key
4. Veranda, Fort Myers
5. Café L'Europe, St. Armands Circle, Sarasota

Creative Cuisine

1. The Perfect Caper, Punta Gorda
2. Chops City Grill, Bonita Springs
3. Fred's, Sarasota
4. Michael's on East, Sarasota
5. Traders Store & Café, Sanibel

Ethnic Eats

1. Bha! Bha!, Naples
2. Blu Sushi, Fort Myers
3. Manni's, Fort Myers
4. Cilantro Tamales, Naples
5. Siam Hut, Cape Coral

Old Florida Funk
1. Cabbage Key Inn, Cabbage Key
2. Phillippi Creek Village Oyster Bar, Sarasota
3. JT's Island Grill & Gallery, Chokoloskee Island
4. Old Marco Lodge Crab House, Goodland
5. Rotten Ralph's, Anna Maria

Breakfast
1. Broken Egg, Siesta Key
2. Gulf Drive Café, Bradenton Beach
3. Amy's Over Easy, Sanibel Island
4. Manna From Heaven, Naples
5. Skillets Sunrise Café, Naples

Deli/Food Markets
1. Morton's Market, Sarasota
2. Blue Pepper, Fort Myers
3. The Gourmet Market, Sarasota
4. Wynn's, Naples
5. Mario's Italian Meat Market & Deli, Fort Myers

Architectural Gems
1. Cà d'Zan, Ringling Estates, Sarasota
2. Gamble Plantation Mansion, Bradenton
3. Sarasota Opera House
4. Gasparilla Inn, Boca Grande
5. Van Wezel Performing Arts Hall, Sarasota

History Alive
1. Historic Spanish Point, Osprey
2. Edison & Ford Winter Estates, Fort Myers
3. De Soto National Memorial Park, Bradenton
4. Koreshan State Historic Site, Estero
5. Collier County Museum, Naples

Kid Cool
1. G. WIZ, Sarasota
2. Imaginarium, Fort Myers
3. King Richard's Family Fun Park, Naples
4. J. P. Igloo, Bradenton
5. Sunsplash Family Waterpark, Cape Coral

Quirky Museums
1. Teddy Bear Museum, Naples
2. Gasparilla Island Maritime Museum, Boca Grande
3. Ringling Museum of the Circus, Sarasota
4. Sarasota Classic Car Museum, Sarasota
5. Bailey-Matthews Shell Museum, Sanibel Island

On Stage
1. Van Wezel Performing Arts Hall, Sarasota
2. Asolo Center for the Performing Arts, Sarasota
3. Philharmonic Center for the Arts, Naples
4. Barbara B. Mann Performing Arts Hall, Fort Myers
5. Circus Sarasota

Night Prowling
1. Luna, The Registry Resort, Naples
2. Gator Club, Sarasota
3. Crow's Nest Lounge, 'Tween Waters Inn, Captiva Island
4. Bimini Beach Club, Marco Island
5. McCabe's Irish Pub, Naples

Boating Adventures
1. Florida Sailing & Cruising School, North Fort Myers
2. Offshore Sailing School, Captiva Island
3. Grande Tours, Placida
4. *Lady Chadwick*, Captiva Island
5. Everglades National Park Boat Tour

Nature Preserved
1. Everglades National Park
2. J. N. "Ding" Darling National Wildlife Refuge, Sanibel Island
3. Rookery Bay Preserve, Naples
4. Corkscrew Swamp Sanctuary, Naples
5. Collier-Seminole State Park, Naples

Eco-Attractions
1. Mote Marine Laboratory, Sarasota
2. Babcock Wilderness Adventures, Punta Gorda
3. Rookery Bay Environmental Learning Center, Naples
4. Manatee Park, Fort Myers
5. Naples Nature Center

Bikeways
1. W. J. Janes Memorial Scenic Drive, Fakahatchee Strand Preserve, Naples
2. Sanibel Island
3. Longboat Key
4. Cape Haze Pioneer Trail, Cape Haze
5. Historical Manatee Riverwalk, Bradenton

Paddle Happy
1. Wilderness Waterway, Everglades National Park
2. Great Calusa Blueway, Greater Fort Myers
3. Myakka River, Greater Sarasota
4. Tarpon Bay/J. N. "Ding" Darling National Wildlife Refuge, Sanibel Island
5. Matlacha Aquatic Preserve, Pine Island

Take a Hike
1. Fakahatchee Strand Preserve State Park, Naples
2. Big Cypress National Preserve, Everglades City
3. Collier-Seminole State Park, Naples
4. Oscar Scherer State Park, Osprey
5. J. N. "Ding" Darling National Wildlife Refuge, Sanibel Island

Shell-Shocked Beaches
1. Bowman's Beach, Sanibel Island
2. Cayo Costa Island State Park/Johnson Shoals
3. Bonita Beach
4. Key Island, Naples
5. Venice Beach

Secluded Beaches
1. Cayo Costa Island State Park
2. Key Island, Naples
3. Stump Pass Beach State Park, Englewood Beach
4. Lovers Key State Park, Fort Myers Beach
5. Palmer Point Beach, Siesta Key

Playful Beaches
1. Siesta Key County Park, Siesta Key
2. Lynn Hall Memorial Park, Fort Myers Beach
3. Manatee County Park, Holmes Beach
4. Coquina Beach, Bradenton Beach
5. Lowdermilk Park, Naples

Fishy Places
1. Boca Grande Pass, Boca Grande
2. Nokomis Jetty, Nokomis Beach
3. Venice Fishing Pier, Venice
4. Naples Pier, Naples
5. Fort Myers Beach Pier, Fort Myers Beach

Shopping Arenas
1. St. Armands Circle, Sarasota
2. Fifth Avenue South, Naples
3. Downtown Sarasota
4. Village at Venetian Bay, Naples
5. Downtown Punta Gorda

Art Appreciation
1. The John and Mable Ringling Museum of Art, Sarasota
2. Naples Museum of Art
3. Towles Court Artist Colony, Sarasota
4. Village of the Arts, Bradenton
5. Von Leibig Art Center, Naples

Swanky Jewelry

1. Port Royal Jewelers, Naples
2. Thalheimers Fine Jewelry, Naples
3. Tilden Ross Jewelers, St. Armands Circle, Sarasota
4. Congress Jewelers, Sanibel Island
5. Wm. Phelps, Custom Jeweler, Naples

Bookworm Holes

1. Main Bookshop, Sarasota
2. Sarasota News & Books, Sarasota
3. MacIntosh Books, Sanibel Island
4. The Bookstore at the Pavilion, Naples

Festivals

1. Edison Pageant of Light, February, Fort Myers
2. Medieval Fair, March, Sarasota
3. Everglades Seafood Festival, February, Everglades City
4. MangoMania, July, Pine Island/Cape Coral
5. Sharks' Tooth Seafood Festival, April, Venice

Homey Hometowns

1. Goodland
2. Punta Gorda
3. Englewood
4. Everglades City
5. Matlacha

Index

LODGING BY PRICE

DINING BY PRICE

DINING BY CUISINE

FOLLOW THE COUNTRYMAN PRESS
TO YOUR FAVORITE DESTINATIONS!

Explorer's Guide & Great Destination Series

NORTHEAST

The Adirondack Book: A Complete Guide
The Berkshire Book: A Complete Guide
Berkshire Hills & Pioneer Valley of Western
    Massachusetts: An Explorer's Guide
Cape Cod, Martha's Vineyard & Nantucket:
    An Explorer's Guide
The Coast of Maine Book: A Complete Guide
Connecticut: An Explorer's Guide
The Hamptons Book: A Complete Guide
The Hudson Valley Book: A Complete Guide
Hudson Valley & Catskill Mountains: An
    Explorer's Guide
Maine: An Explorer's Guide
The Nantucket Book: A Complete Guide
New Hampshire: An Explorer's Guide
New York City: An Explorer's Guide
Rhode Island: An Explorer's Guide
Touring East Coast Wine Country

MID-ATLANTIC

The Chesapeake Bay Book: A Complete Guide
The Finger Lakes Book: A Complete Guide
Maryland: An Explorer's Guide

MIDWEST

The Shenandoah Valley Book: A Complete Guide

SOUTHEAST

Blue Ridge & Smoky Mountains: An Explorer's
    Guide
The Charleston, Savannah, & Coastal Islands Book:
    A Complete Guide
The Sarasota, Sanibel Island & Naples Book:
    A Complete Guide

WEST

The Monterey Bay, Big Sur & Gold Coast
    Wine Country Book: A Complete Guide
The Napa & Sonoma Book: A Complete Guide
Oregon: An Explorer's Guide
The Santa Fe & Taos Book: A Complete Guide
The Texas Hill Country Book: A Complete Guide

General Travel

NORTHEAST

Adirondack Odysseys
The Colors of Fall
Covered Bridges of Vermont
A Guide to Natural Places in the Berkshire Hills
Dog-Friendly New England
Dog-Friendly New York
Eating New England
In-Line Skate New England
Hudson River Journey
Hudson Valley Harvest
Maine Sporting Camps
New England Seacoast Adventures
New England Waterfalls
New Jersey's Great Gardens
New Jersey's Special Places
Off the Leash
The Other Islands of New York City
The Photographer's guide to the Maine Coast
Shawangunks Trail Companion
Weekending in New England

MID-ATLANTIC

Waterfalls of the Mid-Atlantic States

WEST

The California Coast
The Photographer's Guide to the Oregon Coast
Weekend Wilderness: California, Oregon,
    Washington

INTERNATIONAL

Bicycling Cuba
Switzerland's Mountain Inns

We offer many more books on hiking, fly-fishing,
travel, nature, and other subjects. Our books are
available at bookstores and outdoor stores every-
where. For more information or a free catalog, call
1-800-245-4151 or write to us at:
The Countryman Press, P.O. Box 748
Woodstock, Vermont 05091.
You can find us on the Internet at
www.countrymanpress.com.